DEADLY LANDSCAPES

Squaw Creek Ruin on Perry Mesa, Arizona. Standing on the meter-wide, chest-high perimeter wall, fourteenth-century club-wielding defenders of this site would have had a height advantage over similarly armed attackers. They could also have used the wall for protection during exchanges of arrow volleys. (Photograph courtesy of Jerry Jacka, Phoenix, Arizona.)

Deadly Landscapes

CASE STUDIES IN PREHISTORIC SOUTHWESTERN WARFARE

Edited by

Glen E. Rice and
Steven A. LeBlanc

THE UNIVERSITY OF UTAH PRESS

Salt Lake City

06 05 04 03 02 01
5 4 3 2 1

Library of Congress Cataloging-in-Publication Data
Deadly landscapes : case studies in prehistoric southwestern warfare /
edited by Glen E. Rice and Steven A. LeBlanc.
   p. cm.
Includes bibliographical references and index.
  ISBN 0-87480-676-3 (cloth : alk. paper)
   1. Indians of North America—Wars—Southwest, New. 2. Indians of
North America—Warfare—Southwest, New. 3. Indians of North
America—Southwest, New—Antiquities. 4. Southwest, New—
Antiquities. I. Rice, Glen. II. LeBlanc, Steven A.
  E78.S7 D33 2001
  979.004'97—dc21   00-011203

CONTENTS

CHAPTER ONE

Southwestern Warfare

The Value of Case Studies

Steven A. LeBlanc and Glen E. Rice

War is not a pleasant topic. Few people want to dwell on warfare or its consequences, and archaeologists are no exception. Yet in spite of our desire to wish intersocietal conflict away, it is clear that warfare is a common aspect of human behavior and that it has played a major role in shaping social systems. Like it or not, we must deal with warfare objectively and include it, where appropriate, in our models.

Because the southwestern United States is one of the best archaeologically understood areas in the world and also has a substantial body of ethnographic information, it is a particularly good place to consider warfare. Moreover, southwestern archaeologists have long regarded warfare as virtually nonexistent or irrelevant as a factor effecting change in the region. If we have failed to recognize warfare in the Southwest—where it turns out to be commonplace and important—then what must be the situation elsewhere in the world?

There have been some notable overviews and syntheses of southwestern warfare, discussed in greater length below. But such overviews are only as good as their data. Of the several approaches to this problem, one involves the use of case studies. Well-documented, carefully considered cases are central to much archaeological understanding. For example, that old workhorse, the Starr Carr site in England, is still widely used as an archaeological case study. In our view, one impediment to recognition and understanding of southwestern warfare is the absence of such well-worked-out, published examples that include cultural implications. The best to date is Haas and Creamer's (1993) study in the Kayenta area.

With this volume we seek to follow their example and advance the rigorous examination of war in the Southwest by developing a corpus of specific cases. In so doing, we hope to provide models for how studies of this type can be constructed. Because the literature here is so thin, and because much interpretation involves breaking new ground, we expect that the case studies in this book will undergo close scrutiny. In fact, Lawrence Keeley begins the process in the closing chapter.

We also hope the outcome will be a sharpened awareness of methodologies as well as a refined understanding of the specific cases of warfare in the Southwest. Readers will note the broad divergence among the contributions to this volume. There are different definitions of warfare and varying ideas about its causes. Nor do contributors use the same types of data (even when available) to test for the presence of warfare. These are all indications that the study of prehistoric warfare in the Southwest is still in its infancy.

THE CASES

The case studies in this volume include examples from the Hohokam, Sinagua, Mogollon, and Anasazi regions (Figure 1.1). They are clustered in the Hohokam and Sinagua region, in part because the volume grew out of a symposium on Hohokam warfare organized by Glen Rice for the 1998 Society for American Archaeology annual meetings. Given the interest generated by the symposium, Steven LeBlanc (the symposium's discussant) suggested adding examples from other parts of the Southwest to create a volume of case studies on southwestern warfare. This proposal led to the addition of studies from the Mogollon, Cibola, and Mesa Verde regions, as well as a panregional study of iconography (Helen Crotty) covering all the Colorado Plateau and the Rio Grande Valley.

These studies all focus on a narrow time frame, from the A.D. 1200s to the early 1400s. It is in this time span that evidence for warfare is most pervasive in the Southwest (see Haas and Creamer 1996; LeBlanc 1999; Spoerl 1984; Wilcox 1989). In several regions this period was preceded by about a century of gradually increasing hostility: By the early 1200s there was a noticeable increase in the level of warfare, and by the early 1300s war was ubiquitous throughout the Southwest. It is not surprising, then, that the case studies presented here all derive from this time period, and some of the arguments, in fact, rest on comparisons with conditions of the previous centuries.

Several of the case studies suggest local or panregional explanations

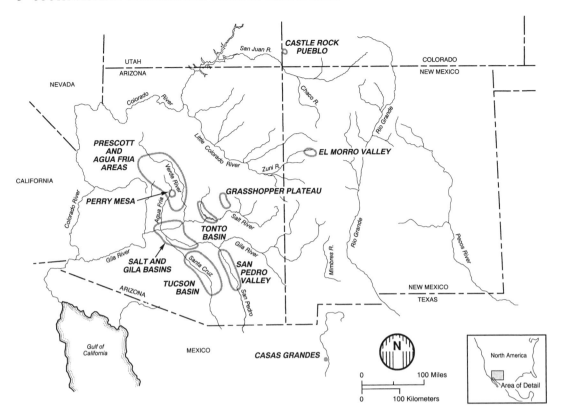

Figure 1.1. Locations of the Southwestern case studies of the Hohokam, Sinagua, Mogollon, and Anasazi areas in this volume.

for the thirteenth- and fourteenth-century developments, ranging from shifts in weather patterns, to increasing population density, to changes in ideology. But the stronger contribution of these case studies lies not only in the clear demonstration that such a pattern of significant warfare in the late prehistoric period does exist but also in the presentation for the first time of detailed data from a wide number of regions in support of this observation.

One implication of the prolonged period of warfare in the thirteenth and fourteenth centuries is that there ought to have been a significant decline in population. Several of the chapters discuss population movements and abandonments of areas. Although there was some reshuffling of people, it is also likely that warfare actually killed significant numbers of people. In particular, it is quite possible that much of the Mesa Verde area population and the Grasshopper population did not survive as intact communities. Conversely, the people of El Morro and the Hohokam farmers on the Gila River seem to have been polities that did survive—to become the Zuni and Pima of today.

The focus in this book on the late time period developed from happenstance, and it ought not to be considered a full characterization of the history of warfare in the Southwest. Studies from earlier periods are also critically needed.

An earlier period of endemic war involved at least part of the Southwest between A.D. 200 and 900. The evidence is strongest for the Anasazi and Mogollon regions, where it takes the form of palisaded villages, villages in hilltop refuges, burned settlements, and death by violence (LeBlanc 1999). It is not clear to what extent the Hohokam also participated in war during this early period, although Rice (this volume) presents cases of conflict in Hohokam villages dating to the tenth and eleventh centuries. In general, however, the cases presented here do not provide detailed discussions of this earlier period of endemic warfare, and it is a period that warrants more detailed study.

We draw attention as well to the importance of the two centuries of apparent peace that held throughout the Southwest from A.D. 900 to 1100 (LeBlanc 1999). In trying to understand the role that war has played in the evolution of human populations, it is just as important that we also understand the conditions associated with periods of prolonged peace (Keeley 1996). A few of the case studies in this volume touch on that period, usually for the purpose of drawing contrasts with conditions of the 1200s to 1400s. Case studies are needed for this apparently "peaceful" period as well, especially since it was a time of considerable trade, settlement expansion, and migration across much of the Southwest.

GENERAL CONSIDERATIONS OF WARFARE

The very term *warfare* causes some difficulty with anthropologists in general. It is thought by some to imply complex organizations and thus is considered inappropriate for use with less complex societies. *Raiding* is often used as a terminological substitute for *warfare*. We believe such a distinction does more harm than good. It subtly assumes not only that different types of societies have different types of conflicts, which is obvious, but also that the importance and consequences of such conflicts are different, which is not necessarily the case. In fact, implicit in the "raiding" model is that bands and tribes do not have "real" warfare but only minor skirmishes and raids, and therefore warfare is of minor consequence. It is perhaps this underlying implicit assumption that all conflict in the Southwest was of this "minor" type that has caused most archaeologists working in the region to ignore or downplay the significance of warfare.

Mervyn Meggitt (1977:10) provides a straightforward definition of war: "A state or period of armed hostility existing between politically autonomous communities, which at such times regard the actions (violent or otherwise) of their members against the opponents as legitimate expressions of the sovereign policy of the community." This definition does not make a distinction between *raiding* and *warfare*, and thus we can separate the methods of warfare from its existence.

As Keeley (1996) recently made clear, the difference between *raiding* and *pitched battles* is one of tactics. If prolonged raiding can result in the annihilation of a competing group, how can it be considered any lesser a form of warfare than pitched battles that, in fact, may be less conclusive? If we object to the term *warfare* because it implies organization and resource expenditures that are not often associated with band and tribal "raiding," this is a misreading of reality. The time spent over one's lifetime building defenses, training boys to fight, preparing weapons, and actually fighting appears to be every bit as great in the New Guinea highlands as it is on a per capita basis in most industrial societies. Among industrial societies wars are periodic with long intervals between massive efforts. Wars among bands and tribes seem to be more continuous, so at any point in time they appear less intense than, say, the height of the First World War's trench warfare. Yet, on a long-term basis, probably the opposite is true.

Keeley (1996) argues that anthropologists have downplayed the importance of warfare because of a desire to see the world as Rousseauian—a world of peaceful noble savages living in harmony with one another and nature. Such anthropologists have rejected a Hobbesian view of constant conflict. Beyond accusing anthropologists of assuming what they should be trying to find out, Keeley goes on to characterize nonstate-level warfare. What one finds is that warfare in nonstate societies is more deadly and more common than in state-level situations, including Western societies in the last century. One is initially shocked to learn that the expectation is that about 25 percent of the men and perhaps 5 percent of women die from warfare in nonstate societies and that societies in which warfare is not chronic are rare and exceptional. With this sobering thought one must reconsider much of the archaeological record.

In spite of the general avoidance of the topic, there is an anthropological literature on warfare. In addition to Keeley, the reader is referred to Fried et al. 1968; Ferguson 1984; Tkaczuk and Vivian 1989; Haas, ed. 1990; and Ferguson and Whitehead 1992. These works are all collections; in spite of their explicit interest in warfare, to a large extent many of the authors are guilty of Keeley's criticisms. In some cases the chapters are far too general to deepen our understanding of warfare in the past. Other authors are Otterbein (1989, 1994, 1997), Vayda (1960, 1968, 1976), and Knauft (1991).

Beyond these standard works, Ember and Ember (1992) provide a useful cross-cultural summary of warfare. The role of warfare as a force in culture change was considered some time ago by Service (1962, 1975) and Carneiro (1970) and more recently by Kirch (1984) and Earle (1997). However, Turney-High's old classic, *Primitive War* (1949), should now be recognized as very misleading and of little utility. Highland New Guinea provides a rich source of ethnographic examples that are particularly relevant to nonstate warfare. Meggitt's *Blood Is Their Argument* (1977) is the most lucid; Heider (1979), Morren (1984), Sillitoe (1977), Berndt (1964), Shankman (1991), and Knauft (1992) offer other examples and debate on various interpretations of highland

New Guinea warfare. Chagnon (1968, 1992) supplies similar information for the Yanomamö.

MODELS OF WARFARE

The literature on warfare raises several issues of interest which at a distance seem tangential to the case studies presented here. These questions are ultimately very relevant, however. The first broad issue is, Why is there warfare? Although this topic is multifaceted, one way to summarize the various arguments is to place them in three categories: the scarce-resource model, the innate-human-nature model, and the revenge model.[1] Archaeology is limited in the contribution it can make to this question (it's hard, for example, to query the archaeological record about the need for revenge), but it can provide useful information on the scarce-resource model. For example, we can look for changes in population size, climate, new technologies, and so on, all of which should have an impact on resources. To what extent do changes in the intensity of warfare correlate with changes in the availability of resources? Archaeology can certainly contribute to this topic. Most of the contributions to this volume do not address the underlying causes of the warfare they describe, although there are various appeals to both the scarce-resource and human-nature models.

The second topic of general anthropological interest (in many ways it's a subtopic of the first) is whether most ethnographically recorded warfare was just a consequence of colonial impact on nonstate societies. Put another way, some argue that Keeley is wrong and the reason archaeologists do not find evidence for warfare is that Rousseau was right: the world used to be a wonderful place, and warfare should be rare or nonexistent in the archaeological record. Colonialism as a prime cause of ethnographically recorded warfare is associated with Brian Ferguson (1984; Ferguson and Whitehead 1992), but not exclusively (see, e.g., Blick 1988). Ferguson variously argues that it is the radical changes in social systems brought about by colonial impact that caused the warfare we find from the Yanomamö to the Great Plains. Archaeology must play a critical role in resolving this issue. With few exceptions, the ethnographic literature exists in a colonial milieu. It does not follow, however, that even if warfare took place in colonial situations because of colonial impact, warfare did not previously take place—and was not as common, or even *more* common—in the precontact situation. Without archaeological time depth, it is very difficult to address the precontact situation, and an understanding of it is critical to interpretations of postcontact warfare.

This volume addresses this second issue squarely. It is easy to see southwestern ethnographic warfare as being caused by population movements, new weapons, slave raiding, horses, and other impacts, direct or indirect, of the Spanish and then American arrival in the area. That does not mean there was peace before the arrival of the Spaniards, however, as the contributions to this volume demonstrate. Before the Spanish entrada people may have fought for different reasons, but they fought nonetheless. So in one sense these case studies are in themselves part of a single, more encompassing case study pertaining to the situation in the Southwest before European contact.

The third broad issue found within the literature on warfare has to do with how war affects the organization of society. With this topic we move beyond matters of definition and recognition and begin the consideration of warfare as an important, perhaps critical, process in the shaping of human societies. A number of the case studies presented here address this question at a local level, and together they provide a basis for developing comparative analyses and syntheses at the regional level.

Much of the existing archaeological literature on war-as-process has focused on its role in the development of complex societies and the rise of centralized bureaucracies (Carneiro 1970, 1978; Haas 1982). Success in war enables aspiring leaders to control larger territories and greater quantities of resources, providing them with the power to consolidate and centralize their authority. With the passage of time the increasing centralization transforms tribes into chiefdoms and chiefdoms into states (Carneiro 1990:208).

Unfortunately, such processes are not observed to any noticeable degree among the peoples of the Southwest, a situation perhaps related to the difficulty researchers have in fitting southwestern societies to the organizational stages invoked by neo-evolutionary models, or because other factors kept the process from progressing very far. To be sure, there were influential and prestigious leaders in the Southwest, but their authority was often based on ritual knowledge rather than secular power, and influence tended to be context specific. The tribal chief was seldom a war captain, and neither one was likely to be the ditch boss who oversaw the cleaning of canals or the shaman-like diviner who foresaw the location of the enemy. Even among the Classic period Hohokam, where archaeologists find obvious examples of elite residential architecture (residences built on platform mounds required an order of magnitude more material to construct than residences built without a platform), such elites exercised no measurable control over economic production and were not organized as bureaucracies, even for purposes of controlling the irrigation systems (Rice 1998, 2000; Rice, ed. 1998).

Warfare affected southwestern societies in other ways, especially in the organization of subsistence practices. In the context of systems that make use of complementary opposition, war may have been instrumental to the operation of the Hohokam irrigation systems (Rice 1998, this volume), whereas elsewhere war rendered some subsistence strategies inoperable. The twelfth-century increase in the intensity of warfare across the Southwest apparently curtailed the use of agriculturally marginal terrain by small, single-family settlements (LeBlanc this volume), bringing to an end several centuries of highly flexible subsistence and settlement practices. The thirteenth- and fourteenth-century development of large aggregated settlements, the abandonment of extensive areas, and the clustering of settlements into subregions resembling polities (LeBlanc this volume; Wilcox et al. this volume) were also very likely outcomes of the increase in warfare. Changes in architecture and in the spatial layout of communities may have been additional responses to war. It is possible, and we think highly likely, that war had far greater impact in these areas than trade, subsistence technologies, or, for that matter, the development of high-status leadership roles.

Warfare is also a process that can generate changes among unrelated groups dispersed over a vast region. One property of battle is that, all else being equal (technology, terrain, and strategies), success tends to go to the group with the larger number of combatants. If a relatively bellicose group in one area makes an organizational change that enables it to field larger forces, that change is likely to precipitate an organizational response among neighboring groups (or those groups are overrun and subsumed). The organizational responses need not be identical, and this is indeed a highly intriguing feature of thirteenth-century warfare in the Southwest: groups reacted in quite different ways to the need for increased organizational strength in war. In the south the Hohokam used organizational principles that enabled them to *mass* forces from within territorial blocs while retaining a relatively dispersed settlement system. In the central mountains and on the Colorado Plateau populations *aggregated* into very large settlements as a means of ensuring the presence of a sizable fighting force.

Populations employing these differing strategies bordered each other on the upper Salt River. Hohokam-related populations with a massing capability occupied Tonto Basin (and also seem to have assimilated people from the surrounding mountains and the Sinagua area) and faced off against the aggregated Mogollon pueblos on the Grasshopper Plateau. Both massing and population aggregation are strategies for building large forces in the field; the current chronological evidence suggests that the Grasshopper Plateau was abandoned in the late fourteenth century whereas occupation of Tonto Basin may have continued into the fifteenth century. Although they may have persisted slightly longer than their Mogollon counterparts, the populations of Tonto Basin were themselves eventually defeated in war and forced to flee.

A third strategy was being employed in the nineteenth century by the Apache and Yavapai and may have been used as well by prehistoric populations in the Prescott area (Wilcox et al. this volume). Faced with overwhelmingly large forces sent out periodically by the Pima and Maricopa, the Yavapai and Apache used a stratagem of failing to engage in battle on their own territory, tending to withdraw unseen in the face of the advancing enemy force.

The studies in this book illustrate the very different ways in which prehistoric populations in the Southwest sought to ensure the availability of combatants or, alternatively, sought to avoid facing overwhelming odds. In some areas competition and war selected for larger canal systems, in others for aggregated settlements, and in yet others for systems of hilltop lookouts and retreats. Steven LeBlanc (1999) has shown that from the thirteenth century onward, many of the characteristics of settlement patterns on the Colorado Plateau and the central mountains can be explained as a response to a period of endemic warfare. The case studies in this book expand on his findings by showing how local variation in ecology, technology, and landscape influenced the response of different groups to war. A single process—the pressure of war—apparently selected for very different kinds of settlement patterns and group responses across the southwestern landscape.

LOOKING AT WARFARE IN THE SOUTHWEST

Much of the literature on southwestern warfare has focused on rather general statements as to whether it existed or not. This literature has been reviewed by Haas and Creamer (1995, 1997), Haas (1990), and LeBlanc (1999). Some researchers have felt that there is evidence for warfare in the archaeological record, but considerably more either find no evidence or consider warfare to have been infrequent enough to be essentially irrelevant for the explanation of events. It was probably in the 1970s and 1980s that warfare reached a nadir as an explanatory mechanism, although the trend seems to have reversed quite rapidly. Evidence for warfare has been seen by archaeologists since the late 1800s, but it is only quite recently that such data have been dealt with at a meaningful level in most broad-based syntheses. The contrast between Cordell 1984 and Cordell 1994, and finally Cordell 1997, is significant. The consideration given warfare by Plog 1997, especially if we go back and contrast it with McGregor 1965, is also striking. In all fairness, various authors represented in these chapters have also evolved their thinking. One of us, Rice, when confronted with a data set that strongly suggests warfare, is far more willing to pursue those implications now (Rice 1998) than he was when confronted with evidence of fortified refuges in a study conducted earlier in his career (Rice 1974). Similarly, Reid (1989) and his co-workers (Reid and Whittlesey 1990; Reid et al. 1996) have not accepted the strong evidence for warfare in the Grasshopper region until very recently (Tuggle and Reid this volume).

Nevertheless, the study by Haas and Creamer (1993) that focuses on Kayenta warfare is a glaring exception to most previous fine-grained analysis of the culture history of particular areas or sites. Another study that dealt with warfare directly is Spoerl 1984, for central Arizona. John Ravesloot and Patricia Spoerl (1989) also present a carefully argued case concerning warfare at Casas Grandes, although the implications of their observations have been essentially ignored in larger syntheses of that area. Most recently, Regge Wiseman (1997) provided considerable evidence for warfare and related it to the presence of competing ethnic groups.

Jonathan Haas and Winifred Creamer (1997) summarize the extensive ethnographic evidence for warfare in the northern Southwest (see also Ellis 1951). For the southern Southwest, Clifton Kroeber and Bernard Fontana (1986) provide considerable data as well as detailed accounts of nineteenth-century battles waged by the Yuma and Mojave against their adversaries on the Gila River, the Pima and Maricopa. Christopher White (1974) presents an interesting model of how ecology structured the patterns of alliances and hostilities across a broad part of southern Arizona and California. Several ethnographic reports on specific tribes (e.g., Russell 1975; Spier 1933; Underhill 1938b) also deal with the matter of Native American warfare in the nineteenth-century southern Southwest and provide valuable written accounts of native oral traditions.

Given the considerable evidence for ethnographic warfare, just how the perception of peaceful native peoples has become so widespread is a topic of interest. Clearly, our views are affected by the impact of the Spanish and the Americans on the nature of conflict in the historic period, as well as the presence of native people who see themselves as peace-loving and who prefer not to have their ancestors depicted as war-like. As yet, no one has carefully evaluated how the common perception of a "peaceful prehistoric Southwest" evolved.

A Regional Perspective of War in the Southwest

The intensity of warfare in the Southwest seems to have fluctuated over time. There is significant but scattered evidence for warfare from the very first part of the first millennium, with evidence for the intensification of warfare around A.D. 700–900. This evidence is strongest for the Anasazi area and is also found in the Mogollon region, but little evidence has been put forth for the Hohokam area.

There is little evidence of warfare across the Southwest for the next two centuries, from A.D. 900 to about 1100. What has been called "pax Chaco" seems to extend over the entire Southwest. Although Wilcox (1993) holds a minority point of view, he argues, with some justification, that Chaco was not as peaceful as it superficially appears.

Beginning in the late A.D. 1100s or early 1200s, there was a marked increase in the level of warfare in the Southwest, and by the early 1300s one finds strong evidence for its ubiquity and significance wherever one looks. It is this period in Southwest history, the thirteenth and fourteenth centuries, that is documented by the case studies in this book. We present several contrasting explanations for this period of warfare and, not unexpectedly, note the kinds of additional data that need to be collected for empirical tests.

The current models make use of what Keeley calls the "bad apple" effect. This is the notion that it takes only one particularly bellicose group in an area to invoke a defensive response across the entire region. The warfare of the thirteenth and fourteenth centuries may have spread as a chain of events and responses until much of the Southwest was involved. The development of warfare in one region necessitated a defensive response in neighboring regions. A local cause leading to warfare in one area could, by this process, result in a response involving the entire region. The case studies provide the beginning of a data base for assessing the degree of contemporaneity of these events across such a vast region.

LeBlanc (1999) finds evidence of a north-to-south time differential in the initial shift to greater defense, with changes in the Mesa Verde area predating those in the Grasshopper Plateau and Tonto Basin areas. He relates this to an earlier global change in weather patterns known as the Medieval Warm period. Helen Crotty (this volume) suggests that perhaps the earliest depictions of shield bearers occur in the Great Basin and are gradually adopted in the Colorado Plateau and Rio Grande areas, but she does not advance a particular factor responsible for this west-to-east spread.

Rice (1998) and Wilcox (1989) propose that the Hohokam irrigation agriculturists on the Salt and Gila Rivers were early belligerents and that their actions prompted defensive reactions to the north (Wilcox et al. this volume) and south (Wallace and Doelle this volume). And, possibly, by sending migrants to join existing populations in Tonto Basin, they elicited a similar defensive response on the Grasshopper Plateau (Rice 1998; Rice, ed. 1998).

The two sets of models (north-first vs. south-first) agree in the one area where they overlap (the Tonto Basin and Grasshopper Plateau areas), and perhaps both reconstructions are valid. Warfare may have spread from the north and south until, by the fourteenth century, it involved the entire Southwest. The difficulty with this integrated reconstruction lies in the suggestion that the intensification of warfare began in the A.D. 1100s in two very distant parts of the Southwest: the Kayenta and the Hohokam regions. The case studies in this volume provide some of the best data sets researchers have to deal with such regional issues.

Turning to the particulars of the increase in warfare in the late prehistoric period, we find some fairly clear patterns and some unresolved issues. In almost every area where the increase has been seriously investigated, we see a staged response. There is an initial shift in settlement pattern to somewhat more defensive arrangements. This interval is often short, and it is not accompanied by abandonments or the formation of unoccupied zones. That is, settlement locations, configurations, and distributions initially do not seem to be sensitive to defensive needs; they are followed by some relocation of sites, or reconfiguration of sites, that increase defensibility but not by very much. This interval is, in turn, followed by much more dramatic changes in community size, layout, location, and the opening up of empty zones. This pattern, or parts of this pattern, can be seen in the chapters by Wilcox et. al. (especially in a comparison of the two contributions), Tuggle and Reid, LeBlanc, and Oliver. Other chapters, such as those by Doelle and Wallace and Lightfoot and Kuckelman, focus on the later, most defensive aspect of the sequence but often have evidence for an earlier, less defensive site and settlement pattern.

LeBlanc (1999) proposes that the intensification of thirteenth-century warfare was triggered by developments in the preceding centuries. The period from A.D. 900 to 1150 was a climatic optimum, labeled the Medieval Warm period in Europe. The population of the Southwest grew substantially—see the population growth curves in Dean 1996—but carrying capacity of the region had expanded because of the optimal climate conditions, so the growth could be accommodated with little or no conflict. Beginning in the late 1100s, however, the population may have caught up with the increased capacity, and by the middle 1200s the climate began to deteriorate into what has been called the Little Ice Age. (These climate issues are discussed in Chapter 2 [LeBlanc].) Thus we seem to have had a classic case of a population exceeding the long-term carrying capacity, coupled with a sharp drop in that capacity—the worst of all possible scenarios. The intense warfare, LeBlanc believes, was directly related to the deteriorating environment and the population's imbalance with the resource base. Conflict over the entire Southwest was the consequence. The cases presented here seem to derive from the same underlying cause, although how the situation played itself out varied greatly from area to area.

If this model turns out to be correct, then these case studies are examples of competition over scarce resources. Other models may eventually prove to be more appropriate as explanations for the late period of endemic warfare. Nevertheless, it is of considerable theoretical interest whether the examples presented here are all the result of a single region-wide cause or can be explained fully by local factors.

The "south first" models propose that the Hohokam irrigation farmers increased their military pressure on the populations of neighboring regions, leading to a subsequent series of events extending northward up the Verde River, southward to the Tucson Basin, and eastward through Tonto Basin to the Grasshopper Plateau. There are at least two variants of this model to be tested with the collection of additional data.

Rice proposes (1998, this volume; Rice, ed. 1998) that the Hohokam irrigation farmers had a systemic proclivity for the use of force and that their ability to field large forces increased in direct proportion to the growth in the size of their canal systems. The practice of irrigation agriculture in the Hohokam environment (marked by a limited number of good locations for canal headgates) created an ecological base for the complementary opposition of settlements using the same canal. Because populations living on a canal were joined in their common commitment to retaining control of the headgate, they tended to act as a single territorial unit when facing a force from beyond their canal. Thus the maximum unit of natural massing for war was not the individual settlement but the entire canal system. And as the canals grew in length, they eventually supported populations far larger than those occupying any individual settlements in the desert periphery. The people living on large canals would also be accustomed to frequent disagreements over the distribution of water and to frequent displays of force in the course of intracanal feuding. By the late Sedentary period, therefore, there were perhaps a half-dozen or so cradles of bellicosity along the Salt and Gila Rivers containing populations that were both accustomed to the use of force and capable of fielding forces of extraordinary size, much larger than those that could be advanced by individual villages located in the surrounding desert or occupying short irrigation canals on side drainages.

One expectation of this model is that the proclivity of irrigation farmers to resolve differences through the threat of hostility should appear shortly after the establishment of the canal systems and to have intensified with the growth of the canals. For that reason, there should be evidence of occasional warfare in the Hohokam core area starting as early as A.D. 800 or 900. Led by this implication, Rice (this volume) looked at several large excavated Hohokam sites on Canal System Two in the Phoenix Basin and found that major portions of those villages were burned at sporadic intervals during the tenth through thirteenth centuries; each burning event was preceded and followed by periods in which only occasional structures were burned. It is possible the Hohokam irrigation farmers on the Salt and Gila Rivers had not heard of the pax Chaco of 900 to 1100.

The scale of warfare should have increased as the numbers of people living on the canal systems grew. By about A.D. 1100 the populations on the largest canal systems had become a threat to those living in independent villages in the periphery (populations also labeled Hohokam because of their use of Hohokam buffwares), and the increased threat of hostilities led the independent villagers to move into hilltop settlements of the kind described by Wilcox et al. in this volume.

Two sets of phenomena suggest that the A.D. 1200s were a period of intense warfare for the Hohokam of the Phoenix Basin. First, there was extensive burning of structures in Hohokam villages on the canal systems (Rice this volume). And second, the hilltop villages in the desert periphery around the canals were abandoned by the end of the century (Wilcox et al. this volume). The apparent victors were the populations living on the canal system. By the early 1300s settlements on the canal systems were fortified by adobe walls, there were far fewer occurrences of burned structures, and the desert regions around the edges of the irrigated zone had been completely abandoned.

David Wilcox and his colleagues (this volume) suggest a variation on this model in proposing that the earliest belligerents were the populations living on fortified hilltops in the periphery of the Hohokam core area and that their occasional raids into the Hohokam core area were, at first, simply endured. Sometime after A.D. 1200 the reorganization of the Hohokam core area into a single large polity, seen in the appearance of platform mounds and walled compounds, led to a more aggressive and politically integrated system that was determined, according to Wilcox et al., to "end the endemic raiding that . . . had gone on for a century and a half." Hohokam attacks against populations in the periphery and in the Prescott area became increasingly successful, and the populations of these areas retreated to well-defended locations on Perry Mesa. The Wilcox model differs from that of Rice in its perspective on the internal organization of the Hohokam: it posits a large polity (rather than a half-dozen or so) incorporating the entire Hohokam core region (i.e., the irrigated areas) during the fourteenth century, and it proposes a late emergence of warfare as a response to raids from the periphery.

Populations living on large canal systems were capable of fielding extremely large military forces. This ability created a considerable disparity in power between the Hohokam occupying the canal systems and the Hohokam living in the surrounding desert who relied on runoff (ak chin) agricultural techniques and were organized only at the level of the individual village. Eventually, the populations in the periphery were forced to abandon the area, and by the fourteenth century the Hohokam irrigation farmers were protected by an unoccupied zone that encircled almost all the irrigated portion of the Salt and Gila river valleys. The unoccupied zone cut across both good and marginal agricultural land. It included, for instance, a portion of the Santa Cruz River to the south of the Gila River that had abundant water and had been continuously occupied since the Late Archaic period but was abandoned after about A.D. 1300 (Wallace and Doelle this volume; Rice 1998).

By historic times, the Salt River was abandoned and was used by the Apache, Yavapai, and Pima as a hunting and gathering area. The Pima irrigation farmers on the Gila River still followed the earlier Hohokam practice of massing at the tribal level, however. At the first sign of a threat, warriors from settlements located as far as 40 km from the scene of battle would assemble to face the enemy as a single force.

Categories of Evidence

If war was as common as we purport it to be, why have so few archaeological models and syntheses dealt with it as a factor in cultural change, migration, abandonment, or even settlement distribution? One reason seems to be that there is no agreed-on methodology for recognizing or evaluating warfare in the prehistoric record.

Although this volume is not a focus on method, it is useful at the outset to enumerate briefly some different lines of evidence for the existence and nature of warfare. Not all are used in our case studies, but most of the types of evidence that have been proposed are represented in one or more of the studies. It is worthwhile pointing out some categories of evidence that were used here—and then to mention those that were not.

Fortifications and site configurations are one of the most archaeologically visible forms of evidence of warfare and are probably the most widely considered around the world. The studies presented here provide examples of fortified refuges, fortified settlements, and fortified elite residences in a variety of cultural contexts. This diversity is a measure of the considerable variation in the organizational abilities of the studied systems. Of Keeley's (1996:57) four categories of fortifications, one type— purely military forts—is not known for the prehistoric Southwest. Examples of various other fortifications are discussed for the Zuni region (LeBlanc), the Tonto Basin Salado (Oliver), the Phoenix Basin Hohokam (Rice), the Tucson Basin Hohokam (Wallace and Doelle), the Hohokam and Sinagua (Wilcox et al.), the Mesa Verde region (Lightfoot and Kuckelman), and Mogollon settlements on the Grasshopper Plateau (Tuggle and Reid).

Another broadly observed category of evidence of warfare is the development in the thirteenth and fourteenth centuries of unoccupied zones separating clusters of settlements. Such zones are good indicators of warfare and alliance formation, especially when they occur in areas that had been extensively occupied before the thirteenth century. Unoccupied zones separating clusters of settlements are discussed in considerable detail for the Tucson Basin Hohokam (Wallace and Doelle), the Sinagua (Wilcox et al.), and the Colorado Plateau (LeBlanc).

Site burning and the presence of unburied bodies are more difficult categories of data to obtain. Rooms can burn for a number of reasons, and differentiating warfare-caused burning from other causes requires good excavation data and analysis, as exemplified by Oliver in his discussion of Tonto Basin. The case study presented by Lightfoot and Kuckelman is without doubt the most solid example of the presence of nonformally buried bodies and warfare in the Southwest.

Iconographic representations of themes associated with warfare are still more indirect types of evidence of such conflicts. Crotty describes wall murals and rock art panels of the Colorado Plateau and Rio Grande Valley that depict warriors using shields or actually engaged in combat.

Line-of-sight links between settlements provide another type of evidence that is readily available but usually ignored or not collected. LeBlanc, Tuggle and Reid, and especially Wilcox et al. consider line-of-sight links between sites to be important evidence for defensive tactics. This was one of the significant kinds of evidence of warfare presented by Haas and Creamer (1993) for the Kayenta area. It is probably one of the more easy to collect yet underutilized categories of data relating to warfare.

Interestingly, many lines of evidence of warfare—such as settlement patterns, line-of-sight, and trade patterns—involve alliance formation. The importance of alliances has been underplayed in the Southwest, with notable exceptions being Wilcox (1981, 1989, 1991a, 1995b, 1996), Upham (1982), Upham and Reed (1989), Creamer (1996), and LeBlanc (2000), although they do not all deeply consider the warfare aspects of such alliances.

Trade is also frequently an arena for competition, and at times such contests can be only slightly less extreme than war. An intriguing example is provided by Simon and Grosser for Tonto Basin: by the thirteenth and fourteenth centuries the villages in the basin had grouped into a spatial cluster in an apparent reaction to the possible threat presented by two other, similar groups of settlements, one consisting of the 11 Mogollon villages on the Grasshopper Plateau (Tuggle and Reid this volume) and the other of settlements in the Globe area (Wilcox et al. this volume). It is very likely that the settlements in Tonto Basin were capable of showing a united front in an attack from either of these two other groups, but it is also apparent that relationships among the settlements within the basin were far from harmonious. Settlements at opposite ends of the basin essentially competed against each other for access to long-distance trade contacts and conducted only a modest level of trade among themselves (Simon and Gosser this volume; see Rice et al. 1998).

Another aspect of information relating to prehistoric warfare is the use of ethnohistoric data and oral traditions. These sources can provide insights into the process of warfare, such as alliance formation, the use of fire in attacks and the like, and even who might have been fighting whom. Rice effectively uses this type of information for the Hohokam, but similar sources could be investigated in many other areas as well.

It is interesting to note that in this volume only the study by Lightfoot and Kuckelman refers to extensive evidence for violent death in the form of skull contusions, embedded projectile points, or informal burials. Some of the other case studies point out the existence of evidence for violent deaths, but none use it as a major form of evidence. Violent deaths are strong evidence for warfare, but the presence of skeletal data for violent deaths is apparently relatively uncommon in the Southwest. This situation is in contrast to studies from California (Lambert 1997), where such evidence is perhaps the primary source used to monitor warfare. There are also notable examples of violent deaths from elsewhere in North America (e.g., Owsley et al. 1977; Owsley and Jantz 1994; Milner et al. 1991). There is a difference, however, between a few dramatic examples of violence in death and a common occurrence of violent deaths. This distinction is important because it is too often thought that the primary means of recognizing warfare archaeologically is the direct evidence of violent death. Yet the overwhelming amount of evidence for warfare presented in these case studies is not in the form of violent deaths. The case study by Lightfoot and Kuckelman aside, the next most extensive use of such evidence is by Oliver: most of his evidence involves individuals who seem to have met a violent death but for whom there is no evidence of contusions or embedded points. David Tuggle and J. Jefferson Reid make reference to scalped individuals at Grasshopper, but it is a minor piece of their data. The relatively low visibility of violent death has implications for the study of prehistoric conflict in other parts of the world (see Keeley's comments in the final chapter).

Several classes of potential evidence for warfare are notably missing from these case studies. Some occur so rarely that they need to be considered on a regional basis—such as the imagery considered by Crotty—and so are not appropriate to many of these localized case studies. However, the omission of some of the possible information is probably due to our lack of ability to recognize and interpret such evidence. Missing is the use of deviations in the sex ratios of skeletal populations. There are notable examples of deviations from 50–50 sex ratios that are likely a result of warfare. LeBlanc (1999) presents the logic behind such interpretation and several examples. And in fact, the burial sample from Grasshopper Pueblo shows just the type of deviance from 50–50 that we would expect under the circumstances described by Tuggle and Reid.

Also missing is evidence for warfare from weapons themselves. Crotty makes reference to the depiction of shields in rock art and murals, but unfortunately, there are only three actual prehistoric shields from the Southwest, all which predate her depiction data. Nevertheless, there are changes in bow form (LeBlanc 1997), arrow-point sizes and shapes, the possible existence of wooden "swords" (Lutonsky 1992), and a number of clubs, club heads, knives, daggers, and the like that have never been accorded serious study as weapons. How can we include their distributions in space and time as meaningful evidence if we do not even recognize them as objects relevant to the discussion of warfare? Other lines of evidence—such as the use of human body parts as trophies (other than scalps) and possible human sacrifice—have been noted for the Southwest but fall outside the scope of the case studies present here.

In summary, there are a number of lines of evidence for warfare in the archaeological record. No single site or study is likely to produce all lines of possible evidence, but all should be considered when they occur. In particular, it is the co-occurrence of multiple independent lines of evidence that provides the strongest evidence for warfare and its nature. It is this point that has been most lost on those who are unwilling to see evidence for warfare in the Southwest and elsewhere. It is easy to argue that a hilltop site is not defensive. But if that site is also built with a defensive configuration and is located to facilitate line-of-sight communication with other sites, and if some of these sites are massively burned and some have unburied bodies, the argument for warfare is vastly stronger.

Moreover, archaeology provides a diachronic framework. If in the previous period sites were not situated on hilltops or defensively laid out, if burning was very rare and unburied bodies unknown, the case for warfare in the subsequent period becomes overwhelming. The argument that one line of evidence can be explained by other factors becomes no longer relevant. One is obligated to explain the conjunction of all lines of independent evidence and the change from the preceding period. The difference between many earlier discussions of warfare and some of the cases presented here is that the studies in this volume appeal to multiple independent lines of evidence.

CONCLUSIONS

The prolonged period of thirteenth- and fourteenth-century conflict in the Southwest did not always lead to adjustments in settlement configurations and locations or to migrations to other areas. In many instances, war during this time undoubtedly led to the killing of significant numbers of people. As archaeologists studying this period, we are likely witnessing numerous cases of group extinction. Under this interpretation, warfare takes on a new importance. It would imply that a large number of independent polities must have become extinct between A.D. 1250 and the Spanish entrada. It is likely that even languages were lost during this interval.

The warfare described in these case studies had major impacts on the peoples involved and the modern peoples who are the descendants of the survivors of that difficult time. It is necessary to understand the native southwestern people of both past and present in that light. These particular examples have implications far beyond the events themselves. There is a "big picture" behind these case studies, and this overall view is important—both for building general models of human behavior and for understanding the overall history of the Southwest. Researchers must not lose sight of the fact that although the overall view may be more important than the particulars, it is only through well-worked-out specific examples such as those presented here that we are able to build a big picture with confidence.

NOTE

1. The innate-human-nature model can be simplistic and easily refuted (e.g., Ardrey 1966) or based on careful consideration of selection over several million years (Boehm 1992; Ehrenreich 1997; van der Dennen 1995; Wrangham and Peterson 1996), although it is counterargued that warfare has no evolutionary significance (Bock 1980; Gould 1996; Keeley 1996; Power 1991; Sussman 1997). These arguments are not mutually exclusive. In fact, one could argue that humans resort to warfare in the face of scarce resources only because there has been selection for the propensity to do so. The point is not that we propose one explanation over another, only that the case studies presented here provide information relevant to the scarce-resource model.

CHAPTER TWO

Warfare and Aggregation in the El Morro Valley, New Mexico

Steven A. LeBlanc

The El Morro Valley of west-central New Mexico witnessed one of the clearest instances in the prehistoric Southwest of warfare and its consequences. Although the idea that the late prehistoric people of the valley were involved in warfare is not new, we now understand much more clearly the dynamics of what took place and how to interpret this evidence for warfare and its aftermath.

BACKGROUND

Evidence for prehistoric warfare in the Southwest is more common than generally recognized (Wilcox and Haas 1994; LeBlanc 1997, 1998, 1999, 2000; LeBlanc and Rice this volume), but much of it is indirect or probabilistic in nature. Moreover, in well-documented cases of conflict, such as at Castle Rock (Lightfoot and Kuckelman this volume), there is no evidence for what happened after a successful attack. That is not the case for El Morro. In addition to the ample evidence of defensive measures and of actual attack, there is good evidence for the nature of the response to the conflict.

It has long been recognized that conflict or its threat was of importance to the late prehistoric residents of El Morro. Site locations and layouts in the El Morro area were sufficiently striking that Woodbury (1959) was prompted to consider the likelihood of inter-Puebloan warfare on the basis of his work at Atsinna (Woodbury 1956; Woodbury and Woodbury 1956) in one of the pioneer considerations of this topic. Subsequently, work undertaken in 1972 and 1973 by the Cibola Archaeological Research Project (CARP), directed by Patty Jo Watson, myself, and Charles Redman, produced a very clear case of a successful attack on a settlement and its consequence in the late A.D. 1200s. In addition, settlement patterns determined from systematic survey, village plans based on intensive systematic wall trenching, and a good number of tree-ring dates have allowed us to characterize what took place in the valley during the mid to late 1200s and the early 1300s. This research has produced papers, dissertations, and theses, and a final report is in progress (Skinner 1981; Marquardt 1974, 1978; McGarry 1975; Potter 1997; Watson et al. 1980; LeBlanc 1976, 1978).

Warfare was not the focus of the CARP research project, and the existence of the burned and stone-robbed Scribe S site, a key component of the following discussion, was not known or even expected until found on survey. In fact, the initial research design virtually ignored the possibility of warfare as an important factor in the valley's prehistory. That is one reason why it has taken so long to build an overall model of what happened and why.

The Culture History and Environment of the El Morro Valley

The El Morro Valley floor lies at about 2,200 m (7,200 feet). It is made up of relatively flat alluvial valleys, which geologists refer to as "race-track" valleys, demarcated by tilted mesas (cuestas) that rise gently from the south and drop off sharply on their north sides. The most famous of these mesas is El Morro, known for the numerous early inscriptions carved on its north face. Some volcanic flows are found in the valley; and in places the water table is very high, leading to cienega-like areas; much of the area has no drainage at all. What drainages do exist form the headwaters of the Zuni River. The ponderosa-clad Zuni Mountains form the north edge of the valley. The area was probably more favorable than most in the Southwest for wild game (Potter 1997), and the altitude must have resulted in more rain than in many other areas. Nevertheless, the high altitude would have produced short growing seasons and slow plant growth because of the cold nights. Today attempts at growing corn are met with failure more times than not. It must have always been a very marginal area for agriculture.

In spite of the considerable amount of research that has been done in the Cibola region in general, as summarized in Tainter and Gillio 1980, Kintigh 1985 and 1996, and LeBlanc 1989, the details of the cultural historical sequence in the El Morro Valley are not well worked out. There is little evidence for the nature of the occupations before Pueblo II. There does appear to be one Pueblo II (or early PIII) community that may have had a great house like those found elsewhere in the region (Fowler et al. 1987; Huntley and Schachner 1999), but Pueblo II occupation, including several great houses, is far more common down the Zuni drainage. The most famous of these is the Village of the Great Kivas (Roberts 1932). But because only the late Pueblo III and early Pueblo IV periods are directly relevant here, these earlier times can be ignored.

Leslie Spier (1917), in a truly amazing site survey, recorded all the large PIII-PIV sites in the valley and roughly worked out the ceramic seriation. Thus, when we began work, we already knew the locations and general characteristics of the large, late sites. The CARP project undertook a two-component, systematic site survey. First, complete or partial samples were surveyed around most of the large sites. Second, a random sample of units was surveyed for the rest of the valley. We found that each of the large sites was associated with a group of discrete room blocks that preceded it in time, but clearly all dated to the A.D. 1200s. These room blocks were closely spaced and formed discrete communities. The rest of the valley was almost devoid of habitation sites at this and most other times, except for the occasional field house (see Figure 2.1).

We termed the earlier discrete room block occupation the Scribe S phase, and the later occupation characterized by large pueblos the Muerto phase.

The Scribe S Phase

Before the Scribe S phase in the El Morro Valley, as noted, there seems to have been very light occupation. The Jones Ranch Road sites (Anyon et al. 1983) farther west represent the time period around A.D. 1215. Sites of this time period in this area seem to be small and not defensive. One of these sites, NM:12:V2:7, had a burned pit structure with an unburied body on the floor, but the site as a whole was not burned. Slightly farther away, the Hinkson Ranch seems to represent the late 1100s, as does the less well understood PII/early PIII community in the valley mentioned above; there is no evidence for defensive locations or site layouts at this time either (Kintigh et al. 1995). Thus, before about 1250, there is little evidence for sites either being in defensive locations or laid out to be defensive.

The initial Scribe S phase occupation in the mid A.D. 1200s in the El Morro Valley consisted of seven communities, each made up of clustered room blocks. These communities were very evenly spaced over the valley, approximately three miles apart. As noted, site survey included random samples within the valley as well as samples around the later larger pueblos (Watson et al. 1980; LeBlanc 1978). No substantial sites were encountered other than these seven communities. Although the valley was sampled rather than completely surveyed, if there were additional com-

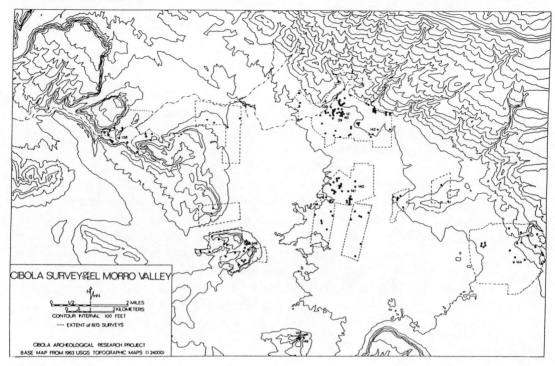

Figure 2.1. El Morro
Valley.

munities, there could not be many of them. All but one of these seven
communities were near large later sites. Moreover, this pattern is repeated outside the valley itself. Chris Zier (1976) excavated a series of
small room blocks—in particular NA11,530—of this same time period
very near the large late site of Heshotauthla (see Stone 1992) down the
Zuni drainage from El Morro (discussed later). There is evidence for
clustered room blocks that are apparently Scribe S phase at Miller
Ranch, and perhaps a lookout site as well, the Shoemaker Ranch site, a
17-room community on a defensive hilltop (Kintigh 1980, 1985).
Farther south, Sandstone Pueblo (Barnett 1974b) may be the same kind
of site relating to the three later sites in the Techado area (McGimsey
1980).

More enigmatic is a suite of sites near the town of Ramah just west of
the El Morro Valley. Some of these sites were excavated as part of the
Michaels Land Exchange, in particular AR 03-03-03-518, -519, -520,
and -788. (These excavations are currently unpublished, and information was graciously provided by Emily Garber, LuAnn Wandsnider, and
Roger Anyon.) As discussed below, these sites date to the Scribe S phase
but consist primarily of jacal structures and deep pithouses (which have
many kiva-like aspects). I refer to this group of sites as the Ramah
Reservoir sites because of their proximity to the reservoir. They lie 2.5 to
3 miles from the now destroyed later Ramah Schoolhouse site. As described below, the Ramah Reservoir sites are farther from a later larger
site than most other Scribe S phase sites, and they are smaller and less
substantial as well.

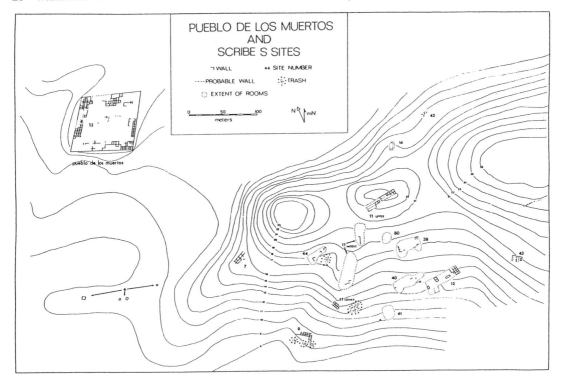

Figure 2.2. Scribe S site.

The seven Scribe S phase communities in El Morro are similar in several ways. Each consisted of discrete room blocks. It is difficult to determine the number of room blocks because the survey was incomplete, and some of the room blocks are so stone-robbed that their size cannot be ascertained without excavation. Also, it appears that some of the large later sites were built right over one or more of the small earlier room blocks. Nevertheless, minimum estimates of the number of room blocks are available. For the Scribe S site itself, there were at least 14 room blocks ranging in size up to about 40 rooms (Figure 2.2). Table 2.1 lists currently known room-block and room estimates for these communities.

The room blocks at these various sites differ considerably in how far apart they are. The average spacing varies from 30 to 900 m. The communities with higher average distances have the most incomplete survey, however, and so the average spacing between room blocks is probably smaller. A maximal average distance between room blocks of 300 m is probably more realistic. The maximal spread of these communities ranges from about 0.5 to 2 km. In spite of this dispersion, the sites are tightly clustered when the valley as a whole is considered. That is, the sites are not evenly distributed over the valley, but there were discrete clusters of room blocks that surely represent integrated communities.

The room blocks ranged in size from a half-dozen rooms to more than forty. Most were two rows of rooms wide, but a few room blocks were three rows deep. A kiva within a room block has been found at the Pettit site, but it is a rare example. Kivas or pithouses probably lay in front of

TABLE 2.1. Characteristics of Scribe S and Muerto Phase Communities in the El Morro Valley

Site or community name	Minimum no. of Scribe S phase room blocks	Estimated minimum no. of Scribe S phase rooms	Average distance between room blocks	Muerto phase pueblos	Room counts for Muerto phase pueblos[a]
Scribe S (Pueblo de los Muertos)	18	410	45 m	Pueblo de los Muertos	880
Cienega	11[b]	205	450 m	Cienega	500
				Mirabal	743
El Morro Rock	7[b]	unknown	900 m	Atsinna	875
				North Atsinna	180
Togeye-Pettit (Kluckhohn)	48	945[c]	265 m	Kluckhohn	1142
CS 142	10	317	30 m	none	—
Tinaja	7[b]	163–211[d]	not meaningful	Tinaja	—
Hole-in-the-Rock (Lookout)	11	270	325 m	Hole-in-the-Rock	300

[a]Based on Kintigh 1985 room counts.
[b]Probably represent significant undercounts because of only partial surveys.
[c]Based on Saitta 1994.
[d]Kintigh's (1985) room count is 163; Watson et al. (1980) have a room count of 211.

the room blocks more commonly than is currently recognized, but no extra-large kivas are known from these sites. There is some evidence for very orderly construction, in particular at the east end of the Pettit site, but for the most part, a few rooms were built and added onto room blocks at one time. The room blocks were otherwise typical for the time range, with habitation and storage rooms and no evidence for second stories.

Several of these communities had at least one room block that was perched on a high place. The most dramatic is one of the room blocks of the Togeye Canyon community, known as the Pettit site, which is located on a mesa remnant in the center of the canyon. The rest of the community lies at the foot of the mesa and in other low areas in the canyon. A similar but less dramatic pattern holds for other Scribe S phase communities. The highest room blocks on the Scribe S site, the upper room block on site CS142, an apparent room block on the mesa top at El Morro rock, and rooms on the small mesa at Tinaja are all high enough to provide excellent views. No particularly elevated room block is in evidence at Hole-in-the-Rock or the Cienega complexes, but in the former case they may have been using the hole in the mesa (discussed below) for viewing at this period as they could have later, and there is no high ground near the Cienega to build on. That is, each of these sites had good line-of-sight capabilities, either through the use of high points or because of the very nature of the location itself.

Therefore, by the beginning of the Scribe S phase, there were discrete large communities in the El Morro Valley, each already strategically located for viewing the other communities. What these communities lacked were defensive site layouts. Although the mesa-top Pettit site was defensive, the community as a whole was not, with several room blocks lying at the foot of the mesa. None of the other communities was built or located to be entirely defensible. This also seems to be the case at the Scribe S phase communities near Heshotauthla and near Ramah, and as noted, the Miller Ranch complex had one defensive room block, very much like the Pettit site, but again the entire community was not defensible.

We can be more specific about the dates of the Scribe S phase than just the mid to late A.D. 1200s, although the picture is not as clear as it might be (Table 2.2). The Scribe S site itself has clusters of dates in 1211, 1228–29, 1235–38, 1240, 1244, 1249, and 1256. None of these clusters is very strong, and the lack of large or deep trash deposits suggests that the site was not intensively occupied for a long time span. Conversely, there do not seem to be any nearby earlier sites that could have been beam-robbed for its construction. It is possible that because of the low use of the area before the founding of the site, dead wood was readily available and incorporated into the roofs, thus accounting for the earlier dates.

There was certainly major construction activity in A.D. 1264–67 at the Scribe S site and a final significant episode of building in 1275–76. NA11,530, the Scribe S phase component near Heshotauthla, has construction dates in the mid-1270s and was occupied at least as late as 1277. The Scribe S phase Ramah Reservoir sites seem to have construction episodes in the 1268–72 time range, which fits the same overall trend. Unfortunately, the Pettit site and other room blocks of this Scribe S phase site, the only other one in the El Morro Valley that has seen extensive excavation (Saitta 1991), have not yielded any tree-ring dates. In summary, although there is evidence for possible earlier construction, the three Scribe S phase communities for which we have information all have dates in the mid-1260s to the mid-1270s, with the last date being 1277 or shortly afterward.

Thus not only are these communities quite similar in layout and settings, but they seem to have significant building going on in the same decade. It is highly likely that these communities' large size, high density, and ideal situation for line-of-sight communication existed because there was a significant threat of warfare. This prediction is in keeping with what we know of the same period elsewhere in the Southwest. At the time these sites were constructed—after A.D. 1250—similar adjustments in settlement patterns and site layouts were being made over much of the northern Southwest. In fact, in the 1260s–70s there is a very notable increase in such evidence (LeBlanc 1999). That is, the Scribe S phase sites seem to have been built during an initial shift to more defensible com-

TABLE 2.2. Tree-Ring Dates from Scribe S and Muerto Phase Sites
(cutting dates and v dates in italic, vv in roman).

Scribe S Site
100_ 7
107_ 2
~
111_ 7
112_
113_ 0 6
114_ 9
115_ 2 5 7
116_ 0 1 3 4 4
117_ 0 5 9
118_ 0
119_ 2 6 7 7
120_ 0 2 2 2 2 3 6 7 9
121_ 0 1 1 1 1 1 1 6 9
122_ 4 6 6 8 8 8 9 9
123_ 0 0 1 1 2 3 3 5 5 6 8 8
124_ 0 0 0 0 0 1 2 3 4 4 4 4 5 6 7 7 9 9 9 9
125_ 0 0 2 2 3 4 5 5 6 6 6 6 6 6 8
126_ 0 0 1 1 1 2 3 4 4 4 4 4 4 4 4 4 4 4 5 5 5
   5 5 5 5 5 5 5 5 6 6 7 7 7 7 7 9
127_ 3 5 5 5 6 6 6 6

Pueblo de los Muertos (CS139)
108_ 7
109_ 6 6
~
115_ 4
116_
117_ 8
118_ 5 8
119_ 8
120_ 3
121_
122_ 8
123_
124_ 5 6 9
125_
126_ 0 2 2 3 4 4 6
127_ 1 4 7 8
128_ 0 0 1 2 4 4 5 7 8

Cienega (CS140)
110_ 3
111_ 7
~
116_ 1
117_ 9
118_ 8
119_ 0 1
120_
121_
122_
123_ 2 3
124_ 9
125_ 9
126_ 2
127_ 0 4 6 9
128_ 2 3 6 7

Mirabal (CS141)
114_ 1
115_ 3
116_
117_ 6
118_ 4
119_ 0
120_ 5
121_
122_ 8 9
123_ 9
124_ 7
125_ 5 8
126_ 0 2 7
127_ 0 9
128_ 3 5 6

TABLE 2.2. Tree-Ring Dates from Scribe S and Muerto Phase Sites
(cutting dates and v dates in Italic, vv in roman). CONTINUED

Tinaja (CS144)	Atsinna (CS149) and North Atsinna (CS149)	NA11,530
103_ 0	105_ 9	108_ 9
111_ 9	~	~
~	111_ 8	117_ 7
114_ 2	~	118_ 8
115_	117_ 1 2 7 9	119_ 5 9
116_ 7	118_ 3	120_
117_ 3	119_	121_ 5
118_	120_ 0	122_ 2 3 6 7
119_	121_ 2	123_ 1 2
120_ 4	122_ 9	124_
121_	123_ 1 2 6	125_ 1 2 5 9
122_	124_ 2 9	126_ 6 7 7 8 9
123_ 4	125_ 7	127_ 1 3 4 5 7
124_ 6	126_ 0 0 6	
125_ 1	127_ 2 3 3 4 6 6 7 7 9	
126_ 2 5 9	128_ 7 7 8	
127_ 0 0	129_ 6 9	
128_ 4	130_ 0	
	131_ 2 2	
	132_	
	133_	
	134_ 9	

Ramah Reservoir	Heshotauthla
112_ 6	111_ 6
115_ 4 6	116_ 5
116_ 2	~
117_ 0 3	123_ 9
118_ 4	124_ 5 7
119_	125_
120_ 0	126_ 2 5
121_ 7	127_ 5
122_ 4	128_ 6 6
123_	129_ 1
124_ 5	
125_ 4 4	
126_ 2 8 8	
127_ 1 2 2	

munities over much of the region. By *more defensible* is meant the clustering of large numbers of people close together, the ensuring of a good view from at least one site, and line-of-sight communication with one's neighbors. The Scribe S sites were more defensible than previous sites, but not as impregnable as the ones that followed. It is likely these communities were built to be as defensible as was thought adequate for the time, but ten to twenty years later this level of defensibility was inadequate. At the Scribe S site, at least, the recognition of such inadequacy was not made until after the site was successfully attacked.

DESTRUCTION OF THE SCRIBE S SITE

Destruction of the Scribe S site and subsequent building of Pueblo de los Muertos provide the most graphic example of warfare in the valley. The Scribe S site was attacked and many room blocks burned (Figure 2.3). There is no evidence of unburied bodies, and although people were undoubtedly killed, the community seems to have survived. One important aspect of the postdestruction period is that stone was removed from most of the Scribe S room blocks, apparently to build nearby Pueblo de los Muertos. Other Scribe S phase sites were also stone-robbed, including room blocks at the Pettit site near the Kluckhohn ruin and NA11,530 near Heshotauthla. Also, NA11,530 was extensively burned, and considerable burning was recorded on the Ramah Reservoir sites. (We would not expect stone-robbing of these sites because of their distance to the later Ramah Schoolhouse site.)

Evidence for burning at the Scribe S site comes from rooms that had in situ deposits, including quantities of bowls, ladles, and storage jars on floors (Figure 2.3). Other rooms had large quantities of burned corn. Fires were so hot in some rooms that the floors were burned purple. There is no evidence from any room block that there was any occupation after this burning episode. Although apparently not all rooms were burned, we have multiple cases of burned rooms from discrete room blocks spaced well apart. All room blocks are stone-robbed to some degree, and in situ assemblages in both living quarters and storage facilities were present in both burned and unburned rooms. I believe this combination of factors to be a signature for warfare. As I have argued elsewhere (LeBlanc 1999), accidental burning should be random and should not affect separate room blocks at the same time. Deliberate burning on site abandonment should not result in foodstuffs and other valuables left in place. Ritual burning should be confined to a few special rooms. Thus the co-occurrence of massive extensive burning, in situ deposits, and site abandonment is best explained by warfare. The dismantling of the Scribe S site and the prompt building of the defensive Pueblo de los Muertos nearby is further evidence for conflict, as discussed below.

Figure 2.3. Scribe S
burned room.

There are several lessons to be drawn from these El Morro sites that
are relevant to understanding warfare in an archaeological context.
Some burned rooms were essentially empty of artifacts, perhaps because
items were salvaged during or after the destruction. Or perhaps the
rooms were simply empty at the time of destruction. Perhaps they were
cleaned out for some particular task just before the attack or even looted
by the attackers before burning. Thus the absence of in situ artifacts in
the presence of extensive burning does not automatically mean that warfare was not involved. A second point is that large groups of people were
susceptible to devastating attacks, not just minor raids. This point is
often missed by researchers who believe that tribal-level warfare involves
only intermittent skirmish and ambush and that formal or pitched battles
are rare or merely symbolic. A careful reading of the ethnographic litera-

ture shows that whereas raiding, ambushing, and even "formal" fights could take place almost continually or at least annually, massive attacks intent on the total destruction of one's enemy also occurred (see Keeley 1996; for a literature summary, see LeBlanc and Rice this volume). Just such attacks are vividly remembered by contemporary New Guinea people, for instance. Evidence for massive attacks is to be expected; lack of such is surprising.

THE SCRIBE S–MUERTO PHASE TRANSITION

There are enough tree-ring dates to determine fairly closely when the attack on the Scribe S site took place and to date the consequent building of Pueblo de los Muertos. It turns out that this one event was not isolated but was part of the transition from the Scribe S phase to the subsequent Muerto phase over much of the Zuni area. The relevant tree-ring dates are summarized in Table 2.2. As previously discussed, various Scribe S phase sites, including the Scribe S site itself, saw significant construction in the mid A.D. 1270s. The most plausible interpretation of the dates is that Pueblo de los Muertos was built no later than 1284 with intensive construction from then to 1288. The alternative is that the 1284 beam from Pueblo de los Muertos was robbed from the Scribe S site and Pueblo de los Muertos was built in 1288. It seems quite certain that the abandonment and new construction occurred between 1277 and 1288, based on the youngest dates from the Scribe S site and those from Pueblo de los Muertos. The Cienega site seems to have had major construction between 1279 and 1282. The Mirabal site, although it has one beam that dates to 1260, like the other large sites has a cluster of dates between 1279 and 1286. The Atsinna dates are a little less clear, but a case for very late 1270s construction and certainly by 1287 can be made. Dates from the Tinaja site do not help much, although the site does have a 1284 date.

As discussed above, building was taking place on the Scribe S phase sites in the mid A.D. 1260s to the mid-1270s, with the last date being 1277, and the large defensive sites have evidence for building from 1279 to the early 1280s. Therefore, there is a very strong likelihood that sometime in the five years between 1279 and 1284, the Scribe S, Ramah Reservoir, and NA11,530 sites were abandoned and Pueblo de los Muertos, Atsinna, Cienega, and Mirabal were built. It is even possible that all these events took place in the same year, and if so, then A.D. 1279 is the most likely year.

Given the closeness of the dates from all these different sites, the transition from Scribe S to Muerto phase was essentially synchronic over the entire Zuni area. Most likely, all seven Scribe S communities in the valley were affected, as well as the downstream Ramah and Heshotauthla communities and a number of others considered below.

THE MUERTO PHASE

The Muerto phase is characterized by very large sites built around central plazas with high exterior walls formed by the outermost row of rooms (see Table 2.1). Other aspects of these communities are also of interest: their locations, the use of rapid building methods in their construction, a concern for secure domestic water supplies, and an increase in the types of special-purpose (ceremonial?) structures.

Several of the sites, including Atsinna, North Atsinna, Pueblo de los Muertos, and Hole-in-the-Rock, are large rectangles of room blocks. Two, Cienega and Mirabal, consist of large circular room blocks. The Kluckhohn site combines a rectangular and a circular room block (Figure 2.4). The remaining site, Tinaja, is more enigmatic. It consists of a small room block on a low mini-mesa with several room blocks at its foot. It is probably a Scribe S phase cluster of sites that was modified by adding a more defensive room block on the mini-mesa, and so bridges the gap between the Scribe S phase and the Muerto phase. It seems to have been abandoned and the upper part cleaned out, not burned as the Scribe S site was, very early in the Muerto phase, and it does not fit the characteristics of the other Muerto phase pueblos.

The other Muerto phase sites are remarkably similar in their construction. As noted, each has a high exterior wall created by the outer wall of the outermost rooms of the pueblo. In each case, the rooms were laid out in a rectangle or circle with a large central, empty plaza. The first row of rooms against the plaza was single-storied so that the rooms formed an amphitheater-like structure with rooms stepping down into the central plaza. In some cases, such as Atsinna, part of the plaza was filled in with additional rows of rooms, complicating the picture just described, but the overall plan of high exterior walls formed by rooms and a large central open space was preserved.

Looked at in terms of changes over time and in comparison with contemporary events in the Southwest, these architectural developments can be explained as necessary for defense. The back row of rooms in use during the historic period at Acoma pueblo presents an analogy for the high outer wall: its defensive value is immediately apparent (Figure 2.5), and this aspect of these prehistoric sites has long been recognized. The value of the large open plazas is often overlooked, however. Warfare at this level of social complexity includes frequent raids and ambushes, and although there are usually only one or two victims from such raids, they can occur with such frequency that the total number of individuals killed per decade can be quite great. Women are particularly vulnerable to such raids. This topic is considered in more detail by Keeley (1996) and for the Southwest by LeBlanc (1999). The large enclosed plazas would have provided safe places to conduct many daily activities without risk.

Other characteristics of the Muerto phase sites are also relevant. A se-

Figure 2.4. Muerto
Phase site plans: A.
Tinaja, B. Hole in the
Rock, C. Kluckhohn,
D. Puerto de los
Muertos, E. Atsinna,
F. Cienaga, G.
Mirabal.

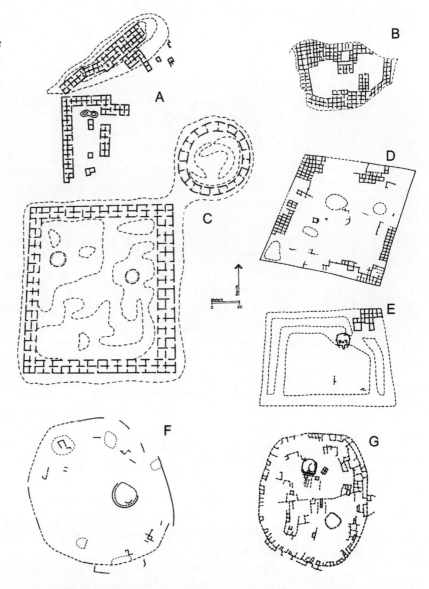

cure domestic water supply was very important. We have for evidence a
walk-in well within the plaza at the Cienega site, and perhaps there was
one at the Mirabal site as well. Pueblo de los Muertos was adjacent to a
stream, but this was apparently not secure enough: a short canal diverted
water from the stream to the very west edge of the site, right up to the
only opening in the exterior wall. This stream emanates from a spring
upslope and was probably quite reliable in the past, although the flows
may not have been great. The location of the Kluckhohn ruin in the bottom of the drainage might have permitted a walk-in well to function in
that plaza or there may have been access to domestic water just outside
the walls; the lack of excavation prevents us from confirming this possibility. Finally, Atsinna has cisterns cut into the mesa-top bedrock, which

Figure 2.5. View of back of last roomblock at Acoma Pueblo around turn of the century. Photo courtesy of Peabody Museum, Harvard University.

presumably collected rainwater usable for domestic purposes and eliminated the need to descend from the mesa to the famous pool at its foot (Woodbury 1956; Woodbury and Woodbury 1956). It is unknown whether North Atsinna had similar features. It is not clear whether any special efforts were made to secure domestic water at Hole-in-the-Rock. In summary, the majority of the sites have some evidence of concern with safe access to domestic water.

Another aspect of these large towns is the consistent use of what has been called "ladder" construction (Roney 1996), which is a method of building large pueblos rapidly that is found at this time over a large area of the Southwest. It consists of laying long parallel walls and later adding the cross-walls that form the rooms (Figure 2.6). At some sites, such as Pueblo de los Muertos, the layout was more complex: the long parallel walls were built two room spaces apart, cross-walls were added which made cells that were twice as long as standard rooms, and then these rooms were subdivided by another cross-wall into the final room cells. Although there are some differences in the particular form this construction method took, one thing is very clear: it was a communal or work-gang–based building method. Room sizes are highly standardized, as are door placements. At Pueblo de los Muertos even the location of wall niches was highly regular. One aspect of the construction is that no one could move in until everyone could. That is, the construction produced rooms en masse rather than piecemeal. A high level of standardization can also be seen in the existence of kivas within the room blocks. At

Pueblo de los Muertos these consist of two standard room cells in which the partition wall was either not built or later removed. That is, no special consideration was given to room-block kivas in the building plan. They had to be based on the standard module size and were not laid out separately.

Cooperation was necessary and is the key to the building method. Interestingly, the outer wall of the pair of long parallel walls was always thicker than its interior counterpart. Because the outer room wall was the defensive wall of the pueblo, the extra thickness was probably added to ensure its strength. Building with "ladder" construction is known from Pueblo de los Muertos, Atsinna, Cienega, and Mirabal in El Morro. It was also used elsewhere in the Southwest, from the Homolovi sites, to the Hopi area, to Gran Quivera (see LeBlanc 1999 for a full discussion). The only documented instance of the use of this construction technique that does not date to the A.D. 1275–1325 time range is Old Kotyiti in the Rio Grande near Cochiti, which was built in the historic period as a defensive refuge. Thus the use of this building technique seems to correlate with the rapid building of defensive sites.

One consequence of this building plan was that the resultant room blocks had a width of three to four rows of rooms. Each of the four sides of Pueblo de los Muertos had four rows of ground-floor rooms. The greater the number of rows of continuous rooms, the more walls a particular room shares with its neighbors. The greater the number of shared walls, the less wall stone is needed per room. One can compute a measure of such wall sharing by determining the average number of walls needed per room. A free-standing room needs four walls, but two connected rooms need only three and a half walls each because they share one wall. One can compare the average number of walls per room for the double-rowed room blocks of the Scribe S phase site with that of Pueblo de los Muertos. We get a Scribe S phase average of about 2.5 walls per room and a Pueblo de los Muertos average of only 1.17 walls per room.

If, as is argued, the Scribe S phase site was dismantled to build Pueblo de los Muertos rapidly, the builders would not have had to quarry and shape stone, saving a great deal of time. Reducing the average number of walls per room would make the stock of already cut stone extend much further. It also meant that construction would have been faster because fewer walls per room needed to be built. I have shown elsewhere (LeBlanc 1999) that building Pueblo de los Muertos with already prepared stone that did not have to be moved far, and with a high degree of room-wall sharing, meant that the three outer rows of rooms could have been built in about two weeks. Although this undertaking would have been a tremendous and exhausting effort and is not in keeping with our notions of rather haphazard and casual construction of historic pueblos, one has only to look at the massive construction projects of Chaco times to convince oneself that if the need arose, such an achievement was feasible. The actual speed of construction has not been demonstrated, but we

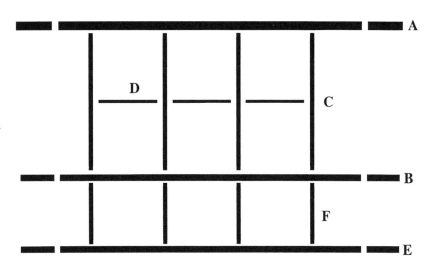

Figure 2.6. Ladder type construction. Ladder type construction in El Morro consisted of long parallel walls, with cross-walls added later. The form depicted here is as seen on Pueblo de los Muertos. The "double ladder" consists of an extra-thick exterior wall (A). A parallel wall (B) was laid two room-widths away. Then cross-walls (C) were added, making extra-long room cells. These extra-long cells were turned into standard rooms by adding perpendicular dividing walls (D). An additional single ladder was appended to the double ladder by laying a long parallel wall (E) and then adding short cross-walls (F).

know that the outer three rows of rooms at Pueblo de los Muertos were built on sterile soil. No trash of any kind accumulated before any of these rooms was built. In contrast, the fourth innermost row of rooms was built over a layer of trash. Given the large number of people that must have been living in the pueblo, such trash layers must have accumulated quickly. The fact that none was found beneath any of the outer three rows suggests they must have been built fast, and simultaneously.

The line-of-sight locations of the Muerto phase pueblos are even more striking than those of their predecessors. Atsinna and North Atsinna have exceptional views, enabling observers there to see at least three other sites. Hole-in-the-Rock, as the name implies, is built up against a narrow mesa remnant where there is an opening in the mesa wall that allows one to see three other sites. Although it is not clear whether the hole is completely natural or not, the pueblo was located to take advantage of it. It may be argued that the other sites were simply fortuitously located to be able to see one another, but it's hard to accept such an argument for the Hole-in-the-Rock site. Two other locations are more difficult to evaluate. It appears that from the second story of Pueblo de los Muertos one could have seen the second story of Kluckhohn, but this possibility has never been tested. Similarly, it is unclear whether one could have seen Hole-in-the-Rock from Atsinna. Thus the visual links are not necessarily perfect: not all sites could see all other sites. These links seem to be much more than chance, however.

A final interesting aspect of these sites is the number of different types of special-function rooms that are known. The big sites have four classes of kivas or kiva-like rooms, including rooms within the room blocks which have benches, airshafts, and deflectors but which could have held only a handful of people. These are made from a standard room cell, as noted above; the modular plan was not adjusted to accommodate such needs. Large kivas are also found within room blocks, however, and are at least twice the size of the standard room cells. They would have required construction or remodeling efforts after the main building activity was completed. Atsinna and the Mirabal site also have extra-large kivas in the plazas. These are about 9 m in diameter, distinctly smaller than Chacoan and earlier Great Kivas. They could not have held the entire community but would have contained a substantial number of people—and can be referred to as "Grand Kivas" for our purposes here. Finally, located between the Mirabal and Cienega sites is a very large, unroofed feature that would appear to be an "unroofed great kiva." As I have shown previously (LeBlanc 1989), these are known elsewhere from slightly earlier to about the same time at Site 143—the Hubble Corner site—(McGimsey 1980), the Box S site (see Kintigh 1985), and Hinkson Ranch (Kintigh et al. 1995). No Grand Kivas or Great Kivas—roofed or unroofed—are known from any Scribe S phase site. Given the limited amount of excavation that has taken place on the large sites, the number of kiva-like structures associated with them is significant.

Thus, at the same time that the people of these communities were pushed very close together, or entire communities themselves were suddenly juxtaposed, we find an increase in the number of kiva-like features and an increase in their size ranges. This phenomenon is probably related to the new proximity of great numbers of people. Ultimately, of course, the pueblos themselves become kiva-like in that the stepped rooms become the viewing area for performances in the enclosed plazas. Some researchers (e.g., Cameron 1995) have argued that the function of this type of large site was to facilitate such activities. Surely this is backward, however. The people were suddenly forced to live very close to one another in very large numbers, and they consequently and rapidly evolved mechanisms to cope with the social problems that ensued. One of the mechanisms was public ceremonies involving lots of participants. These large sites were not built to enable public ceremonies in their plazas with lots of participants, but instead such ceremonies evolved to cope with the existence for the first time of such large communities. It is quite likely that the Kachina Cult (Adams 1991) developed partly in response to these problems, but that topic is beyond the scope of this chapter (see LeBlanc 1998, 1999).

The shift to the Muerto phase resulted in some adjustments to community locations in the valley. One location was abandoned at the time of the transition (CS142), another apparently soon thereafter (Tinaja). At the same time, however, two locations in the valley wound up with two large sites instead of one. The large Cienega and Mirabal sites were only 300 m apart, and Atsinna and North Atsinna were even closer to each other. Both these sets of sites seem to be cases of site pairs. Such close pairings of large pueblos are relatively common at this general time on the Colorado Plateau and in the White Mountains. The Pescado Springs sites downstream are a similar example: at least three sites seem to be contemporary and very close together around the springs. Other examples include the Bidahochi South sites, the Chavez Pass South complex's East and West pueblos, and the multiple "room blocks" at Kinishba, Grasshopper, and Q Ranch. This community pattern is discussed in more detail in LeBlanc 1999. Of course, modern Zuni (Halonawa) is a historic example in which six separate communities came together to form a single village. The six kivas of historic Zuni pueblo may relate to the initial separate Prehispanic villages.

Paired sites are closely related to a second community pattern, one that is much more subtle. For some large, late sites in the Zuni region and beyond, the site is a single monolithic construction, but one with discrete parts. The circular and square room blocks on the Kluckhohn Ruin, which are linked by a suite of rooms several rooms wide, are the best example of this pattern (Figure 2.2). Archeotekopa II has similar merged circular and square room blocks (Kintigh 1985). I have argued elsewhere (LeBlanc 1998, 1999) that Kin Tiel, according to Mindeleff's (1891) map, is really two circular sites that have been merged. The Newton site is also made up of linked circular and square room blocks (Frisbee 1973). Thus we find in El Morro both these patterns: namely, two site pairs—Atsinna and North Atsinna, as well as Cienega and Mirabal—and one "merged pair"—Kluckhohn.

If, as I argue below, each of these site components originally represented a discrete community, then we actually have represented at these five Muerto phase locations a total of eight original communities: Pueblo de los Muertos, Cienega, Mirabal, Atsinna, North Atsinna, Hole-in-the-Rock, Kluckhohn rectangle, and Kluckhohn circle. There were seven known discrete communities in the same area during the Scribe S phase.

EXTERNAL RELATIONS

The large sites in El Morro did not exist in a vacuum. The presence of the small room-block sites—the Scribe S phase—have been hard to recognize without systematic intensive survey, but the large sites in the area have long been known (Spier 1917; Kintigh 1985). Thus one can look at the regional settlement pattern for the Muerto phase. The El Morro sites seem to be part of a much larger cluster of sites. One can make a case that at one time there were about 18 sites in the cluster. That would make this the largest cluster of sites in the Southwest, matched only by an equal number of sites in the Hopi mesas area. These 18 Zuni sites are spaced over an area of about 45 km by 26 km.

Along the Zuni River there are a number of these large sites. Yellow House, the most westerly, had 425 rooms. (All Zuni-area site room counts are from Kintigh 1985 except as noted above.) Upstream is Heshotauthla (875 rooms). Farther upstream is the Pescado group: Lower Pescado Village (420 rooms), Pescado West (425 rooms), Lower Pescado Ruin (180 rooms), and Upper Pescado Ruin (405 rooms), the last three of which are all very close together near the reliable Pescado Springs. Upriver, the site disturbance around the town of Ramah confuses things somewhat, but there was the Lower Deracho site (609 rooms), Day Ranch (574 rooms), and the somewhat smaller Ramah Schoolhouse site (186 rooms). Finally, the previously discussed El Morro group contained Pueblo de Los Muertos, Cienega, Mirabal, Hole-in-the-Wall, Atsinna, and North Atsinna. These later sites are spaced some 2.5 miles apart, whereas the large Kluckhohn ruin is 5.5 miles from the nearest El Morro site and 4.3 miles from the Deracho group.

One can see these sites either as being somewhat clumped or as simply a single string of sites from Yellow House on the western, downstream side to Atsinna upstream in the east. This string of at least 14 sites has no gap of more than 4.5 miles (7 km) between sites. There are also two other slightly outlying sites—Kay Chee (225 rooms and on a ridgetop) and Pescado Canyon (723 rooms)—but they are also no more than 4.5 miles (7 km) from other sites.

There are another four sites on the southeast edge of the Zuni Reservation with a spacing of about 3 to 4 miles between sites: Jack's Lake (245 rooms), Archeotekopa II (1,412 rooms), the Fort Site (144 rooms), and Ojo Pueblo (222 rooms) (Kintigh 1996). Jack's Lake, Archeotekopa II, and Ojo Pueblo are all very close to water or have a source inside the pueblo. The Fort Site is relatively small and the only one that is defensively located. This group is, incidentally, a good example of large sites next to water and small sites on high places.

In addition, there were a few sites that were either outside this cluster or tangential to it. As is universally the case in the Southwest at this time, such outlier or "unattached" sites are very short-lived. The best known of these is the Big House site (500 rooms; Stein and Fowler 1996) in Manuelito Canyon (Fowler et al. 1987; Weaver 1978). Another such example is the Box S site (473 rooms) near Nutria (Spier 1917; Kintigh 1985). Though not too far from the El Morro group of sites, it does seem to be rather isolated. Spier's site 61 (122 rooms) north of Zuni is another. Each is at least 7.5 miles (12 km) from another possibly contemporaneous site. All three sites are very close to domestic water with a possible walk-in well at Box S.

The obvious question is whether all these sites were contemporary. Keith Kintigh (1985) and I see the evidence somewhat differently. I believe all or almost all these sites were occupied during the very late A.D. 1200s. Clearly, not all have the same ceramic frequencies, and some survived longer than others. But I believe there was one generation when the bulk of them were contemporaneously occupied. Unlike the case in the El Morro Valley, there are almost no tree-ring dates from these other sites in the Zuni area. Therefore, I base my argument on the level of ceramic similarity and the actual overlapping tree-ring dates from the El Morro sites and an extrapolation to the entire cluster. These other sites are close enough architecturally and ceramically that, I believe, for at least a generation most of them were contemporaneously occupied, as can be argued from tree-ring data for the ones in El Morro.

It should be noted that the interpretation of the settlement pattern changes and social dynamics does not require that these sites all be perfectly contemporary, only that most of the large sites be occupied in the last decade of the 1200s.

SITE CLUSTERS NEAR THE ZUNI CLUSTER

Outside the large group of sites that make up the Zuni cluster—of which El Morro is a part—are several nearby clusters that probably figured in the overall external relationships of the Zuni cluster. The seven immediately surrounding site clusters are tallied in Table 2.3 and Figure 2.7. Excavation data are available for only a few of the sites in these other clusters. The Newton site in the Newton-Rattail cluster was intensively burned; it is unclear whether there were significant unburied bodies. Two sites in the Techado cluster, Horse Camp Mill—McGimsey's site 616—and Techado Springs, were both burned; apparently, each had in situ deposits and unburied bodies, at least one of which died a traumatic death (McGimsey 1980; LeBlanc, personal communication from pothunters, 1998). No excavations have taken place on the Jaralosa Draw sites or on the Upper Puerco. Although some limited testing took place on sites in the Cebolleta cluster (Dittert 1959; Ruppé 1953), there is no published information about extensive excavations on the Calabash site. Our knowledge of a cluster farther to the west—the Upper Little Colorado cluster—is much better, the majority of sites having witnessed some excavation, although sometimes early or poorly reported (see Duff 1995, 1996, and Kintigh 1996 for syntheses).

We can summarize the relations among these clusters. None of the clusters was nearly as large as Zuni, and none had sites as large as the largest Zuni cluster sites. We see then that the sites in El Morro were closely spaced and, as argued below, made up an alliance cluster. Not far removed were another dozen sites or so that were probably also loosely allied. Separated from them by gaps of 20 miles or more were five other site clusters, each probably constituting a separate alliance of sites that may have been intermittently allies or enemies with the Zuni cluster. Thus each large site in the El Morro Valley was embedded in a much larger social milieu, with strong allies in the valley and probably weaker but still significant allies outside the valley but not far away. Outside this alliance was a series of other alliances that could have been friend or foe over time but were probably generally competitive. Still farther away was the Upper Little Colorado cluster, which seems to have lasted a long time and was probably more often an ally of the Zuni cluster than a competitor.

TABLE 2.3. Site Clusters near the Zuni Site Cluster.

Cluster and Sites with Map No.	Evidence for Conflict	No. of Rooms	References and Notes
Zuni Cluster			See text
Upper Puerco, West Cluster			Stein and Fowler 1996
Isham		50	
Sanders/Rocky Point, K:15:2	?		This is a questionable member of cluster
Emigrant Springs	?		
Taylor Springs	?		
Jaralosa Draw			Fowler et al. 1987
Fort Atarque, LA55637	200		
Ojo Bonito, LA11433	225		
Techado			
Veteado Pueblo, LA44918	?		Fowler et al. 1987
Techado Spring, LA6010	Some burning, large number of unburied bodies	500	Fowler et al. 1987, pothunter informants
Horse Camp Mill, LA10983, McGimsey 616	Very extensive, two unburied bodies	500	McGimsey 1980
Newton-Rattail		Roney 1996	
Rattail, 68112	200		
Newton, LA13422	Some burning, child skull in "special" room, other possible unburied bodies	165	Frisbie 1973
Cebolleta Mesa			Roney 1996
Ranger Station		150	
Calabash, LA1331		367	
Penole, LA11677		100	
Kowina, LA1334		86	
Upper Little Colorado			Kintigh 1996

WHAT HAPPENED?

Based on the information above, one can construct a "just so" sort of story about the events in El Morro and the surrounding region. During the mid A.D. 1200s people moved into the El Morro Valley, probably from areas downstream. They constructed seven communities, and the fact that they were carefully placed to view one another implies that the move was rather orderly and the people already had an alliance relationship or formed one as they settled. The close clustering of the individual

Figure 2.7. Regional map showing site clusters near the Zuni cluster.

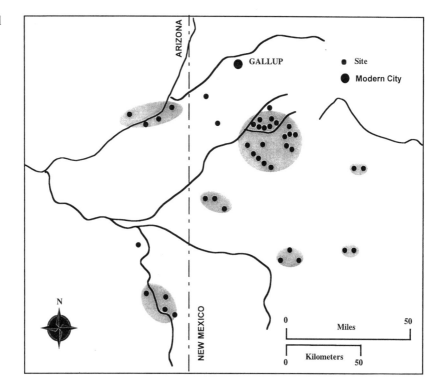

room blocks suggests a concern with defense, as does the line-of-sight village placement. But except for the room block on the top of the mesa remnant at the Pettit site, there was apparently no particular concern with defensive construction. For example, at El Morro rock itself some room blocks were on the mesa, but most were at its foot in undefensive locations.

Room blocks were single-story, did not enclose plazas, and were often quite small—ten rooms or fewer. All over the Southwest at this time similar defensive adjustments were being made, and these communities responded much as the others did. The occupation lasted for a generation or so, and then sometime very close to A.D. 1279 one of these communities—the Scribe S site—was attacked and burned. Similar successful attacks seem to have taken place at the communities near Heshotauthla and Ramah Reservoir. It appears that some or most of the population survived these attacks, although elsewhere in the Southwest people were not so fortunate, as was the case at Castle Rock (Lightfoot and Kuckelman 1995, this volume). Members of these communities as well as people of other communities quickly dismantled the room blocks, used the stone to build massive defensive sites, and fundamentally changed the nature of their communities. The architectural transformation took less than a decade, and probably only a few years, to complete over a large area.

In the process, some communities such as the CS142 and Tinaja sites abandoned their locations and probably formed some of the site pairs found in the valley. This must have been an even more difficult decision for the community members to make with an even greater impact on their lives. The wall stone could not have been reused and so building the new pueblos would have been more work. Also, the right to farm land would have had to have been negotiated with the already extant community at that location. (Hopi oral traditions are filled with just such integration efforts and problems.) Tinaja was always relatively isolated from the other sites and may have been vulnerable so far away. It does not seem that there was any place to build a large settlement at the location of CS142 that could have had line of sight with the other pueblos, or possibly the community felt too small to go on alone. Interestingly, the Mirabal site had a larger population than the Cienega site, and North Atsinna is much smaller than Atsinna. It is quite possible that one of these sites was built by CS142 site people who felt the need to be very close to a much larger community.

In any case, by A.D. 1286 the process was complete and all the inhabitants of the valley were living in large, defensive, intervisible sites. There is no evidence that any more successful attacks took place, but sometime in the early to mid-1300s these sites and the valley were abandoned and the historic Zuni villages were built or greatly expanded.

Events in the surrounding region took on a very different cast. A similar process of abandoning small discrete pueblos and building large fort-like communities was taking place in all the surrounding clusters and in the other communities in the Zuni area cluster, although no examples as clear as El Morro have been worked out. Unlike El Morro, however, where most of the communities survived intact at least for a while, outside the Zuni area both communities and entire site clusters were fast disappearing. Of the five surrounding clusters, we have useful but limited excavation data from only three. On the basis of surface sherds, it appears that the entire Rio Puerco West cluster and the Jaralosa cluster were short-lived. The Rio Puerco West cluster in particular seems to have been completely abandoned by A.D. 1300; part of the Jaralosa cluster may have lasted into the early 1300s. Nothing else can be said at this time about these sites.

Of the three sites in the Techado cluster, two have been partially excavated: McGimsey's Site 616, also known as Horse Camp Mill, and Techado Springs (McGimsey 1980). Both these sites were intensively burned, and Horse Camp Mill revealed considerable in situ assemblages and some unburied bodies (McGimsey 1980; John King, personal communication 1975). Pothunter informants have described Techado Springs the same way with a considerable number of unburied bodies. There is little evidence that any of these sites existed as late as A.D. 1300. Similar destruction is known from the Newton site in the Newton-Rattail cluster, and it also seems to date no later than 1300. Some sites of the Cebolleta cluster probably lasted into the early 1300s, but not as late as 1350

(Roney 1996). That is, four of these five clusters were abandoned or destroyed by around 1300, and the last one did not survive much longer.

We have no evidence for any successful attacks in the Zuni cluster after the A.D. 1270s, but it is clear that the number of sites declined. As noted, there were initially about 18 sites in the cluster. Although Kintigh (1985) does not believe that all these were necessarily contemporary, all or almost all seem to have been occupied in the very late 1200s. That is, a reasonable case can be made that for a brief time nearly all were in use. More important, regardless of the exact number initially, by 1350 there were clearly fewer sites, and by 1400 there were fewer still. Even if it turns out that several were not built until later, the number of sites declined substantially in the next hundred years. Ultimately, of course, the number fell to 6, the communities encountered by Coronado in 1540. Thus, whether the number fell from 18 to 6 or from 14 to 6 is in many ways irrelevant. The original number of sites in the Zuni cluster was larger than for the surrounding clusters, and the average site size was as large as or larger than any of the other clusters. The other clusters all declined to nothing; the Zuni cluster declined also but continued to exist.

Also of interest is that the decline was rapid. There is little evidence based on sherds or dates that the Jaralosa, Techado, Newton-Rattail, Cebolleta, or Puerto West clusters survived more than a decade or so into the A.D. 1300s, if that long. Thus by 1350 there was only one surviving cluster out of the original six, namely Zuni. The slightly more distant Upper Little Colorado cluster also survived. These two clusters had a dynamic relationship for the next 75 years or so before the Upper Little Colorado cluster died out, but that is beyond the scope of the present chapter. In short, as the number of sites and clusters declined, so apparently did the military threat. The later Zuni sites are less defensive than their predecessors, and there is no evidence of successful attacks.

The number of people involved is hard to determine with much precision (see Kintigh 1985 and Ferguson 1996 for extended discussions). Their numbers must have declined substantially, however. There is no evidence that the people from these seven clusters migrated to any other area in large numbers. Five of the clusters declined to zero, and the average number of rooms for the historic six pueblos was lower than for the more numerous ca. A.D. 1300s sites. I think that between 1275 and 1540 the total population of these six clusters declined to 25 percent of its initial figure, but this is open to debate. That there was a substantial decline, however, is quite clear.

WHAT DID NOT HAPPEN

It is sometimes easier archaeologically to determine what could not have happened rather than what did. Turning to the El Morro Valley itself, we find that all evidence indicates the communities in the valley did not attack one another. This can be seen by the closeness in their locations and by the placement of new large pueblos. As has been discussed, the Scribe S phase sites were located to be able to see one another. Such viewing has no offensive benefit, as individual movements cannot be seen at these distances, but it has important defensive aspects. That is, intervisibility makes sense only if the communities were allied and intended to aid one another if necessary. Nevertheless, it is possible that they were originally allied but the alliance came apart. If intravalley conflict had followed, we would not expect the subsequent sites to have also been built so close to one another and again with intervisibility apparently a concern. Surely the combatants would have moved farther apart. This suggestion is confirmed by the lack of evidence for further conflict at these sites. A state of intravalley conflict during the Muerto Phase would certainly have left some evidence. If one questions the likelihood that such large, fortress-like pueblos could have been successfully attacked, one must confront the evidence for such attacks found over much of the Southwest at this time, often involving large defensive sites. Two-thirds of the 27 site clusters for which we have information underwent one or more successful attacks. Clusters around the Zuni area, including the Techado, Rattail-Newton, and Upper Little Colorado, all have evidence that one large community was successfully attacked (LeBlanc 1998, 1999).

These successful attacks did not necessarily all emanate from Zuni. There were still other clusters around these five clusters, and the Zuni cluster was only one of many potential enemies. What we can conclude, however, is that the Zuni cluster communities do not seem to have fought one another on a major scale. If that had been the case, we would expect the sites to have begun to be relocated and to open up no-man's-lands as found earlier between the six clusters. This would have been especially likely to occur as the other clusters disappeared, opening up areas for settlement. That does not seem to have happened.

Such an analysis is rather simplistic, however, because we know that the Hopi cluster witnessed internal conflicts up to the 1700s and yet remained intact. The general point is that such conflict did not result in the development of new separate clusters at Hopi, nor, if such conflict existed at Zuni, did it result in separate clusters there. It would appear that the Zuni cluster remained an effective alliance throughout this period, unlike its neighbors, and that the El Morro alliance remained intact while the valley was occupied.

WHY DID IT HAPPEN?

The question why the series of events just described took place forces us to confront the issue of causes in general. At the local level, one can suppose that some small group of leaders in one community decided to attack the Scribe S site. They may have had knowledge of other attacks that had recently taken place in the Southwest, at Castle Rock, Sand

Canyon, Salmon, and the like (see LeBlanc 1999 for a discussion). Nevertheless, their reasons must have been local: a threat real or imagined or a perceived opportunity. Extreme food stress coupled with the perception that the Scribe S site was vulnerable could have been specific motivations, for example. From a broader perspective, however, warfare was probably on the rise during the previous generation, and the Scribe S site was built on a ridgetop in response to such warfare. Attack, counterattack, death, and revenge death were probably ongoing. The successful attack on the Scribe S site may have been just a lucky hit by attackers intent on more limited gains.

Viewed at a broader level, the El Morro case is but one of many encountered over the Southwest at this time. There can be little doubt that warfare intensified over the entire area in the late A.D. 1200s and early 1300s. Thus its overall cause cannot simply be local revenge or similar motives. Something changed substantially over the entire area, and warfare was one of the consequences. One can actually argue that warfare intensified over much of the entire continent at this general time and that the Southwest was one of many examples of this intensification. I have argued elsewhere (LeBlanc 1999) that the overall cause was climatic deterioration—with consequent economic collapse—known world wide during the Little Ice Age (Grove 1990; Lamb 1995; Le Roy Ladurie 1971). In short, the climate of the world appears to have been warm and wet during what is termed the Medieval Warm period, beginning around A.D. 900 and lasting into the 1100s. Then the climate seems to have rapidly become drier and colder, culminating in the Little Ice Age. The peak cold probably occurred in the 1500s, but by the early 1300s it was significantly colder in the British Isles. How closely the Southwest tracked these general world patterns in both timing and severity is open to debate.[1]

The El Morro population response was multifold. The movement into the higher-elevated valley may have been an attempt to deal with rainfall shortages at lower elevations. But increased cold, with concomitant increased failure of crops to mature, probably resulted in the abandonment of this high-altitude strategy in a generation or two.

The initial response to increased threat of attack was probably a compromise solution. Move into large communities, place them close (3 miles from each other) and in line-of-sight locations, but continue the previous pattern of living in separate, small room blocks. People would have had to make social adjustments to living with so many others in one general location, but friction would have been reduced by the separate housing units. This response was widespread over much of the Southwest at this time. There was aggregation, but not full integration in most areas that later saw such integration. One can see both willingness and resistance to moving close together in increasingly larger units.

In any case, this initial response was inadequate, and the building of the large defensive pueblos subsequently took place. In El Morro and elsewhere community size influenced to some degree how such defense was implemented. In general, if the community was large, the pueblo was built on low ground, focusing on a secure water supply. This strategy is seen clearly in Pueblo de los Muertos, Kluckhohn, and Mirabal. It is also found in dozens of other examples over the northern Southwest. Smaller communities also built fort-like structures but often placed them on high points or places with additional defensive characteristics. This approach would seem to describe the Hole-in-the-Rock site and even perhaps the room block on the small mesa at Tinaja. The other response to small community sizes was to locate the pueblo in the shadow of a larger community, as was done by North Atsinna and at the Cienega site.

What is not clear from just the single example of El Morro is that bigger was better. Over an enormous area it is the small hilltop or otherwise more defensively located sites that are abandoned first. That may be the case for Tinaja, but it is harder to determine for Hole-in-the-Rock. Some sites were both large and well protected, such as Atsinna. These sites seem to be especially long-lived, and Atsinna was certainly the last surviving site in El Morro. The Pescado Canyon site, also part of the Zuni cluster, seems to be somewhat similar. It is relatively large with 413 rooms, it is on a mesa top, and it apparently lasted longer than many other sites in the cluster. The Chavez Pass pueblos are a similar example farther to the west. The early abandonment of smaller sites does not mean that they were always, or even often, destroyed in attacks. Instead, it seems that the decision would be made that the community was too small to be viable and the people would relocate.

POPULATION DECLINE

The settlement shifts described above are relatively easy to document and, I believe, to explain. Coming to grips with the social and demographic consequences of these changes is much more difficult. Several of these issues have been touched on and are worth summarizing here. First, this must have been an exceedingly difficult time for these people. Even movements within the general area must have been traumatic. Groups that previously had lived farther apart were thrown together. Who owned which land? How were new types of disputes settled? Did new values, such as the authority of and rewards for war leaders, have to evolve? The presence of very large, grand, and regular ceremonial structures as well as very small ones may be evidence of an increase in social complexity to cope with these changes. The Kachina cult itself seems to have developed at about this time and may have been another response. The finding that leadership positions seem to be manifested by warrior-related weapons and symbols at Hawikuh (Howell 1996) in the subsequent century or so may be a consequence of this process.

Second, and perhaps most important, the response was maladaptive. Living very close together in large groups was a poor response to the nutritional stress that must have accompanied the changing climate. Although large groups can share food more effectively than small ones, the area being exploited by each group was much smaller than would previously have been the case, and crop failure for one most likely meant crop failure for all. Also, the immediate area around each large site must have been rapidly denuded of firewood, small game, and wild plants. Foraging away from the pueblo was dangerous, especially for women, and thus one can only surmise that the diet would have declined in quantity, quality, and variety. Virtually every study on health and nutrition in the Southwest points to such declines at this time (e.g., Berry 1983; Clark 1998). Because the time period is so short in the valley, and comparisons have to be made outside the valley, this contention is hard to document for the valley itself, but there is limited evidence supporting it. Population decline, due partially to actual warfare but much more to famine and declining nutrition, must have taken a heavy toll. As smaller sites declined in size, they may have reached a threshold at which they could not defend themselves and the remaining people would have moved into nearby communities. A case can be made that the smaller Cienega, Tinaja, Hole-in-the-Rock, and North Atsinna sites were abandoned and that the larger Pueblo de los Muertos, Atsinna, and Kluckhohn lasted longer. There is no reason to believe that the full complement of people present at these sites in A.D. 1288 were still there to migrate downstream in the early 1300s.

Unfortunately, part of the reason we can see the settlement patterns so clearly in El Morro is its short occupation: we cannot follow these important aspects of the evolving adaptation and response in the valley itself. El Morro provides a clear view of one aspect of the overall situation, but only a quick, almost momentary snapshot. We will have to look elsewhere for a fuller understanding of the overall series of developments and their consequences.

It is most likely that the movement of people into and out of the valley was prompted by a combination of factors. The movements involved significant elevation changes. As noted, El Morro is high, over 7,000 feet, and the population moved up in elevation into the valley, then down in elevation when it left. The choice of settlement must have been partly determined by environmental factors, but the locations of these communities were also dictated by the location of other members of the alliance.

IMPLICATIONS FOR THE STUDY OF WARFARE

The evidence from El Morro points out several important aspects for recognizing warfare in the prehistoric record. Probably most important is that the best method is comparative. By looking at changes in settlement patterns, site configurations, and so on, one can see that such changes are in the direction of increased defensibility, for example. Second, as with any scientific inquiry, the use of multiple independent lines of evidence provides the strongest support for inferences about warfare, as it does with other questions. In the case of El Morro, independent findings show several patterns: an increase in settlement clustering, settlements arranged for line-of-sight visibility, settlements becoming more defensive over time, increases in site size over time, increased concern for secure domestic water, and smaller sites being more defensively located than larger ones. Each of these patterns can be explained by increased concern with warfare. Some of them also have other possible explanations, but there is no other explanation that accounts for all these simultaneous trends so well. Similarly, the burning of the Scribe S site could be attributed to other causes. However, the rapid rebuilding of the subsequent fortress-like Pueblo de los Muertos, combined with several other instances of burning followed by the rapid and virtually synchronous building of large fortress-like sites, is difficult to explain in terms of other causes.

When we combine the overall valley trends with the particular instances of burning and rebuilding, the evidence points overwhelmingly to warfare as the cause. Looking at just the Scribe S site or at just Pueblo de los Muertos without noting how they fit valleywide and regionwide patterns would result in missing the major significance of events at these sites. That is, like many other aspects of archaeology, warfare is far better recognized and understood when we examine regional and temporal patterns rather than just a single site. Finally, this entire argument has been made in the absence of unburied bodies or bodies with fatal wounds. Although such evidence exists for approximately this time at other locations in the Southwest, no such "smoking gun" indication for warfare is necessary to demonstrate its presence or importance, and such evidence is very likely to be lacking even when warfare was intense and catastrophic.[2]

CONCLUSIONS

The example of El Morro shows that there is a surprising amount of relevant information available to document warfare if one looks for it. Much of it is comparative in nature and necessitates a regional rather than site-specific perspective. Equally important, the presence or absence of warfare is not the issue of ultimate interest. Changes in intensity and relation to the overall social milieu are more interesting questions. We can see from El Morro that the threat and actuality of warfare had a dramatic impact on the daily lives of the people and on their chances of survival. Their settlement locations, settlement configurations, subsistence, daily activities, and social structure were all affected by warfare, which must have been so thoroughly a part of their lives that it cannot be treated separately in discussing the archaeology and culture history of the El Morro Valley or of any other part of the Southwest at this time.

NOTES

1. Why a Little Ice Age is not part of our general perception of the Southwest's climate history is a good question. Some researchers, such as Petersen (1988, 1994), using pollen and treeline data, find good evidence for it. Others, such as Dean (1988, 1994), using tree-ring data, do not. Tree-ring data have normally been used to examine short-term variability, however, and they need to be statistically manipulated to reveal long-term climate trends.

2. High incidence of skeletal trauma has been associated with warfare in southern California (Lambert 1997) and in particular cases in the Midwest (Owsley et al. 1977; Owsley and Jantz 1994; Milner et al. 1991). In Europe, however, there is ample evidence for warfare in the Mesolithic-Neolithic transition with little skeletal evidence, especially on the Neolithic side (Price et al. 1995; Keeley and Cahen 1989). In the Southwest there is also not the degree of skeletal evidence one might expect. Even in situations such as Cave 7 (Hurst and Turner 1993), Casas Grandes (Ravesloot and Spoerl 1989), Te'ewi (Wendorf 1953; Reed 1953), and Awatovi (Fewkes 1893, Peabody Museum Archives), where it is clear a large number of people were killed, there is little skeletal evidence. Whatever the cause of this relative paucity of cases—the fact that physical anthropologists have not looked for evidence of violence, or that southwestern weapons and tactics did not tend to leave archaeologically visible skeletal remains, or other reasons—it is an interesting and as yet unanswered question.

CHAPTER THREE

A Case of Warfare in the Mesa Verde Region

Ricky R. Lightfoot and Kristin A. Kuckelman

In the Mesa Verde region of southwestern Colorado and southeastern Utah (Figure 3.1) archaeological indications of warfare are abundant and have been recognized for more than a century (Holmes 1981; Jackson 1981:373, 381, Plate 5; Newberry 1876:88; Nordenskiöld 1979:58). In the late 1800s explorers and scholars observed the ruins of thirteenth-century Pueblo villages, noting the defensiveness of the architecture and the defensibility of site locations (Figure 3.2). That these villages were built for defense seemed so obvious as to merit little discussion, being apparently taken for granted. In this chapter we examine evidence of warfare from the thirteenth-century village of Castle Rock Pueblo in the context of the Mesa Verde region.

Castle Rock Pueblo was a small village built around the base and on top of a prominent sandstone butte overlooking the McElmo Creek floodplain near the mouth of one of its tributaries, Sand Canyon, in southwestern Colorado. Castle Rock Pueblo consisted of at least 16 kivas, 37 rooms, 9 towers, a D-shaped enclosure around a kiva, two dams that impounded small reservoirs, two plazas, and numerous segments of walls that partly enclosed the site (Figure 3.3). An estimated 75 to 100 people lived in the village.

Although we believe that 16 is an accurate count of the number of kivas, the village probably contained many more than 37 rooms originally. Much of the surface rubble that would typically be used to esti-

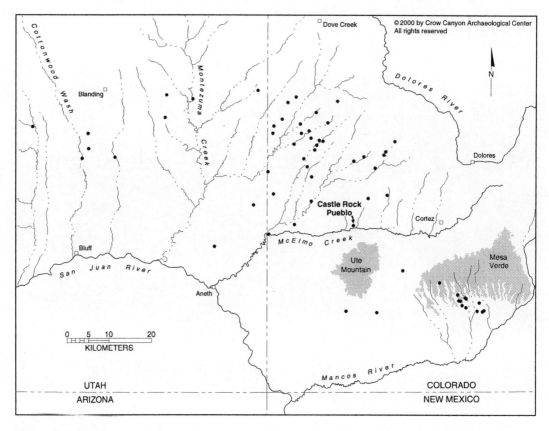

Figure 3.1. Mesa Verde region villages occupied in the period A.D. 1250–1300.

mate quantities of rooms was salvaged from the site in historic times (Kuckelman 2000); many historic structures in McElmo Canyon were constructed with sandstone rocks.

Analysis of tree-ring samples collected during excavations produced 409 dates, with the best date assemblages coming from eight structures (Kuckelman 2000). These dates indicate that construction at Castle Rock Pueblo began in A.D. 1256 and reached its peak in the 1260s. Based on a noncutting date of 1274, we estimate that construction in the village continued well into the 1270s and that the village occupation probably ended by the early to middle 1280s.

SITE SAMPLING

Crow Canyon Archaeological Center conducted excavations at Castle Rock Pueblo from 1990 to 1994 (Kleidon 1999; Kuckelman 2000). The excavations began with a random sampling strategy in which each square meter on the site was assigned to one of six sampling strata: (1) room block, (2) inner periphery, (3) kiva, (4) courtyard/plaza, (5) midden/wall fall, and (6) outer periphery (Varien 1999). From each of these sampling strata, a random sample of 1-m squares was selected for exca-

Figure 3.2. Castle
Rock Pueblo; pho-
tographer: William
H. Jackson in 1873,
looking southeast.
Photo (WHJ-164)
courtesy of the
Colorado Historical
Society.

vation. Sixty-six randomly selected 1-x-1–m units were excavated. An
additional 324 m² of the site were excavated in units that were judgmen-
tally selected. Judgmental units were selected for one of three reasons: (1)
to expand a randomly selected unit and expose more of a given feature,
structure, or stratigraphic profile; (2) to improve sample size and spatial
coverage in middens and other nonstructural areas; or (3) to sample
kivas that had not been tested by random sampling.

Seven of the randomly selected squares were excavated in six kivas. In
addition, we excavated a 1-x-2–m unit in each of the remaining ten
kivas. The 1-x-2–m excavation units in these kivas were excavated to
learn more about the architectural style, structure use, and abandonment
history and to obtain a collection of associated artifacts, tree-ring samples, and ecofacts from the floor, fill, and hearth of each structure.
Included in the 324 m² of excavations were two areas of more intensive
excavations. Based on what we learned from the initial samples, we selected one kiva (Structure 103) in the southern portion of the site and
one kiva (Structure 302) in the northern portion of the site for more intensive excavation. The intensive excavations included all of Structure
103 and its associated surface rooms and courtyard areas as well as half
of Structure 302, its courtyard area, half of an associated tower
(Structure 305), and a 1–x-2–m unit in an associated room (Structure
308). A complete report of the excavations, results, and interpretations
of Castle Rock Pueblo can be found in Kuckelman 2000.

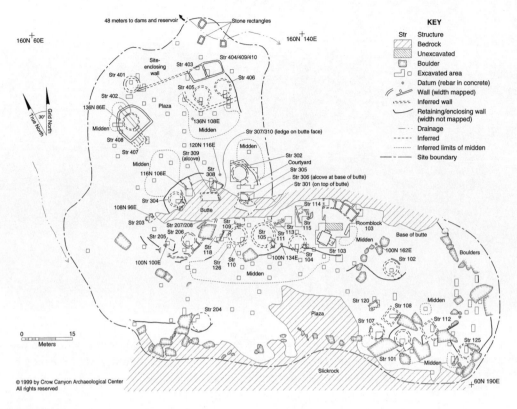

Figure 3.3. Castle Rock Pueblo architecture and cultural features.

ORAL HISTORY

Castle Rock Pueblo is of particular interest in this volume because of a published, nineteenth-century account of an ancient battle that purportedly occurred in this village and ended its habitation. Castle Rock Pueblo was first recorded in 1874 by a government-sponsored exploring expedition known as the Hayden Survey (Jackson 1981:379–380). The members of the Hayden Survey included famous photographer William Henry Jackson and a reporter, Ernest Ingersoll, who wrote about the discoveries of the expedition and published his accounts in newspapers and magazines back East. Led by a local guide named John Moss, the members of the Hayden Survey traveled down McElmo Canyon, and Castle Rock Pueblo caught their attention. They referred to the site as the "Fortified Rock on the McElmo" (Figures 3.2 and 3.4) and "Battle-Rock, in the Cañon of the McElmo" (Jackson 1981:Plate V).

John Moss, a former Hopi Indian agent (Dockstader 1979:525), told the exploring party a legend about the site that he said had been told to him by a Hopi Indian. Ingersoll recounted the story in an article published by the *New York Tribune* on November 3, 1874:

Figure 3.4. Castle
Rock Pueblo; pho-
tographer: William
H. Jackson in 1873,
looking southwest.
Photo (WHJ-163)
courtesy of the
Colorado Historical
Society.

Formerly, the aborigines inhabited all this country we had been
over. . . . They had lived there from time immemorial. . . . They culti-
vated the valley, fashioned whatever utensils and tools they needed
very neatly and handsomely out of clay and wood and stone, not
knowing any of the useful metals; built their homes and kept their
flocks and herds in the fertile river-bottoms, and worshiped the sun.
They were an eminently peaceful and prosperous people, living by
agriculture rather than by the chase. About a thousand years ago,
however, they were visited by savage strangers from the North, whom
they treated hospitably. Soon these visits became more frequent and
annoying. Then their troublesome neighbors—ancestors of the present
Utes—began to forage upon them, and, at last, to massacre them and
devastate their farms; so, to save their lives at least, they built houses
high upon the cliffs, where they could store food and hide away till the
raiders left. But one summer the invaders did not go back to their
mountains as the people expected, but brought their families with
them and settled down. So, driven from their homes and lands, starv-
ing in their little niches on the high cliffs, they could only steal away
during the night, and wander across the cheerless uplands. To one who
has traveled these steppes, such a flight seems terrible, and the mind
hesitates to picture the suffering of the sad fugitives.

At the *cristone* they halted, and probably found friends, for the
rocks and caves are full of the nests of these human wrens and swal-
lows. Here they collected, erected stone fortifications and watch-

towers, dug reservoirs in the rocks to hold a supply of water, which in all cases is precarious in this latitude, and once more stood at bay. Their foes came, and for one long month fought and were beaten back, and returned day after day to the attack as merciless and inevitable as the tide. Meanwhile, the families of the defenders were evacuating and moving south, and bravely did their protectors shield them till they were all safely a hundred miles away. The besiegers were beaten back and went away. But the narrative tells us that the hollows of the rocks were filled to the brim with the mingled blood of conquerors and con-quered, and red veins of it ran down into the cañon. It was such a vic-tory as they could not afford to gain again, and they were glad, when the long fight was over, to follow their wives and little ones to the south. There, in the deserts of Arizona, on the well-nigh unapproach-able isolated bluffs, they built new towns, and their few descendants, the Moquis, live in them to this day, preserving more carefully and purely the history and veneration of their forefathers than their skill or wisdom. It was from one of their old men that this traditional sketch was obtained. (Jackson 1981:380)

There are several aspects of this account that are remarkably accurate, given the state of knowledge of southwestern culture history in the 1870s when the story was told. Based on archaeological data and especially the precision of tree-ring dating, we now know that for more than a millen-nium ancestral Pueblo people occupied the arable uplands of the north-ern San Juan region. During Pueblo III times they left their scattered upland homes and built cliff dwellings and aggregated villages. After about A.D.1250 most of the population was aggregated in villages, and virtually every settlement had defensive features. The story told by Moss is essentially correct in that it accurately portrays the general sequence of Pueblo prehistory. But this sequence would not be determined by archae-ologists until the 1890s, and not until 1929, with the completion of the Southwest tree-ring chronological sequence, would archaeologists know the true age of the ancient ruins of the northern San Juan. Without the benefit of modern dating methods it is remarkable that Moss's story specified the time of regional conflict and migration as accurately as it did.

The details of Moss's story that can be verified appear to be accurate, and from this we propose three hypotheses for further consideration. First, Moss could have heard this story from an elderly Hopi person, as he said he did, and the accuracy might be explained if the story had been retold in detail generation after generation by the descendants of the peo-ple to whom these events happened. Second, it is likely that, as the story indicates, raiding and hostility were important factors that shaped the re-gional events just before the migration from the region, when Castle Rock was occupied. Third, the end of the occupation of Castle Rock Pueblo in particular might have been associated with a significant battle.

ROCK ART

Evidence of conflict, or at least a concern about conflict and defense, can be seen in a rock art panel in a prominent location at Castle Rock (Figure 3.5). The panel depicts three anthropomorphic figures of similar size, positioned side by side. The three figures have rectangular or globular bodies that may represent warriors' shields. The two figures on the right hold bows and arrows, stand back to back, and appear to be defending each other. The figure in the center seems to be shooting an arrow toward the figure on the left. The figure on the left, with his legs in front of him, appears to be falling away from the central figure and to be holding up a shield in defense against the arrow.

The typical anthropomorphic figures created in this region during the time of the Castle Rock occupation are front-view "lizard men" with stick-like arms and legs out to the side and bent at elbows and knees (Cole 1990:143; Schaafsma 1980:135–136). The bodies of these figures are usually stick-like or narrow rectangles. The Castle Rock figures are not typical of this style, in that the bodies are not stick-like and are depicted in side view. Figures far more similar to the Castle Rock figures have been recorded near Moab, Utah (Cole 1990:Plate 60; Schaafsma 1980:Figure 126). Many of the Utah figures are also depicted in side view, have similar shields or backpacks, and in some cases have "antennae" like those of the central figure in the Castle Rock panel. It is possible, then, that the panel at Castle Rock shows influence from southeastern Utah. Additional evidence of contact with that area is present at Castle Rock in the form of a Bull Creek projectile point. Bull Creek points are typically found in the Colorado River drainage of southeastern Utah (Fetterman and Honeycutt 1990:58).

Anthropomorphic figures with bows and arrows have been reported on other rock art panels in the Southwest. Figures wielding bows and arrows are usually depicted in animal hunting scenes (Cole 1990:Plate 85; Hurst and Pachak 1989:16; Schaafsma 1971:Figures 32, 33, 121; Plates 14, 16; 1980:Figure 65); other possible depictions of human violence are not unknown, however (Hurst and Pachak 1989:10). The Castle Rock panel could have been created for any of several reasons. It could have

Figure 3.5.
Petroglyph panel at Castle Rock Pueblo depicting human figures interacting, bearing bows and arrows and shields or backpacks.

been made by one or more residents of Castle Rock during the occupation of the village to reflect the conflict and unrest in the area during that time. Or it could signify an agreement among the villagers to defend one another in case of attack or a warning to possible intruders. Alternatively, the panel could have been created after the violent attack that ended the occupation of the village, either by a survivor or by a friend or relative of a survivor from a different village, or even by one of the attackers. One function of rock art was to record historic events (Hurst and Pachak 1989:24; James 1990:137). The panel at Castle Rock is significant because it provides further evidence of conflict in the region, if not at the village itself.

SETTLEMENT PATTERN

Defensible Locations

Throughout the Pueblo III period there was an increase in the occupation of defensible locations (Kenzle 1995:Table 2; Varien et al. 1996). Examples of such locations are canyon rims, buttes, mesa rims, prominences, cliff overhangs and boulders. At Mesa Verde the shift from mesa tops to cliff overhangs was so dramatic that during Pueblo III times almost everyone lived in cliff dwellings (Hayes 1964:109; Rohn 1977:243; Smith 1987:67). The priority for settlement locations seems to have shifted from those with the best farming soils in early Pueblo times to those with good defensibility after about A.D. 1200.

Aggregation

During the A.D. 1250s and 1260s Castle Rock Pueblo emerged and grew rapidly into a small village of about sixteen households. This growth reflected a general trend in the locality and in the region in which there was a shift in settlement size from small one-to-two-family farmsteads in early Pueblo III to large aggregated settlements in late Pueblo III. Throughout most of their occupation in the Mesa Verde region ancestral Pueblo people lived in small hamlets that were dispersed across the landscape. During only two periods, the A.D. 800s and the 1200s, did the majority of the people in the Mesa Verde region live in aggregated villages. In the 1200s families moved from small farms on deep arable soils to aggregated villages consisting of 15 to 100 households. Varien and others (1996) compiled data on Pueblo III villages in the Mesa Verde region, and they identified only eight villages with 50 or more rooms that date to the late 1100s. In the first half of the 1200s there were at least 29 aggregated settlements in the region, including 5 that had 200 to 500 rooms each. These occurred in a more or less linear band that extended northwest from the Mesa Verde escarpment into southeastern Utah. The largest villages and densest clusters of villages were in the McElmo Creek and Montezuma Creek drainage basins. In the last half of the 1200s this trend toward increasing aggregation became even more pronounced. Varien and others (1996) identified 47 villages that were occupied between 1250 and 1300, including 11 that had 200 to 500 rooms (Figure 3.1). These villages were even more densely clustered than villages had been in the previous half-century.

Access to Domestic Water

Castle Rock Pueblo is less than 1 km from the current channel of McElmo Creek, which was probably a seasonal stream before modern irrigation practices. Two dams were built in a small arroyo that bordered the north edge of the village, and these dams would have captured runoff water from a large area of exposed bedrock into two small ponds, or reservoirs. Nevertheless, these ponds would have provided water only for short periods of runoff following rains or during snowmelt.

Throughout the Mesa Verde region during the Pueblo III period there was an emphasis on access to or control of domestic water; Pueblo III sites are generally nearer water than earlier sites are (Fetterman and Honeycutt 1987:127; Haase 1985:24; Neily 1983:122). Late Pueblo III villages were commonly built around springs, and reservoirs were often built in or near these villages (Varien et al. 1996:28). Having a permanent water supply within a village would have clearly enhanced its defensibility. Castle Rock Pueblo did not have a permanent spring or reservoir within or immediately adjacent to the village, however. The residents apparently sacrificed control of a permanent water source to gain the defensive advantage offered by the butte.

DEFENSIVE ARCHITECTURE

In addition to the advantages that the butte at Castle Rock offered for defense, the layout and construction of buildings and walls in the village were clearly defensive in design and intent. For example, enclosing walls surrounded much of the village, and towers enhanced the ability of residents to protect themselves. Many of the rooms and room suites were built against the butte with their associated kivas on terraces in front of them. Two rooms (Structures 306, 309) were built into alcoves on the north face of the butte. Several kivas (Structures 101, 102, 107, 112, 125, 204, 206) were built alongside large boulders or nestled in clusters of boulders. These positions against the butte face or among boulders reduced the number of directions from which an enemy could attack and provided natural lookout positions for the residents. Structures were built on top of the butte, on a ledge midway up the north face of the butte, and on a huge boulder alongside the butte. Even if these buildings were used for domestic or storage purposes most of the time, their locations and the restriction of access to their entrances clearly presented a defensive posture.

Access-Restrictive Features

At Castle Rock Pueblo there are many masonry wall segments that define the boundary of the site, though the wall apparently was never continuous around the village. In addition, the structures that were built on the talus slope at the base of the butte had retaining walls or structure walls that, in combination with the steep slope, would have created a formidable barrier. Enclosing walls were common at late Pueblo III habitations in the Mesa Verde region, both in villages and in smaller cliff dwellings (Kenzle 1995). One such cliff dwelling is Balcony House, which was built in an even better defensive location than most of the other large Mesa Verde cliff dwellings (Nordenskiöld 1979:66). Balcony House was built predominantly in the A.D. 1240s, but it underwent an intensive construction episode in the 1270s in which many defensive and access-restrictive features were added (Fairchild-Parks and Dean 1993:5). Most settlements in the Mesa Verde region that were built or occupied in the late 1200s had some means of restricting access to the pueblo.

Towers

Masonry towers, which have obvious defensive attributes, came into existence in the late Pueblo II period. During Pueblo III times almost every hamlet or village had one or more towers. How towers were used is poorly understood, but they could have contributed to a site's defensibility (Farmer 1957; Mackey and Green 1979; Schulman 1950; Wilcox and Haas 1994). Towers could have been used to reinforce vulnerable areas or as locations from which to signal the approach of an enemy. Towers, often connected by tunnels to other structures, would have allowed residents to move between structures without being exposed outdoors. Excavations in towers have provided evidence that some towers were used for storage (Mackey and Green 1979). Interior features and artifacts in two towers tested at Castle Rock Pueblo indicate that some domestic activities occurred there. Many archaeologists have suggested that towers in the Southwest were used for lookout and defense (Farmer 1957; Hibben 1948:36; Lancaster and Pinkley 1954:44–47; Mackey and Green 1979; Schulman 1950), and remains of people who died violent deaths have been found in towers (Mackey and Green 1979:146–147; Shipman 1980:255–258).

The locations of towers at Castle Rock appear to be significant from a defensive point of view. Structures 401 and 404/409/410, towers at the northwest and northeast corners of the site, respectively, were in strategic defensive locations in the event of an attack from the north. Two towers

(Structures 305 and 307/310) against the north face of the butte provided restricted access to the top of the butte. One tower (Structure 207/208) built between the south face of the butte and a huge boulder provided a restricted access route to buildings on top of the boulder. The towers that provided access to the tops of the butte and the large boulder were important because they served as pathways to the most restricted and protected locations in the village.

At least two towers (Structure 301 and an unnumbered structure known only from historic photographs) were built on top of the butte, which gave them the most protected and access-restricted location in the village. In the event of an attack, noncombatant residents, such as children and the elderly, could have been moved to these buildings while other residents defended the points of access to the butte. One of the buildings on top of the butte is completely gone, and only a little of the other remains. The buildings on top of the butte were probably not residences, as they would have been difficult to get in and out of on a regular basis. If the buildings were used only in the event of an attack, they would have sat empty and unused most of the time. However, such buildings could have been used to store food and water, without conflicting with their use as defensive structures, thus providing necessities during an attack or siege.

EVIDENCE OF CONFLICT IN HUMAN REMAINS

Human remains at Castle Rock Pueblo indicate that violence and interpersonal conflict occurred during the occupation of the village and that the occupation ended with a violent event. The evidence includes disarticulated skeletons, and bone damage caused by trauma, weathering, and carnivore activity. A minimum of 41 individuals were identified in the human bone assemblage of approximately 1,300 bones and identifiable bone fragments that are inferred to have been deposited as a result of the violent event that ended village occupation. Three individuals were represented by mostly complete, articulated skeletons. A minimum of 25 people were represented in commingled bone clusters that contained a total of approximately 500 bones. An additional 13 people were represented by isolated bone clusters or single bones. No formal burials were encountered during testing at Castle Rock.

Trauma

Several types of physical trauma are represented in the human remains at Castle Rock Pueblo, including healed as well as fatal cranial depression fractures, broken limb bones, broken teeth, and a broken nose. Not all these forms of trauma are necessarily fatal or limited to warfare, but the healed fractures on four skulls indicate an endemic pattern of interpersonal violence. Two skulls have depression fractures that are likely to have been the cause of death. Direct evidence of fatal trauma appears only sporadically in the archaeological record, but cranial trauma has also been identified as a cause of death of individuals in a number of other late Pueblo III sites in the Mesa Verde region (Lightfoot and Kuckelman 1994; Martin et al. 1999; Morley 1908:607; Morris 1939:42, 82).

Postmortem Neglect

Although human remains were relatively abundant at Castle Rock Pueblo, none of them occurred in formal burials. That is, no complete bodies had been carefully positioned, covered with dirt, and protected from weathering and carnivores. Also, none of the human remains had any associated artifacts or grave goods that would indicate a respectful burial.

Postmortem neglect, which is the failure to bury, cremate, or otherwise respectfully dispose of the dead, is indicated at Castle Rock Pueblo by a high incidence of carnivore damage, weathering, and the skeletal disarticulation resulting from these forces. At Castle Rock Pueblo only three individuals were found with their skeletons articulated. In general, human remains at Castle Rock were disarticulated and mixed. Postmortem neglect has been documented in other late Pueblo III period sites in the Mesa Verde region (Lightfoot and Kuckelman 1994; Morris 1939:42; Nordenskiöld 1979:170).

CONTEXT OF HUMAN REMAINS

Nearly all the human remains documented at Castle Rock Pueblo were deposited as a result of the violent attack that ended the occupation of the village sometime in the early to middle A.D. 1280s. All but a few of the structures in the village were still in use at that time. A portion of nearly every kiva roof was burned either during or after the attack; in many cases, however, the portion burned was very small and did not include cribbing beams. The remains of 38 of the 41 individuals documented in abandonment contexts at the site were found inside structures, on the floors, in the collapsed roofing material, or just above the collapsed roofing material. The remaining 3 individuals were represented by miscellaneous bones outside structures but in contexts that suggest that these individuals had been left outdoors either on prehistoric ground surface or on the butte when occupation of the village ended.

The number of individuals documented during testing at the site suggests that many of the village inhabitants were in residence at the time of the attack. Our limited testing of the site indicates that at least 41 of the estimated 75 to 100 village residents died in the attack. Table 3.1 shows the age and sex distribution of those 41 individuals. This distribution in-

TABLE 3.1. Age and Sex Distribution of the Human Remains Documented at Castle Rock Pueblo That Are Associated with the End of Village Occupation.

Age	Male	Female	Unknown Sex	Total
Fetus				
Newborn–.9 years			1	1
1–4 years			4	4
5–9 years			7	7
10–14 years			1	1
15–19 years			2	2
20–34 years	1		3	4
35–50 years	3	2	2	7
50+ years		1		1
Subadult			2	2
Adult	1		10	11
Unknown			1	1
Total	5	3	33	41

cludes men, women, and children and suggests that the entire village might have been wiped out in what should be referred to more properly as a massacre.

CONCLUSIONS

Evidence from Castle Rock Pueblo indicates that a catastrophic attack took the lives of many if not all of the residents of the village. This massacre ended the occupation of the village at a time when other settlements in the region also experienced endemic conflict, raiding, and warfare and when the occupations of other settlements in the region were also ending. By the late A.D. 1280s it appears that the entire Mesa Verde region was devoid of population.

In the mid A.D.1200s climatic conditions for dryland farming in the Mesa Verde region were deteriorating. In the previous six centuries the climate had alternated between sustained periods of cool, moist conditions and warm, dry conditions. The Pueblo farmers of the region survived and flourished by moving to higher or lower elevations in response to these changing climatic conditions. Petersen (1988) portrays the late thirteenth century as a time of cool, dry climate that squeezed the dryland farming belt in the region completely out of existence. Petersen argues that the combination of cool and dry conditions dealt these Pueblo farmers the death blow by pushing together the high- and low-elevation boundaries of the farming belt. Other researchers (Ahlstrom et al.1995; Van West 1999) have also concluded that climatic changes, particularly changes in rainfall patterns, adversely affected agricultural productivity in the Mesa Verde region in the mid-1200s. As the climate deteriorated, domestic water sources would have been less dependable, farming more risky, and crop failure more frequent. The environmental stage was set for survival stress, intercommunity raiding, and conflict.

There was also abundant potential for social and political stress between the residents of different villages in the Mesa Verde region, especially after A.D. 1250 (Haas and Creamer 1996). During the 1200s the number of villages increased, which caused the available resource catchment area for each village to decrease (Varien 1997). At the same time, the populations of these villages grew larger, necessitating larger catchment areas to provide the food and other resources necessary to sustain the larger number of people. As population grew denser and more aggregated and per capita catchment areas decreased, the potential for competition and conflict between communities would have increased.

Although the oral history account of the battle at Castle Rock specifies the ancestors of the Utes as adversaries of the local Pueblo population, there is little archaeological evidence of non-Puebloans in the region in the A.D. 1200s. Thus the possibility seems remote that intruding bands of foragers from outside the region could defeat and oust a large, resident population of sedentary Puebloans. More likely, the violence at Castle Rock Pueblo was part of a far-reaching pattern of competition and conflict between residents of communities and regions during the thirteenth and fourteenth centuries across the entire Southwest (Haas and Creamer 1996; LeBlanc 1999; Morris 1939; Turner and Turner 1999; White 1992; Wilcox and Haas 1994) and from northern Mexico (Ravesloot 1988) to the northern Great Plains (Gregg et al. 1981) and across the Midwest (Milner et al. 1991). Though the processes by which violence became so widespread during this time are not understood, deteriorating climatic conditions almost certainly played an important role. An understanding of violence in the Southwest will emerge from studies that look at individual cases, such as the attack on Castle Rock Pueblo, and those that study broader patterns of conflict.

CHAPTER FOUR

Shields, Shield Bearers, and Warfare Imagery in Anasazi Art, 1200–1500

Helen K. Crotty

Militaristic imagery in Anasazi rock art and kiva murals emerges around the mid A.D. 1200s, coinciding with the beginning of a period of intense conflict, described by LeBlanc (1999). Among the earliest of the images are large pictographs of shield-like forms prominently displayed near a number of late Pueblo III alcove habitation sites in the Kayenta region of southeastern Utah and northeastern Arizona. Depictions of shield-bearing warriors in the same area lend credence to the identification of the large circular motifs as representations of shields, although other interpretations have been proposed. Shields and shield bearers are even more common in Pueblo IV petroglyphs in the Rio Grande region. In kiva art a single rather anomalous example is known from the late 1200s, but shields and shield bearers are abundantly represented in kivas dating to the late 1300s and early 1400s, gradually diminishing during the 1400s. Although rock art images that cannot be directly dated may have persisted longer, we know that shield bearers are not pictured in kivas dating after 1500. Militaristic imagery in prehistoric art, therefore, fits very well chronologically with LeBlanc's Late period of prehistoric southwestern warfare (A.D. 1250–1500s). It is first associated with obviously defensive sites of the Tsegi phase of the Kayenta Anasazi and later with large pueblos in the

Hopi and Rio Grande areas. Despite its absence from many Anasazi sites of the period, the imagery provides some additional lines of evidence for the prevalence of prehistoric warfare at that time.

SHIELDS AND SHIELD BEARERS IN PUEBLO III ROCK ART AND KIVAS

Shield Forms in Anasazi Rock Art

Toward the end of the Pueblo III period, large-scale paintings of shield-like forms are placed in or near the alcoves that shelter defensible cliff dwellings in the Kayenta Anasazi area of what is now southern Utah and northern Arizona. Several authors have suggested that the shield forms symbolize socioreligious or clan affiliations (Anderson 1971:24; Cole 1990:147; Schaafsma 1980:148; Cole and Schaafsma citing Hopi ethnographic sources). Though the shield forms may indeed mark the residence of a particular religious or kinship group, it is not inconceivable that the same symbol would be used to decorate the shield of a warrior or of several warriors belonging to that group. Evidence suggesting that actual shields are represented is discussed below. For convenience, the shield-like pictographs are referred to henceforth as shields.

Shields are most closely identified with the Tsegi phase (A.D. 1250–1300) of the Kayenta Anasazi, when a number of well-dated villages were constructed in cave shelters in Tsegi Canyon (Dean 1970). They are so common and so striking that in an early survey of Tsegi Canyon rock art, Schaafsma (1966:35) describes the white clay paintings of large, usually circular, motifs that dominate the right-hand end of the cave as "characteristic of Tsegi Phase rock art." In a later work Schaafsma (1980:145–146) gives the name Tsegi Painted Style to the large-scale shields and other motifs executed—sometimes rather sloppily—with thick clay mixtures, most commonly in white but sometimes in tans and various shades of pink and purple. In Tsegi Canyon the shield motif often consists of white concentric circles as large as 90 cm in diameter. Concentric-circle shields are present at Betatakin, Lolomaki, Bat Woman, and Twin Caves, where a pair of them is recorded (Schaafsma 1966:35–36). In addition to the concentric-circle shields, there are a few large white circular paintings in Tsegi Canyon with more elaborate decoration: one from Turkey Cave that Schaafsma (1966:22, Figure 35) describes as having a "face like a death's head" set inside a wide outer circle, one from Bat Woman House decorated with two downward-turning crescents (Schaafsma 1966:Figure 20), and two from Betatakin (Figure 4.1a, b). One of the Betatakin shields is painted pink and decorated with a quartered circle design; the second is decorated with an anthropomorphic figure that, as Wright (1976:4) observed, bears some resemblance to the decoration of an actual Pueblo III basketry shield re-

Figure 4.1.
Depictions of shields or shield-like images from various locations. (*a, b*) Betatakin, Navajo National Monument, Arizona: (*a*) negative anthropomorphic figure on white enhanced with red and yellow, ca. 1 m diameter; (*b*) pink-and-beige with negative quartering lines, ca. 75 cm diameter. (*c–e*) Shields from Jailhouse Ruin, Grand Gulch, Utah, all 60 cm diameter: (*c*) enhanced with green; (*d, e*) white with negative decoration. (*f–j*) Shields from Cow Canyon, Glen Canyon National Recreational Area, Utah, all ca. 45–55 cm diameter: (*f*) painted in red pigment; (*g–i*) white caliche with red pigment enhancement. (*k*) White painted circular form with human facial features in black and green, ca. 50 cm diameter, from Canyon Creek Ruin, Fort Apache Indian Reservation, Arizona. (*l*) White painted circular form with floral or star decoration, ca. 30 cm diameter, from Soldier Creek, Sierra Ancha, Arizona. (*a–e*) Drawings by Deborah Kelley after photographs by the author. (*f–j*) Redrawn by Deborah Kelley from Geib 1996: cover art and Figure 81. (*k, l*) Redrawn by Deborah Kelley from Haury 1934: Figure 26c, d.

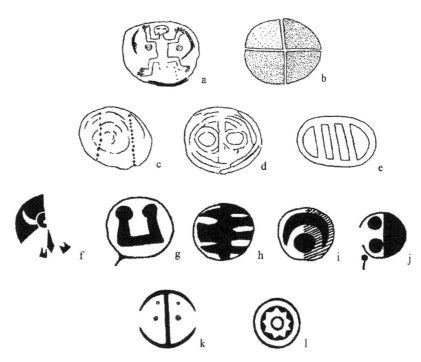

covered from Mummy Cave in Canyon del Muerto (Morris and Burgh 1941:51–52, Figure 31f). The shield decorations are all negative designs; that is, the area occupied by the decoration is left unpainted.

Despite the frequent occurrence of shield pictographs in Tsegi Canyon, they are not present at every habitation site. There is no shield, for example, among the pictographs at Kiet Siel, the largest and longest-occupied of the Tsegi Canyon cliff dwellings.

Tsegi Style shields occur sporadically outside Tsegi Canyon, in other parts of northern Arizona and also in southern Utah. Schaafsma (1966:36) reports large white circular paintings associated with Inscription House in Navajo Canyon and with Pueblo III cliff dwellings in Long Canyon, and on Chinle Wash in Arizona. In Utah they are also found in Grand Gulch, where there are three at Jailhouse Ruin (Figure 4.1c–e) and another plain white one at an unnamed site (William Hyder, personal communication 1998). Cole (1990:145–146) mentions numerous examples associated with cliff dwellings and storage structures on Cedar Mesa with "as many as eight with different interior designs at one Slickhorn Canyon site," and at various sites in Butler Wash and along the San Juan River.

Possible Fremont Origins of the Shield Motif in Anasazi Art

The Fremont shield seems to have been the model for shield designs appearing in late Anasazi work. As Schaafsma (1980:171) suggests, the motif (and possibly the artifact itself) enters the Anasazi iconography during a period of Kayenta expansion across the Colorado in late Pueblo II and early Pueblo III times. Schaafsma (1978) reports large circular designs associated with Pueblo II–III rockshelter habitation sites in the White Canyon Basin in the Natural Bridges area. At one site two shields are painted white and blue; at a second a white circular design is painted on a red background. Farther north, in the Escalante drainage north of the Colorado in Glen Canyon Recreation Area, Geib and Fairley (1996: 192–193) found five shield images (Figure 4.1f–j) in a shallow overhang along the principal overland access into Cow Canyon, the most direct route of communication to the Red Rock Plateau and contemporaneous Horsefly Hollow phase (A.D. 1210–60) communities. The habitation sites in Cow Canyon were scattered small units located in the open rather than cliff dwellings, and they are believed to have been abandoned by 1250. The five shields have varied designs and range from 45 to 55 cm in diameter, about half the size of the usual Tsegi Style shields, and the technique is apparently unique to the site. The panel was created mostly by rubbing or scraping away a thin veneer of mud to expose a white caliche stain on the sandstone and then enhanced with red pigment in a few instances. Four of the shields are readily visible from the trail; a fifth is hidden. Geib and Fairley (1996:193) suggest that the visible shields may have been "heraldic household emblems used to identify various families residing in the canyon" and the fifth "could have symbolized the larger kin group or lineage comprising the various families living in the canyon." Some evidence, however, that the shields might be related to warfare appears in rock art of the same period at Defiance House in Forgotten Canyon in Glen Canyon National Recreation Area, where three large warriors executed in white paint brandish shields and weapons (Figure 4.2), discussed below. Painted in red in the same shelter is a "large set of concentric circles, apparently a shield design" (Castleton 1979:325).

Depictions of shield bearers and shields occur very early in the Uinta Fremont area centered around Vernal, Utah, and Dinosaur National Monument, where Fremont occupation is dated by Marwitt (1970:141–142) from A.D. 750 to 950. The rock art in the Uinta area, classified as Classic Vernal Style, includes many representations of shield bearers and shields (e.g., Castleton 1978:Figures 2.1, 2.6, 2.14, 2.18, 2.27, 2.28, 2.29, 2.60, 2.61, 2.62, 2.63; Cole 1990:Plates 81, 83, 84, 87, 88, 89, Figures 81, 85, 86; Schaafsma 1971:Plates 2, 3, 4, 7, 10, Figures 6, 9, 10, 11, 12; 1980:Figures 132, 133). Classic Vernal Style rock art is carved rather than painted, although painted embellishment may be added. Shield decoration is usually geometric and generally more intricate than on the shields of the Tsegi Style, although concentric circles and spirals also appear. Most Classic Vernal Style anthropomorphic figures have facial features indicated and appear to be attired in ceremonial dress. They wear headdresses, earbobs, necklaces or breastplates, and kilts. The warriors hold their shields at arm's length, and in several panels they carry what appear to be trophy human heads, which is certainly indicative of

Figure 4.2. White-painted shield bearers ca. 1 m tall, from Defiance House, Forgotten Canyon, Glen Canyon National Recreation Area, Utah. Drawing by Deborah Kelley after Castleton 1979:Figure 9.37.

warfare, although combat is not represented. A few of the shield bearers from the Uinta area are much closer to the Anasazi imagery than the ceremonial warriors and may date from a different time. These figures are portrayed with bucket-shaped heads, and their shields cover their bodies. Unlike the later Anasazi representations, facial features of the Uinta Fremont are usually indicated and the feet normally point outward.

Sinagua Shield Form Pictographs

Another possible source for the Tsegi Style shield motifs, if not for shield bearer depictions, lies south of the Anasazi territory in the red rock canyons near Sedona, Arizona. Large cream-colored or whitish painted circular designs are present near cliff dwellings and in pictograph sites. These pictographs are attributed to the Sinagua, who occupied the area from about A.D. 1150 to 1300 (Pilles 1994). The designs, most of which are about 80 cm in diameter, with some smaller (30–40 cm), occur individually and in pairs (Peter Pilles, personal communication 1998). Most have some sort of decoration, usually a negative design, at the center, and some have a fringe around the periphery. Because images of shield bearers are absent in the Sinagua pictographs, the shield-like forms here may represent suns or they may be emblematic of social groups, as Pilles (personal communication 1998) believes, rather than associated with warfare. Though it is doubtful that the Sinagua shield forms inspired those of the Tsegi area, there may be a link between them and some fourteenth-century examples from Canyon Creek Ruin and the Sierra Ancha to the southeast, discussed in the next section.

Shield Bearers in Rock Art

Shield bearers are definitely present in Anasazi art of the late thirteenth century and, as we have seen with the three shield-and-weapon-

Figure 4.3. Shield bearers from various sites. (*a*) Pecked shield figure, ca. 70 cm diameter, Indian Creek, Canyonlands National Park, Utah. (*b*) White-painted shield figures, ca. 45–50 cm diameter, Trail Arch, Needles District, Canyonlands National Park. (*c*) "All American Man," painted in red, white, and blue, Needles District, Canyonlands National Park. (*d*) White-painted "Batwoman," ca. 1.5 m tall, Batwoman House, Tsegi Canyon, Arizona. (*e*) Shield figure, ca. 75 cm diameter, Canyon Creek Ruin, Fort Apache Indian Reservation, Arizona. (*a*, *c*) Drawings by Deborah Kelley after photographs by Owen Severance. (*b*) Drawing by Deborah Kelley after photo by Deborah Kelley. (*d*) Drawing by Deborah Kelley after Schaafsma 1980:Figure 108. (*e*) Drawing by Deborah Kelley after Haury 1934:Figure 26b.

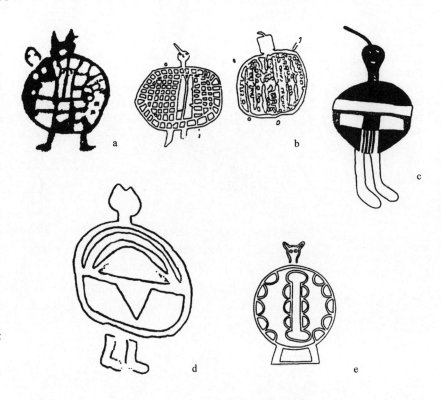

brandishing warriors from the Horsefly Hollow phase Anasazi habitation site of Defiance House, even earlier. Although the Defiance House figures are Anasazi in scale (ca. 1 m tall) and in medium and lack facial features, they also exhibit Fremont characteristics. They hold their shields at arm's length and their feet point outward in the Fremont fashion. Another apparently Anasazi shield figure found below a small cliff dwelling in Indian Creek in the Canyonlands area exhibits both Fremont and Anasazi characteristics. The figure is pecked rather than painted, and his feet turn outward (Figure 4.3a). The shield is elaborately decorated in a girded pattern edged with positive and negative disks. A looping form at the figure's right shoulder may represent a weapon. His Anasazi affiliation is suggested by the body-covering shield and the featureless head with eared or horned helmet. At Trail Arch in lower Salt Creek Canyon in the Needles District of Canyonlands National Park are two white painted figures with shields about 45 to 50 cm in diameter decorated with elaborate geometric patterns reminiscent of the Fremont shields (Figure 4.3b). The figure on the left has a small round head, a possible feather decoration, and partial legs. His patterned shield resembles a turtle shell. His companion has a Fremont-style bucket-shaped head with possible feather decoration and a possible weapon at his left shoulder. No legs are visible below the striped and dotted shield. About 14 miles farther up Salt Canyon in an alcove near a Pueblo II–III habitation site is a polychrome 1.2-m-tall shield bearer known as the "All American Man" (Figure 4.3c). His small round head with a feather protruding

Figure 4.4. Incised
shield figures, ca. 25
cm tall. Kiva K, Cliff
Palace, Mesa Verde
National Park.
Redrawn by
Deborah Kelley from
Ives 1980.

from it is similar to that of the left figure farther down the canyon, but
here features are represented, although both feet point in the same direction in the Anasazi fashion. The figure derives its name from the red,
white, and "blue" striped decoration of his shield. The "blue" is actually
a mixture of charcoal and a white pigment, and a spalled sample recovered from the shield was recently subjected to radiocarbon dating, yielding a calibrated date of A.D. 1295 (Chaffee et al. 1994). Another
well-dated Anasazi shield figure is the popularly named "Batwoman"
from Batwoman House, a site in Tsegi Canyon that also contains shields,
as mentioned above (Figure 4.3d). The 5-foot (1.5-m) figure is rather
crudely rendered, but the decoration of its shield is slightly more complex than most of the Tsegi Style shields. Its eared head is reminiscent of
the petroglyph shield figure from Indian Creek. Schaafsma (1966:16)
notes the remnants of a similar figure nearby, of which only the eared
head and part of the circular design of the body remain. Tree-ring dates
from construction beams at Batwoman House show cutting dates of
1275 and 1279.

A number of other shield bearer figures attributable to Pueblo III
Anasazi are known from southeastern Utah (e.g., Castleton 1979:Figures
7.66, 7.67, 7.75, 8.23; Wormington 1955:Figures 64d–l; 65a–c).

Shield Bearers in Kiva Art

The only known example of shield bearers portrayed in kiva art during
Pueblo III times is engraved in the final plaster layer of Kiva K at Cliff
Palace, Mesa Verde National Park (Ives 1980). Unlike their Kayenta
counterparts and Pueblo IV kiva murals, these figures are rather stylized,
relatively small, and incised rather than painted. All but one lack heads.
The feet of two of the figures definitely point in the same direction, another is ambiguous, and another has no feet. The legs of two figures are
joined at about the knee line, forming an "H" shape, and all the shields
have versions of the same decorative motifs (Figure 4.4). This suggests
that warriors belonging to the same social or kinship group could have
had their shields decorated with variations of that group's symbol.

MILITARISTIC IMAGERY IN PUEBLO IV ANASAZI ART

Datable Fourteenth-Century Images

Very few rock art depictions of shields or shield bearers can be securely dated to the early fourteenth century A.D. in the Anasazi area, but several are reported by Haury (1934) from Canyon Creek Ruin and from other sites in the Sierra Ancha below the Mogollon Rim in east-central Arizona. Like the Tsegi Style pictographs, they are associated with cliff dwellings situated high on canyon walls and difficult of access. At Canyon Creek Ruin, which is dated from about the 1320s to 1350 (Haury 1934:156), two possible shields are represented on the cliff wall below the ruin along with some handprints and complex geometric designs. One of the possible shields consists of concentric circles in white, red, and brown, with an outer fringe like rayed feathers that resembles the peripheral decoration of some of the shields depicted in fifteenth-century kiva murals, but it is small, only 6 inches (15 cm) in diameter (Haury 1934:Plate 82b). The second shield-like pictograph is 20 inches in diameter and appears to be a stylized face, with black and green features on a large white field (Figure 4.1k). Among the other pictographs Haury (1934:Figure 26a, b) illustrates are another shield, 60 cm in diameter, consisting of concentric circles and a rather unusual shield bearer, 75 cm in diameter with legs ending in a horizontal bar (Figure 4.3e). Although the caption for Haury's Figure 26 identifies these pictographs as "in and near the Canyon Creek Ruin," they are not further identified in the text. A relatively small (30 cm) circular form with a stylized nine-pointed star or floral motif is identified as from the cliff wall near a ruin at the head of Soldier Creek in the Sierra Ancha (Figure 4.1l).

In kiva mural art, representations of shields and shield bearers are among the earliest paintings recorded at Awat'ovi, a large Western Anasazi pueblo in the Jeddito Wash area of northeastern Arizona believed to have been settled in part by Kayenta Anasazi (Smith 1971:608). The paintings are from Rooms 218 and 229, two rectangular kivas located in the Western Mound of Awat'ovi and dating between A.D. 1350 and 1400 (Crotty 1995:48; Smith 1952:317–318, 1972:10). The shield bearer portrayals are recognizable because of their similarity to earlier and later examples; one is only fragmentary, and the other is crudely rendered and rather bulbous (Figure 4.5a, b). The fragmentary figure is from the second mural painted in Room 218, and the bulbous one is from the second mural painted in Room 229. On the next plaster layer above the fragmentary figure from Room 218 is a painting of two shields, one with a concentric circle motif and one with a more complex design incorporating four-pointed stars (Figure 4.5c). As we have seen, concentric circles were the most popular design represented in the Tsegi Style pictograph shields. On the painted plaster layer beneath the bul-

Figure 4.5. Early murals from Awat'ovi and Pottery Mound. (*a*) Painting in white, green, and red of fragmentary shield figure from Room 229, Front Wall Design 24, Awat'ovi. (*b*) Crudely painted shield figure from Room 229, Front Wall Design 8, Awat'ovi. (*c*) Painting of shields in red, green, black, and white, Room 218, Front Wall Design 23, Awat'ovi. (*d*) Shield paintings from Pottery Mound, Kiva 7, Layer 36, west wall. (*a–c*) Drawings by Deborah Kelley after Smith 1952:Figures 40d, 46c, 40a. (*d*) Drawing by Deborah Kelley after Maxwell Museum of Anthropology, University of New Mexico, catalogue #76.70.518 and #76.70.510.

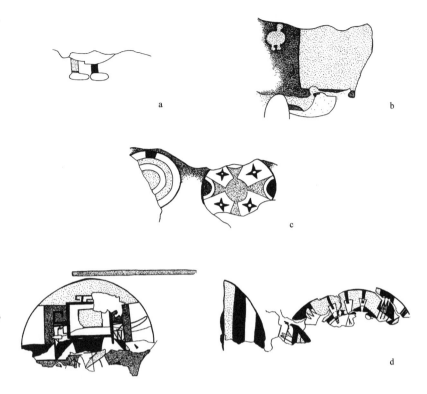

bous shield bearer from Room 229 is a depiction of a mountain lion (Smith 1952:Figure 43a). Mountain lions are associated with warfare as well as with the hunt in Pueblo mythology. A series of four murals from Room 218 may represent shields, although no more than the lower third of any of them is preserved (Smith 1952:Figure 42a–d). Each has a radial design centered in the lower segment, reminiscent of the decoration of the All American Man's shield except that the red and white stripes of the latter are vertical rather than radial. In three of Room 218's murals, this segment is made up of inward-pointing projectile points, or points together with eagle feathers. Heavy black lines frame the segment and in two panels overlap the shield edges. Because this basic design layout appears in later Awat'ovi and Pottery Mound shield depictions (e.g., Hibben 1975:Figure 101; Smith 1952:Figure 56b), I have counted them as shields in my analysis of the imagery. Thus shields appear in 14 percent of the early Awat'ovi murals and shield bearers in 7 percent; mountain lions are portrayed in 4 percent of the Awat'ovi murals from all kivas (Crotty 1995:Tables B.3, B.5).

Shields, shield bearers, and mountain lions also appear frequently in the early murals of Pottery Mound, a large Rio Grande Anasazi site located on the floodplain of the Rio Puerco southwest of Albuquerque, New Mexico. Occupation of Pottery Mound probably began sometime in the A.D. 1300s, but the kiva murals recovered from the site are not from the earliest occupation. They date from perhaps the very late 1300s

Figure 4.6. Mural of warriors from Kiva 9, Layer 12, Pottery Mound. (*a*) Figure holding Sikyatki-style shield and spear, west wall. (*b*) Figure wearing bandolier and holding war club, south wall. Drawings by Deborah Kelley (*a*) after Hibben 1975:Figure 101; (*b*) after Maxwell Museum of Anthropology, University of New Mexico, catalogue #76.70.802.

a

b

and into the 1400s, although an earlier date is often given in the literature. The full argument for dating the earliest murals around 1400 is presented elsewhere (Crotty 1995:52–54). In brief, the earliest recovered murals cannot date much before 1400, the suggested date for the appearance of the fully developed Sikyatki Polychrome pottery style in the Hopi area. This is because the earliest plaster layers of nearly all the Pottery Mound kivas are decorated with the distinctive motifs and asymmetrical layouts of the Sikyatki style (e.g., Hibben 1975:Figures 6, 13, 22, 35, 36, 50, 51, 52, 54). The presence of large amounts of Hopi yellow wares on the site together with strong similarities to the Awat'ovi murals in style and iconography point to an as yet little understood alliance between the inhabitants of the two sites.

Arrays of shields, some with Sikyatki-like decoration, are depicted on the first painted layers of Kiva 7, which appears to be one of the earliest Pottery Mound kivas (Hibben 1975:Figures 53, 56) (Figure 4.5d). Shields superimposed by mountain lions appear in the next layer, and another array of shields a few layers later (Crotty 1995:Table A.56). In Kiva 9, another early Pottery Mound kiva, shields are portrayed on an early layer, and a pair of fierce-looking male figures brandishing shields and weapons is found on the next painted layer (Figure 4.6a, b).

Figure 4.7. Murals of combat scenes from Kawaika'a and Awat'ovi: (*a*) Kawaika'a Test 14, Room 4, right and back walls, Design 2; (*b*) Awat'ovi Test 13, Room 3, front wall B, Design 2. Drawings by Deborah Kelley after Smith 1952:Figure 52.

Fifteenth-Century Kiva Murals

Several depictions of warriors apparently engaged in single combat appear in the early-fifteenth-century kivas of Awat'ovi and the neighboring village of Kawaika'a. In a mural that continues across two walls from Test 4, Room 4, at Kawaika'a, a warrior almost hidden by a huge shield decorated with eagle feathers stands over his enemy, who falls backward, dropping his rectangular shield and apparently dying from an arrow or spear in his side (Figure 4.7a). The victorious warrior seems to be dressed in leggings with stockings or gaiters held up by garters below his knees; his opponent wears leggings and sash but lacks the garters. His shield and dress might be intended to indicate that he is an outsider. In a probably contemporaneous kiva, Test 13, Room 3, from the intermediate occupation of Awat'ovi, two warriors are shown engaged in combat with a single shield between them (Figure 4.7b). In this case both warriors are garbed in ceremonial kilts, suggesting that what is depicted is a ceremonial reenactment of a historic or mythological event. The shield is undecorated, but the bodies of three birds are magically superimposed over its lower edge, neatly framed by the feather-bedecked shafts of four arrows that disappear behind the shield. Other portrayals in Awat'ovi and Kawaika'a show kilted figures with shields and weapons or shields alone with birds or projectiles arranged around the lower edge in defiance of gravity—testimony, perhaps, to their magical powers (Smith 1952:Figures 51d, 54a, 54b, 56a, 73a). In general, the impression conveyed is of symbolic rather than actual warfare, with the possible exception of the figures from Kawaika'a, as Smith (1952:312) suggests (Figure 4.7a).

In contrast, many of the murals of Pottery Mound virtually bristle with imagery that seems intended to impress the viewer with the bel-

Figure 4.8. Murals of
warriors and shields
from Pottery Mound,
Kiva 2, Layer 3.
Drawings by
Deborah Kelley after
Hibben 1975:Figures
101, 102, 103.

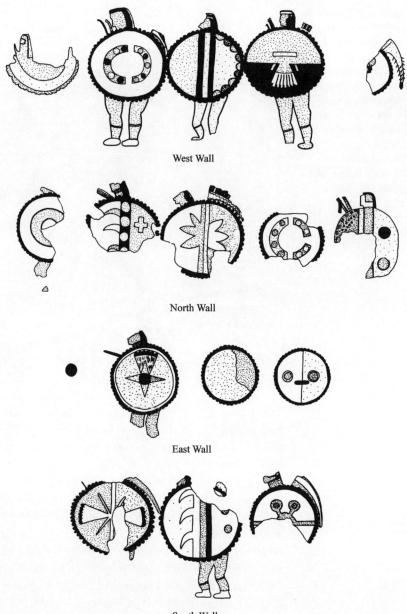

West Wall

North Wall

East Wall

South Wall

ligerency of the village. The most striking of these is a relatively late
painting, probably dated toward the end of the fifteenth century A.D.,
that covered all four walls of the third painted layer of Kiva 2 (Figure
4.8). It shows a line of warriors carrying their shields and weapons. No
two shields are decorated exactly alike, and where preservation permits,
the warriors can be seen to be attired in leggings with garters below the
knees. Three of the shields are slightly smaller than the others, and no
traces of warriors can be seen near them. Perhaps these represent warriors or kinship groups or allies absent for one reason or another. My in-

Figure 4.9. Possible shields from Las Humanas, Kiva N, Gran Quivira Unit, Salinas Pueblo Missions National Monument, New Mexico: (*a*) Quiver and shield with diamond pattern decoration from Layer 18, northeast wall; (*b*) shield or mask (?) from Layer 11, northeast wall. Drawings by Deborah Kelley after Peckham 1981:Fiches B3, A9.

a

b

terpretation is only speculation, of course, but if these shields were depicted without bearers, it suggests that at Pottery Mound at least, the shield device had a meaning closely associated with the warrior who carried it. Further, that at least at Pottery Mound each warrior had his own distinctive shield. This may not have been intended so much for personal identification as for the protective powers the device would provide the warrior. This possibility would not, of course, preclude the use of clan or sodality emblems in the design, nor does it explain similar devices portrayed in rock art at widely separated locations in New Mexico. In all, shields appear in 9 percent of all Pottery Mound murals, shield bearers in 2 percent, and mountain lions in 7 percent (Crotty 1995:Tables B.3, B.5).

Militaristic imagery appears also at Las Humanas (Gran Quivira) on the eastern fringe of Anasazi territory, one of the group of Salinas pueblos believed to have been involved in trade with Plains groups (Hayes 1981:11). The kiva in which these images were found is the best-dated of all the fifteenth-century painted kivas. It was built with logs cut in A.D. 1416, repaired with one cut in 1467, and subsequently burned (Hayes et al. 1981:52). Two possible shields are represented from the kiva (Figure 4.9a, b). The first, on the eighteenth painted plaster layer, is recognizable as a shield because of the presence of an arrow-filled mountain-lion skin quiver beside it. The second, on the eleventh layer, is identified as a mask by Peckham (1981:22), but because of the possible stylized quiver behind it and the frequent decoration of shields with human facial features at other sites, I suggest it represents a shield. Peckham (1981:20, 34) reports a very small incomplete figure bearing a shield decorated with concentric circles on the sixth layer of the same kiva. No shields or shield bearers were found in murals from the other kivas of the intermediate occupation or in the murals of the late occupation of Las Humanas.

Sun Shields

Omitted from the discussion above are examples of "sun shields" from Awat'ovi, Kawaika'a, and Pottery Mound. Many of these are unaccompanied by life forms and consist of simple undecorated disks from which eagle feathers radiate (Smith 1952:Figures 48a, 49b, 63d, 70c, 72a, 86b, 89c). A few are elaborately decorated and apparently involve the transformation of human or animal figures pictured as jumping through them (Hibben 1975:Figures 28, 78; Smith 1952:Figures 47b, 56a, b, 72b, 72c, 73c, 89a). As the animals depicted are usually felines, they may well have militaristic connotations as well.

Also omitted is a small concentric circle design, the only shield-like form from Kuaua, and a series of possible shields or sun symbols from Pueblo del Encierro. The Kuaua example was identified by Dutton's Zuni consultant as "the sun, or sunshine" (Dutton 1963:51, Figure 100). Kuaua is dated by Dutton from the late fifteenth century A.D. into the sixteenth; whereas, for reasons discussed elsewhere (Crotty 1995:61–64), I have dated the murals perhaps a century later. The Pueblo del Encierro suns are simple concentric circles consisting of an inner disk and an outer ring separated by lines and occasionally embellished with an outer ring or fringe. They occur in pairs on either side of the ventilator and are the only images recovered from a kiva dated from about 1450 into the 1500s (Schaafsma 1965; Warren 1979). For a more complete discussion of possible sun shields in Anasazi mural art, see Crotty 1995:238–242.

Fifteenth-Century Rock Art Depictions

In the rock art of the Galisteo Basin north and east of Pottery Mound are numerous petroglyph representations of shield bearers and shields. These images are found in many other Pueblo IV Anasazi rock art sites in New Mexico as well (e.g., Schaafsma 1980:Figures 200, 201, 207, 208, 223, 237; 1992b:119, 147, 157, 169, 170, 178). The motifs decorating the rock art shields are often remarkably similar to those seen in the Pottery Mound paintings, as Schaafsma (1992a:159) observes with regard to a Galisteo Basin site. The most spectacular and best-known warrior images of the Galisteo Basin are the two nearly life-size figures elegantly pecked on a panel of a 3.5-mile-long volcanic dike known as Creston, or

Figure 4.10. Warriors and other depictions from Creston, Gallisteo Basin, New Mexico State Trust Lands. Drawing by Lay Powell.

popularly as Comanche Gap (Figure 4.10). The two figures have horned or eared helmets or headdresses and wield menacing war clubs. Their warlike posture clearly conveys that their function is protective rather than ceremonial. They were most likely made by inhabitants of nearby Pueblo Blanco, a large site composed of some 1,450 to 2,000 rooms which was occupied, perhaps intermittently, from the late A.D. 1300s and into the 1500s, with the greatest population density probably in the fifteenth century (Winifred Creamer, personal communications 1996, 1998). Pueblo Blanco lies at the western end of the dike, and near it is a sandstone cliff that bears a number of rock art panels, several of them decorated with shields and shield bearers. It appears that militaristic imagery was preferred by earlier occupants of Pueblo Blanco, for several shields are superimposed by later depictions of very large horned serpents. Because the serpents are quite similar to depictions in fairly early Pottery Mound kiva murals, the superimposed shields would seem to date in the early 1400s, but with rock art, dating must always be approached with caution.

DISCUSSION

Images of shields first appear in Anasazi art in the Glen Canyon region sometime in the A.D. 1200s at a time when Anasazi populations were already retreating from their previous expansion into the southern reaches of the Fremont area (Gumerman and Dean 1989:121; Lister l964:81). There is little doubt that Fremont depictions of shields and shield bearers were the inspiration for the new imagery that the Anasazi began to use at this time. The fact that the Fremont shields were most often associated with human figures who carried them indicates that the shield depictions stemmed from militaristic imagery, but we cannot be certain that the Anasazi adopted the ideology along with the iconography. Certainly they did not adopt the art style completely, choosing painted imagery over pecked, expressing their designs in negative unpainted areas, using shields to cover the bodies of the bearers, adding horned or eared headdresses quite different from those of the Fremont models, and pointing the feet in the same direction rather than outward. The shield and shield bearer imagery persisted in Anasazi art into the fifteenth century and perhaps beyond. Some of the pictorial details of the earliest Anasazi examples of shield bearers from southeastern Utah can still be seen in the Galisteo Basin petroglyphs. There was clearly something in the new imagery that satisfied a need in Anasazi society. Was this simply a desire to express socioreligious or clan affiliations, or was it more basic to survival?

The warrior panel from Defiance House indicates that the militaristic imagery of the Fremont had become germane for the Anasazi at that particular time. The spread of the imagery into other areas of Kayenta occupation in the drainages of the left bank of the Colorado is strong evidence that it continued to have meaning for them as they retreated southward and into the heads of the canyons in the Tsegi. As Haas and Creamer convincingly argue: "The residents of the canyons did not abandon all their open-air sites, abandon their most accessible shelters, or abandon the natural wealth of Bubbling Springs Canyon in response to low-level conflict among friends. The people of the canyon were under the overt threat of physical attack, and they faced the threat with the utmost seriousness" (Haas and Creamer 1993:127).

Contemporaneous depictions of shield-bearing warriors support the interpretation of large circular pictographs as shields, yet many authors (Anderson 1971; Cole 1990; Geib and Fairley 1996; Pilles 1994; Schaafsma 1966, 1980) are reluctant to accept that interpretation. I have suggested that the use of a shield device to indicate the residence of a particular religious or kinship group is not incompatible with its use on actual shields by one or more warriors from that group, and this is confirmed in part by the example of the shield figures from Cliff Palace, but only from that single site, and this still leaves a number of questions. There is ethnographic evidence for the use of certain symbols to identify the shield of a particular sodality in the Soyal observances at Hopi (Fewkes 1898:70), but this is a ceremonial occasion rather than an actual warfare situation. If the same practice were observed at Pottery Mound in the 1400s, it is hard to imagine that 16 different societies would be taking part in a ceremony in a single rather small kiva. Also troubling is the explanation that the shield devices identify the kinship or lineage of the residents of individual houses, for if five shields are needed for the small open Pueblo III sites in Cow Canyon, why are there only one or two or three for large sites in Tsegi Canyon and none at all at Kiet Siel? Why choose a particular location at the right-hand side of the cave, at least in Tsegi Canyon? Why the frequent appearance of the concentric circle motif at so many widely separated cliff dwellings, and even paired at Twin Caves Pueblo, if the shields represent societies or kinship groups? As we saw, concentric circles are often associated with the sun in Pueblo thought, and the sun, father of the War Twins, is a power for war as well as for fertility (Tyler 1964:143, 161). Perhaps it is possible to resolve these questions by suggesting that the shield representations were perceived as magical protective devices for the residents of that particular house. With the exception of the Cow Canyon examples, which are early and anomalous in location, technique, and scale, the shields are associated with defensive cliff dwellings, which, as Haas and Creamer (1993) state, were built in inaccessible locations because the inhabitants of the canyons believed themselves to be in constant danger of physical attack.

Curiously, so far as I know, there are no examples of shields and shield bearers in the rock art of the Cibola region, where dramatic changes in settlement patterns in the late A.D. 1200s strongly suggest a perceived need for defensive potential in site location and size (LeBlanc 1989, 1999). Murals were discovered in an apparently secular room at Atsinna, one of these defensive sites, which was occupied between 1275 and 1350, but the paintings follow an earlier Anasazi tradition of decorating walls with geometric designs, some of which were derived from pottery decoration (Crotty 1995:43, Table A.2). The only southern instances of militaristic imagery to my knowledge are the cliff houses of the Sinagua near Sedona and those of Canyon Creek and the Sierra Ancha area. It may be that this was a Kayenta tradition that moved with the Kayenta population to Hopi and thence to southern Arizona. It seems to have reached the Rio Grande through the still unexplained ties between Awat'ovi and Pottery Mound.

The Anasazi adoption of Fremont shield bearer imagery made a lasting change in the art, not only in iconography but also, perhaps because of the desire to make the shields visible over a long distance, in scale. The Anasazi, who since Basketmaker III times had been content with relatively small images apparently haphazardly arranged, now began to think big. The new concept of scale may have contributed to the florescence of mural art in the Pueblo IV period since the larger figures required more compositional organization and allowed for more detailed rendering.

The new imagery appears almost immediately in the first kiva murals of Awat'ovi, and though dominant at the very beginning, it was soon supplemented or replaced by other themes. By the early A.D. 1400s at Awat'ovi, depictions of reenactments with the combatants in ceremonial dress seem to have replaced the more simple depictions of shields and shield bearers like those seen in rock art. Depictions of ceremonial events are, after all, appropriate for a kiva setting, and as LeBlanc (1999:236) suggests, they may reflect the evolving social role of the warrior. In the kivas of Pottery Mound, and also at Las Humanas, a more bellicose iconography continues well into the 1400s. This may reflect nothing more than regional or ethnic disparities or a more prolonged period of instability in the Rio Grande area, but another possibility is that this iconography expressed the socioeconomic concerns of the residents. As noted earlier, shields in early Pottery Mound murals are decorated with Sikyatki style designs, and a significant amount of Hopi yellow wares were found at the site. What went back to Awat'ovi in return? LeBlanc (1997, 1999), in his examination of technological innovation in southwestern warfare, argues that the introduction of the sinew-backed bow sometime between the 1100s and the 1400s resulted in the replacement of the basketry shields of Pueblo III times with hide shields, and that apparently the only acceptable hide for the new shields was buffalo. LeBlanc (personal communication 1997) has further proposed that Pottery Mound, because of its location near the edge of the plains, might have been in a position to obtain buffalo hides, perhaps from Las Humanas, to exchange for the Hopi yellow wares. The presence of Sikyatki style designs on Pottery Mound shields has always been puzzling because such designs are not found on shields pictured in the Awat'ovi and Kawaika'a murals. Similarly, murals composed of Sikyatki style designs are far more prevalent in Pottery Mound kivas than at Awat'ovi. In addition, Sikyatki style decoration was applied to Pottery Mound Polychrome, a local imitation of the Hopi wares (Brody 1964). One of the few sites where Pottery Mound Polychrome is intrusive is Las Humanas. The Pottery Mound depictions of Sikyatki style designs may have expressed a trade relationship with the Hopi area or proclaimed the association with powerful allies, or perhaps the Sikyatki designs had even acquired religious significance. If Pottery Mound was supplying buffalo hides for shields, it would, in a sense, have a vested interest in active warfare, or the threat of it, which was expressed in the overt militarism of the murals from that site.

Whatever the motivation for the militaristic imagery of the Pottery Mound murals, it seems likely that the same sort of imagery in the petroglyphs of the Galisteo Basin and other New Mexico sites reflects the existence of warfare among the Rio Grande pueblos of the fourteenth and fifteenth centuries, or whenever the petroglyphs were made. Better methods of dating rock art and a better understanding of the interactions among the protohistoric Rio Grande pueblos may one day pinpoint the association. It is possible that images of shields and shield bearers may have been pecked into rock surfaces long after they had disappeared from kiva walls.

CONCLUSIONS

The adoption of Fremont militaristic imagery around the mid A.D. 1200s by the Kayenta Anasazi appears to be a response to the increasing hostilities between neighboring groups as they withdrew from their northern expansion and gathered in larger settlements in the homeland areas. Increasing environmental deterioration in the decades that followed would have intensified the hostilities. Shield bearer images are more prevalent at Anasazi settlements in the drainages of the right bank of the Colorado, however, than they are in Tsegi Canyon, where the display of large shields in a preferred location on the right side of the alcove may have been perceived not only as a warning to enemies but also as a protective device. Although the practice of placing shield pictographs in visible areas near cliff dwellings apparently spread to east-central Arizona in the Sinagua and Sierra Ancha regions, similar paintings seem to be absent at defensive sites elsewhere. With the exception of the anomalous Cliff Palace incised figures, representations of shield bearers in rock art or murals are not known from other locations occupied during the late thirteenth and early fourteenth centuries. Shields and shield bearers of the Pueblo III period appear to be most closely identified with the Kayenta Anasazi.

Shields and shield bearers figure prominently in the kiva murals of the late fourteenth century at Awat'ovi, which is believed to have been settled at least in part by Kayenta Anasazi, and Pottery Mound, where mural artists were obviously heavily influenced by Awat'ovi iconography and Hopi pottery decoration. Depictions of combat in the Hopi kivas of the fifteenth century appear to be ceremonial reenactments perhaps associated with the increased social importance of warriors, unlike the depictions of shields and shield bearers at Pottery Mound, which convey a sense of militancy. The militaristic imagery is found to a more limited extent in the contemporaneous pueblo of Las Humanas. It is speculated that buffalo skins, perhaps obtained from Las Humanas, were traded for Hopi yellow wares found at the Pottery Mound site. This type of trade, however, would flourish only if the need for hide shields persisted, which suggests that warfare, or the threat of warfare, continued in the Western Pueblos well into the fifteenth century. The less securely dated petroglyph representations of shields and shield bearers in the Galisteo Basin and many other locations in the Rio Grande area are also indicative of endemic warfare that may have lasted even longer.

Although hostilities among the various Anasazi pueblos may not always have found expression in kiva or rock art depiction of shields and shield bearers, the imagery is certainly an apt representation of militaristic concerns. It serves both to illustrate how the conflicts were decided and to suggest the growing social importance of the warrior in a troubled era.

CHAPTER FIVE

Conflict and Defense in the Grasshopper Region of East-Central Arizona

H. David Tuggle and J. Jefferson Reid

Armed conflict, although varying in form and intensity, is virtually a human universal (Ember 1978; Keeley 1996), but ironically, it often leaves little mark on the archaeological record—and any mark that may be left is frequently ambiguous and thus disputable.[1] In discussing prehistoric conflict in the Grasshopper region of east-central Arizona, part of the Mogollon culture area (Figure 5.1), we take a simple approach to this problem: we assume that conflict of some sort was a component of the prehistoric social system and thus we develop a model based on the evidence that is consistent with this assumption. This is obviously only one component of research and analysis (involving multiple hypotheses and working models), but we leave the development of alternative models to lengthier presentations.

Conflict in prehistory has not been a dominant theme in Mogollon investigations, although general reference to it is not completely absent (e.g., Danson 1957; Farmer 1957; Longacre 1962; Rinaldo 1964; Lindsay 1969). The burned room block at Point of Pines Pueblo has been interpreted as one of the most substantial examples of this type of event (Haury 1958).

For the Grasshopper region of Arizona, the University of Arizona field school research program (which ran from 1963 to 1992) gave little at-

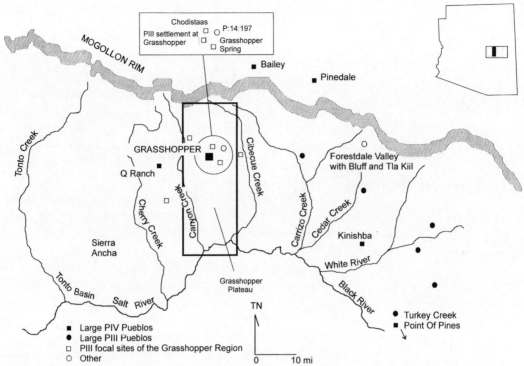

Figure 5.1. East-central Arizona, with major Pueblo III and Pueblo IV sites, and focal PIII sites of the Grasshopper area. Rectangle outlines the Grasshopper research area of the University of Arizona field school, 1963–92.

tention to warfare or conflict during its first decade of research. Investigation focused on the large Pueblo IV period (PIV) Grasshopper Pueblo, first in a cultural-historical context and later in the context of so-cial organization (Thompson and Longacre 1966; Longacre and Reid 1974). The question of conflict and warfare in the region was raised as an element of settlement analysis when systematic survey of the Grass-hopper region was undertaken in 1969 (Tuggle 1970). The settlement model proposed increasing community interaction under pressures of population increase, competition for arable land, and possible environ-mental deterioration. Armed conflict was included as one dimension of this interaction, based on cross-cultural ethnographic models and on the defensible character and positioning of the large PIV period sites of the Grasshopper region (Tuggle 1970:61–64).

In subsequent years of research, excavations were expanded beyond Grasshopper Pueblo to small sites of the Pueblo III (PIII) and PIV peri-ods, accompanied by an extensive survey program. These combined re-search realms produced an increasing amount of evidence for conflict, and it became one of the critical elements in the interpretation of re-gional history, settlement pattern and settlement system, and the pro-cesses of change (Reid and Tuggle 1988; Reid 1989).

The present chapter, a synthesis of the Grasshopper regional model, focuses on the evidence for conflict and its role in cultural dynamics for the period from around A.D. 1000 to about 1400. The argument for con-flict in this region is based not only on specific archaeological data but on an understanding of the cultural-historical events occurring over the extensive area of the Mogollon Rim and adjacent regions.

THE GRASSHOPPER REGION AND THE RESEARCH DOMAIN

The Grasshopper region is a research area of 830 km² extending from the Mogollon Rim south to the Salt River and from the Cibecue Valley west to Canyon Creek (see Figure 5.1). For the time of the early A.D. 1300s, this area may also be described as a regional interaction system, balanced against the Q Ranch region to the west and the Kinishba region to the east.

The topography of the area is dominated by the Grasshopper Plateau (Figures 5.2, 5.3), whose southern and western edges are sharply defined by the 1,500-foot-high cliffs of the Salt River and the aptly named Canyon Creek. The eastern side of the plateau is marked by a series of terraces and drainages dropping into the Cibecue Valley. The plateau has an elevation range of about 6,300 feet asl at the base of the Mogollon Rim, dropping to about 4,000 feet asl overlooking the Salt River. Grasshopper Pueblo lies in the upper elevation of the plateau at about 6,000 feet asl and is in the approximate center east to west.

The Grasshopper region is part of the vast circum-Sonoran uplands (Shreve 1951), a biotic and physiographic province that is characterized by heavily dissected terrain, semiarid conditions, a high water table, and numerous springs. The area is comparatively rich in game and wild plants but is highly variable for cultivation. It has small regional pockets that provide soil, water, and a temperature range suitable for horticulture, but there are vast areas of harsh, uncultivable terrain (Welch 1996).

When we look at east-central Arizona within the larger circum-Sonoran uplands, it is useful to compare the eastern and western zones, roughly corresponding to what is today the eastern and western sections of the White Mountain Apache Reservation (and a portion of the San Carlos Reservation). In general terms, the agricultural potential diminishes from east to west. In the White River and Cedar Creek areas the water resources are greater and bottomlands more extensive than in the Grasshopper region. The water and arable soil resources of Cibecue Creek and the Canyon Creek/Oak Creek drainages are relatively limited, with the Grasshopper Plateau even more restricted in soil, water, and frost-free days. At the western edge of this area are the formidable cliffs and canyons of the Sierra Ancha. Nineteenth- and early-twentieth-century Apachean settlements, which centered on garden plots, reflect this patterning of resource potential, with the larger settlements in the east; the villages in the Grasshopper region were concentrated in the Cibecue and Oak Creek/Canyon Creek drainages, with a small transitory settlement on the Grasshopper Plateau (Goodwin 1942; Tuggle 1970; Graves 1982; Welch 1996).

Survey of the Grasshopper region and a portion of the Q Ranch re-

Figure 5.2.
Topography of the
Grasshopper region,
with large pueblos
(more than 45
rooms) and defensive
settlement of the
Pueblo IV period.
Except for the large
pueblos, PIV sites in
the interior of the
Grasshopper Plateau
are not shown.

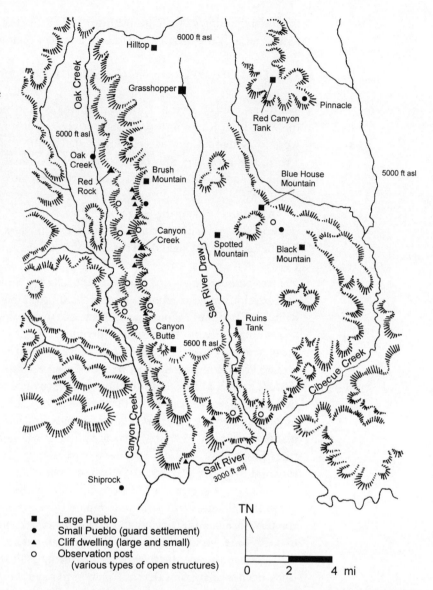

gion includes intensive coverage of 466 km² and topographic-transect coverage of an estimated 150 km of ridgelines, finger ridges, and other rugged topographic forms. Some 779 sites and 713 artifact scatters have been recorded. Intensive excavations have been conducted at the Grasshopper Pueblo (PIV, 500 rooms), Chodistaas (late PIII, 18 rooms), Grasshopper Spring (late PIII, 10 rooms), and AZ P:14:197 [ASM] (late PIII, 5 rooms), with testing at eight other sites and tree-ring coring of numerous cliff dwellings. Before the University of Arizona field program, the only significant excavation in the region was the work at the Canyon Creek Pueblo cliff dwelling (Haury 1934). The sites in the Grasshopper region that are noted here or used in the analysis are summarized in Appendix 5.1.

Figure 5.3. Western side of the Grasshopper Plateau, facing east. Site P:14:263 is on the prominent knoll just left of center.

SETTLEMENT, AGGREGATION, AND CONFLICT

The archaeological record seldom shows change that is rapid enough to measure by a human generation or two, but the transition from late PIII to PIV in the Grasshopper region has left such a record. In the A.D. 1270s groups were small in number, occupying scattered settlements on a seasonal basis. By the early 1300s population had exploded and numerous large, permanent pueblos had been constructed. There is archaeological evidence for conflict during the transition period, and there is a clear attention to defense during the PIV period. The character of the defense, however, emphasizes protection and warning rather than defense through fortification.

Pueblo II and Early Pueblo III Periods

In the PII and early PIII periods (defined by ceramic cross-dating) sites in the Grasshopper and adjacent Q Ranch regions are small and scattered. There is substantial evidence of interregional contact and possibly population movement during this period, indicated by the presence of red-on-buff, micaceous plainware, and carbon painted whiteware (Reid 1982; Tuggle et al. 1982).

There are no archaeological indicators of conflict during this time, which may be a function of the nature of the site types and the form of conflict that may have existed. The sites consist of clusters of a few pithouses and two- to three-room low-walled cobble structures and a variety of isolated scatters of chipped stone and ceramics. Detailed analysis of survey data and surface artifacts (primarily from the Q Ranch region) indicates that this was an era of low population, consisting of highly mobile groups relying on a mixed subsistence base in which hunting was the core, supplemented by gardening (Wood 1980; Graybill and Reid 1982; Reid 1982; Tuggle 1982; Whittlesey et al. 1982). Limited clashes between small groups, along with small-scale raiding and ambush, would be expected, based on ethnographic generalization, but none of these would

leave much substantial evidence in the archaeological record, at best isolated instances of burned thatch structures or damage to human skeletons. Excavation of sites of this time range in the Grasshopper and Q
Ranch regions has been too limited to provide a basis for evaluating evidence for conflict, however.

During this period, sites in the Forestdale Valley and Point of Pines
areas indicate that population was probably greater than in the Grasshopper region, and there is much more evidence for settled semiagricul-
tural communities. For example, the site of Tla Kii (Haury 1985) is a
twenty-one–room pueblo, tree-ring-dated in the A.D. 1100–1150 range.
There is no site of the time period in the Grasshopper region that is re-
motely similar to Tla Kii in size or architecture. This difference is consistent with the greater agricultural potential of the eastern area and is
indicative of a process of cultural development that had substantial implications for the Grasshopper region in the late PIII period. There is no
direct evidence of conflict in this eastern area, but the earlier Bluff Village
is in a defensible location (Haury and Sayles 1947; Haury 1985; Reid
1989:71), and the aggregation at sites such as Tla Kii may be indicative
of a concern with defense.

This region of Arizona has not been surveyed extensively or systematically, however, and thus the larger pattern of site destruction and positioning is uncertain. What is certain is that by the A.D. 1200s there were
numerous large pueblos in this area and that population movement and
settlement expansion in the eastern area began to press on the peoples of
the Grasshopper uplands.

Late Pueblo III Period and the Transition to Pueblo IV

In the mid to late A.D. 1200s the Grasshopper and Q Ranch regional
population remained low and villages small, an isolate in a world of
rapid growth. In the eastern area there were numerous pueblos in the
100-room range (Reid and Tuggle 1988), with at least one (Turkey Creek
in the Point of Pines area) as large as 335 rooms (Lowell 1991). How far
the large eastern pueblo development extended toward Grasshopper is
unknown because of the limited amount of survey data from the intervening Cedar Creek and Carrizo areas, although some large PIII sites are
reported from the Carrizo drainage. To the north, above the rim, pueblos
such as Pinedale and Bailey were developing; to the west, cliff dwellings
were being constructed in the Sierra Ancha; and to the southwest, there
were large communities in Tonto Basin (Ciolek-Torrello and Lange
1990; Ciolek-Torrello 1997).

This explosive growth of the surrounding areas, particularly to the
east, was probably a result of internal population increase based on
greater agricultural dependence, accompanied by a substantial influx of
peoples from the Colorado Plateau who were driven south to the rivers
below the rim by the disastrous years of the late-thirteenth-century Great

Drought (Reid and Whittlesey 1997:147). The regional complex below the Mogollon Rim from Carrizo to the Black River has not been well recorded or studied, so there is no evidence concerning the development of defensive systems or the extent to which conflict took place. The fact that conflict did occur at nearby Point of Pines is well documented in a burned room complex (Haury 1958), however, and future excavations in the eastern area will probably demonstrate that this was not an isolated incident. Further, pueblo aggregation occurring at this time itself has been commonly seen as a defensive feature and an indicator of conflict or threat of conflict (e.g., Kidder 1924; Hunter-Anderson 1979; Lowell 1989:188–192; LeBlanc 1999), a position we share (Reid and Tuggle 1988; Reid 1989:81).

Although their numbers were not growing rapidly in the late PIII period and they had lost their contacts with the desert south, the people of the Grasshopper region were by no means out of touch with the rest of the mountains and the rim country. The area had developed a new source of black-on-white ceramics (Tuggle et al. 1982; Zedeño 1994), so it was part of a ceramic network involving Cibola Whiteware and White Mountain Redware (Triadan 1997) which included the villages in the eastern region. There can be little doubt that the involvement with this interaction sphere to the east meant forays from these larger communities into the range of the people of the Grasshopper region. These forays occurred for a variety of reasons, including resource collection, trade, search for new settlement locations, and raiding. The consequences for the Grasshopper region become obvious in the detailed information collected from sites of this period and of PIV, the temporal focus of the Grasshopper program.

In the Grasshopper region the first significant sign of aggregation occurs in the late A.D. 1200s (Tuggle 1970; Reid et al. 1996). This is seen in the construction of small pueblos (10 to 20 rooms),[2] usually in room blocks connected to a low-walled plaza or plazas (probably the western-area expression of the great kiva). Each of these is adjacent to a spring or stream and arable soil. These appear to be focal villages in discrete, isolated settlement clusters that also include a few scattered rooms or room sets and small activity areas indicated by sherd and artifact scatters; each cluster was some one to two kilometers in diameter (Reid and Tuggle 1988; Reid 1989:77–80; Welch 1996:Figures 4.3 and 4.4). There were three late PIII focal settlements on the Grasshopper Plateau (see Figure 5.1): the sites of Chodistaas (Figure 5.4) and Grasshopper Spring Pueblo (which lacks a walled plaza but is considered a focal settlement for a variety of reasons) and a settlement in the location that would become the massive Grasshopper Pueblo (Reid and Whittlesey 1999:32). There is also one focal village in each of three other locations in the region: Cibecue Valley, Oak Creek Valley, and Campbell Creek (in the Q Ranch region),[3] all with walled plazas (Reid et al. 1996; Tuggle 1970, 1982).

These aggregations are associated with a rise in regional population,

Figure 5.4.
Chodistaas Pueblo
(late PIII),
Grasshopper Pueblo
(PIV), and Canyon
Butte Pueblo (PIV).

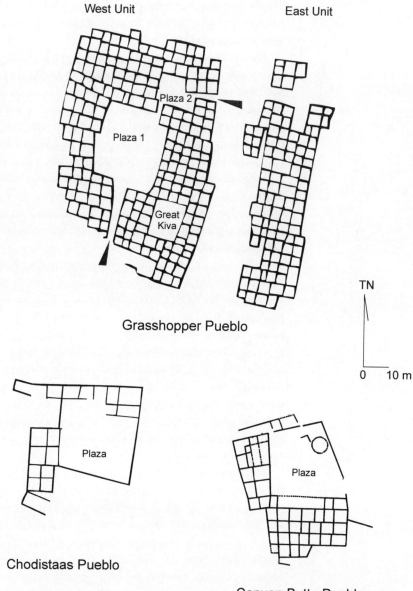

increased sedentism, and movement of new peoples into the area, processes that are demonstrated by the work at Chodistaas (Crown 1981; Montgomery and Reid 1990; Montgomery 1992; Zedeño 1994). Technological analysis of ceramics indicates that Chodistaas was probably a settlement of people having strong contacts with the Colorado Plateau (Zedeño 1994). The changes occurred during a time of environmental stress and extensive demographic shifts on the Colorado Plateau (Dean and Robinson 1982), as some people moved into the well-watered areas to the east of Grasshopper and others made their way into the Grasshopper region, which had a low population and open arable lands.

This is a setting for conflict. As Keeley (1996:127–141) notes, a "moving frontier" and hard times are two of the most common conditions associated with warfare.

Three sites of the late PIII period in the Grasshopper region have been intensively excavated: Chodistaas, AZ P:14:197, and Grasshopper Spring Pueblo (see Figure 5.1). Chodistaas and Grasshopper Spring are two of the three focal villages of the area, and P:14:197 is a small room site in the Chodistaas settlement cluster. All three of these sites were burned to the ground (Montgomery and Reid 1990; Reid et al. 1996). Chodistaas was burned sometime after A.D. 1285, probably in the 1290s, and the others about this same time (Reid and Whittlesey 1999:40). The destruction of two of only three central places[4] (and a satellite) on the Grasshopper Plateau at this time can be seen as a result of the conflict that was occurring in an era of widespread economic stress, high demand for land and other resources, and social tensions resulting from immigration (Reid 1989:81). At Grasshopper Spring Pueblo a disarticulated body with an associated projectile was found on the floor of a proto-kiva, also suggestive of conflict (although ritual dismemberment is an alternative explanation).[5] This was also the time when the use of the atlatl in the region was completely abandoned (Lorentzen 1993). Atlatl dart points are found at Grasshopper Spring Pueblo and arrow points at the coeval Chodistaas, but only arrow points are present at Grasshopper Pueblo, occupied immediately afterward. Atlatls and bows have advantages and disadvantages as hunting weapons, but the bow is unquestionably a more effective weapon of war. The loss of the atlatl in the cultural inventory is consistent with the other evidence of increased conflict at this time.

The people of the Grasshopper region were hardly unaware that along the Mogollon Rim and through the uplands they were in a small minority of folk still living in small pueblos. This situation did not last long. The archaeological evidence indicates that the aggregation began immediately after the burning of the villages, with people from Chodistaas and Grasshopper Spring constructing new settlements as the beginnings of room blocks at Grasshopper (Reid and Whittlesey 1999:66). Thus disastrous conflict and subsequent defensive aggregation may have occurred in a time span counted in single years, sometime from the A.D. 1290s to the early 1300s. At the same time, with large numbers of other peoples moving to the plateau, additional aggregated settlements were being founded, and within a generation after the burning of Chodistaas there were ten major pueblos on the Grasshopper Plateau, ranging in size from 46 to 500 rooms.

Pueblo IV

Grasshopper Pueblo is not where it should be. That is to say, if Grasshopper is considered in terms of ecologically based settlement patterning, the largest village in the region with a substantial agricultural base would be expected in Cibecue Valley, not on the Grasshopper Plateau. This is one of several anomalies in the PIV settlement of the Grasshopper region that, on the one hand, suggest the importance of defense in the development of this system and, on the other, are the outcome of a specific set of historical events. And at the end of this remarkable set of events it turns out that Grasshopper is exactly where it should be.

The cluster of the ten large PIV pueblos[6] on the Grasshopper Plateau (see Figure 5.2) is not consistent with the patterning of agricultural potential in the larger area. The plateau is not a good agricultural locale and is certainly inferior to watered lands available in the Cibecue Valley to the east and Oak Creek/Canyon Creek to the west, where, in contrast, there is only one small PIV site in each of these comparatively rich riverine locations.[7] The significance of this is made striking by the fact that on the plateau the location of Grasshopper Pueblo is predictable as the largest settlement associated with the largest zone of arable soil, a rank-order pattern that holds for all the large pueblos on the plateau (Tuggle et al. 1984; also see Welch 1996:Figure 4.2). Further, the total population of the region was not exclusively concentrated in large pueblos. In addition to the 10 major pueblos (including Canyon Creek Pueblo, a 120-room cliff dwelling), there were 58 small open sites and 24 cliff dwellings in use during this time (based on ceramic types and tree-ring dating). Certainly many of the smaller sites were special-activity areas and temporary camps, but the trash and architecture of several of them also indicate permanent residence. This PIV development of the early fourteenth century has to be seen as well in light of the fact that local aggregation also entailed an influx of large numbers of new groups, coming from above the rim and from the east, as indicated in part by White Mountain Redwares that appear in large quantities in the region for the first time (Tuggle 1970; Reid and Tuggle 1988; Triadan 1997), with additional ceramic evidence of groups from the southwest. This interregional migration is also indicated by other characteristics of the archaeological data from Grasshopper (Reid and Whittlesey 1982, 1999), with strong support from the geochemical analysis of tooth enamel of 69 adults from the Grasshopper population (Ezzo et al. 1997).

A strong model interpreting this pattern suggests that, as peoples moved into the area, regional settlement became concentrated on the Grasshopper Plateau because of its defensive potential and that, as immigrants interacted with local populations, aggregation was chosen as another component of defense. The core of this development resided in the small local PIII period settlements, whose residents undoubtedly were part of the initial aggregation at Grasshopper following the destruction of their villages (Reid and Whittlesey 1999). Cibecue Valley and Oak Creek[8] were probably largely abandoned at this time, and people from these villages may also have joined the Grasshopper community. The defense and aggregation pattern that is evident in the Grasshopper region is in fact part of the much larger picture of conflict and drastic settlement change for much of the Southwest (LeBlanc 1999).

PROTECTION AND WARNING ON THE GRASSHOPPER PLATEAU

If we look at warfare in terms of the cultures of the area, it was certainly in the range of "deadly raids, ambushes, and surprise attacks on settlements" that Keeley (1996:174) defines as the preferred combat of tribal warriors. Expressed emphatically, this is "war reduced to its essentials: killing enemies with a minimum of risk, denying them the means of life via vandalism and theft" (Keeley 1996:175). From this standpoint, the defense of the people of the Grasshopper region can be seen centered not on fortification but on protection, warning, and increasing the risk to aggressors. And in a period of economic stress, it is food that demands the greatest protection, stored food and food as localized subsistence resources (including gardens).

The settlement information[9] constitutes the bulk of evidence for the nature of conflict and defense during this period. Figure 5.2 shows the relevant settlement distribution, and a listing of large pueblos and defense-related sites of the region during the PIV period is presented in the chapter appendix.

The Grasshopper Plateau as Protection

The Grasshopper Plateau itself provides the first component of protection. Access to the region for about three-fourths of its perimeter is comparatively difficult (Figure 5.5), and the population concentration on the plateau was an inherent defense against small raids. The topography of the plateau combined with the large population also created some measure of security for the smaller settlements scattered about the area. The settlement pattern also indicates that although villages on the plateau may have been wary of one another, their main worries were directed outward.

Grasshopper Regional Settlement

The most definitive evidence for defense comes from the western edge of the plateau (see Figure 5.2). Much of this area is a high, rugged escarpment (some of it two-tiered), and the ridge ends and canyon edges are dotted with small isolated open pueblos, cobble structures, and cliff dwellings of various sizes.[10] Many of the small room sets (dated to PIV by ceramic types) are placed in rugged terrain (usually cliff edges), overlook major drainages, and have relatively small quantities of surface artifacts, with no suggestion of permanent occupation (Figure 5.6). A room in one of these sites was tested, producing no evidence of trash deposi-

Figure 5.5. Schematic
terrain profiles of
Grasshopper Plateau
with selected site lo-
cations.

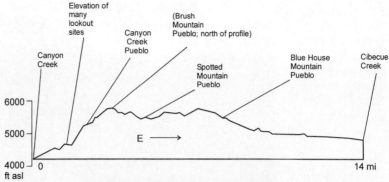

Profile of Grasshopper Plateau, (west to east) south of Grasshopper Pueblo,
with Cibecue Valley and Canyon Creek drainage

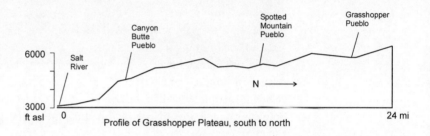

Profile of Grasshopper Plateau, south to north

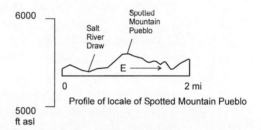

Profile of locale of Spotted Mountain Pueblo

tion or burning, but three in situ large corrugated brownware storage
jars were found, indicative of the storage that would be associated with
short-term use of the location. In some cases, access routes through
cracks in the adjacent cliff face have been blocked with stone. None of
these can be considered forts or refuges.[11] They were observation posts
that would have served to provide warning of approach up Canyon
Creek by people who could be coming from the south, from the east
(along Salt River), or from Tonto Basin to the west.

In addition to the sites that served as observation posts, there are two
small pueblos on knolls at the edge of the plateau (see Figure 5.3) that
were permanent villages but combined this function with defensive/ob-
servation positions. These are considered possible guard settlements (see
Figure 5.2)—that is, villages of normal settlement activities augmented
with a role of observation and warning.

Figure 5.6. A site on a cliff edge of the lower tier of the Grasshopper Plateau's western escarpment, facing north, 300 m above Canyon Creek.

There are also at least 25 cliff dwellings that are scattered along the cliffs of the Oak Creek/Canyon Creek drainage, Salt River, and lower Cibecue Creek (see Figure 5.2; note that many of the smallest cliff dwellings are not shown). These range in size from 2 to 120 rooms and range in function from permanent settlements to small, unobtrusive storage facilities. The presence of these cliff dwellings greatly expands the physical extent, density, and complexity of the protective settlement along the edges of the plateau, as these are inherently defensive structures[12] but also add more permanent residences to the set of observation posts along the canyon rim. Some of the smaller, nonpermanent cliff dwellings may also have been hidden lookouts. The larger cliff dwellings that were settlements might also be considered guard villages (see Wilcox and Haas 1994).

There are also at least three sites not on the plateau that may be classified as guard villages and included as a component of a defensive boundary. These are relatively small, open pueblos with evidence of intensive, perhaps permanent occupation which are located in isolated and defensive positions. One of them (Pinnacle Pueblo), on the eastern flank of the Grasshopper Plateau, stands on a very narrow, steep-sided, finger ridge (Figure 5.7). The rooms are small and built to the edge of the ridge, leaving no space for exterior activity areas. A combination of defense and observation provides justification for construction in this difficult position. This is the only site of this type on the eastern side of the Grasshopper Plateau, but it has a very broad view of the large terrace separating Cibecue Valley from the Grasshopper Plateau, allowing it to function as an observation post. At the same time, the quantity of trash

Figure 5.7. Pinnacle Pueblo, located on the end of the ridge, facing west. The ridge is part of Spring Ridge, which joins Grasshopper Plateau, seen in the background.

indicates an intensive occupation, possibly permanent, and not short-term use simply as a sentinel position. A pueblo that lies off the plateau on the west side (Oak Creek Pueblo) may also have been a combination permanent settlement and defensive observation post. It lies in an area of relatively easy access to the plateau but is placed atop a rock outcrop in a defensive location along the creek. The third site in this category (Shiprock Pueblo, Figure 5.8) is in the drainage of Canyon Creek near the confluence with the Salt River and is placed on the edge of a rocky bluff overlooking the Salt River.

The manner in which the occupants of any of these observation posts, isolated pueblos, or cliff dwellings communicated with one another or with the main villages on the plateau is a matter of speculation. The field-work related to this problem has never been conducted in the Grass-hopper region. This work would involve line-of-sight determinations (as estimated in the Q Ranch region; Reid 1982:137–138), surface evidence for signal fires, and detailed studies of surface artifacts and excavation to determine the full range of activities and intensity of occupation of the lookout sites.

If the large pueblos of the plateau are reconsidered from the stand-point of topographic distribution, they can also be seen as playing a role in defense not only by their size but by their geographic positioning. It is clear that their distribution is primarily related to arable soils of the plateau (Tuggle et al. 1984; Welch 1996), but the effect of this distribu-tion is to provide an additional element to the defensive patterning of the plateau (see Figure 5.2).[13] In other words, the distribution of small de-fensive sites and observation posts (and cliff dwellings) creates a sentinel system, with the locations of many of the larger pueblos effectively plac-

Figure 5.8. Shiprock Pueblo, located on the top of the knoll, facing north. Grasshopper Plateau is in the background to the right.

ing massed populations along access routes, serving as protection and warning. Access routes from the east are blocked by Black Mountain and Blue House Mountain Pueblos; from the north and northwest by Hilltop Pueblo; from the south by Ruins Tank and Canyon Butte Pueblos (see Figure 5.4); and from the west and southwest by Brush Mountain and the two largest cliff dwellings in the region, Canyon Creek and Red Rock House.

Pueblo Setting and Structure

The individual setting and architecture of some of the large pueblos also served to enhance defense, conceived as protection and warning. Spotted Mountain (see Figure 5.5) and Hilltop Pueblos are in elevated locales with a defensive component. Three of the large pueblos (Brush Mountain, Black Mountain, and Canyon Butte; see Figure 5.5) stand at the edge of the plateau or at the heads of canyons. At Blue House Mountain Pueblo there is a massive wall, possibly defensive, along one side of the structure parallel to a room block, the only known feature in the region that suggests some form of fortification (although its function has not been investigated by excavation or detailed architectural analysis). This aspect of pueblo structure is little understood, however; the architectural organization and special features of the pueblos related to topographic position need to be examined much more carefully to test possibilities that locations are defense related.

The large pueblos are defensive by nature. The size and population of these structures were deterrents to the raids and surprise attracts expected of the warfare of this time. They were also resistant to damage; a full-standing pueblo was not easily burned. They protected food stores within them (Lowell 1989). Their proximity to gardens meant that larger numbers of people would usually be near anyone working in the fields, adding a measure of protection to the fields themselves. Further, two-story room blocks add to the defensive character of these villages. Two-story room blocks were commonly built as the first major architectural unit of most of the large pueblos in the region (as indicated by architectural seriation; Reid and Tuggle 1988). This was certainly the case at Grasshopper Pueblo, where the two-story room block was built on a low hill, enhancing the impression of structural presence.

Grasshopper Pueblo (see Figure 5.4) is the largest structure in the region but is unique among the large pueblos by being positioned in indefensible topography—that is, not placed on a substantial rise or canyon edge. Its size alone provided an element of protection, augmented by the architectural layout. The main room cluster of the pueblo, the western unit, has no known exterior doorways into the rooms but was entered by two roofed corridors opening into plazas. This is a common defensive feature of village architecture around the world and is found in a number of other sites in the Southwest (LeBlanc 1999:61). The Grasshopper corridors did not have baffles, but temporary blocking devices could have easily been prepared.

The Social System

Identification of the social organization related to war is of course dependent on the larger question of village and community social structure. The Grasshopper data indicate that community decision making was structured by restricted sodalities (Reid 1989; Reid and Whittlesey 1982, 1990, 1999). One of the archaeologically identified sodalities has been termed the Arrow Society, which probably was an organization dedicated to war and hunting, with the most prominent member of this sociality (Burial 140; Griffin 1967) identifiable as a war chief. Based on the work of Jorgensen (1980:226–290), the prominence of the Arrow Society is consistent with a cultural setting stressing defense.

The structure of the defensive settlement indicates a regional concern for defense. This concern could have been operationalized in the social system in a number of ways, based on the general nature of village interaction, which in turn rested on settlement history. The present understanding of the village development and settlement history is that it was a relatively complex process involving a combination of settlement budding, niche filling, and some degree of continuing immigration (Reid and Tuggle 1988; Reid 1989; Ezzo et al. 1997). This undoubtedly resulted in social ties among the villages which were maintained by a network of intermarriage, economic reciprocity, and religion. For example, some degree of ceremonial connection is suggested by the fact that Grasshopper Pueblo has the only great kiva in the region and there is no evidence for a kiva of any kind at Canyon Creek Ruin. In this framework, defense was a loose system of pragmatic cooperation, one in which the common interest in a comparatively secure locale had created the settlement distribution to begin with. The massed settlements provided a substantial amount of protection, and there were sufficient places to locate observation posts and outlying small villages to provide a general warning of the approach of people with questionable intentions.

It should also be emphasized that for two reasons it is not immediately evident that real cooperation, and certainly any well-structured organization, was necessarily present. First, there is no evidence that any conflict actually took place (as discussed below), which is to say that there is no indication that the system ever functioned; and second, the period of maximum population and settlement density was brief, probably only two decades or so (Reid 1989; Welch 1996).

Enemies, Aggressors, and Acts of War

It is necessary to ask, protection from whom? Almost certainly each major pueblo was concerned about the others, as would be expected in a social setting in which an interaction complex could involve marriage, trade, and raiding. But the larger pattern of defensive positioning clearly indicates a protective attention directed outside the plateau. The ceramic production history at Grasshopper Pueblo may be instructive in this regard, in that imported ceramics in the early years (probably brought by immigrant groups) are replaced by locally made ceramics in the later years. This replacement suggests that exchange contact with other villages outside the Grasshopper region may have diminished or been severed in the later years of increasing economic strain and growth of potential enmities.

To the east, the aggregation that occurred during the preceding (thirteenth) century appears to have generally advanced to another phase of consolidation, one of extremely large pueblos (such as Point of Pines and Kinishba) with associated abandonment of many of the PIII sites. Thus in the mid-PIV if there was any threat from the east, Kinishba would have provided the greatest potential for raids.

The defensive settlement pattern, however, suggests that the greatest concern for security was focused toward the south and west, the Salt River with access up Canyon Creek, as well as possibly from the Q Ranch area. The threat from Q Ranch would have been equivalent to that from Kinishba, pueblos in the general size class of Grasshopper. At the same time, not all threats were necessarily equal. The size and structure of Grasshopper and the other large pueblos of the plateau may have been seen as sufficient to deter raiding parties from Q Ranch, Kinishba, or the Sierra Ancha. The observation posts, possible guard villages, and cliff dwellings may be extra features of protection and warning directed toward peoples viewed with more serious concern, those who had developed the large villages and platform mounds of Tonto Basin (see Ciolek-Torrello 1997).[14]

But whoever the enemy was, there are no significant indications at Grasshopper of any real acts of war (Allen et al. 1985:30; Reid and Whittlesey 1997). There are no burned room blocks that would indicate an attack, with the roofed corridor into Plaza 1 (see Figure 5.4) the only place where there is a suggestion of nonaccidental burning.[15] However, the record of excavations in this area has never been analyzed in detail sufficient to evaluate its nature or possible causes. There is also virtually no evidence of violence in the large skeletal population (674 individuals; the notable exception being three cases of scalping [Allen et al. 1985]), but the fact that there is a greater number of women than men in the burial population (3:2 ratio; Reid and Whittlesey 1999:106) raises the possibility that men were killed in warfare away from the pueblo (see LeBlanc 1999:86). This takes us back to the problem that war at this scale often leaves little evidence. It may be that the enemy or enemies never ventured into the Grasshopper region, or that if they did their actions were primarily looting that produced no archaeological result, or that the attacks were not at the massive Grasshopper Pueblo. If any raids and surprise attacks took place, many of them most likely occurred at the smaller villages along the boundary of the plateau, such as Oak Creek Pueblo or Canyon Butte Pueblo, locations for which no excavation data are available.

Finally, there is the question whether the people of Grasshopper were themselves aggressors. There are foreign goods at Grasshopper, and although these are considered trade items or items brought by immigrants, the possibility that they were obtained by raiding should not be dismissed (see Keeley 1996:126). This problem simply needs more consideration, warranting a renewed look at the material at Grasshopper, the nature of the sodalities, the extraregional indications of defense and warning that might be focused in the direction of Grasshopper, and the evidence from nearby areas, such as Q Ranch, where ongoing excavations demonstrate extensive pueblo burning (LeBlanc 1999:301). The fact that there are defensive observation posts and guard villages on the Q Ranch side of Canyon Creek as well as on the Grasshopper side raises the strong possibility that these two major pueblos and their regional populations were at odds.

Abandonment

The collapse of the Pueblo IV settlement in the Grasshopper region probably occurred over about the same time span as its development, a generation or two, as families and small groups left the villages sporadically; there is some indication that people even returned to the sites temporarily before total abandonment. The system collapse came about through a combination of excessive demand on the limited resources of the region and associated decline of the subsistence base, indicated in skeletal abnormalities (Hinkes 1983) and changing dietary patterns of the population (Ezzo 1992, 1993); a period of poor rainfall after A.D. 1330 (Graybill, in Reid and Whittlesey 1997:164); nearly complete emphasis on agriculture in a region ill-suited for it (Welch 1996); and an ultimate failure of the mechanisms of social integration that were part of the solution to the problems of protection through aggregation. Although there is no direct evidence of warfare during this dispersement era, with the disintegration of the large pueblos and whatever system of large-scale defense that existed with them, it is quite probable that there was conflict among the small scattered groups. Continued use of cliff dwellings, probable use of cliff storage areas, and temporary settlement in open sites all suggest a defensive mode.

CONCLUSIONS

Subsistence stress and population relocation in the late A.D. 1200s well into the 1300s is evident in the Grasshopper region of Arizona. A variety of cultural groups, including local Mogollon, came together on the Grasshopper Plateau during the early 1300s, creating the largest settlements and highest population density that have ever existed in the region. There was a mutual accommodation of villages and cultural groups, one in which the settlement system provided some sense of protection and potential warning by the concentration of a large regional population, the use of aggregated villages, the choice of village location and architecture, and the distribution of sites that served as observation posts and guard villages. This cultural pattern occurred in most of the areas around the Grasshopper region before developing on the Grasshopper Plateau. At the height of population and settlement expansion in the region, in the mid-1300s, security concerns were focused to the south and west, probably directed toward the cultural developments in Tonto Basin. To what extent the perceived threats ever became reality is unknown. There is no unequivocal evidence of conflict in the 1300s. The abandonment of the region also occurred without evidence of violence. Groups gradually departed from the region, leaving behind no indications that they were forced out by internal violence or external aggression.

ACKNOWLEDGMENTS

We have greatly benefited from the comments of Stephanie Whittlesey, John Welch, David Wilcox, Myra Tomonari-Tuggle, and the volume reviewers, including Steve Plog. Thanks to all of them.

NOTES

1. One of us (HDT) also does research in Polynesia and Micronesia, which have well-documented pre-Western oral traditions that tell of societies nearly constantly at one another's throats. These traditions include explicit descriptions of military campaigns and pitched battles between armies. Nevertheless, the archaeological evidence is slim indeed. In the exceptional cases in which clear evidence of warfare exists, primarily dramatic fortifications, the strained efforts to explain them away provide fine examples of what Keeley (1996:vii) has called artificially pacifying the past.

2. Some of these are not true pueblos, as defined by high walls with viga-supported roofs; they have walls of intermediate height and roofs that are pole and thatch. They are, however, puebloid in concept and clearly distinguishable from low-walled cobble rooms and structures.

3. It should be emphasized that this is the entire set of focal villages (room clusters with plazas) recorded in the Grasshopper–Q Ranch research domain. Given the nature of the survey, it is probable there are few, if any, additional ones yet to be identified.

4. The limited evidence for the PIII site that underlies Grasshopper Pueblo is insufficient to address the question whether or not it was burned.

5. This was the only significant human skeletal material found in the three burned sites. By policy (see Reid and Whittlesey 1999), no burials at these sites were excavated, and thus there are no skeletal remains available for the study of violence-induced trauma for the PIII period in the Grasshopper region.

6. This includes the cliff dwelling of Canyon Creek Pueblo and excludes Oak Creek Pueblo, which is not on the plateau.

7. In a previous examination of this pattern, environmental factors other than arable capability were considered as an explanation (Tuggle 1970), but the broader view resulting from additional research subsequently changed the interpretation.

8. There is a small PIV pueblo in each of these locations, but the ceramic data indicate that they are probably late PIV in the regional time scale; that is, they were not established until well after A.D. 1300.

9. The question of settlement contemporaneity is a legitimate concern for studies of war and defense (e.g., Cordell 1994). The Grasshopper data for the PIV period clearly indicate that regional changes and settlement expansion took place but that there was a period of perhaps a generation in the early to mid-1300s when population was at its peak and most of the PIV sites were occupied, although in some cases on a part-time basis (Reid 1989).

10. In the adjoining Q Ranch region there are also sites atop buttes and at ridge ends that are certainly defensive, but the survey in this re-

gion has not been sufficient to determine the entire network of such structures.

11. Numerous terms have been used for defensive structures in the southwest (e.g., Farmer 1957; Spoerl 1979; Wilcox and Haas 1994; LeBlanc 1999); a limited selection is used here.

12. There are exceptions. The Sanrace cliff dwellings along the Salt River are at the base of the canyon wall, a place affording no particular protection.

13. The distribution of all the PIV sites in relation to arable soils is shown in Welch 1996:Figure 4.3, demonstrating the wide distribution of small sites well removed from potential farming locales.

14. As described above, the eastern side of the Grasshopper Plateau is less amenable to the construction of lookout positions than is the western, but nonetheless there are places where other such sites could have been built on the eastern side.

15. See LeBlanc 1999:74–83 for a detailed discussion of the issue of room burning, room-block burning, and warfare.

APPENDIX 5.1: TABLES OF SITES IN THE GRASSHOPPER REGION

The three tables in the appendix are the data set of sites used in the analysis presented in the chapter. Note that only sites relevant to the question of conflict and defense are included and thus the tables do not include all the sites in the Grasshopper Region.

The sites in each table are ordered by total room number, not by site number. Canyon Creek Pueblo is listed in Table 5.1 as one of the major pueblos of the plateau and is also listed in Table 5.3 as one of the cliff dwellings of the region.

Only site names mentioned in the text are listed below. Many names assigned to sites refer to nearby named geographic features such as springs or buttes, providing a guide to their location. Thus as a part of efforts to restrict information about site location, the names are not given except where necessary.

TABLE 5.1. Large PIV Pueblos and PIII Focal Sites of the Grasshopper Plateau.

Site Type	Name	Site No.	No. of Rooms
Large PIV pueblos			
	Grasshopper	P:14:1	500
	Brush Mountain	P:14:13	200
	Blue House Mountain	V:2:3	136
	Canyon Creek (cliff dwelling)	V:2:1	120
	Ruins Tank	V:2:7	97
	Spotted Mountain	V:2:3	85
	Black Mountain	GFS-86-3	70
	Canyon Butte	V:2:49	65
	Hilltop Site	P:14:12	62
	Red Canyon Tank	P:14:25	46
PIII focal sites			
	Early Grasshopper	Part of P:14:1	?
	Chodistaas	P:14:24	18
	—	P:14:197	
	Grasshopper Spring	P:14:8	15

TABLE 5.2. Sites in Defensive Positions Associated with the Grasshopper Plateau.

Name	Site No.	No. of Rooms	Site Type[a]	Topography	Function
Oak Creek	P:14:15	35	Pueblo	Knoll	Guard settlement
—	P:14:273	14	Pueblo	Cliff, knoll	Guard settlement
Shiprock	V:2:87	14	Pueblo	Knoll	Guard settlement
—	GFS-81-87	11	Pueblo	End of ridge, cliff	Observation post
Pinnacle	P:14:71	10	Pueblo	End of ridge	Guard settlement
—	V:2:62	10	Pueblo	Cliff, knoll	Guard settlement
—	GFS-81-6	9	Cobble	Knoll	Observation post
—	V:2:73	7	Cobble	Knoll	Observation post
—	V:2:82	7	Cobble	End of ridge	Guard settlement
—	GFS-81-15	7	Cobble	Cliff, knoll	Observation post
—	GFS-81-133	7	Pueblo	End of ridge, cliff	Observation post, early Apache modification for lookout
—	GFS-80:20	6		End of ridge	Observation post, early Apache modification for lookout
—	GFS-80-56	6	Pueblo	Cliff	Observation post
—	GFS-82-8	6	Cobble	End of ridge	Observation post
—	GFS-82-11	5	Pueblo	End of ridge, cliff	Observation post
—	GFS-81-88	4	Cobble	Cliff, knoll	Observation post
—	GFS-82-12	3	Cobble	Side of knoll, cliff	Observation post

Note: Sites do not include cliff dwellings.
[a]Pueblo = open pueblo; cobble = cobble foundations for pole and thatch structure.

TABLE 5.3. Cliff Dwellings of the Grasshopper Region (Selected, as Shown in Figure 5.2)

Name	Site No.	No. of Rooms
Canyon Creek	V:2:1	120
Red Rock House	P:14:14	30
—	V:2:5	19
—	GFS-81-97	18
—	V:2:79	15
—	V:2:78	15
—	GFS-80-52	10
—	GFS-80-60	10
—	V:2:63	9
—	V:2:75	7
—	GFS-80-64	5
—	GFS-80-61	3
—	GFS-80-63	2

CHAPTER SIX

Antecedents to Perry Mesa

Early Pueblo III Defensive Refuge Systems in West-Central Arizona

David R. Wilcox, Gerald Robertson Jr., and J. Scott Wood

The discovery of a network of small defensive pueblo sites from the Pueblo III era in the Middle and Upper Agua Fria brings the numerous hilltop sites of the greater Prescott area into relation with the line of defensive hilltops found in the foothills north of Phoenix. A comparative analysis of these data is conducted that evaluates several alternative hypotheses to explain the functionality of the hilltop sites. Both internal feuding and "core/periphery" conflict between them and the Phoenix Basin Hohokam are supported, the hilltops providing defensive retreats to associated lowland agricultural settlements from about A.D. 1100 to 1250. The appearance and demise of this pattern is correlated with major organizational changes in the Phoenix Basin and may be explained by changing processes of "core" and "periphery" interaction. The contrast between the early Pueblo III defensive-refuge pattern and the Pueblo IV defensive system identified on Perry Mesa indicates an escalation of the conflict between the populations of west-central Arizona and the Phoenix Basin Hohokam.

Discussions around the campfire during a November 1997 field trip to

Perry Mesa led the authors into a consideration of antecedents to the Pueblo IV Perry Mesa defensive system (see Wilcox et al., Chapter 7, this volume). Our first thought was about the hilltop sites north of Phoenix, and we determined to find out more about them. It was really our interest in the Pueblo IV neighbors of Perry Mesa that led us to examine sites on the west edge of nearby Black Mesa, and it came as quite a surprise to find that they dated to an earlier, Pueblo III, time. A local site steward, Judy Taylor, took Wilcox to one, the Running Deer site, and the three of us visited two others, the Alkali Canyon and Quadruped sites. None of them had any of the diagnostic painted pottery or redware found on Perry Mesa. From other reports and site-file searches at the Museum of Northern Arizona (MNA), the Sharlot Hall Museum, and the Prescott National Forest offices, it became evident that in the Middle and Upper Agua Fria there was a whole series of Pueblo III hilltop sites and small "fortified" pueblos (Figure 6.1; Appendix 6.1). Although a great deal of new research is needed in the Agua Fria just to document the known sites adequately, the current data demonstrate that the pattern of hilltop sites found north of Phoenix extends continuously northward right into the greater Prescott area—where the avocational archaeologist Ken Austin (1977, 2000) recorded more than one hundred hilltop sites that apparently date in the period A.D. 1100 to 1250.[1] Thus the question of antecedents to the Perry Mesa system takes on a much greater significance, involving most of west-central Arizona, not just the foothill zone north of Phoenix.

HILLTOP SITES NORTH OF PHOENIX

Publications by Fewkes (1912a), Dove (1970), Valehrach and Valehrach (1971), Holliday (1974), Rodgers (1978), and Spoerl and Gumerman (1984), together with Bruder's (1982) and Lerner's (1984) dissertations and van Waarden's (1984) Master's thesis, have made the hilltop sites north of Phoenix relatively well known. Diagnostics found on them suggest they were occupied sometime between A.D. 1100 and 1250 (see Appendix 6.2).[2] They appear just at the moment that irrigation communities between the foothills and the Salt River communities are abandoned (Doyel and Elson 1985).[3] In a pioneering study Spoerl (1979, 1984) proposed a four-part classification of these sites into forts, retreats, hilltop habitations, and hilltop centers; van Waarden (1984) applied these concepts to classify all the recorded hilltop sites in the foothills north of Phoenix (Figure 6.2). By a *fort*, Spoerl indicated a small site in a defensible position on isolated buttes or hills which has protective walls or a few rooms; Austin (1977, 2000) more aptly regarded such sites as *lookouts*. A *retreat* is a massive-walled compound on a high butte or hill, and its few rooms and rare artifacts indicate temporary occupation. Both forts and retreats are often far from arable land (Holliday 1974; van Waarden 1984). *Hilltop habitations* usually have defensive walls but also

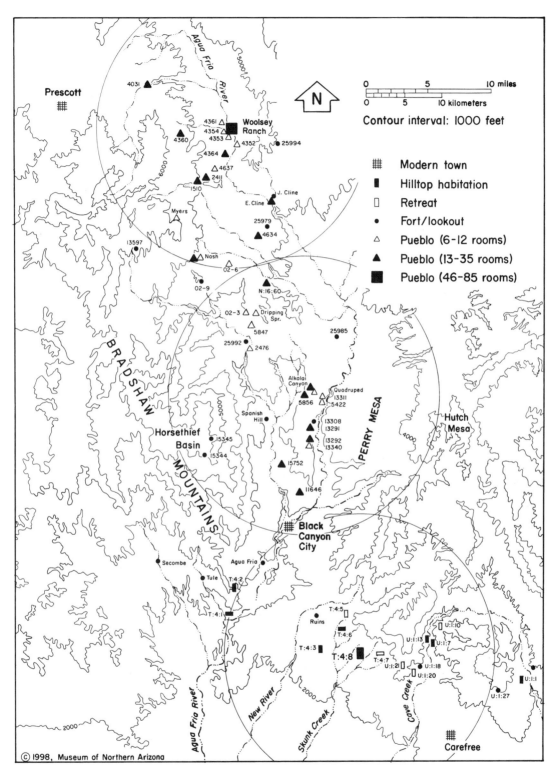

Figure 6.1. Pueblo III sites from Carefree to Prescott, Arizona.

Figure 6.2. Hilltop
sites north of
Phoenix (based on
van Waarden 1984).

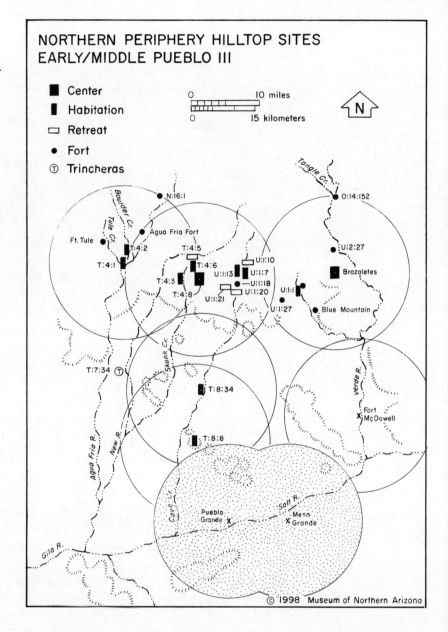

rooms and artifact middens. *Hilltop centers* are much larger sites, AZ
T:4:8 (PC) being the type example. Van Waarden (1984) also classes
Brazaletes Pueblo as a hilltop center. Clustering among the hilltop sites is
evident, and Van Waarden (1984) thought there may have been conflict
among the clusters.

Previous work at the hilltop centers strengthens the defensive refuge
hypothesis. A comparison of the recent site map (Figure 6.3) and a century-
old description shows that Frank Hamilton Cushing and the Hemenway
Expedition visited AZ T:4:8 (PC) on February 6, 1887:

A feature of unusual interest was observable in this structure, in that the part of it set aside for residence, which contained the greatest number of rooms, was situated on the highest portion of the butte, was walled in by itself . . . , yet the outer walls enclosing this portion were extended down to a considerably lower level occupied by a natural terrace to the rear of this more elevated portion. These walls enclosed quite an extensive and almost rectangular space, artificially terraced like the gardens of Zuñi, and doubtless once serving a similar purpose. The upper terrace was occupied by round hut foundations, but the lower space was left free, and in an extreme corner there was evidence that it had been used not less, possibly, for ceremonial purposes than as a gathering place for stone and perhaps pottery working.

Judging from the appearance of distant headlands visible from this there must be a considerable group or else a long line of artificial fortifications or strongholds as this. But a feature of them all, if I may judge from those afterward examined on the lower course of New River [at Fort Mountain], and in Cañon Diablo and other localities, was the presence of outlying walls or enclosures which apparently could have served no other purpose than that of corrals. Sometimes, indeed, these works consisted of such structures, the area occupied by houses being extremely limited and grouped in the one end or one corner of them. Mr. [Frank] Alkire[4] informed me later that this surmise was correct insofar that there were no fewer than five or six localities occupied by similar works. (Cushing in Hinsley and Wilcox n.d.)

What is most interesting about this account is that the hypotheses of agriculture, ceremonialism, and defense are combined into a single interpretation. Cushing's invoking of line of sight to define a system of related sites (documented in Figures 6.1 and 6.2) is also most striking. His "corrals," a common vernacular interpretation in the 1880s, are identifiable today as plazas where people, not animals, could have congregated.

Data from human remains excavated at Brazaletes Pueblo (Valehrach and Valehrach 1971) provide strong support for the claim that violence was a significant factor in the organization of these hilltop settlement systems. Missing crania and other body parts (especially hands and feet), crushed skulls, deposits of miscellaneous teeth and finger bones, and the general absence of evidence for formal burial pits all point to some form of violence (see Appendix 6.3 for details). At the same time, many of the remains had valuables with them: turquoise beads and pendants, shell, and a remarkable painted stick 1.22 m long. Rather than being objects added to the funerary assemblage after death, however, these items probably were parts of the dress of the victims that were left with them at death. A hypothesis that may fit these facts is that these individuals were captives who were either tortured or sacrificed.[5] Their placement to-

Figure 6.3. Site map
of AZ T:4:8 (PC)
(after Spoerl and
Gumerman 1984).

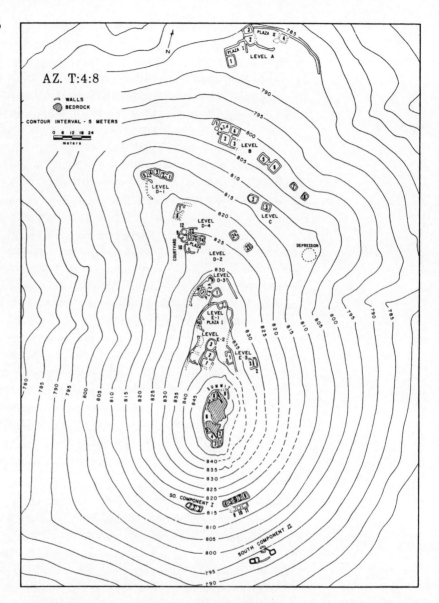

gether in shallow interments suggests that this was a special precinct
where such remains were ritually disposed of.

In Figure 6.2 we have enhanced van Waarden's (1984: 20) map by
keying out the site classifications, adding circles of 18-km (11-mile) radius (the distance one can walk in a day and come back carrying a pack;
see Drennan 1984), and showing the locations of the Salt River Valley
platform mounds of Pueblo Grande and Mesa Grande. Those Hohokam
sites had the two largest platform mounds, and each is situated near the
head of a macro-canal system (Turney's [1929] Systems One and Two;
see Gregory and Nials 1985), yet they are only a half-day apart. The
clustering of platform mounds apparent in Wilcox et al., this volume,
Figure 7.1, leads Wilcox to postulate that the Phoenix Basin, at least dur-

ing the Civano phase—and perhaps earlier—was politically integrated into a single polity (Wilcox 1988, 1999; Howard 1993). This was most likely a corporate rather than a networking system (see Blanton et al. 1996; Muller and Wilcox 1999). The linked circles in Figure 6.2 connecting Pueblo Grande and Mesa Grande symbolize a system that probably employed concepts of dualism or moiety to achieve integration (Wilcox 1999). The emblems of this dualism are beautifully symbolized by the turquoise-mosaic toad and raptorial bird pendants repeatedly but rarely found in graves or caches (Billideau 1986; Wilcox 2000). Complementary opposition, as suggested by Rice (1998), is a related idea that appears to have great promise as a means to reconcile seemingly contrary views (see Abbott 1994a).

Van Waarden's (1984) objective in her thesis was to test three alternative hypotheses about the relationship of the riverine "core" settlements and the northern "peripheral" hilltop sites. Almost no support was found for the hypothesis that exchange characterized the relationship. We would add that a fourth hypothesis, that the hilltops were guard sites on behalf of the Phoenix Basin polity, is not supported for the same reasons: surely, if they were guard sites, much more evidence for exchange from the Phoenix Basin would have been found. Van Waarden thought the hypothesis of "core-periphery" conflict (see Wilcox and Sternberg 1983) was only weakly supported, but she hesitated to reject it. Wood adds that Pueblo III compound sites *north* of the east-west line of foothill forts may constitute a population protected by the defensive sites, hence supporting a core-periphery conflict hypothesis. Van Waarden's third hypothesis was that there was "intra-peripheral" conflict, or what we call here feuding among local systems. This is an excellent proposal, supported also by Bruder (1982:247–248). Thus current data support multiple working hypotheses.

Figures 6.1 and 6.2 illustrate the clustering of local groups around drainages, and the strong tendency of the forts (lookouts) and retreats to lie on the edges of the groupings of hilltop habitations and centers strengthens this conception. The close proximity of the Skunk Creek and Cave Creek groups, however (only 7 km apart), and the fact of line of sight among their sites (van Waarden 1984) point toward the close alliance of these groups, as the 18-km circle around them emphasizes. The sites on the Lower Agua Fria and Camp Creek are only slightly farther away (15 km), and they might also have been allied. The contrast Wood sees in the Brazaletes ceramics compared with those in the sites from Camp Creek west may be better evidence of a social boundary than spatial proximity alone. We recently learned, however, that a lookout on St. Clair Peak provides a line-of-sight link between Brazaletes and Sears-Kay, and the latter group is only 11 km from the Cave Creek group.

Ciolek-Torrello (1997:573–574) shows that the district north of Brazaletes to the north end of today's Horseshoe Reservoir has many sites that he calls "defensive habitation sites."[6] One of them, the Citadel

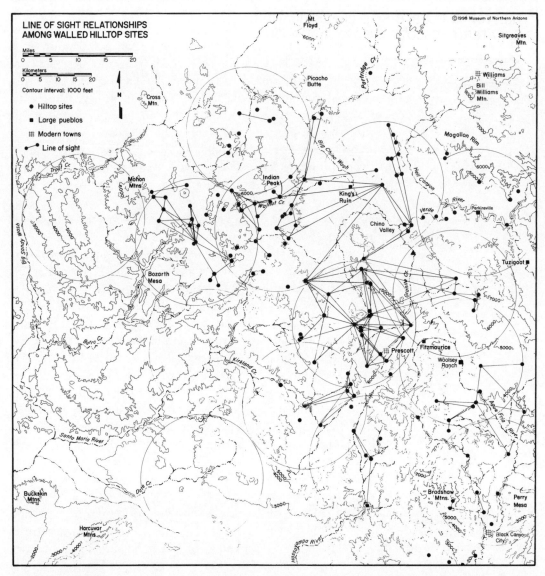

Figure 6.4. Local settlement systems in the greater Prescott area, ca. A.D. 1100–1300.

(AR 03-12-01-188), has a site structure much like that of Brazaletes (Richard Ciolek-Torrello, personal communication 1998). Much more intensive study of these hypothetical local systems is needed to define their extent and to test hypotheses about their interaction. Tentatively, we use the 18-km circles to define three local groups but believe they could easily have been members of a larger alliance or confederacy.

PUEBLO III LOCAL SYSTEMS IN THE GREATER PRESCOTT AREA

Once the continuity of the hilltop systems north of Phoenix via the Middle and Upper Agua Fria into the greater Prescott area became ap-

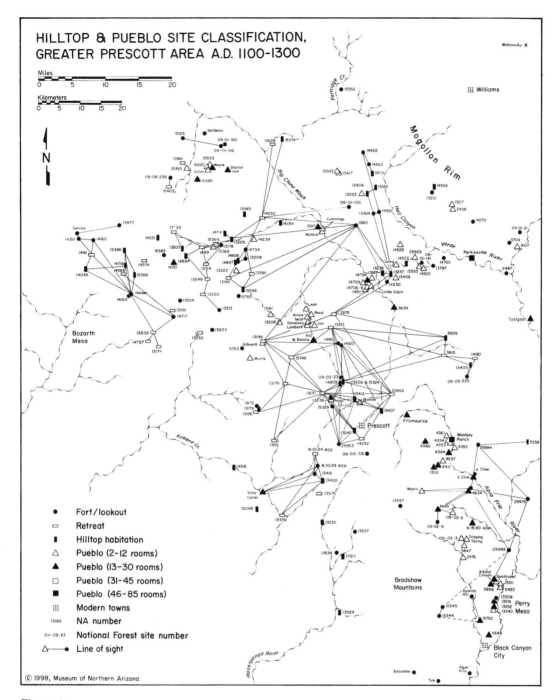

Figure 6.5.
Distribution of hilltop site classes in the greater Prescott area.

parent, an extension of our studies of the antecedents of the Perry Mesa system to the Prescott area became desirable. Working first with the MNA site files and later incorporating additional data from the Sharlot Hall Museum, the Prescott National Forest, and a recent study by Richard Lundin (1993), together with some limited field checking, we greatly enhanced Austin's (1977, 2000) map of hilltop sites and line-of-sight relationships (Figure 6.4) and we constructed detailed data tables that document the data in the map and provide greater specificity (Appendix 6.4). Applying a version of Spoerl's (1984) classification to these data permits the distribution of these classes to be examined (Figure 6.5).[7] In Figure 6.5 we also plot the distribution of what Austin called "house mounds," most of which apparently are pueblo homesteads.

The first attempt to define local settlement systems employed circles of 18-km (11-mile) radius centered on agricultural areas, clusters of hilltop sites, and networks of line-of-sight connections. When it was discovered that Austin had made additional line-of-sight studies[8] and later site cards also had more such data, a more connected graph of line-of-sight connections could be drawn (on the study of graphs, see Hage and Harary 1983). A preliminary analysis of this graph brought into focus those sites that had the maximum number of line-of-sight vertices, and experimentation suggested that 18-km (11-mile) circles centered on them produced interesting results (Figure 6.4; Table 6.1).

We thus have produced the first comprehensive model of what may be local settlement systems in the Prescott region. Appendix 6.4 spells out these hypotheses in detail. Much further work will be necessary to determine whether this model works well as a synthesis of other data sets. Pending such studies, the image Figure 6.4 presents helps us see that the same issues of local feuding versus alliance discussed for the foothill area north of Phoenix apply here. Robertson points out that the Prescott systems were probably not built all at once but were more likely begun and then elaborated over some time, perhaps over a century or more. Feuding, as a process, could explain this, and also why the settlement systems did not pull back from one another across wide no-man's-lands (Mera 1935) or buffer zones (see Hickerson 1962, 1965; DeBoer 1981), which function to reduce conflict (Hally 1993).

A radically different hypothesis, J. M. Sanford's (*Arizona Miner* 1875) inference of "temples" of sun worship, at least for some of these sites, also remains viable (see Wilcox et al. this volume, Chapter 7). Studies that would help to resolve these issues include the following:

1. Re-recording the known hilltop sites, scouring them for diagnostics to improve the chronological assessments, and making better maps, such as at the Indian Peak Site (see Wilcox et al., this volume, Figure 7.2), that more thoroughly record the number of rooms and their arrangements.

2. The so-called retreats, which are massive-walled compounds with few rooms and fewer artifacts, are the best candidates for "temples." Closer examination of them for "altars" or other facilities that may have served functions of astronomical observation, as Bostwick and Plum (1996), for example, have recently done at Shaw Butte, would be most interesting. Robertson and Wilcox have visited the Milligan site (NA1899; Fewkes's [1912a] "Fort below Aztec Pass"), and we cannot see how it could have functioned effectively as a "fort" unless it had

Table 6.1. Analysis of Line-of-Sight Connectivity, Greater Prescott Area.

Rank	Settlement System	NA No.	Austin Name	Position	No. of Vertices
First	Prescott	13,171	Albee	*Center*	13
Second	"	25,953	[Big House]	South	8
"	"	14,910	Wainwright	Internal	8
"	"	13,206	Janet	Internal	7
"	"	13,186	Coulter	West	7
"	"	25,952	[Wilkinson]	East	6
"	"	14,909	Bleibtreu	Internal	5
"	"	13,407	Storm	ESE	5
"	"	13,176	Antonich	Internal	5
"	"	15,749	Denny	Internal	5
"	"	13,240	Necessity	Internal	5
"	"	13,238	Nabhan	Internal	4
"	"	13,412	Tewkesbury	Internal	4
"	"	13,126	Kelley	SE	2
"	Upper Kirkland Creek	13,115	Christopherson	North	2 (+?)
Third	Prescott	13,175	Ann T.	North	5
"	"	13,213	John T.	Internal	8
"	"	14,252	Howard	SE	2
"	"	15,238	Quentin	Internal	2
"	Chino/Hell Canyon	13,183	Cheryl	*Center*	7
"	"	14,530	Wells	South	4
"	Coyote Springs	14,548	Aiken	NW	5
"	"	6654	Emilienne	*Center*	6?
" ?	Upper Kirkland Creek	13,376	Vicky Carter	*Center*	3 (+?)
Fourth	Walnut Canyon	14,250	Olsen	NE	6
"	Chino/Meath	13,236	Molly G	Internal	3
"	"	13,237	Morgan	SSE	6
"	Walnut Canyon	822	Jackson	Internal	4 (+?)
Fifth	Partridge Creek	13,628	Rhea	SW	1
"	Chino/Hell Canyon	14,521	Holt	Internal	3
"	"	13,404	Stricklin	Internal	2
Isolate?	Upper Hassayampa	13,513	Carter	*Center*	
Isolate?	Mount Hope	14,150	Harper	*Center*	8
Isolate?	Turkey Canyon	—	On Turkey Creek	*Center*	?
Isolate?	Perkinsville	2440	[Perkinsville]	*Center*	?
Isolate?	Humboldt/Mayer	4364	—	*Center*	?
Isolate?	Bumblebee/Black Mesa	—	[On Bumblebee Creek]	*Center*	?
Isolate?	Trout Creek/Aquarius Mtns	—	[East edge of Aquarius Mtns]	*Center*	?
Isolate?	Lower Burro Creek	—	[On Burro Creek]	*Center*	?
Isolate?	Lower Kirkland Creek	—	[On Kirkland Creek]	*Center*	?
Isolate?	Date Creek	—	[On Date Creek]	*Center*	?

wooden parapets. It does have excellent line of sight to other hilltop sites but no obvious "altar."

3. All the high spots in each local system should be checked out and what can be seen from each should be compared with what can be seen from those that were culturally modified. Why some hilltops and not others were selected for sites may thus be clarified.

Studies of the communication potentials in these line-of-sight systems should more systematically document not only the network connections but also the capacity for communication. What kinds of messages can be sent using smoke signals, loud noises, blankets, or other means? Did nineteenth-century military officers or others write reports analyzing such matters? Experimentation would also be highly revealing.

Nineteenth-century pioneer William Hardy, who opened a toll road from Hardyville in the Mohave Valley to Prescott in 1864, had some interesting things to say about the communication capability of Yavapai smoke signals:

> Each Indian when on the warpath carried two sticks, one a dry stock of beargrass with notches cut in it, the other a hard stick like an old-fashioned fog-horn ramrod. They would place the sticks with notches on the ground, put their feet on it and set the other stick with the end in the notch, then roll fast between the hands. Within half a minute they would start a blaze of fire, caused by friction. These sticks the Indians call "ocacha." Sometimes they use flints. These the Indians call "otavia." When the fire was started they would sprinkle a little pulverized pitch or resin on it. It started a black smoke quick. They would spread a handful of green woods or grass on the fire and a white smoke or steam would follow. Again they would remove the grass and blow the fire a little and add pitch. Thus dots and dashes might be made, quite like the old-fashioned way of telegraphing on paper. Again at night I have seen signal fires on the side or top of mountains and a blanket or robe passed in front of it conveyed information. There was no patent covering the way of conveying news by the savages. I have seen on a calm day a column of smoke with black and white spots rise near one thousand feet high. *I have known correct news* concerning the movements of U.S. troops in war times *to be smoked through at least three hundred miles in two or three hours*, and news by courier five or six days later would prove the news by Indians to be correct. (Hardy 1888:5–6; emphasis added; note that the couriers could run about fifty miles per day)

What was done during rainy days remains to be learned.

Recent research by Wilcox and Robertson, and site stewards Judy Taylor, Judi and Rollie Myers, Don Mather, Tom and Sue Weiss, Joe Vogel, Sharon Olsen, Terry Julin and others, has now demonstrated the presence of a macroregional network of signaling capacity that linked

Indian Mesa, just north of Lake Pleasant and west of New River, with Little Granite Mountain in the midst of the Prescott area. Both by predicting where hilltop sites should be and by flying over likely areas using Joseph Vogel's small planes, we have discovered six new sites that are nodes in a continuous series of line-of-sight relationships. From north to south these sites are Boulder Maze, Lower Stoddard, a bulldozed site, Townsend Butte, Horseshoe Butte, and Rosalie Lookout. From south to north, the connections established now are Indian Mesa and Boulder Creek (north of Lake Pleasant) to Henrie (at the south end of Black Mesa) to South Fort and then East Fort (in Horsethief Basin), then to Horseshoe Butte (northwest of Perry Mesa) and on to Copper Mountain (near Mayer) and Boulder Maze (east of Humboldt). From a ridge 50 to 75 m northeast of Boulder Maze one could signal to Nordwall and thence to Emilienne (Coyote) and to Janet and on to Little Granite Mountain (Albee). The establishment of these observations strengthens the hypothesis that local systems throughout this area were closely integrated, thus making Wood's (1987) conception of a Central Arizona Tradition more intriguing. Much more work is needed to fully chart these connections and their geographical extent.

THE GREATER PRESCOTT AREA BECOMES A BUFFER ZONE

Currently, the best guess, based mainly on ceramic cross-dating of associated sites below them, is that these sites were abandoned by the middle A.D. 1200s (Jim McKie, personal communication 1998; see also Wilcox et al. 2000). Did an escalation of feuding cause this abandonment, or the environment, or were other factors involved? We suspect that conflict on a regional rather than only a local scale was a crucial factor. The result was that the greater Prescott area became a buffer zone, and the boundary of pueblo-like settlement in the Southwest shifted eastward to Perry Mesa and the Verde Valley. To the west lay the Mohave Valley.

A series of multiple working hypotheses can be formulated to account for this process. Neighbors external to the greater Prescott area included the Cohonina on the northeast (although they were gone by A.D. 1150 [Mc.Gregor 1951]), proto-Hokan speakers to the west, the Middle Verdeans on the east, and the Middle Agua Fria populations on the southeast. Way to the south were the Hohokam in the Phoenix Basin.[9] Looking at Figure 6.4, we would make a thumbnail estimate that the average population of each 11-mile circle was about 300 to 500 people. If so, we have a hard time understanding how upland proto-Hokan speakers, presumably organized in hunter-gatherer bands of 25 to 50 people, could have driven out the Prescott folk. They might have been a contributing factor, and they did ecologically replace the Prescott populations, perhaps sometime around 1300 once the Prescott folk had moved on (Pilles and McKie 1998). Some refugees might also have been absorbed by the hunter-gatherers. The proto-Hokan Hakataya villagers in the Mohave Valley and points south along the Colorado River, however, would have been a more powerful force, comparable to the Hohokam (Warren 1984).

The large Honanki phase populations in the Middle Verde (Pilles 1996) may have been a bigger political factor, and so, too, the Pueblo III populations in the Middle and Upper Agua Fria. In the late A.D. 1200s, at Fitzmaurice Pueblo (Barnett 1974a) and King's Ruin (Spicer and Caywood 1936), small pueblos were built adjacent to or in the grasslands along the eastern third of the greater Prescott area. Ceramically, these sites are closely related to the Middle Verde or Agua Fria. In Austin's words about several other small sites south of King's Ruin: "[The Matson site] is the last of four sites at average intervals of 1000' south of King's ruins, with indications of a Southern Sinagua [Verde Valley] prehistoric occupation succeeding a Mountain Patayan [Prescott] presence, the others being [the] Spicer, Cummings and Caywood sites" (Austin 1979a).

The pattern of small-pueblo distributions documented in Figures 6.1 and 6.4 suggests the hypothesis that populations from the Perkinsville and Middle Agua Fria areas, in the middle to late A.D. 1200s, pushed into the eastern grassland areas of the greater Prescott region, occupying different niches than those of the earlier hilltop-oriented local systems. Argillite Pueblo, the Del Rio sites, and a set of small pueblos on Mint Creek may all be part of a thrust into the Prescott area from the Upper Verde at Perkinsville (see Appendix 6.4 and Figure 6.5).

The largest pueblo in the Upper Agua Fria is 52 m^2 with 80-plus rooms; it lies directly under the ruins of King S. Woolsey's 1863 ranch, just north of Humboldt, Arizona.[10] Woolsey built his ranch using stones from the pueblo, and although this fact has long been known (Hodge 1877:191; Barnes 1935:58; Simpson 1982), the existence of this site, and its importance, have gone unrecognized until now. Much larger than the nearby and possibly contemporaneous Fitzmaurice Ruin (NA4031; Spicer and Caywood 1936; Barnett 1974a), the Woolsey Ranch Pueblo appears to be the center of what we suspect was a Pueblo III settlement system that in the late A.D. 1200s intruded into the eastern Prescott area.[11] The Coyote Springs subsystem may be part of the system centered on the Woolsey Ranch Pueblo, and a recent visit to the Emilienne (Coyote) site revealed that it occupies a highly defensible position on a rocky butte, all surrounding hills lacking such an outcrop; the Fitzmaurice site, on Lynx Creek, is also highly defensive, lying on a high ridge spur. Better dating of the Coyote Springs sites is crucial to a test of this hypothesis, as are detailed ceramic analyses.

A step in this direction was made when Wilcox visited all the Coyote Springs sites in May 1999. He observed that the pottery is not Prescott Grayware but a local brownware, although occasional sherds of Prescott Gray are present. Although across a wide grassland, line-of-sight relationships exist between the Coyote Springs sites and hilltop sites in the Prescott area; we wonder if signaling was intended or whether they merely allowed the two groups to monitor one another's signals. More work continues to be needed on these intriguing issues.

One conclusion is clear: by the early A.D. 1300s, Perkinsville was the westernmost pueblo still occupied; all the others in the greater Prescott area had been abandoned, and the frontier of agricultural settlement had shifted eastward to the Middle Verde Valley and Perry Mesa. Up to this point we have discussed largely local factors to explain these transformations. Perhaps we should give some consideration to a more radical, macroregional factor that may also have been critically important if we are to understand the abandonment of the greater Prescott region.

THE HOHOKAM FACTOR

Even if the early Pueblo III hilltop defensive refuge system had largely to do with patterns of local feuding, raiding against outside neighbors, such as the Hohokam in the Salt River Valley or the Hakataya in the Mohave Valley, may also have happened. This dual pattern was true of the Western Apache in the nineteenth century (Goodwin 1942; Basso 1971), and there is little reason to doubt it during early Pueblo III times. If so, we would have to infer that the Hohokam and Hakataya during the early Classic period were relatively weak militarily or that there was a trade/raid pattern that was tolerable. The striking fact is that both the hilltop sites north of Phoenix and those in the greater Prescott area were abandoned ca. A.D. 1250, just at the moment that compounds began to be built and structures were placed on top of the platform mounds in the Phoenix Basin (see Gregory 1991). This timing may not be a coincidence. Uniquely among the neighbors of the foothill populations north of Phoenix and the people in the greater Prescott area, those in the Phoenix Basin were demographically large enough to destroy these hilltop retreat systems. Perhaps the reorganization indicated by the construction of compounds and platform-mound structures also indicates the emergence of a more aggressive, politically integrated Hohokam system that determined to end the endemic raiding that we postulate had gone on for a century and a half.

The defeat of the Navajo in 1863 by Col. James H. Carleton and his lieutenants Kit Carson and Alfred W. Pheiffer with about a thousand men may provide a suitable analogy. Six thousand Navajo surrendered and were transported to Bosque Redondo, and many others fled as refugees, causing a regional abandonment until they returned after the treaty of 1868 (Bailey 1964). What brought about this success against a worthy enemy was a scorched-earth policy in which cornfields and grain supplies were systematically destroyed in the late summer and fall. This was followed by a winter campaign in which housing and peach orchards were destroyed. Facing famine as well as serious harassment from the Utes, Pueblos, and Hispanics, the Navajo had little choice but to surrender or flee (Bailey 1964).

Suppose, then, that the newly organized Hohokam could put 1,000 warriors in the field (and with a politically integrated population of something approaching 24,000 [Wilcox 1991], we see little reason to doubt their capacity to do so). Direct attacks against the hilltop sites north of Phoenix could have destroyed them, leaving the refugees to flee northward, perhaps to Perry Mesa. If the Prescott populations, too, were perceived as enemies because of intermittent raiding over many decades, we can picture the possibility of a large Hohokam force running over to the Wickenburg area, regrouping there, and then going in the "back door" up the Hassayampa, into Peeples and Skull Valleys, and then into the heart of the Prescott area and on to Walnut Creek, burning cornfields, destroying houses and grain supplies, killing or wounding a few people, and taking a few captives. Moving fast, they then could have returned home, leaving devastation and the start of famine in their wake. It would not have taken many blows of this kind to cause the abandonment of the greater Prescott area and the decision to reorganize into much more defensible formations like the one we have described on Perry Mesa (see Wilcox et al., this volume, Chapter 7). Now intermittent raiding had escalated into all-out warfare.[12]

CONCLUSIONS

The defensive hilltop sites documented in pioneering work by Austin (1977, 2000) and Spoerl (1979, 1984) are shown to be parts of a larger whole by the site data assembled from the Middle and Upper Agua Fria. Spoerl's classification is readily extended to Austin's data, and an analysis of it has produced a comprehensive model of local systems in the greater Prescott area. Models of local, regional, and macroregional conflict have been proposed to explain these data, and numerous ways to pursue the testing of relevant hypotheses have been suggested. What is most striking in these data is the contrast with the kind of settlement organization documented on Perry Mesa (Wilcox et al., this volume, Chapter 7). It evidences an escalation of warfare on regional and macroregional scales, which, we argue (Wilcox et al., this volume, Chapter 7), is supported by the settlement distribution data during the Pueblo IV period in all of central Arizona. A great spectrum of new research possibilities is thus established that we hope will stimulate both those who are inclined to accept such views and those who are not.

ACKNOWLEDGMENTS

Many people made this chapter possible. Glen Rice's invitation to prepare it stimulated our fruitful collaboration. Peter Pilles's three decades of accumulated knowledge about Perry Mesa, the Verde Valley, the Agua Fria, and much else added immeasurably to the synthesis presented here. James McKie, Judy Taylor, Connie Stone, Richard Lundin, Judi Myers, Don Mather, Todd Bostwick, Stephen Germick, Donald Weaver, George Alkire, Joseph Vogel, and others provided critical data. The members of the staff of the Sharlot Hall Museum deserve special thanks for their courtesy and helpfulness, and we want to single out Mona McClusky, Michael Wurtz, Sandra Lynch, and Director Richard Sims in this regard. David Schaepe helped prepare the Ken Austin base map. Michael Barton at Arizona State University and Sharon Urban at the Arizona State Museum kindly provided access to site files at those institutions. Special thanks go to Mary Spall, Yavapai Archaeological Society, for arranging for us to see the Fitzmaurice and Emilienne sites. Jodi Griffith, Museum of Northern Arizona Exhibits Department, drafted the figures in her usual exquisite fashion. For any errors in the text, the authors take full responsibility.

NOTES

1. This dating is the current consensus based on the few diagnostics found on the hilltop sites and the association of these sites with farmsteads and hamlets below them (James McKie, personal communication 1998). Clearly, better chronological resolution is needed.

2. No polychromes or black-on-whites beginning in the middle or late A.D. 1200s, such as Tusayan Black-on-white or Tusayan Polychrome, are found on these sites. There is thus no good reason to think they date later than about 1250.

3. In fact, ca. A.D. 1100, not only was the irrigated zone north of Phoenix abandoned but also the lower Verde Valley below Bartlett Dam, a string of ball-court sites along the base of the Superstition Mountains, and the Buttes Dam area along the Gila River (Wilcox 1979a; Wilcox and Sternberg 1983). Thus a no-man's-land or buffer zone was established at the beginning of the Classic period that set off the Phoenix Basin from its northern, northeastern, and eastern neighbors. We remain uncertain how to explain this fundamental fact.

4. Frank Alkire and his brother George were the owners of the Triangle Bar Ranch, one of the largest in Arizona Territory; its location can still be seen north of the New River exit to Interstate 17 where three palm trees stand on the east side of New River (George Alkire Jr., personal communication 1998). The Alkires later became important businessmen in Phoenix, and Frank Alkire lived until 1964.

5. To put this another way, the valuables found with these remains may indicate the wealth of neighboring enemy populations rather than that of the local Horseshoe Basin groups who did the disarticulating.

6. Ciolek-Torrello called our attention to these data at the 1998 Society for American Archaeology meetings. His Figure 14.10 (1997)

also identifies "defensive locales," and he supplied us with their Tonto Forest numbers. Checking on these sites, we found that many of them are field houses on ridges, which we do not regard as "defensive"; several that fit our criteria have been added the Pueblo IV map and data tables that are presented in Wilcox et al., this volume, Figure 7.12 and Appendix 7.2B.

7. Forts/lookouts are about 120 m² or less; retreats are compounds of several shapes, usually with few or no rooms and few artifacts; hilltop habitations have three to four rooms or more, and more artifacts. Our experience at the Indian Peak Ruin (Figure 7.1) suggests that Austin did not always record all the rooms or other habitation structures that are present on these sites. Field examination of his Stannard Dillard site led to a similar conclusion. From a military point of view, Robertson points out, observation or listening posts are commonly established to warn of any approach toward a defensive perimeter. Some of the "forts/lookouts" may have been observation posts or something else; conversely, some places that were observation posts may have little or no archaeological signature. For example, though Austin's Henrie site cannot be seen from his Euler site, at the end of a ridge south of the latter there is line of sight; a cleared space there about 7 m in diameter could have been a good place from which to signal, but no artifacts were found.

8. These studies are in two loose-leaf notebooks at the Sharlot Hall Museum. The detailed sketch maps are color coded, and the line-of-sight lines to hilltop sites are shown in relation to petroglyph sites, apparently in a study of cultural boundaries (see also Austin 2000). Data tables accompany the maps.

9. Much closer to the south is the Middle Hassayampa Valley. Its Tucson-like appearance and fertile valley suggest that it should have been the focus of large Hohokam villages with irrigation canals and ball courts. Because this area became private land in the 1860s, however, and is far from any university, almost nothing is known about its archaeology. Was it, like the Lower Verde, occupied intensively during the Late Pioneer to Sedentary periods, only to be abandoned ca. A.D. 1100, thus becoming a buffer zone? Only future investigations can address this and many similar questions.

10. Hodge (1877:191) reported that "on the site of the present residence of Mr. Nathan Bowers, there was a very large ruin of a stone building, which was one hundred and sixty feet square. From the debris of this building, a large double stone house, one smaller one, and much stone wall have been erected, and there yet remains on one side, a pile of debris four or five feet in height." When Wilcox stopped by to look at this site in March 1998, the pueblo could be clearly seen, just as Hodge described it, *under* the ruins of the Woolsey-Bowers ranch buildings. Mae Statler, who has lived across from the site for sixty years, told him that a former owner had removed some of the stone from the ranch ruin to try to save an irrigation head, but it washed out anyway. What now appears to be a

west plaza may originally have been rooms, the stone from them having been taken to construct the ranch buildings.

11. NA4364 was reported by Milton Wetherill as having 70 rooms, but we have not been able to relocate this site to confirm this; in Figures 6.1 and 6.5 it is shown as less than half that size.

12. Alternatively, the Hakataya from the Mohave Valley, rather than the Hohokam, might have been an agent of such a process. Regrettably, too little is known about these groups to consider such a hypothesis further.

APPENDIX 6.1. PUEBLO III SITES, MIDDLE AND UPPER AGUA FRIA DRAINAGE.

Upper Black Mesa
[PIII: 111+ rooms; ca. A.D. 1100–1250; PIV: 70+ rooms; ca. A.D.1300–1450]

NA No.	JJ No.	Other No.	Elevation (ft.)	No. of Rooms	Comments
25,981	23		3,320	19+11	**Alkali Canyon Ruin**
25,982			3,320	12+6	**Quadruped Site**
5856	24		3,060	20–30	**Running Deer Site;** 2 stories? 1 room burned
5855			3,060	30-50 jacal	**Little Rattler Site**
13,311			3,440	9–12+	
5422	27		3,450	6–8	**Richinbar Site (A)**
5424			3,490	?	Kayenta B/w
13,322			3,420	2–5	
13,308	29		3,560	2	Fort

Middle Black Mesa [44+ rooms; ca. A.D. 1100–1250]

NA No.	Other No.	Elevation (ft.)	No. of Rooms	Comments
13,294		3,390	1–2	
13,320		3,410	2	
13,291		3,390	15	
13,292		3,340	16	
13,342		3,350	1–3	
13,340		3,330	10	

Above Black Canyon City [PIII?]

NA No.	Other No.	Size (m²)/No. of Rooms	Type	Comments
11,646	N:16:1 (PC); JJ No. 30	775; ca. 22 rooms	Hilltop habitation	**Henrie Site**; enclosed plaza; 2,885 ft.
15,752		20 rooms	Hilltop habitation	**Euler Site** (near Bumblebee exit)
25,975		2 rooms	Retreat	**Spanish Hill**
—		No rooms	Retreat	**Water Tank**

Horsethief Basin [PIII?]

NA No.	Other No.	Size (m²)	Type	Comments
15,344	09-02-1		Hilltop fort	**South Fort (aka Dunbar)**; 45-ft. wall
15,345	09-02-2	650	Hilltop fort	**East Fort (aka Galatti)**; walled enclosure with corner room

Dugas Area

NA No.	Other No.	No. of Rooms	Type	Comments
25,978		4 rooms	Hilltop fort	Estler Peak

Cleator/Cordes Area [PIII]

NA No.	Other No.	Size (m²)/No. of Rooms	Type	Comments
2476	09-02-15	ca. 12 rooms	Pueblo	**Golden Turkey Pueblo**; 3,000 ft.
5847	09-02-10?	9 rooms	Pueblo	"Easily defensible"
—			Hilltop habitation	**Dripping Springs**
—	N:16:60 (ASM)	743;16 rooms	Hilltop habitation	**DeNoyelles Site**; oval house mound; plaza (4,175 ft.)
—	09-02-3	rooms	Fort/Lookout	**Mesa Site**
25,992			Fort/Lookout	**Townsend Butte**

Mayer Area [PIII?]

NA No.	PNF No.	Size (m²)/No. of Rooms	Type	Comments
25,973		5 rooms	Fort/Lookout	**Myers Fortress**
25,976		88	Fort/Lookout	**Joanne Cline Site**; rectangular compound; 4,000 ft.
25,977		14+ rooms	Hilltop habitation	**Earl Cline Site**; pueblo; enclosed plaza; 4,260 ft.
25,980		3 rooms	Fort/Lookout	**Copper Mountain North**; 4,840 ft.
25,979		175	Fort/Lookout	**Copper Mountain South**; 5,026 ft.; small walled enclosure
4634		23–30 rooms	Hilltop habitation	**Jagged Tooth Ruin**; on high outcrop; Flagstaff B/w, Tusayan Poly; PIII
25,954	09-02-08?	ca. 15 rooms	Hilltop habitation	**Nash Site**; on high outcrop; 5,142 ft.; 12-room site at foot of hill (NA25,955)
—	09-02-06	ca. 10 rooms	Pueblo	**Triangle M Site**
—	09-02-9		Fort/Lookout	**Fence Tank Fort**; on ridgetop; few artifacts
4636		5+ rooms	Pueblo	On knoll (not plotted)

Humboldt/Poland JunctionArea [PIII]

NA No.	Other No.	Size (m²)/No. of Rooms	Type	Comments
				Lower Stoddard Ruin
1510	09-03-6	743	Pueblo	Walnut B/w
2411	09-03-7	20+ rooms	Pueblo	
4364		70 rooms	Pueblo	Some maroon redware
4637	N:12:9ASM	18 rooms	Pueblo	**Humboldt Ruin (aka McMahon Site)**; compound wall; Sunset Red; PM

Humboldt/Poland JunctionArea [PIII], continued

NA No.	Other No.	Size (m²)/No. of Rooms	Type	Comments
4363	N:8:1 & 8 ASM	2,704; 80+ rooms	Pueblo	**Woolsey Ranch Pueblo;** Hodge 1877:191; redware
4365		19+ rooms	Pueblo	"Fortified"; not plotted
4352		Small	Pueblo	**O'Brien Ruin**
4353		ca. 10 rooms	Pueblo	PM plainwares; some redware
4354		9,750	Pueblo	4 small pueblos
4361		ca. 7 rooms	Pueblo	Early PIII
4360	09-03-9	ca. 19 rooms	Pueblo	2 pueblos, 1 is 2 stories
25,994		5	Fortified pueblo	**Boulder Maze**
13,597	09-03-153	1,115	Lookout	**Poague Lookout;** 2 walls across mtn top (6,798 ft.)
3339 & 4031	—	25+	Fortified pueblo	**Fitzmaurice Ruin;** late PIII (5,100 ft.); burned; partially 2-storied

APPENDIX 6.2. SITE DATA ON PUEBLO III HILLTOP SITES NORTH OF PHOENIX, FROM THE VERDE VALLEY TO THE LOWER AGUA FRIA.

Agua Fria from Lake Pleasant North (ca. A.D. 1100–1250)

NA No.	Other No.	Size (m²)/No. of Rooms	Type	Comments
T:3:1 (ASM)		rooms	Hilltop habitation	[Now an island in Lake Pleasant]; 3 defensive walls; oval rock-ring houses
T:4:1(PC)	NA15,754	17–22 rooms	Hilltop habitation	**Indian Mesa Site (aka Dobyns Site)** (2,340 ft.)
T:4:2 (PC)		1793	Hilltop retreat	**Boulder Creek Ruin**
—	—	82	Fort/Lookout	**Fort Tule** (2,330 ft.); 2 peepholes; oriented northward
—	NA25,990	ca. 1,000; 1 room	Religious?	**Agua Fria Ruin;** walled enclosure
—			Lookout	**Secombe Site** (2,405 ft.)

Miscellaneous Hilltop Sites below Lake Pleasant and Cave Creek Dam

Site No.	Other No.	Size (m²)	Type	Comments
T:7:34 (ASU)		?	Fort/Trinchera	Near Calderwood Butte; see Fewkes 1912a
			Hilltop habitation	Near Frog Tanks (reported by Fewkes 1912a)
T:8:34 (ASU)		2500	Hilltop retreat	**Fort Mountain** [probably visited by Cushing et al., April 4-5, 1888]; Soho phase? [Casa Grande R/b in low-lying sites]
T:8:88 (ASU)	T:8:2 (PG)	586	"	**Shaw Butte;** has astronomical associations; petroglyphs on nearby Moon Hill possibly visited by Cushing et al. April 6, 1888;

Daisy Mountain/Cave Creek System [ca. A.D. 1100–1250]

Site No.	Other No.	Size (m²)/No. of Rooms	Type	Comments
T:4:8 (PC)		4212; 87 rooms	Hilltop habitation center	*Strombus galeatus;* Flagstaff & Walnut B/w; 6 Sacaton R/b; 31 modeled spindle whorls; macaw bone; A.D. 930 +/-80 (I-8950); A.D. 1095+/- 80 (I-8951)
T:4:3 (PC)	NA2311	1,080	Hilltop habitation	
T:4:6 (PC)		7,412	"	Modeled spindle whorl
T:4:7 (PC)		531	Fort	
U:1:7 (ASU)		4,050	"	30 rooms; Gila Red; Gila Shoulders
U:1:13 (ASU)		4,048	"	40 rooms; Gila Red; modeled spindle whorl
U:1:18 (ASU)		312	"	No ceramics
—			Hilltop "Ruins"	T7NR2E Sec 12, south center
T:4:5 (PC)		1,092	Hilltop retreat	1 modeled spindle whorl
U:1:21 (ASU)		?	"	No ceramics; overlooks field houses in Paradise Valley
U:1:10 (ASU)	01-09	465	"	Redware; Gila shoulder
U:1:20 (ASU) No. 84	Schroeder	3,000	"	No ceramics
U:2:27 (ASU)		2,560	"	Redware

Camp Creek System [ca. A.D. 1100–1250]

Site No.	Other No.	Size (m²)/No. of Rooms	Type	Comments
U:1:1 (ASU)	12-01-74	8,097; ca. 40 rooms	Hilltop habitation	**Sears-Kay Site;** enclosed plaza; redware
12-01-65	AZ B:1:3(GP)	ca. 3,000	Hilltop habitation	**Blue Mountain;** 15 rooms
U:1:31(ASU)			Habitation	"Commands clear view in all directions"; destroyed by fire
U:1:27 (ASU)		?	Fort	
—		None	Fort	Kentuck Mtn. Fort; **circular; peepholes**

Lower Verde Hilltop System [ca. A.D. 1100–1250+]

Site No.	Other No.	Size (m²)	Type	Comments
U:2:1 (ASU)	NA13577	4,849	Hilltop habitation center	**Brazaletes Site;** 100+ rooms; Casa Grande R/b; Flagstaff & Walnut B/w; redware; modeled spindle whorl
U:2:2 (ASU)	12-01-166		Hilltop habitation	20–35 rooms
—	—		Fort/Lookout	**St. Clair Peak Fort;** lookout
—	12-01-188		Hilltop habitation	**The Citadel**
	12-01-1245		Compound	On Horse Creek; ca. 25 rooms
O:14:152 (ASU)	12-01-642	416	Fort/Lookout	**Tangle Fort;** compound wall; entry

APPENDIX 6.3. BRAZALETES PUEBLO HUMAN REMAINS AND ASSOCIATED FUNERARY
OBJECTS (AFTER VALEHRACH AND VALEHRACH 1971).

Burial No.	Sq. No.	Condition	Associations
1	D2	No skull, hands, feet, or vertebrae	Large Verde Smudged bowl by left arm; small crude Verde Red jar near feet with bottom punched out
2	D3	No skull, no feet	2 Verde Smudged bowls, one on each side of the shoulders; 2 Tuzigoot W/r bowls, one at left hand, one between legs below knee; shell bracelets at right wrist and large number of scattered turquoise beads around right elbow; projectile point near left elbow
3	E3	No skull, no feet, no hips	Earring; Verde Red pot off right shoulder; 2 Verde Smudged pots, one by left ankle, one where head might have been
4	E2		13 *Glycymeris* red-painted bracelets on left wrist; 2 Verde Red and 1 Verde Smudged pot
5	E3	Early 20s male with base of skull smashed; no feet	Large cardium with cut hole above head; bone awl by right elbow; 2 Verde Smudged pots, one by left neck, one by right ankle
6	E3	Elderly female with skull deformation; no hips, vertebrae, or most ribs	5,000+ minute black beads and perforated turquoise beads in 7-strand necklace; abalone shell near head; 3 Verde Smudged pots, one by left arm, one by left knee, one by lower right leg
7	D3	Torso only; under south wall	2 large *Glycymeris* bracelets on humerus of left arm; *Conus* tinkler inside left arm
8	D3	2 ribs and humerus; under south wall	Verde Smudged pot; B/w sherd; stone-pendant bird
9	C2	Young child: no skull; no hips; 5 milk teeth in place of skull	4 frog shell necklace; 216 (1.27 m) *Olivella* at ankles; red ochre covered; Verde Brown pot; Verde Smudged pot
10	C3	Crushed skull	102 turquoise bead necklace; 17 turquoise inlay; Verde Red bowl; burial pit cut into rock
11	C3	Crushed skull	Sacaton Red-on-buff sherd; burial pit cut into rock
12	C3	Only front of skull, no mandible; no torso or left arm	Several 100s turquoise beads and inlay forming two ear bobs; other turquoise around head; 17.7-cm [human femoral?] bone awl along head; Tuzigoot W/r jar & 23 grouped arrowpoints [quiver?] near right shoulder; 1.22-m-long "staff of authority" with blue and red bands with green separations along right arm; 6 obsidian and chert points along arm; 3-strand turquoise-bead bracelet; semibasin metate left of head; Verde Smudged pot between femora [associated with Burial 13?]; burial pit cut into rock
13	C3	Flexed leg and foot only (rest removed by pot-hunter?); adult	No associations; superimposed above legs of Burial 12

Brazaletes Burial Data, continued

Burial No.	Sq. No.	Condition	Associations
14	D3	Few scattered long bones and ribs	No associations
15	B3	Few hand bones in pot	Verde Red or Smudged bowl
16	B3	Parts of a cranium	Verde Red or Smudged bowl
17	F3	Large number of human teeth and great number of finger phalanges near north wall	No associations
18	D3	Scattered bones	Sherds
19	D3	Scattered bones	Verde Smudged pot
20	E1	Pile of human bone fragments, some charred	No associations

APPENDIX 6.4. KEN AUSTIN'S PRESCOTT-AREA HILLTOP SITES, WITH ADDITIONS (CA. A.D. 1100–1300).

Mt. Hope/Windy Mesa System

NA No.	Austin Name	Elevation (ft.)	Size (m²)/No. of Rooms	Classification	Comments
	Sunrise	6,075		Fort/Lookout	
14,159	Jack	5,830	110	Fort/Lookout	Triangular compound
14,160	Jane	6,040	19	Fort/Lookout	Compound
14,161	John [Indian Hill]	6,170		Retreat	Compound; gate
14,045	Irwin	5,830	7 rooms	Hilltop habitation	3 compounds
13,977	Reynolds	5,810		Fort/Lookout	Triangular compound
15,383	Danson	6,505	120	Fort/Lookout	Compound
15,386	Eckel	6,540	251	Hilltop habitation	8-ft.-high mound
14,156	Don	5,320	312; 5 rooms	Hilltop habitation	
14,569	Hargrave	4,730	383; 2 rooms	Retreat	Compound; entry
14,574	Watson	5,720	279	Retreat	Compound
15,388	Lindsay	5,385	502	Hilltop habitation	
14,148	Harper [Black Butte]	6,000	2 rooms	Fort/Lookout	
14,150	Ronnie	5,850		Fort/Lookout	Triangular compound
13,174	Anderson	5,680	195; 2 rooms	Retreat	Compound; gate
13,638	Vandervoort	5,515	175	Retreat	Compound; gate
14,757	Hooks	5,460	464	Retreat	Compound; entry
14,717	Dave; 09-06-217	6,108	93	Fort/Lookout	Compound
13,591	Tourtellot; 09-06-83	4,885	1115	Retreat?	N:1:7(PC); compound
13,554	Metzger; 09-06-146	6,220	3 rooms	Fort/Lookout	

APPENDIX 6.4. KEN AUSTIN'S PRESCOTT-AREA HILLTOP SITES,
WITH ADDITIONS (CA. A.D. 1100–1300), CONTINUED.

Turkey Creek System

NA No.	Austin Name	Elevation (ft.)	Size (m²)/ No. of Rooms	Classification	Comments
15,403	Rhoda May	6,355	376; 2+ rooms	Retreat	Compound
—	Valerie [Haystack Peak]; 09-06-236	6,315		Fort/Lookout	Compound within compound
13,967	Marshall; 09-06-80	5,950	480	Retreat	Compound?
—	Aaron	5,355	93	Fort/Lookout	
15,515	Cowden; 09-06-232	5,640	60	Fort/Lookout	Square enclosure
—	Nettleton	5,325		Fort/Lookout	
—	Vista; 09-01-160	5,530		Lookout	No artifacts
—	Larry Adams; 09-01-156	6,045	38	Fort/Lookout	No artifacts
—	Sharlot Hall	5,850	ca. 14 rooms	Pueblo	3 room blocks
—	Wayne	6,063	ca. 16 rooms	Pueblo	
15,553	Carrie	6,200	80	Pueblo	
—	Victor	6,193	ca. 2 rooms	Pueblo	
15,520	Tommy	6,120	ca. 10 rooms	Pueblo	
15,395	Blake	5,770	ca. 16 rooms	Pueblo	
15,393	Curtin	5,670	ca. 6 rooms	Pueblo	On small butte

Walnut Creek/Santa Maria Mountain System

NA No.	Austin Name	Elevation (ft.)	Size (m²)/ No. of Rooms	Classification	Comments
14,051	Sherri	6,435	748	Hilltop habitation?	Rock mound; associated brush houses
14721	Homer	6,310	ca. 15 rooms	Pueblo	2 room blocks
13,229	Mayes [Aztec Pass]	6,950	314	Retreat	Compound
13,203	Hunt's Knoll	6,225	280; 6+ rooms	Hilltop habitation	Walled enclosure with 3 divisions
14,894	Hunt's Twins	6,230	474; 8 rooms	Hilltop habitation	2 pueblo enclosures
1899	Milligan; 09-06-23	6,250	276	Retreat	Compound
13,194	Ferguson; 09-06-15	5,835	465	Retreat	
14,907	Triangle Top	5,535	929	Hilltop habitation	
13223	Lorna H	5,390	3 rooms	Pueblo	
14,908	U Site	5,350	669; 4 rooms	Hilltop habitation	100-ft. wall
—	Sue Chamberlain	5,300	14	Fort/Lookout	
—	Jerry; 09-6-289	5,350	2,208	Hilltop habitation	

Walnut Creek/Santa Maria Mountain System, continued

NA No.	Austin Name	Elevation (ft.)	Size (m²)/ No. of Rooms	Classification	Comments
822 & 13,205	Jackson	5,455	1,040; 21 rooms	Hilltop habitation	Compound; entry; tower
15,364	B & B; 09-06-183		15–20 rooms; +20 rooms	Pueblo	Whipple 1856
15368	Rodda	5,325	ca. 3 rooms	Pueblo	
3626	—			Compound and pueblo?	Fewkes 1912a
3627	—			Pueblo	**Marx Ranch Ruin;** Fewkes 1912a
3628	—			Pueblo	Fewkes 1912a
14239	Ann Olsen	5,050	3+ rooms	Pueblo	
13,178	Avant	5,400	100; 1 room	Fort/Lookout	Double-walled enclosure
13,209	Johnson	5,460		Fort/Lookout	Entry in wall across mtn tip
13,983	Laurie	5,215	3 rooms	Hilltop habitation?	Compound?
14,734	Warren	5,325	111	Fort/Lookout	Rectangular compound
13,395	Roxie; 09-06-03	5,369	500	Retreat	Compound; gate
14,250	Olsen; 09-01-162	5,460	2,439	Retreat	Compound; entry
3629 & 14,056	Rogers	4,715	520; 2 rooms	Hilltop habitation	Compound; entry; Fewkes 1912a:215
13,549	Hunt; 09-06-145	6,020	372; 1 room	Retreat	Irregular compound; entry
13,220	Lerchen; 09-06-119	5,984	669; 2 rooms	Retreat	7-sided compound
13,113	Ostrander; 09-06-147	6,150	420	Fort/Lookout	Walls on 3 sides
13,230	McGroatry; 09-06-36	5,150	440	Retreat	Circular compound; gate
13,634	Elson; 09-06-74	5,270	98	Fort/Lookout	Square compound; entry
13,195	Fiero; 09-06-5	5,240	350	Retreat	Compound; entry
13,548	Hanson; 09-06-76	5,200	111; 4 rooms	Hilltop habitation	
5782	09-06-168	5,150	3 rooms	Fort/Lookout	**Brushy Site**
5353	Kimball [Jones Mt]	5,740	557	Fort/Lookout	Walls linking outcrops

Partridge Creek System

NA No.	Austin Name	Elevation (ft.)	Size (m²)/ No. of Rooms	Classification	Comments
13,628	Rhea	4,640	1,617; 1 room	Retreat	Compound; entry

Partridge Creek System, continued

15,374	McBride	5,255		Hilltop habitation	3 small room blocks
15,552	Mesa; [Smith Butte]	5,650	35	Fort/Lookout	"Walled hilltop structure"; Archaic?

Big Chino Valley/Meath Creek/Upper Hell Canyon System

NA No.	Austin Name	Elevation (ft.)	Size (m²)/ No. of Rooms	Classification	Comments
14,552	Everall	5,310	1 room	Fort/Lookout	
14,562	Sarvis	5,385	2 rooms	Fort/Lookout	
13,231	Meath; 09-01-36	5,070	600; 4 rooms	Hilltop habitation	Compound; gate
4358; 13,182	Blanton; 09-01-59	5,200	600; 5 rooms	Hilltop habitation	Compound; 2 peepholes
13,408	Stricklin; 09-01-37	5,800	900; 4+ rooms	Hilltop habitation	Walls at hilltop; rooms below
13,233	Merne	5,650	6 rooms	Pueblo	
15,522	Stewart	5,825	ca. 3 rooms	Pueblo	
13,417	Wilma	5,800	4 rooms	Pueblo	On narrow point
13,404	Stanley A	5,420	225; 4 rooms	Hilltop habitation	Compound; entry
14,521	Holt; 09-01-85	5,020	3 rooms	Fort/Lookout	
—	Jim & Carma; 09-01-130	5,720	54; 2 rooms	Fort/Lookout	
13,183	Cheryl; 09-01-31	5,350	2 rooms	Fort/Lookout	
14,529	Thomas; 09-01-7	4,650	ca. 7 rooms	Pueblo	
13,236	Molly G	4,470	2,081; 5 rooms	Hilltop habitation	Compound; 2 entries
13,237	Morgan	4,700	613; 16+ rooms	Hilltop habitation	Enclosed plaza
14,530	Wells	5,165		Fort/Lookout	Wall on one side of pinnacle; 2 peepholes
13,406	Steve	4,970	2 rooms	Pueblo	On butte
—	Carma	4,485	ca. 10 rooms	Pueblo	3 room blocks
13,187	Dahlberg	4,500	5 rooms	Pueblo	On hilltop
—	Linda Gilpin	4,490	273; ca. 5 rooms	Pueblo	**George Banghart's Ruin;** compound; Hodge 1877:189
14706–8	Del Rio	4,470	11 + rooms	Pueblo	3 room blocks
14754	Zulu	4,380	ca. 12–16 rooms	Pueblo	
14709	Gilpin	4,465	ca. 5 rooms	Pueblo?	Compound?
14511	Bunker	4,550	ca. 2 rooms	Pueblo	
1587	—	4,460	12+ rooms	Pueblo	**King's Ruin;** late PIII; 2 stories
—	Cummings	4,465	ca. 12 rooms	Pueblo	Late PIII
—	Matson	4,465	ca. 4 rooms	Pueblo	Late PIII

Perkinsville/Upper Verde System

NA No.	Austin Name	Elevation (ft.)	Size (m²)/ No. of Rooms	Classification	Comments
14,522	Kimmet	4,445	3+ rooms	Hilltop habitation	
25,929	Shannon Dillard; 09-03-112	4,260	6–10 rooms	Pueblo	On knoll
15,555	Cecil	4,125		Defensive pueblo	
14,520	Hilton	4,110	ca. 11 rooms	Pueblo	6 room blocks
—	Peg; 09-01-141	4,295	120	Fort/Lookout	Square compound; entry
11,761 & 13,797	Paul	4,050	138; 2–3 rooms	Fort/Lookout	**aka Fort Monolith;** compound?
14,703	Cort; 09-01-40	3,915	3 rooms	Fort/Lookout	
14,558	Mills; 09-01-104-106	5,350	7+ rooms	Hilltop habitation	Excellent view to south
13,201	Helen; 09-01-83	5,130	?	Fort/Lookout	
13,217	Ken; 09-01-95	5,400	10 rooms	Pueblo	On hilltop
2438	—	5,280	10 rooms	Pueblo	
—	09-01-21		rooms	Fort/Lookout	
14,270	Favour #2; 09-01-147	4,815	?	Fort/Lookout	
5704	Perkins; 09-01-386			Fort/Lookout	
4107	Gail; 09-01-02	4,925	ca. 8 rooms	Pueblo	Cliff dwelling; PIII
3500	—		4 rooms	Pueblo	**Hidden House;** cliff dwelling; PIII
2487	—		8 rooms	Fort/Lookout	PIII
2440	—		ca. 50	Pueblo	**Perkinsville Ruin**
3639	—	4,740	38 rooms	Pueblo	**Piedra Roja Ruin (aka Lou Curtis Site);** PIII

Middle Williamson Valley Pueblos

NA No.	Austin Name	Elevation (ft.)	Size (m²)/ No. of Rooms	Classification	Comments
13,181	Betsey	4,700	6 rooms	Pueblo	
13,208	Joan	4,650	6 rooms	Pueblo	
—	Leah	4,650	ca. 8 rooms	Pueblo	
—	Reed	4,765	2 rooms	Pueblo	
—	Arrowhead	4,720	ca. 10 rooms	Pueblo	
—	Dennison	4,750	ca. 8 rooms	Pueblo	
—	Lombard	4,730	ca. 4–5 rooms	Pueblo	
—	Jan	4,935	ca. 7 rooms	Pueblo	
—	Bill & Bonnie	4,795	ca. 15 rooms	Pueblo	

Prescott/ Upper Williamson Valley System

NA No.	Austin Name	Elevation (ft.)	Size (m²)/ No. of Rooms	Classification	Comments
3625 & 13,175	Ann T.	5,225	442	Retreat	**aka Limestone Butte Ruin;** entry; compound (Fewkes 1912a:204-206)
13,213	John T.	5,400	450; 2 rooms	Retreat	Compound; blocked entry?
14,910	Wainwright D	5,567	465; 1 room	Fort/Lookout	100-ft. wall & 50-ft. wall
14,922	Wainwright	5,507	2 rooms	Fort/Lookout	
13,186	Coulter; 09-06-297	5,300	1156	Retreat	Compound; gate
—	Gilbreath	5,000	ca. 6 rooms	Pueblo	
—	Morris	5,210	ca. 4-5 rooms	Pueblo?	Compound?
15,749	Denny; 09-03-135	5,150	813	Retreat	Compound
13,176	Antonich [Tonto Mt]; 09-03-18	5,630	3,600	Retreat	Compound
—	09-03-23			Fort/Lookout	
13,206	Janet; 09-03-78	5,490	12+ rooms	Hilltop habitation	Compound; 3 entries
15,324	Janet D	5,510	480; 7 rooms	Hilltop habitation	
14,909	Bleibtreu; 09-03-143	5,610	3 rooms	Fort/Lookout	No artifacts
—	Kuehn; 09-03-130	5,920		Fort/Lookout	
13,238	Nabhan; 09-03-25	6,450	500	Retreat	Compound
—	—			Hilltop habitation	Walled enclosure on Judge Fleury's land; Hodge 1877:188
—	Brutinel	5,365	11–15 rooms	Pueblo?	Black Mesa B/w? (Lundin 1993)
13,171	Albee; 09–03–27	7,089	1,239; 6+ rooms (Lundin 1993)	Retreat	Compound; entry; 600-ft. racetrack? Prescott B/g; Jeddito Orange
15,328	Quentin; 09-03-131	6,035	None	Fort/Lookout	Walls on 3 sides
13,412	Tewksbury	5,840	15+ rooms	Hilltop habitation	Enclosed plaza with entries; loopholes
—	N:7:2ASM		20+ rooms	Hilltop habitation	Sosi B/w?
25,952	[Wilkinson]	5,630	None	Retreat	Compound; entry (Lundin 1993)
13,407	Storm A	5,450	435; 3 rooms	Hilltop habitation	Compound; 2 gates (Cline and Cline 1983)
14,252	Howard	5,866	2,550; 5 rooms	Hilltop habitation	Spiral compound; gate (Lundin

Prescott/ Upper Williamson Valley System, continued

NA No.	Austin Name	Elevation (ft.)	Size (m²)/ No. of Rooms	Classification	Comments
—	09-03-331	6,488	ca. 4 rooms	Fort/Lookout	**Bean Peak;** walled enclosure; few artifacts
13,240	Necessity	5,700	Large	Hilltop habitation?	**(aka Indian Hill;** Fewkes 1912a); compound; few artifacts; now badly disturbed
25,953	[Big House]	6,103	2-3 rooms	Fort/Lookout	Walls on several levels (Lundin 1993)
13,172	Allen	4,700	4+ rooms	Fort/Lookout	
13,179	Becky; 09-03-62	4,770	8 rooms	Hilltop habitation	
13,126 & 14,251	Kelley; 09-03-05	5,100	908; 1 room	Retreat	Rectangular compound; gate; other walls block approaches

Kirkland Valley System

NA No.	Austin Name	Elevation (ft.)	Size (m²)/ No. of Rooms	Classification	Comments
13,115	Christopherson	4,680	8,700	Hilltop habitation	3 plazas, entry; outrider walls
14,916	Ritter A	4,145	8 rooms	Hilltop habitation	
—	Vicky Carter	4,110	14 rooms	Hilltop habitation	Enclosing wall
15,096	Rigden	4,175		Hilltop habitation?	
—	09-03-40	5,575	Small structure	Fort/Lookout	
N:10:24 (ASU)	Jeter	5,320	1 room	Retreat	**Copper Basin Site**
N:10:28 (ASU)	Weaver	5,299	3 rooms	Fort/Lookout	
N:10:29 (ASU)	—			Retreat	
13,416	Willy; 09-03-53	5,160		Fort/Lookout	
13,400	Shea; 09-03-35	5,500	2,000; 5+ rooms	Hilltop habitation	Double compound
13,376	Walter	4,225	1,421	Retreat	Triangular compound; entry; peephole
13,575	Lowell	4,932	2,331	Retreat	Compound? walls uncertain
13,376	—	4,492	625	Retreat	Compound; no artifacts

Upper Hassayampa System

NA No.	Austin Name	Elevation (ft.)	Size (m²)/ No. of Rooms	Classification	Comments
13,235	Mir; 09-03-2	4,272	10 rooms	Hilltop habitation	Compound
—			2 acres in walled enclosure; ca. 14 rooms	Hilltop habitation	[2 mi. N of Walnut Grove, in sight of Cpt. Bartlett's; Hodge 1877:187]
13,537	Waters	4,200		Fort/Lookout	[Battleship Butte] 60-ft. wall
13,513	Carter	4,075	5 acres in walled enclosure; 24 rooms; with tower	Hilltop habitation	[6 mi. SE of Bartlett's; on E side of Milk Ck; (natural) stone causeway 50 yds. long from S spur
to					main summit; Hodge 1877:188]
13,534	Veater	4,081	105	Fort/Lookout	
13,529	Mayer	3,905	920; 3 rooms	Hilltop habitation	

Coyote Spring System [These sites may be part of a late Pueblo III System centered on the Woolsey Ranch Pueblo]

NA No.	Austin Name	Elevation (ft.)	Size (m²)/ No. of Rooms	Classification	Comments
3809; 14,548	Aiken	5,483	8–15 rooms	Hilltop habitation	(aka Brady's Fort) South entry
3810 & 6654 & 14,549	Emilienne	5,545	41+ rooms	Hilltop habitation	(aka Coyote Ruin) 2 stories; fortified on rocky butte
11,358 & 13,405	Stansell	5,800	600; 20+ rooms	Hilltop habitation	Compound; dense ceramics; Tusayan B/r; Blk Mesa B/w
14,180	Nordwall	7,352	7 rooms	Hilltop habitation	West trail access past wall
—	09-05-225	5,880	no rooms	Lookout	No artifacts; 20-m wall

CHAPTER SEVEN

Organized for War

The Perry Mesa Settlement System and Its Central Arizona Neighbors

David R. Wilcox, Gerald Robertson Jr., and J. Scott Wood

Controversy about the peaceful versus warlike relations between the Hohokam and their neighbors raises scientific questions about how to move the debate forward. This chapter presents the results of a collaboration among two archaeologists and a person with military experience. Beginning with an examination of the Pueblo IV Perry Mesa settlement system, we show that the ways it was organized support the hypothesis that it was organized for war, and that it could have withstood attacks from its more populous Hohokam neighbors in the Phoenix Basin, two days' travel to the south. Turning to Perry Mesa's other Pueblo IV neighbors, we delineate a "Verde Confederacy" that united Perry Mesa with its immediate neighbors against the populations of Chavez Pass and Tonto Basin and the Phoenix Basin Hohokam. Widening the inquiry further to look at the political geography of central Arizona, we show that the pattern of emergence of site clusters bounded by "no-man's-lands" or buffer zones supports a model of regional warfare among multi-settlement-system polities in the early A.D. 1300s. We then discuss comparisons with the spatial scale of polities in the American Southeast. The data thus assembled serve to transform the debate by expanding it from a focus on merely the internal processes of local systems to the external processes operating on regional and macroregional scales as well. Many avenues for new research are proposed, but we expect the controversy to continue.

Interpreting the true meaning of putative "defensive sites" has a long history in Arizona archaeology. The first European interpretation of a hilltop site in southern Arizona was by the Jesuit Eusebio Kino, who reported a religious usage (Manje 1954:137). When settlers of the new Arizona Territory first began exploring the Prescott area, they were fascinated by the numerous "lookouts" found on hilltops there. One settler, George Banghart, in the Del Rio area of Little Chino Valley, excavated a mass grave in a burned room, satisfying himself that an earlier conquest of the area had occurred (Hodge 1877:189–190).[1] J. M. Sanford also gave "the matter much intelligent thought" and expressed the opinion that the "lookouts" were temples of sun worship; he claimed to have found altars in the west ends of these walled-compound structures from which the devotees could face the rising sun (*Arizona Miner* 1875). Ellsworth Huntington (1914), one of the early scientific observers of Hohokam sites in southern Arizona, guided by the ruling theory of environmental determinism, interpreted the walled hillsides of Arizona and Sonora as agricultural terraces. With fine rhetorical flourish, the geographers Carl Sauer and Donald Brand (1931:70) dismissed Huntington's ideas as "quaint," arguing that the *cerros de trincheras* were places of defensive refuge and habitation. They correctly pointed out that the tiny amount of possible arable land behind the walls contrasted absurdly with the vast amount in the bottomlands below. Soon Harold Gladwin's (1930) postulation of a Salado invasion into the Phoenix Basin dramatized the specter of Hohokam warfare, but Emil Haury (1945) effectively banished that idea with what his friend A. V. Kidder (1949) wryly called a "lion and lamb" hypothesis. The idea of the peaceful Hohokam "desert farmers and craftsmen" (Haury 1976) was thus born.

Yet the notion of "defensive refuges" persisted (Larson 1972), and more violent models of Hohokam prehistory were proposed (Di Peso 1956). Having been early impressed by T. C. Chamberlin's (1965) call for the "method of multiple working hypotheses," which Wilcox chose to interpret not only psychologically as Chamberlin did but also sociologically as "controversies," Wilcox welcomed the chance some twenty years ago to study the dry-laid walls of Tumamoc Hill in Tucson (Wilcox 1979b). By both standing on the shoulders of earlier students (see Merton 1993) and producing new data, Wilcox found that a defensive-refuge hypothesis best fit the available facts. Since then, others have argued for an agricultural-terrace hypothesis (Fish, Fish, and Downum 1984; Downum 1993; Downum, Fish, and Fish 1994), but they as yet have failed to show what would have been successfully grown in the areas behind walls that have no soil and the many more with very thin soil.[2] The normative assumption that all the hillside sites in the Tucson area are cerros de trincheras may have obscured a diversity of uses (see Fontana, Greenleaf, and Cassidy 1959:50). On Tumamoc Hill the one wall on the south side lies above a vertical cliff whereas numerous walls occupy the gentler east and north slopes; these facts are easily accounted for by a defensive hypothesis, and it is interesting that an agricultural one may predict this pattern, too—though for different reasons (Downum et al. 1994)![3] The defensive-refuge idea is thus still viable,[4] and with it the implications—because the size of the groups indicated the necessity for early warning—for a *regional* scale of Hohokam warfare (Wilcox 1979b).

The demonstration of two empirical generalizations has subsequently strengthened these claims: (1) the creation of twenty-mile-wide "no-man's-lands" (Mera 1935) or buffer zones (see Hickerson 1962, 1965; DeBoer 1981), first at ca. A.D. 1100 in the lower Verde (below Davenport Wash) and in the Buttes dam areas, and then ca. 1300 between Picacho Peak and the Tucson Basin (Figure 7.1),[5] and (2) the disjunct distribution after 1100 of hilltop "defensive" sites and Hohokam ball courts (Wilcox 1979a, 1989; Wilcox and Sternberg 1983; Doelle and Wallace 1991). A general consideration of the data supporting conflict or warfare in the Southwest (Wilcox and Haas 1994) shows the importance of buffer zones of a day's travel on foot with a pack (which Drennan 1984 gives as 22 miles or 36 km) to models of interpolity warfare during the late pre-historic period (see also Upham 1982; Jewett 1989; Wilcox 1991a; LeBlanc 1999). Similar patterns are characteristic of the same period in the American Southeast, where clusters of palisaded settlements are also found bounded by buffer zones (Hudson and Chavez 1994; Hally 1993; Blitz 1999). In the Phoenix Basin, beginning in the middle 1200s, massive compound walls were built around platform mounds and other kin-group domains (Gregory 1991): what are they if not "palisades"?[6]

Yet the controversy continues, and the only tokens of significant value that will help resolve it are new facts. Without the glyphic evidence that proved so crucial in the Mayan area (Coe 1992), what new facts can move this controversy toward resolution in the Southwest—or the Hohokam area? Where can we turn for inspiration? Two approaches are explored here: a military science approach, and one based on settlement-system analysis and the distribution of buffer zones.

THE MILITARY SCIENCE APPROACH

Military science should provide many insights. But the knowledge of this field by most southwestern archaeologists is secondhand, derived mainly from reading. Wilcox had long thought that collaboration between ar-chaeologists and people with real military experience, both formal train-ing in military science and firsthand knowledge of war, would be a fruitful methodological course to follow. So, beginning in 1992, when he

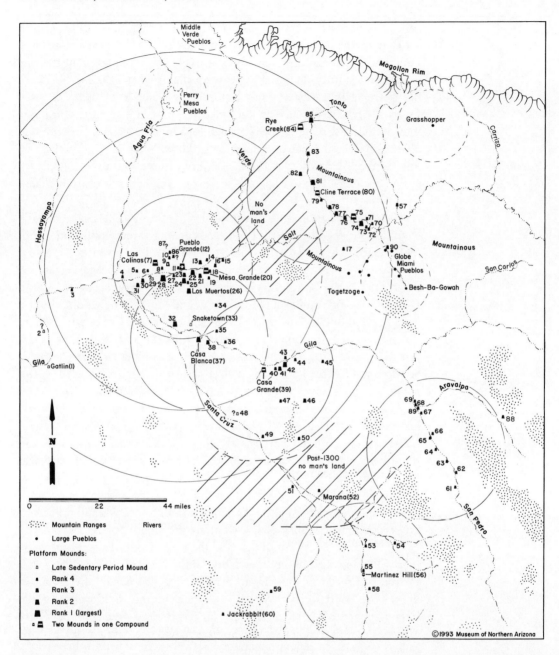

Figure 7.1.
Hohokam platform
mounds in regional
context.

first met the avocational archaeologist Jerry Robertson and learned he
had been the commander of an infantry rifle company in Vietnam, a captain in the 101st Airborne, Wilcox began to ask Robertson to apply his
military knowledge to the interpretation of archaeological sites. Not only
had Robertson been awarded a Silver Star, three Bronze Stars, two
Purple Hearts, and—most unusually—an air medal for valor, he had organized, developed, trained, and led a group of twenty-eight former Viet
Cong, operating for five months in the same area where they had previously been guerrillas. Though he has tried to forget those days and thus

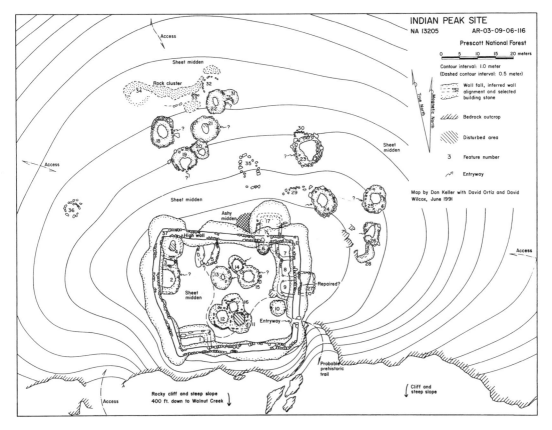

Figure 7.2. Indian
Peak Ruin, Walnut
Creek, Arizona.

found it a little difficult to do as Wilcox asked, he became interested and
has managed to keep his bad memories at bay.

We began at Pueblo III sites such as the Indian Peak Ruin (Figure 7.2),
which lies 400 feet above Walnut Creek north of Prescott (see Wilcox et
al., this volume, Chapter 6). We walked around the massive compound
wall and Robertson described how enfilading fire from the walls and
"plunging fire" from the north tower with bows and arrows could have
held attackers at bay. We assumed a self bow of the kind found in the
Southwest would be effective over about 40 m. At Hatalacva (Figure
7.3), a Pueblo IV site in the Middle Verde Valley north of Tuzigoot,
which we mapped for the Archaeological Conservancy, a three-story
pueblo terraces up from a small enclosed plaza to a two-to-three-room
tower that dominates the approach up a narrow ridge from the south.
Many areas on the ridge to the north could have provided large flat
places to build a pueblo, Robertson pointed out, yet the people chose a
difficult place on the south tip.[7] An advantage of this position is that attackers would be "canalized"—or strung out—by a narrow ridge immediately north of the pueblo, preventing them from bringing all their force
to bear at once. Robertson's rule of thumb is to have three-to-one odds if
attacking. Thus the narrow ridge gave the advantage to the defenders,
who if overrun could have withdrawn to the tower. This is a "defense in

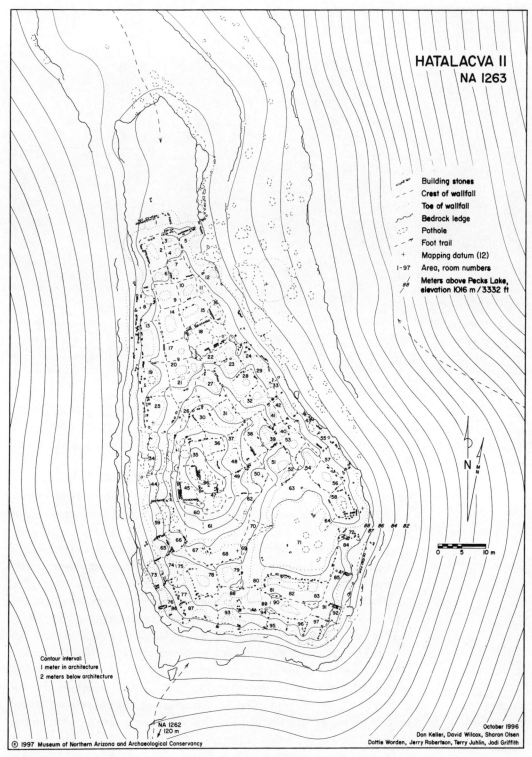

Figure 7.3.
Hatalacva site,
Middle Verde Valley,
Arizona.

Figure 7.4. Perry Mesa, looking northeast, with Black Mesa on the left (photo by Jerry Jacka).

depth." However, it is worth noting that a tower room now exposed by vandals was burned.

PERRY MESA: ORGANIZED FOR WAR

In April 1997 the Arizona Archaeology Society's Verde Valley Chapter, of which Robertson was president, took a field trip to Perry Mesa, a 75-square-mile grassland plateau about 50 miles north of Phoenix (Figure 7.4).[8] J. Scott Wood, the Tonto Forest archaeologist, led the tour and gave us a handout (Wood 1992) that included an interesting map (Figure 7.5). With the Agua Fria and Black Mesa on the west, Perry Mesa is dissected by a series of deep canyons from Silver Creek on the north to Squaw Creek on the south. Small Pueblo IV pueblos characterized by yellowwares, Salado polychromes, and Four-Mile Polychrome are distributed all around the periphery of the mesa in such a way that they could block access up any of the side canyons—except Larry Canyon, Robertson was quick to notice. In general, Robertson's impression was that this was an integrated system, with the people of each pueblo protecting the backs of the others. The absence of such pueblos on the rim of Larry Canyon seemed anomalous.

We visited three of the pueblos on that trip—Baby Canyon, Pueblo Pato, and Squaw Creek Ruin—and we saw the linear cleared areas near each that are called "racetracks." At Baby Canyon (Figure 7.6), which

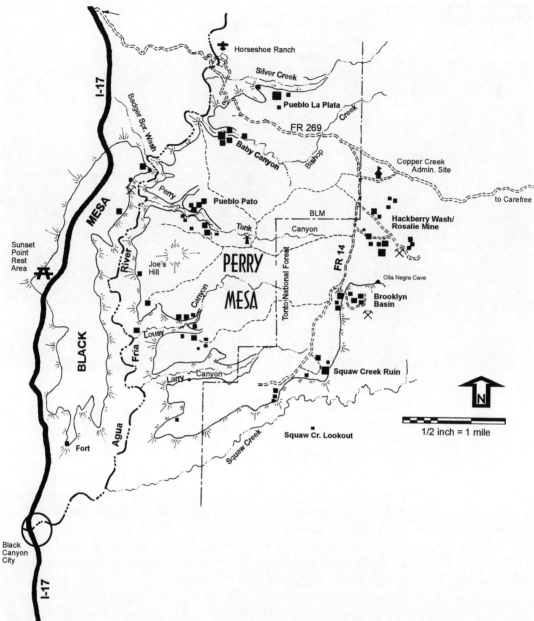

Figure 7.5. Perry Mesa locality (after Wood 1992).

has about 72 rooms, we noticed that north of the enclosed plaza the ruin occupies a small basalt butte, with vertical cliffs on the east side, but where they end, a wall continues the perimeter. We then noticed that a trail zigzags up from the canyon below, only to be blocked and hemmed in by the wall at the top. Defenders, therefore, could effectively interdict any approach from that direction. At Pueblo Pato (Figure 7.7) we saw four pueblos, the largest estimated at 125 rooms with two stories. It is situated above the vertical cliffs of Perry Tank Canyon. Across the canyon are two pueblos of about 50 rooms each, and it appeared to us that together they could effectively block access from the canyon.

Figure 7.6. Baby
Canyon site (after
Wood 1992).

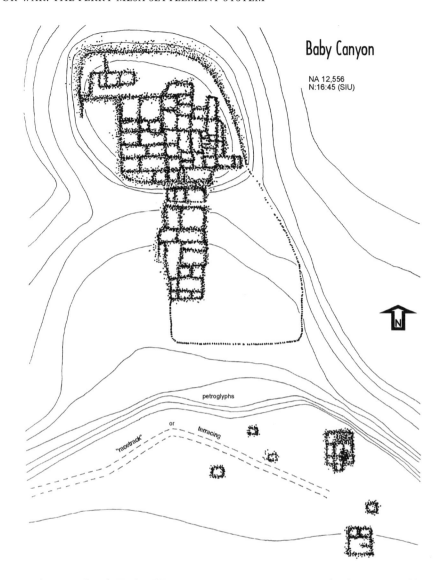

Squaw Creek Ruin (Figure 7.8), at 150 rooms, is the largest pueblo
ruin on Perry Mesa. Perched above vertical basalt cliffs, it was surrounded on three sides by a meter-wide breast-high wall, enclosing a
large plaza. Walking along the cliff edge, we noticed that large boulders
had been placed in all the crevices. Access from the canyon below is possible, and no wall blocks it in the center of the south side, but any attack
up that route would be subject to a devastating cross-fire, and entrap-
ment if the attackers made it into the plaza beyond. Continuing around
the perimeter, Robertson pointed out that attackers approaching the wall
would be coming upslope, giving an advantage to the defenders, who
could also withdraw to the pueblo, providing them a "defense in depth."
Robertson also insisted that the defenders would require early warning,
so we made our way along the cliffs west of the ruin in search of likely
lookout spots. Wood then told us about a massive wall across a mesa tip

Figure 7.7. Pueblo
Pato/Rattlesnake
complex (after
Wood 1992).

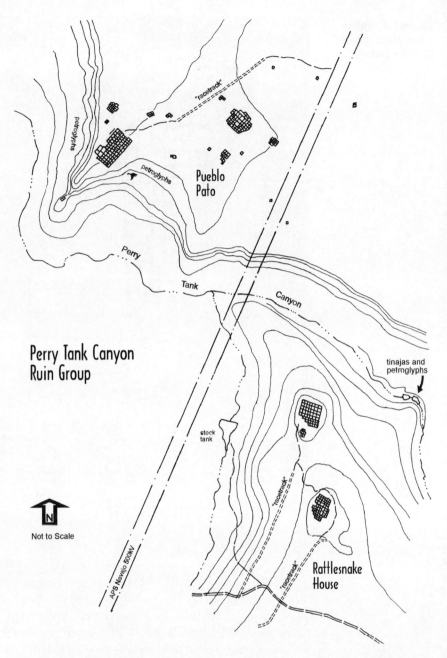

on the south side of Squaw Creek (AR 03-12-01-1364) which he had
spotted from a helicopter: it would have been an excellent lookout.

When Glen Rice invited Wilcox to participate in a symposium on
Hohokam warfare at the 1998 Society for American Archaeology meetings, Wilcox at once proposed a collaboration to Robertson and Wood
in a paper focused on Perry Mesa. They readily agreed, and Robertson,
in particular, became quite excited. When we visited Perry Mesa again in
early November on a three-day field trip, he immediately shared with us
two seminal ideas.

Figure 7.8. Squaw
Creek Ruin (photo
by Jerry Jacka).

First, he mused, why would anyone want to attack Perry Mesa? What
did the people there have that anyone would want? There being no obvious answer to this question, he then said, What if the people of Perry
Mesa were the aggressors? The way they had deployed themselves, therefore, and the way their sites were organized, were designed to repel the
feared retaliation for their actions! Wood and Wilcox thought this was a
marvelous idea.

Second, he said, think of a castle wall—and he shaped his hands accordingly. Now, he said, moving his hands apart, think of Perry Mesa as
the castle. Another brilliant idea! This abstract image transforms our earlier hypotheses into a coherent scientific model that clearly implies that

Figure 7.9. Distance
relationships among
Perry Mesa pueblos.

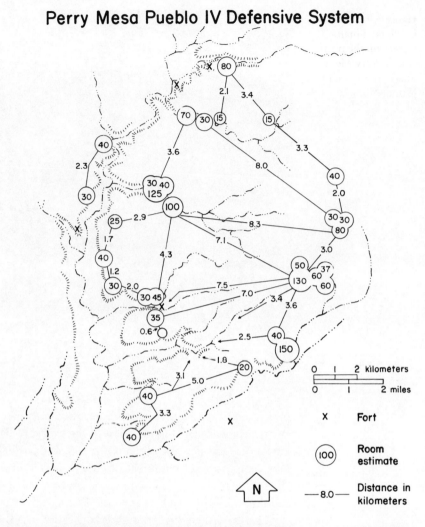

Perry Mesa Pueblo IV Defensive System

the Pueblo IV occupants of Perry Mesa were organized into a single military organization whose "command structure," Robertson suggested, would have been seated at Squaw Creek Ruin.

As a test of these ideas, we wanted to investigate more closely how various of the pueblos were organized and to look for sites around Larry Canyon. Robertson again insisted that there must have been early warning from the lower end of Squaw Creek, though no site was shown there on Wood's map.[9] So we drove down to the tip of the mesa, and sure enough, out on a needle point there was a 20-room pueblo with excellent views of the Agua Fria/Squaw Creek junction and a good line of sight up the canyon to that walled mesa tip (12-01-1364) from which messages could be relayed to Squaw Creek Ruin. As for Larry Canyon, we checked out a few rim areas, and Wood later flew over it, but no pueblos like those along the other canyons were found. Careful mapping of the vertical cliffs in these canyons and of possible access from below still needs to be done. Perhaps approaches up Larry Canyon could be blocked by peo-

Figure 7.10. Pueblo
La Plata, a major
Center on the north
rim of Perry Mesa,
and Fort Silver (after
Wood 1992).

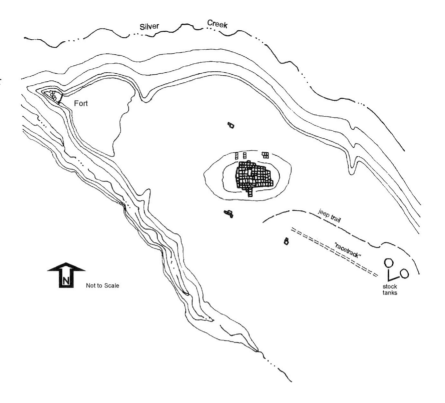

ple coming over from Squaw Creek Ruin and other sites if given sufficient early warning (Figure 7.9). All the sites on Perry Mesa are within 9
km of one another, and often much less, and the deployment of population, as measured by number of rooms, is well calculated to allow each
to provide military support to its neighbors. Many of them are in line of
sight of one another (Ahlstrom and Roberts 1995).

We also visited Pueblo La Plata (Figure 7.10), a compact 80-room
pueblo on the north end of the system where there is also a walled mesa
tip from which early warning could be given. Finally, the Rosalie Mine
and Brooklyn Basin groups, we noted, were well positioned to block access to attackers who might try to come up the canyon past Squaw Creek
Ruin and swing around to the north. Aggressors still would have had to
run a gauntlet to gain access to Perry Mesa. The Brooklyn/Rosalie
groups could also provide a strategic reserve to be called out to help
wherever they were needed on the mesa (Figure 7.11; Appendix 7.1).

When Robertson was first telling us about his ideas, we had stopped
on a dirt road, and it was natural to find a stick and sketch out a map,
the questions being, Who were their neighbors, and who were they
afraid of? The map extended from Black Mesa on the west eastward to
the Globe-Miami area, and from Chavez Pass to the Phoenix Basin. We
also talked about the agricultural potential of this grassland and the climatic conditions that may have favored occupation here. Around the
campfire we raised the question of antecedent systems, thinking at once

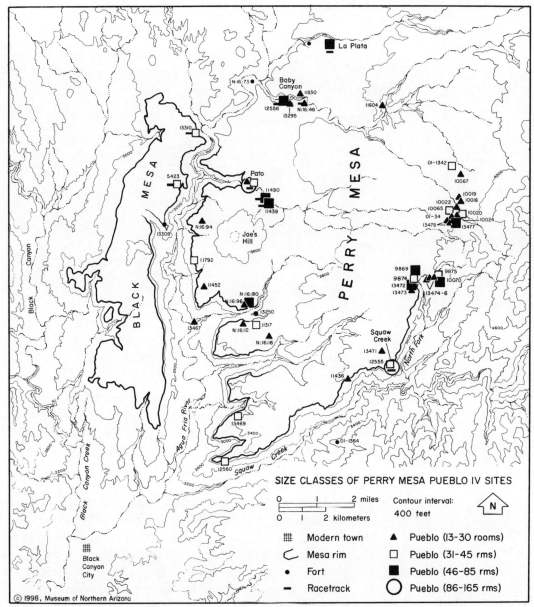

Figure 7.11. Size distribution of Perry Mesa pueblos and "forts."

about the hilltop sites in the foothills north of Phoenix (Spoerl 1979; Spoerl and Gumerman 1984; van Waarden 1984). Unlike Perry Mesa, those sites had seemingly been a "defensive retreat" system in which farming populations living down below resorted to the hilltop sites in time of danger. Given Wilcox's (1991c:263) estimate of 24,000 Hohokam for the Phoenix Basin at its height in the early A.D. 1300s, and the inference that they were politically integrated in some way (Wilcox 1988, 1999; see also Howard 1993), we postulated that the Hohokam were capable of fielding a 1,000-man warrior society, and such a group could have destroyed the defensive retreat system. Why, then, had this not happened until the middle 1200s—when the system apparently was abandoned (see Wilcox et al., this volume, Chapter 6)?

The distribution of pueblos and lookouts on Perry Mesa made it seem that the enemy was expected to come from the south. We considered the Middle Verde Valley to the north and Bloody Basin and the Lower Verde to the east but rejected those hypothetical enemies, Wood arguing that the latter were most likely allied to the Perry Mesa polity. Asked if the Perry Mesa castle could have successfully repelled an attack from a 1,000-man Hohokam force that had good command and control, Robertson unhesitatingly said yes. His argument was that such a force would be canalized or strung out in the canyons below and would not have been able to deliver a strong enough blow at the points where the defenders (with early warning) were waiting for them. They also could be attacked from ambush as they approached and as they left. The Perry Mesa castle was impregnable.

As for its agricultural potential, prehistoric fields, Wood told us, are "everywhere." Perry Mesa is situated where it could intercept storm tracks coming up the Agua Fria; its volcanic formations are capped by clay-rich volcanic and granitic soils that are underlain by an impermeable layer of compressed volcanic ash. Its low-relief topography is a mosaic of rolling hills, gentle slopes, and shallow sediment basins ideal for harvesting soil and water runoff. Water-control devices include rock-wall terraces, banked-earth contour terraces, check dams, and waffle gardens—not to mention rock piles and cleared fields where the gradient did not require runoff control. Though the old A-horizon of topsoil has been pulverized by cattle, no plowing has occurred, and much of the prehistoric agricultural landscape is still intact. Most of these sites, especially the largest ones, remain unmapped—and none has been studied in detail—but limited excavation at a dozen or so sites suggests that they supported a variety of crops, including maize, squash, agave, and a little barley. Today agave, yucca, and prickly pear, as well as grasses, are ubiquitous. Until more detailed analyses are possible, it seems reasonable to assume for now that the Pueblo IV population was agriculturally self-sufficient.

To follow up on our ideas, we initiated three kinds of studies: (1) consolidation of information about Perry Mesa and further field trips to check out particular points; (2) investigation of the antecedent defensive systems (see Wilcox et al., this volume, Chapter 6); and (3) assembling of information on Perry Mesa's late Pueblo III and Pueblo IV neighbors in central Arizona. The third study, a settlement-system and buffer-zone analysis, has taken us far afield from Perry Mesa, including comparisons with the American Southeast, but its fundamentally important findings have situated Perry Mesa in the regional and macroregional context of thirteenth- and fourteenth-century political geography.

Examining what is known about the pottery from Perry Mesa,[10]

Wood noticed that in some of the Baby Canyon and Lousy Canyon sites, Prescott Gray and Wingfield Plain are present in some quantity, and he has proposed that the pueblo system on Perry Mesa began in the late A.D. 1200s, when that pottery was still being made, and that the settlers included populations from the Middle and Upper Agua Fria drainage. Before that time most of the Pueblo III sites on Perry Mesa were field houses, implying that habitation was down below and off the mesa. Hoping to support these findings, Wilcox reviewed all the Perry Mesa site cards and collections at the Museum of Northern Arizona (MNA) but found almost no black-on-white pottery and no late-1200s polychromes (see Appendix 7.1). Much of the Perry Mesa redware looks very much like Salt Red, a late redware in the Phoenix Basin. Discussion with Jerry Jacka, who has seen a good deal of material from Perry Mesa sites, further confirms the observation of the rarity of black-on-white; Jacka also has the impression that Tonto Polychrome is more frequent than Gila Polychrome (personal communication 1998). But why would the plainwares show so much continuity with local Agua Fria wares if there was a great hiatus of occupation? Perhaps the Perry Mesans were "out of the loop" in the late 1200s and did not receive as many exotic ceramics then as later.

In an effort to get more data on this key chronological question, to look again at the Larry Canyon anomaly, to climb Joe's Hill (the highest place on Perry Mesa), and to refine our data on the context and room counts at certain other sites, the three of us returned to the area in August 1998 for three days. Starting with Larry Canyon, we again drove out to the end of the road on the south side, where we had been in November, and then walked another half a mile to a point 0.7 mile up Larry Canyon where Wood had spotted on an aerial photograph a possible pueblo site. Sure enough, at this first access point to the rim coming up Larry Canyon, we found a seven-room site at an excellent lookout location, seemingly guarding a trail from the canyon below where there is also a large pool of water. We also noticed that if a force went farther up Larry, it would come out just west of Squaw Creek Ruin, which has the only massive compound wall of all the Perry Mesa sites. Such a force could then be taken from the rear by forces dispatched by the Rattlesnake sites, or on the flank by forces from Brooklyn Basin. Perhaps, then, early warning was all the defense needed to block attack up Larry Canyon.

Joe's Hill, Robertson thought, might be a signaling place, but when we climbed it we found that it has a very rounded surface and does not allow one to see in all directions at once. There also was evidence of many lightning strikes, suggesting it was not a very safe place to be—so we left. Later, looking south from Estler Peak, along the Dugas Road, we predicted that there ought to be a hilltop site near Cordes Junction, and site stewards Judi and Rollie Myers proceeded to find it on Horseshoe Butte. Subsequent work by Robertson and Wilcox established that

Horseshoe Butte (NA25,985) can be plainly seen from Squaw Creek Pueblo, and from there one can see all the other Perry Mesa sites on the north half of the mesa. Communication regulated by Squaw Creek Pueblo throughout the whole Perry Mesa settlement system was thus certainly possible.

Camping at Brooklyn Basin, we visited all the large pueblos there and counted their rooms (Appendix 7.1). Again Robertson was impressed by how well the terrain had been used for defense and by how effectively the residents could repel a force coming up past Squaw Creek Ruin. One site puzzled us, however. NA10,070 is down in the canyon on a low ridge and consists of three room blocks totaling about 60+ rooms that surround a possible plaza space measuring 94 m east-west by 64 m north-south which has been modified as a historic corral or garden (a mining operation had a house on the southwest edge of the site about fifty years ago). The site is in a highly vulnerable situation. Perhaps it was a place intended to receive strangers: as exchanges were made, the local people were protected by the proximity of kinsmen and retreat by outsiders was cut off by Squaw Creek Pueblo.[11] The only other Perry Mesa site in a similarly vulnerable position, NA13,467 at the mouth of Lousy Canyon, lacks a large plaza.

Perhaps our most exciting find came when we noticed right next to NA9869 (where we were camped) the cobble foundations of jacal structures whose ceramic assemblage contained much less redware than the large pueblos and which also had a series of diagnostics dating to the late A.D. 1200s. One of these late Pueblo III components had a piece of Homolovi Polychrome and a late Tusayan Whiteware. At the Rattlesnake ruins we found a piece of Winslow Polychrome, and at NA13,477, the large Rosalie-area double pueblo, we found another, plus areas with Wingfield Plain, less redware, a Tusayan Whiteware, and a Little Colorado Whiteware. At AR 03-12-01-32 and 1066 we found cobble foundations, pit rooms, compound walls, a low frequency of redware, and a piece of Tusayan Black-on-white. What all this adds up to is that there is a late Pueblo III period occupation on Perry Mesa in the same places that the large pueblos are later built, suggesting an antecedent version of the later defensive *system* we have described. These data clearly open up many new avenues for future research on the evolution of the Perry Mesa defensive system.

THE VERDE CONFEDERACY

The question of neighbors is related to that of the scale on which conflict may have been taking place. Who were friends and who were enemies? Any system can be looked at in terms of both the internal and the external processes that affect it, as well as the interaction between the two. There is also the question of what is internal and what external: what are the boundaries of a system and its subsystems? To answer such questions, we began by looking at Perry Mesa's immediate neighbors and later expanded the inquiry to a macroregional scale—all of central Arizona. The absence of settlements, or the pattern of their abandonment, marks the emergence of buffer zones, which are thought to help *reduce* conflict and provide areas where wild food provisions are accumulated for use in emergency situations (DeBoer 1981; Hally 1993; Martin and Szuter 1999). Buffer zones also may delineate clusters of settlements whose spatial association indicates a political relationship, or polity (Wilcox 1981; Upham 1982; Hally 1993). Additionally, the position of hilltop "fort" or lookout sites proved instructive in defining system and subsystem boundaries. Once such entities are defined, the conflict relationships among them can be addressed (for the methodology of this approach, see Wilcox 1989; Haas and Creamer 1993; Hally 1993).

The first step to define Perry Mesa's neighbors was to put together a comprehensive map of all Pueblo IV sites in west-central Arizona (Figure 7.12). In 1986 Wilcox had organized a Pueblo IV symposium that was presented at both the Pecos Conference in Payson and the Mogollon Conference in Tucson. No publication resulted, but both Wood and Peter Pilles did their homework. When the present study raised the question of who Perry Mesa's neighbors were, collaboration with Wood and superb cooperation from Pilles, together with studies of the MNA site files, made possible the construction of Figure 7.12 and the associated data tables, which are integral to the interpretation of the map (Appendices 7.2A and 7.2B). This study has thus brought about a synthesis of late Pueblo III and Pueblo IV data from three national forests, two museums, and a series of individuals. For the first time, we can now see how all the Pueblo IV sites in west-central Arizona are spatially related to one another.

Previous studies of Pueblo IV site distributions have revealed site clusters separated from one another by buffer zones (Upham 1982; Jewett 1989; Wilcox 1991a; LeBlanc 1999). The biggest surprise evident in Figure 7.12 is that there is *no* large gap or buffer zone along the Verde River from Perkinsville to Davenport Wash. Four or five miles is the largest separation between sites. The territorial size of this continuous entity is an astonishing 105 km from Perkinsville to Davenport Wash and 57 km from Perry Mesa to Polles Mesa. Thus all the Pueblo IV sites from Perry to Polles mesas, and Davenport Wash to Perkinsville, *may* have been allied—or at least sufficiently friendly that no great separation was necessary to reduce conflict. In Appendix 7.3 we explore a considerable amount of local knowledge to argue that this entity can be partitioned into a series of constituent subsystems. We are thus led to infer that they were allied into a "Verde Confederacy."[12]

Sites in the Bridgeport/Oak Creek group are nearly all highly defensible (see Figure 7.2), as are those in the Brown Springs/Hackberry Basin group, Perry Mesa, and the subset of sites below Mercer Ruin. As a group, the Polles Mesa sites are also probably defensive (see Figure

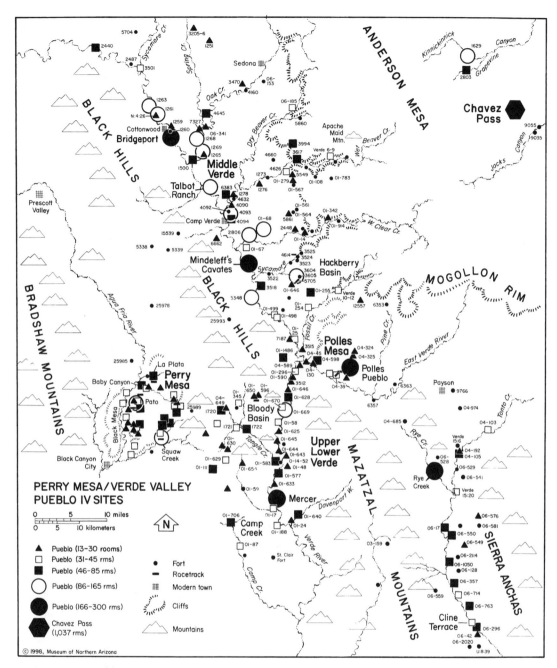

Figure 7.12. Pueblo IV sites in west-central Arizona.

7.13). In contrast, the Bloody Basin sites and most of the Lower Verde ones are not obviously defensive.[13]

Interestingly, the nondefensive sites are in the *middle* of the Verde Confederacy where it probably was the safest. This leaves the middle portion of the Middle Verde, where many of the sites on Wet Beaver and West Clear Creeks are defensive but several of the largest ones apparently are not. No sites in this section are located on the west side of the Verde, though good agricultural land exists there. It is as though the river

Figure 7.13. Aerial view of Polles Pueblo (AR 03-12-04-122) (photo by Jerry Jacka).

was a political boundary, affording some protection from threats coming from the west. That there was a danger from the west seems supported by the fact that the three-story pueblo at Talbot Ranch was burned (Mearns 1890), as was Montezuma Castle B (Jackson 1933). We thus predicted that there should be forts/lookouts along the western approaches along the pass through the Black Hills. The site files showed that three such sites are known there (Figure 7.12); new survey is needed to search for others and to determine if they together could have functioned as an effective early warning system.[14] In general, however, the hypothesis of a Verde Confederacy appears to be supported by current data.

Based on the empirical generalization by Wood and Pilles that the average room sizes of the Pueblo IV sites in our sample is 16 to 20 m², and assuming 10 m² per person (Naroll 1962), we have drawn on the room estimates assembled in Appendices 7.2A and 7.2B to construct Tables 7.1 and 7.2.[15] Taking as a point of reference the estimate of 24,000 people for the whole Phoenix Basin during the Civano phase, A.D. 1300–1360 (Wilcox 1991c:263), we are led to the following inferences: (1) the combined Verde Confederacy of 12,000 people was about half the size of the Civano phase Hohokam of the Phoenix Basin; (2) the Middle Verde subsystem of 4,000 people was twice the size of the Chavez Pass popula-

TABLE 7.1. Perry Mesa/Verde Valley Pueblo IV Population Distribution.

| Middle Verde System (without Salado polychromes or racetracks) | | | | |
Subsystem	Est. No. of Rooms	Pop. Estimate	% of Middle Verde System	% of Whole Verde System
Bridgeport to Perkinsville	568+	908–1,136	25	9
Oak Creek	353+	564–706	15	5
Talbot Ranch/Wet Beaver Creek	548+	876–1,096	24	8
Wingfield Mesa/Clear Creek	815+	1,304–1,630	36	13
Subtotal	**2,284+**	**3,654–4,568**		35

tion of about 2,000 people; and (3) both Perry Mesa and the Lower Verde subsystem (with Bloody Basin), at 3,000 each, were only about one-eighth the size of the combined Phoenix Basin population.

What kind of threat could the Phoenix Basin have posed to the Verde Confederacy? We have argued that although its members feared retaliation from the south, the Perry Mesa subsystem was impregnable.[16] What would have happened, however, if the Phoenix Basin Hohokam attacked the Lower Verde subsystem? The latter's defensive perimeter below the Mercer Ruin would have absorbed the first blow. After that, Robertson points out, the narrow valley with mountains close at hand would have made a "defense in depth" possible, forcing the attackers to run a gauntlet that would have been excruciating. Support from Perry Mesa, Polles Mesa, and the Hackberry Basin subsystems could also have been called on. Thus, even though they were relatively small, the Perry Mesa and Lower Verde subsystems apparently were so organized as to remain viable in the face of any threat from the south.[17]

TABLE 7.2. Perry Mesa/Verde Valley Pueblo IV Population Distribution.

| Perry Mesa to Polles Mesa System (with Salado polychromes and racetracks) | | | | |
Subsystem	Est. No. of Rooms	Pop. Estimate	% of Perry Mesa/Polles Mesa System	% of Whole Verde System
Brown Springs/ Fossil Ck/ Hackberry Basin	457+	731–914	11	7
Polles Mesa	313+	500–626	7	5
Davenport Wash to Fossil Creek	1,208+	1,932–2,416	29	19
Upper Camp Creek	90+	144–180	2	1
Bloody Basin	368+	588–736	9	6
Perry Mesa	1,751+	2,801–3,502	42	27
Subtotal	**4,187**	**6,692–8,366**		65
Grand Total	**6,471**	**10,347–12,934**		

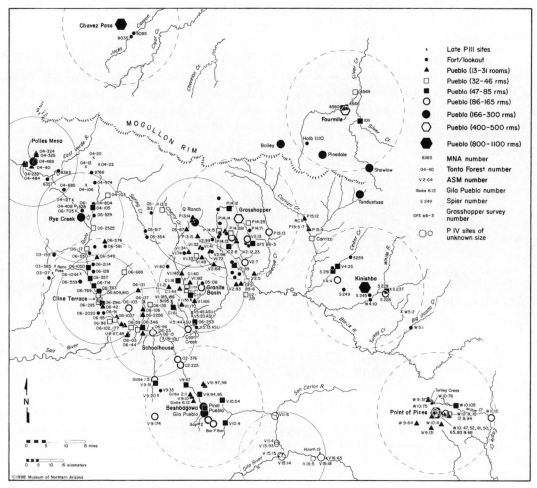

Figure 7.14. Late
Pueblo III and
Pueblo IV sites in
east-central Arizona.

THE POLITICAL GEOGRAPHY OF WARFARE
IN CENTRAL ARIZONA

Figure 7.12 documents the presence of three buffer zones: between the
Middle Verde and Chavez Pass, between Polles Mesa and the northern
Tonto Basin, and between Perry Mesa, the Lower Verde, and the Phoenix
Basin. Widening our inquiry about the neighbors of Perry Mesa, and the
role this "castle" may have played in the evolution of regional warfare in
central and southern Arizona, we next sought to construct a map similar
to Figure 7.12 for the greater Tonto Basin, Globe-Miami, Cherry Creek,
Q Ranch, Grasshopper, Carrizo, Silver Creek, Kinishba, Point of Pines,
and San Carlos areas. Site file searches at Arizona State University and
the Arizona State Museum, a literature review, John Welch's dissertation
(1996), and especially the assistance of Stephen Germick of the Tonto
Forest staff and others made it possible to create Appendix 7.3 and to
draft Figure 7.14.

The data assembled in Figure 7.14 and Appendix 7.4 show that buffer zones indeed developed between multi-settlement site clusters in the late A.D. 1200s and early 1300s. Those site clusters, like analogous ones north of the Mogollon Rim (Upham 1982; Kintigh 1998; LeBlanc 1999), were probably integrated politically, perhaps in several different ways (see Mills 1998). We thus suggest that it is reasonable to call them *polities* and to inquire further about the nature of their political integration. Hally (1993) has applied a similar logic to late prehistoric site clusters and buffer zones in north Georgia, where there is agreement that those polities were a form of chiefdom. In the Southwest no such consensus exists, and it in general seems more likely that some form of "corporate" organization structured power relations (Muller and Wilcox 1999).

The hypothesis of "regional warfare," that is, conflict among these polities, also is supported by the data. The concentration of burned or abandoned sites on the edges of the clusters or in the boundary zones is what we would expect (Wilcox 1991a:132–133; see Appendix 7.4). Thus the possibility that interpolity warfare was one of the principal causes of the macroregional abandonment of all of central Arizona by ca. A.D. 1400–1450 should be given more serious consideration.

The estimated comparative demography of multi-settlement political systems in central Arizona is summarized in Tables 7.3 and 7.4.[18] Although the relative size of the Phoenix Basin populations is in no way

TABLE 7.3. Greater Tonto Basin, Globe-Miami, and Q Ranch/Grasshopper Pueblo IV Population Distributions.

Subsystem	Est. No. of Rooms, 1300–1330	Pop. Estimate, Early PIV	Est. No. of Rooms, 1330–1375	Pop. Estimate, Later PIV
Upper Tonto Creek	340	544–680	340	544–680
Lower Tonto Creek	697	1,115–1,394	651	1,041–1,302
Salt Arm, Tonto Basin	827	1,323–1,654	475	760–950
Subtotal	1,864	2,982–3,728	1,466	2,345–2,932
Globe-Miami	1,689	2,702–3,378	1,689	2,702–3,378
Sierra Ancha/Granite Basin	898	1,436–1,796	783	1,252–1,566
Q Ranch	479	766–958	415	664–830
Grasshopper	1,276	2,041–2,552	1,729	2,766–3,458
Silver Creek	1,346	ca. 2,019	744	ca. 1,116
Kinishba	1,110	1,776–2,220	1,210	1,936–2,420
Point of Pines	1,671	2,673–3,342	1,745	2,792–3,490

TABLE 7.4. Population Comparisons among Pueblo IV Polities in Central Arizona.

Polity	No. of Rooms	Pop. Estimate	% of Perry Mesa (as standard)
Phoenix Basin	?	24,000	7.5 times as large
Verde Confederacy	6,471	10,347–12,934	3.7 times as large
Bridgeport	921	1,474–1,842	53
Mindeleff's	1,464	2,342–2,928	84
Polles	669	1,070–1,338	38
Mercer	1,666	2,666–3,332	95
Perry Mesa	1,751	2,801–3,502	100
Chavez Pass	1,170	1,872–2,340	67
Tonto Basin			
Rye Creek	370	592–740	21
Early PIV Tonto Basin	1,524	2,438–3,048	87
Late PIV Tonto Basin	1,126	1,801–2,252	64
Globe-Miami	1,689	2,702–3,378	96
Central Mountains	1,377	2,203–2,754	79
Sierra Ancha/Granite Basin	898	1,436–1,796	51
Early PIV Q Rancha[a]	479	766–958	27
Early PIV Grasshopper	1,276	2,041–2,552	73
Late PIV Grasshopper	1,729	2,766–3,458	99
Early PIV Silver Creek	1,346	ca. 2,019	77
Late PIV Silver Creek	744	ca. 1,116	42
Kinishba[a]	1,110	1,776–2,220	63
Point of Pines[a]	1,671	2,673–3,342	95
Early PIV Homolovi	1,800	2,880–3,600	103
Late PIV Homolovi	1,600	2,560–3,200	91
Safford Valley[a]	1,000+	1,600–2,000++	57++

[a] Room estimates from these areas may not represent all settlements 13 rooms or larger, more so than in the other areas.

surprising, the relative size of the "Verde Confederacy" is revealed in this work for the first time. Its constituent "subsystems" are much more like in size the settlement systems we have identified from Tonto Basin eastward, supporting the view that they are separate political entities confederated together. Our findings suggest that the "gravity" of the Verde in any models of exchange and its potential power in regional political conflicts must now be taken much more seriously than we have tended to previously.

The "weights" of the late Pueblo IV Grasshopper and Globe-Miami systems appear to be fairly comparable to one another and to the combined Tonto Basin in early Pueblo IV times. Perry Mesa is in this same size category (see Table 7.4), as are Point of Pines and the Homolovi group (Adler 1996:260). However, the substantial reduction of the Tonto Basin population during Pueblo IV times suggests that by middle Pueblo IV times it had become much weaker than its eastern (Grasshopper) and southern (Globe-Miami) neighbors. By themselves, the Polles Mesa, Rye Creek, and Q Ranch clusters appear to be too small to have survived without support from neighbors. They may each have had "guard" functions in larger confederacies (as we argued earlier was the case for Polles Mesa). Squeezed between its larger eastern (Tonto Basin) and western (Grasshopper) neighbors, the Sierra Ancha/Granite Basin and Q Ranch clusters both apparently declined in size during the 1300s while the Grasshopper system apparently grew much larger.[19] We suggest that the Q Ranch sites, like the Grasshopper sites (Zedeño 1994; Triadan 1997), either were part of a Western Anasazi intrusion from the north (which we doubt), were a separate local system, or were local populations allied with the Sierra Ancha cluster. We further suggest that the Q Ranch cluster was either absorbed or eliminated by the Grasshopper polity.

The Silver Creek area also shrank by about half. If we suppose that there was a demographic threshold past which it was felt to be no longer tenable to occupy an area (see Dobyns 1963), such conflicts may explain why some zones were abandoned. Clusters that grew may have done so by absorbing populations of former enemies. If we suppose, further, that such abandonment resulted in a net loss of external energy inputs to the remaining populations from their neighbors, other critical thresholds may have been exceeded, resulting in a domino effect of abandonment. Environmental perturbations could have further exacerbated such a process. New research on these important issues is needed.

COMPARATIVE POLITICAL GEOGRAPHY OF CENTRAL ARIZONA AND THE AMERICAN SOUTHEAST

Hally (1993) has recently employed several empirical methods for measuring the territorial size of southeastern polities, making it possible to compare his results with the data presented here on central Arizona (Figure 7.15).[20] Taking platform mounds as his point of reference, Hally (1993:160) finds that in northern Georgia the "spatial size of site clusters—the straight-line distance separating towns at each end of the cluster—ranges from 10.8 to 23.5 km, while the maximum distance separating mound sites and towns within clusters is 18.7 km [—or half a day's travel]." More generally, he finds that the core areas (site clusters)

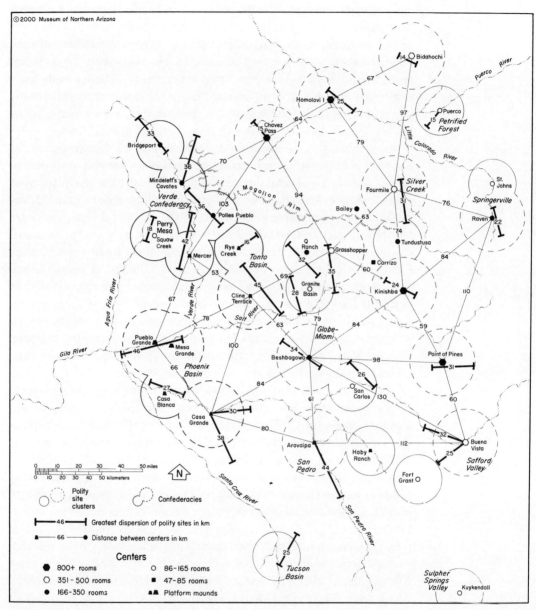

Figure 7.15. Pueblo IV political geography in central Arizona.

"varied in size from as little as 11 km to as much as 29 km [across]" and that they were separated from one another by buffer zones of "at least 10 km across and more commonly 20 to 30 km across" (Hally 1993:162).

The spatial sizes of the Pueblo IV site clusters in central Arizona are expressed in Figure 7.15 as a vector of the dispersion between the most distant sites within each cluster. For 26 cases, the average spatial size is 29.8 km, with only 11 cases less than 30 km. The 4 largest cases, Pueblo Grande–Mesa Grande and Casa Grande in the Phoenix Basin, Tonto Basin, Mercer along the lower Verde, and the San Pedro cluster, exceed a day's travel by 2 to 10 km. Interestingly, these site clusters are contiguous and are made up of platform-mound sites or have centers that have platform mounds. If we treat each site cluster/polity as a node in a macroregional network, we find that the distances between the centers of each node are also instructive: for the 29 cases shown in Figure 7.15, the average is 79.7 km, or a little over two days' travel. It would seem from these data that many of these southwestern polities were individually larger and more powerful than the southeastern cases considered by Hally.

In the Southeast there were also "paramount" chiefdoms such as the Coosa that exercised some form of political hegemony over distances exceeding 200 km in several directions (Hally 1993). How to identify such systems archaeologically is still a moot issue (Blitz 1999). Although this problem goes well beyond the scope of this chapter, several points are worth noting. If we take our 18-km (11-mile) and 24.5-km (15-mile) circles as a measure of territorial control by the different-sized polities, Figure 7.15 clearly shows that considerable buffer zones separate each site cluster from its neighbors—with some interesting exceptions. The concept of a Verde Confederacy has been discussed above. The contiguity of the Phoenix Basin site clusters and their wide separation from other polities point toward their being politically integrated in some way. So, too, Rye Creek with Tonto Basin, and Granite Basin with Grasshopper, as also discussed above. Similar dyadic relationships may link Globe-Miami with San Carlos, the San Pedro with Haby Ranch, Springerville with St. Johns, Bidahochi with Petrified Forest, and Tundustusa with either Silver Creek or Kinishba. The fact that rectangular great kivas embedded in a room block near a large central plaza occur uniquely in each of the site clusters of Point of Pines, Kinishba, Grasshopper, and Chavez Pass suggests a linear network of ritual/political connections among these neighboring polities. It will be most interesting to rethink the artifactual data on interaction in light of these spatial patterns.

The macroregional perspective developed as a result of basic research in this chapter suggests further inferences about the nature of the Perry Mesa system. Unlike most of their central Arizona neighbors, none of the sites in the Verde Confederacy is a primary center. On Perry Mesa, Squaw Creek Ruin is not even twice the size of other settlements there. This implies that mutuality rather than dependency relations characterized the constituent subsystems of the Verde Confederacy. Perry Mesa's spatial size of only 18 km makes it one of the most tightly integrated of all the Pueblo IV polities in central Arizona (see Figure 7.15), yet its population size is as large as much more dispersed polities. Surely, it was not simply the agricultural opportunities of this place that attracted so may people to live there.

When the Perry Mesa "castle" was established on the southwestern flank of the Verde Confederacy, it would have blocked north-south access along the Agua Fria, protecting the flank of the Bloody Basin and Lower Verde subsystems and the Middle Verde. Could it be that this was necessary because the Phoenix Basin Hohokam had been coming northward to attack the Middle Verde, arriving from the west down today's Interstate 17 corridor? We think it is time to give serious consideration to such a possibility and to the political agency indicated by the establishment of the Perry Mesa "castle."

CONCLUSIONS

The controversy about prehistoric conflict or peaceful farmers will no doubt continue. We recognize that what we have reported here is not definitive. But we suggest that the collaboration between archaeologists and a person with real military experience has been fruitful and many new lines of inquiry are identified. The facts generated in the Perry Mesa case study and its contextualization have transformed earlier perceptions of relationships, and we have expanded the arena of debate to include not only local systems but also regional and macroregional ones. The emergence of buffer zones where there once had been viable settlements is patterned on a regional scale and points to the creation of political boundaries that mark the arenas of regional conflict between politics. We thus rest our case for now but look forward to pursuing additional field and archival studies, confident that new data will continue to change the debate and move scientific discourse forward. Perry Mesa and its neighbors have only begun to reveal what they can teach us about the southwestern past.

ACKNOWLEDGMENTS

Many people made this chapter possible. Glen Rice's invitation to prepare it stimulated our fruitful collaboration. Peter Pilles's three decades of accumulated knowledge about Perry Mesa, the Verde Valley, the Agua Fria, and much else added immeasurably to the synthesis presented here. Stephen Germick, James McKie, Judy Taylor, Connie Stone, Richard Lange, John Welch, Richard Ciolek-Torrello, Todd Bostwick, David Gregory, H. David Tuggle, Barbara Mills, Roger Lidman, John Hohmann, Judi and Rollie Myers, Tom Wright, Kyle Woodson, Bob Neily, Keith Kintigh, Dennis Gilpin, Stephen Kowalewski, Donald Weaver, George Gumerman IV, Eric van Hartesveldt (on confederacies), and others provided critical data and comments. Members of the staff of the Sharlot Hall Museum deserve special thanks for their courtesy and helpfulness, and we want to single out Mona McClusky, Michael Wurtz, Sandra Lynch, and Director Richard Sims in this regard. Michael Barton at Arizona State University and Sharon Urban at the Arizona State Museum were unfailingly helpful about our requests for site information. Special thanks go to Carla Sartwell, who flew Wood over Perry

Mesa in her plane; to Joe Vogel, who flew Wilcox and Judy Taylor; and to Jerry Jacka for permission to publish two of his photographs and for providing a print of Squaw Creek Ruin. Jodi Griffith, Museum of Northern Arizona Exhibits Department, drafted the figures in her usual exquisite fashion. Our only regret is that Robertson was not able to attend the Society for American Archaeology meetings in Seattle, where a version of the chapter was presented. For any errors in the text, the senior author takes full responsibility.

NOTES

1. This is Ken Austin's (1979b) Laura Gilpin site. It had about five rooms surrounded by a stone compound wall (Hodge 1877:189–190).

2. The trench placed in an eastern terrace of Tumamoc Hill (Fish et al. 1986), though it yielded much valuable data, including a Late Archaic date on corn, was not well situated to be representative of the cleared areas behind the walls on Tumamoc Hill. The fact that 40 cm of soil occurs in one area in no way demonstrates that this is generally the case.

3. From the perspective of the agricultural hypothesis, one could explain the revetment character of the walls as due to "field" clearing (see Wilcox 1979b). The tiny size of the cleared land behind the walls, compared with the large amount in the bottomlands below, could be addressed by proposing that specialty crops were grown on the hill—agave, perhaps, or datura (for other possibilities, see Downum et al. 1994). Katzer's study (in Downum 1993:91–95) brought new facts to bear on this issue but is inconclusive. Nor have the sites of Linda Vista Hill or Cerro Prieto been evaluated from a military science perspective.

4. Downum et al. (1994) see fit to reject this hypothesis; but without offering definitive evidence against it, they confuse science with opinion (see also Doelle et al. 1995:421). More recently, the Fishes have excavated several structures on Tumamoc Hill and found them to date to the Tortillita phase, about A.D. 300–500. The trench where they found 40 cm of deposit behind one of the walls proved on reexamination to be the fill of a pithouse that intrudes into ancient soil with only about 10–15 cm of later deposits above it (David Gregory, personal communication 1999). The agriculture hypothesis is in no way strengthened by these findings, but the historical context for the conflict that the defensive-walls hypothesis implies is certainly changed, falling in LeBlanc's (1999) early period when warfare was also widespread.

5. Figure 7.1 should be thought of as a poor man's GIS. It is a palimpsest of different data "layers" conflated in one image. To "read" it properly, one should first look at the names of the sites and compare them with the map, getting them fixed in mind. Then notice the multiple cases of two platform mounds in the same compound and their distribution. Finally, look at the relationship of the day circles to gain an understanding of the spatial relationships of the platform mound clusters.

Doelle et al. (1995) have usefully extended this analysis, imposing 11-mile circles and using them to define "local systems." Eleven miles is a measure of the distance a person on foot with a pack can go and come back in a day. They see four in the Phoenix Basin and three in Tonto Basin, where Wilcox (1987, 1999) was trying to make a case for one each.

6. Other explanations are possible—that the walls ensured secrecy, for example. They required quite a lot of labor to build, however, and the rooftops adjacent to the walls and towers may have provided firing platforms from which to ward off attackers. No one to our knowledge has tried to determine whether these walls had parapets, which would have further facilitated defense (see Tropic and Tropic 1987). Because the compounds could be seen from towers or rooftops on the platform mounds, and many of the mounds were intervisible, we suggest that community and polity defense was integrated at several levels above the compound social groups.

7. In research related to this chapter Robertson returned to Hatalacva and, looking at the approaches, figured that he would want to post a lookout at the north end of that north ridge. Exactly where he would expect, he then found a one-room structure overlooking the Tapco area north of the ridge, the perfect place to station a lookout if there was a fear of attackers coming from the north, via Perkinsville or Sycamore Creek.

8. A popularized preliminary account of the study that resulted from this trip has been published with color aerial photographs and maps (Wilcox, Robertson, and Wood 1999).

9. It turned out later that a site named Point Extreme (NA12,560) was earlier recorded there by MNA archaeologists.

10. As is often the case, the plainware and redware found on Perry Mesa sites appear to be locally made, and Scott's work on sites in the Bradshaw Mountains and along the Middle Agua Fria (Wood 1978, 1987) suggests that the Perry Mesa ceramic tradition is a late manifestation of a largely undefined ceramic province centered in these areas. Schroeder's (1954) definition of Wingfield Plain with micaceous schist temper was later unfortunately expanded by others to include the non-micaceous phylite temper characteristic of the Lower Agua Fria and areas to the west. If Wingfield Plain is to be understood as the principal type of a distinct ware, as conferees proposed at the 1996 Prescott Pottery Conference held at the Museum of Northern Arizona, it is obvious that a great many foundational studies along the lines pioneered by Abbott (1994b) and Heidke and Stark (1995) remain to be done.

11. Also relevant is the consideration that we think it is possible to see the point where Squaw Creek Ruin lies from NA10,070, but further investigation is needed to test this supposition.

12. We must stipulate, however, that our map is possibly a "palimpsest," a mixing together of sites of somewhat different ages. It

seems unlikely that all these sites were absolutely contemporaneous throughout the whole Pueblo IV interval. Solving that problem will require considerably more research.

13. We look forward to many field trips on which we can show these sites to Robertson and talk to him about their defensibility or lack thereof. The classifications given in the tables of Appendices 7.2A and 7.2B are a consensus reached between Wilcox and Wood or Pilles, based on the sites being on high hills, having a wall around them, or other obviously defensive features. In a number of cases classified as not defensive, the pueblos were on a mesa edge, and the decision might better be based on an assessment of the direction from which the enemy was likely to come.

14. On visiting them, however, we found that these sites probably were constructed during the Pueblo III period (see Wilcox et al., this volume, Chapter 6). The question of a Pueblo IV early warning system in this area remains to be answered.

15. Given the data available from the Verde Valley, only sites with more than 12 rooms were counted and only the low end of the ranges given for each site. An advantage to these procedures is that the real possibility that all sites are not absolutely contemporaneous can be mitigated. On Perry Mesa about 200 rooms are known in sites of 2 to 12 rooms; the number of such sites in other areas is unknown.

16. Jerry Jacka (1980:273), who in his youth recorded 30 Perry and Black Mesa sites using aerial photographs and site visits, reports that four of these sites had burned rooms and one room had a mass grave in it. Jacka (personal communication 1998) adds that one of the burned rooms was in a site at the mouth of Lousy Canyon (NA13,467) and another was in Squaw Creek Ruin; he also remembers a burial that had, at its feet, an extra cranium under a bowl. None of this evidence appears to weaken the claim that Perry Mesa was impregnable.

17. Bandelier (1892) recorded a platform mound at Ft. McDowell. Little is known about it and most of this site is now built over, but our supposition is that it was late Classic. If this site has any integrity left, it would be highly significant, as its study could shed important light on the political processes of the Pueblo IV period and the relationship of the Phoenix Basin to the Verde Confederacy.

18. The same estimation procedures used in Tables 7.1 and 7.2 were repeated here, except for Silver Creek an estimate of 15 m² per room is used (Mills 1998).

19. Certainly caution is needed here because the survey coverage of the Grasshopper region, for example, is vastly better than that for Q Ranch or other regions (see Tuggle and Reid, this volume, Chapter 5). These comparisons are suitably illustrative, however, of the kind of relationships we should be trying to document.

20. Figure 7.15 synthesizes the data from Figures 7.1, 7.12, and 7.14, together with data from several adjacent polities. Data for these addi-

tional site clusters comes from MNA and ASM site files, and for the Safford Valley from Tom Wright, Kyle Woodson, and Bob Neily; for the Springerville–St. Johns area, from Keith Kintigh and David Gregory; and for Bidahochi, from Dennis Gilpin. Further extensions of this mapping process to the political geography of the whole North American Southwest would be highly desirable.

APPENDIX 7.1. PERRY MESA CLUSTERS OF LARGE PUEBLO IV SITES, BY DRAINAGE.

Brooklyn Basin (370++ rooms; ca. A.D. 1300–1450)

NA No.	JJ No.	Other No.	Elevation (ft.)	No. of Rooms	Comments
9869	16A	12-01-42	4,000	50–65	
9870		12-01-39	4,080	5	Cibola ? WW; Bida. Poly
9871		12-01-38	4,000	10	Bida. Poly
9872	16E	12-01-41	3,820	10	Retaining wall
9874	16B	12-01-43	4,000	44	
9875	17	12-01-44	4,040	37	Bida. Poly
13,472	16C	12-01-72	4,020	70–90	PIV
13,473	16D	"	4,040	20+	PIV
13,474		"	4,090	25+	PIV
13,475		"	4,090	25+	2 room blocks; PIV
13,476		"	4,090	14+	2 room blocks; PIV
10,070A–C	17	12-01-45	3,860	60+	3 room blocks with historic corral(?) between; PIV
25,989			5,510		Walled enclosure

Rosalie Mine/Hackberry Wash (284++ rooms; ca. A.D. 1300–1450)

NA No.	JJ No.	Other No.	Elevation (ft.)	No. of Rooms	Comments
—		12-01-1342		39	
10,067		12-01-28	4,060	20+	
10,019		12-01-29	4,100	28	
10,018	18	12-01-31	4,100	17	Enclosed plaza; 1 b/w
10,020	18	12-01-33	4,120	31+	
10,022`	18	12-01-32	4,120	15	
10,023	18	12-01-34	4,040	8	
10,024	18	12-01-35	4,040	14+	
10,065	18	12-01-31	4,100	32+	
—		12-01-1295	4,290	7	
—		12-01-1349	4,060	10	
13,477a,b	18	12-01-1292		80+	2 plazas, 2 pueblos; cul-de-sac; late PIII/PIV
13,478a,b	18		4,040		PIV
25,989			5,510	None	**Rosalie Lookout;** walled enclosure

Silver Creek (80 rooms; ca. A.D. 1300–1450)

NA No.	JJ No.	Other No.	Elevation (ft.)	No. of Rooms	Comments
11,648	1	02-02-278 (BLM)	3,720	80	**Pueblo La Plata;** racetrack
—			3,600	1+	**Fort Silver;** wall on mesa tip

Horseshoe Butte (ca. A.D. 1100–1400?)

NA No.	JJ No.	Other No.	Elevation (ft.)	No. of Rooms	Comments
25,985	—	—	4,232	5	Walled enclosure; superb lookout

Bishop/Baby Creek (137++ rooms; ca. A.D. 1300–1450)

NA No.	JJ No.	Other No.	Elevation (ft.)	No. of Rooms	Comments
11,830	2		3,610–60	17+	PC dug; 1 Kayenta B/w
11,604			3,750		PIV
12,556	3	02-02-75 (BLM)	3,600	72	**Baby Canyon Site**; PIV; enclosed plaza; racetrack
12,295	4	02-02-76 (BLM)	3,600	18–25	
		N:16:46 (PC)	3,700	30	Cul-de-sacs; racetrack; PIII?
11,786			3,640	6	PIV; 1 b/w

Perry Tank Canyon (417++ rooms [212++ rooms on N side]; ca. A.D. 1300–1450)

NA No.	JJ No.	Other No.	Elevation (ft.)	No. of Rooms	Comments
11,682	—		3,600	10–15	PIV
11,434A	5	02-02-264 (BLM)	3,650	12+	**Pueblo Pato**; PIV; racetrack
11,434B	5A		3,650	42+	" "
11,434C	5B	"	3,650	125+	" "
					Cul-de-sac
11,434D	5	"	3,650	28+	**Pueblo Pato**; PIV
11,419			3,650	4–5	
11,417			3,640	10+	
11,418			3,680	9–12	
11,438			3,760	9–12	
11,440			3,760	5–8	
11,490			3,750	48+	4 pueblos
11,490	6		3,700	48+	**Rattlesnake House II**; racetrack; PIV
11,439	6		3,750	50	**Rattlesnake House I**; cul-de-sac; racetrack; PIV
11,785			3,730	9–12	PIV
13,327			3,700	8	

Between Perry Tank and Lousy Canyon (69+ rooms; ca. A.D. 1300–1450)

NA No.	JJ No.	Other No.	Elevation (ft.)	No. of Rooms	Comments
—	26				Fort
—		N:16:94 (PC)	3,660	25	
—		N:16:95 (PC)	3,800	9-12	
11,792	7		3,650	35–50	PIV

Lousy Canyon (174++ rooms; ca. A.D. 1300–1450)

NA No.	JJ No.	Other No.	Elevation (ft.)	No. of Rooms	Comments
11,452	19		3,650	30+	Joe's Site; PIV
11,420			3,480	3–4	
—		N:16:97 (PC)	3,680	3	
—		N:16:96 (PC)	3,680	30+	
—		N:16:80 (PC)	3,690	40–50	Cul-de-sac
—		N:16:90 (PC)	3,700	4	
13,303			3,690	9–12	
13,329			3,760	5–8	
13,350			3,520	5–8	Fort
13,317	9	N:16:7 (PC)	3,700	38+	PIV
—		N:16:12 (PC)	3,620	15	

Near Junction of Agua Fria and Lousy Canyon (20+ rooms; ca. A.D. 1300–1450)

NA No.	JJ No.	Other No.	Elevation (ft.)	No. of Rooms	Comments
13,467	10		2,520	20+	

Larry Canyon (54+ rooms; ca. A.D. 1300–1450)

NA No.	JJ No.	Other No.	Elevation (ft.)	No. of Rooms	Comments
—		N:16:6 (PC)	3,740	8	
—		N:16:17 (PC)	3,740	14	
—		N:16:16 (PC)	3,700	9–12	
—		N:16:20 (PC)	3,800	10	
—		N:16:57 (PC)	3,800	7+	
—		N:16:59 (PC)	3,840	1–3	
—		N:16:111 (PC)	3,980	5–8	

Between Larry and Squaw Creek (40 rooms; ca. A.D. 1300–1450)

NA No.	JJ No.	Other No.	Elevation (ft.)	No. of Rooms	Comments
13,469	11		3,320	40	

Squaw Creek Canyon (306+ rooms; ca. A.D. 1300–1450)

NA No.	JJ No.	Other No.	Elevation (ft.)	No. of Rooms	Comments
12,560A	12	N:16:47 (PC)	3,240	20	**Point Extreme Site** ; PIV
12,560B	12	"	3,320	20	PIV
—		N:16:54 (PC)	3,300	10	PIII?
—		N:16:49 (PC)	3,480	3–4	
—		N:16:50 (PC)	3,480	3–4	
11,436 & 13,466	13		3,840	20	PIV; Jeep trail to bottom of Squaw Creek here
12,555 & 13,470	14A	12-01-55	4,000	150	**Squaw Creek Ruin:** PIV; compound wall around large plaza; cul-de-sac; racetrack
—	14B			40	Just north of Squaw Creek Ruin
—			3,940	ca. 10	
13,471	15		3,960	30	
—		01-1364	3,640		Fort: wall across mesa tip

Black Mesa

NA No.	JJ No.	Other No.	Elevation (ft.)	No. of Rooms	Comments
13,310	25	N:16:6 (ASU)	3,500	40 (53)	**Badger Springs Site;** PIV; plaza; racetrack
5423	28		3,540	30–40	**Richinbar Site (B);** PIV; racetrack

APPENDIX 7.2A. PUEBLO III AND IV SITES, MIDDLE VERDE VALLEY AND CHAVEZ PASS

Brown Springs/Fossil Creek/Hackberry Basin Subsystem (457+ rooms)

NA No.	Other No.	Age	No. of Rooms	Defensive?	Comments
3515	Verde 10:6; 04-01-521	PIV	26	no	**Fossil Creek Ruin;** Gila Poly
3516	04-01-25	PIII/PIV	42	yes	
7187	—	PIV	ca. 25–30	yes	**Verde Hot Springs Ruin;** Salado polys
18,961	04-01-498	PIII/PIV	30	no	
18,960	04-01-499	PIII/PIV	42	yes	
—	—	?		yes	Fort/lookout; at Burnt Spring
—	04-01-111	?	12	yes	Fort

Brown Springs/Fossil Creek/Hackberry Basin Subsystem (457+ rooms), continued

NA No.	Other No.	Age	No. of Rooms	Defensive?	Comments
—	—	?	9–12	yes	Fort; SE of Hackberry Mountain
19,286	04-01-254	PIV	29	yes	**Salome Ruin**
19,287	04-01-255	PIII/PIV	44	yes	**Boulder Canyon Ruin**; tree-ring date: 1302
—	Verde 10:12	PIV	30+	yes	**'Dobe Flats Ruin**
—	Verde 10:18	PIII	30	yes	Cavates
12557	—	PIV	13–20	no	
6353	—	?	3	yes	Peck's No. 16; fort/lookout; circular compound
—	04-01-646; Verde 10:14	PIII/PIV	25	no	**Needle Rock Ruin**
3604	04-01-100	PIII/ early PIV	50–100	yes	**Doran Castle Ruin**
3605	—		12	yes	**Doran Fort**
3606 & 4625A	04-01-642	PIII	15–20	no	Racetrack [NA5705] nearby; 450 m long
4614	04-01-97	?		no	Racetrack; 200 ft. long; N side Sycamore Creek
—3522?	04-01-569	?	3	yes	Fort/lookout; S side Sycamore Creek; enclosing wall
—		?	9–12	yes	Fort; S side Sycamore Creek
—3523?		?	9–12	yes	Fort; S side Sycamore Creek
—3524?	04-01-1014	?	5–8	yes	Fort; S side Sycamore Creek
—3525?		?	10–12	yes	Fort; S side Sycamore Creek
4087	04-01-199	PIII	6+	yes	Cliff dwelling; 2 stories; 1 Walnut B/w (late); 7 Citadel Poly; 1 Sunset Red; 1 Roosevelt B/w
5348	09-05-201	PIII/PIV	100+	yes	**Brown Springs Ruin**; enclosing wall; 2 enclosed plazas
25,993		PIII	8–10+	Yes	**Gap Creek Pueblo**; Flagstaff & Walnut B/w, Sunset Brown
3518		PIII/PIV	50	yes	**Bull Run Ruin**; 2 pueblos

Wingfield Mesa/ Camp Verde/ Clear Creek Subsystem (815+ rooms)

NA No.	Other No.	Age	No. of Rooms	Defensive?	Comments
1511		PIII/PIV	30; + 256 cavates	no	**Mindeleff's Cavate Lodges**
2494, & 3521 & 3664 & 4624	04-01-67; Verde 5:18	PIV	37	no	**Wingfield Mesa Ruin**; central plaza
6662	—	PIV	20	yes	**Salt Mine Pueblo**; on hill
3520 & 4094	04-01-59; Verde 5:16	PIV	30-50	yes	**CV Hill Ruin**
3519 & 4093	04-01-58; Verde 5:14	PIV	100+	no	**Calloway No. 2 Ruin**
4092	04-01-57; Verde 5:13	PIV	8	yes	**Calloway No. 1 Ruin**; fort

Wingfield Mesa/ Camp Verde/ Clear Creek Subsystem (815+ rooms), continued

NA No.	Other No.	Age	No. of Rooms	Defensive?	Comments
4091	04-01-30	early PIV	12	no	
4090	04-01-31	PIV	15	yes	**Rock Cone Ruin**
2806		PIII/PIV	150	yes	**Clear Creek Ruin**
18,495	01-68; Verde 5:25	PIII/PIV	90	yes	**John Heath Ruin**; 2 plazas
2448	Verde 5:31	PIV	24	no	**Bull Pen Ranch Ruin**
—	—	?		yes	Fort; SW of Blodget Basin
12,533	04-01-14	PIV	23	yes	2 Winslow Orangeware
—	—	?		yes	Fort; Chalk Point Spring
6668	04-01-342	PIV	30–50	?	Cliff dwelling; Fourmile & Homolovi Poly; Tusayan B/w (dates: 1320v, 2 x 1321v, 1323v)
—	04-01-914	?	5	yes	**Maverick Basin Fort**
5861	04-01-95	PIV	10–14	yes	Fort
—	04-01-564	?	5–8	yes	Fort
—	04-01-561	?	5–8	yes	Fort

Cienega Creek; west of Verde River, along pass through Black Hills

NA No.	Other No.	Size (m2)	Type	Comments
5338 & 13,403	09-05-39; N:8:4 (ASU)?	14+ rooms	Hilltop habitation	**Smith Site**; has loopholes; 4,900 ft.; Verde Brn, Tuzigoot Plain
5339		16.25; 1 room	Fort/ Lookout	SE of Interstate 17/Cherry Road exit; 4,650 ft.
15,539	09-05-38		Fort/ Lookout	On butte; 2 peepholes looking N; no artifacts; 4,820 ft.; 1 flake

Talbot Ranch/ Wet Beaver Creek Subsystem (548+ rooms)

NA No.	Other No.	Age	No. of Rooms	Defensive?	Comments
3526, 3535, 3536, & 8959	04-01-28	PIII/PIV	ca. 150+	yes	**Talbot Ranch Site** (aka Middle Verde Site of Mearns 1890); 2 pueblos and ca-vates; NA3526, 3-stories, burned (Mearns 1890:14)
4619		PIII/PIV	19	yes	Cliff dwelling; Winslow O
4608		?	none	yes	Walled promontory
6383	04-01-640	PIII/PIV	45	yes	**Montezuma Castle A**; burned; 14 Gila Poly
1278	04-01-34	PIII/PIV	20	yes	**Montezuma Castle B**
1273	04-01-636	PIII/PIV	17	no	**Montezuma Well (E. rim)**
1274	04-01-305	PIII/PIV	11	no	**Montezuma Well (SW side)**
4632		PIII/PIV	3	yes	Fort/Lookout
1276	04-01-43	PIII/PIV	30	yes	**Jackson Ranch Ruin**
4640	04-01-75	PIII	9+	yes	**Hawk Hill**; fort
4626	04-01-80	PIV	38	yes	**Sacred Mountain**; central plaza
5549	04-01-114	PIV	30	no	**Walker Creek Ruin**

Talbot Ranch/ Wet Beaver Creek Subsystem (548+ rooms), continued

NA No.	Other No.	Age	No. of Rooms	Defensive?	Comments
5550	04-01-69	PIV	20	yes	
—	04-01-279	PIV?	15	no	
—	04-01-567	?	5–7+	yes	Fort; walled enclosure; no ceramics; S of 04-01-279
3617	04-01-85	PIV	40	no	**Casner Canyon Ruin**; enclosed plaza
—	—	?		yes	Fort; junction of Wet Beaver and Long Canyon
—	04-01-108	?	6	yes	Fort; Long Canyon
21,075	04-01-783	PIII	4	yes	Fort; Roundup Basin
—	Verde 6:9	PIV	30	yes	Cliff dwellings
—	—	?	2–3	yes	Fort/Lookout; mouth of Home Tank Draw
—	—	?	5–10	yes	Fort; upper Wet Beaver Creek
3993 & 3994 & 6296	04-01-302	PIII/PIV	53	no	**Riordan Canyon Ruin**; 4 room blocks
3995 & 10,529 & 11,267	01-70	PIII	ca. 75	yes	**Ruin Point**; Walnut B/w
—	04-01-921	PIV?	?	yes	
5860	—	PIII	none	yes	**Rattlesnake Canyon Ruin**; retreat; compound; 1 loop hole; 1 Walnut B/w; redware
18,430	06-185	PIII/PIV	30+	yes	**Horse Mesa Fort**; 200-m defensive wall; 1 Wupatki B/w

Oak Creek Subsystem (353+ rooms)

NA No.	Other No.	Age	No. of Rooms	Defensive?	Comments
1500	04-06-41	PIII/PIV	ca. 50	no	**Oak Creek Site**; 3 stories; 15 cavates; Fewkes 1912
1269	04-06-78	PIII/PIV	50–100	yes	**Sugarloaf Site**; central plaza
1265	04-06-75; Verde 5:11	PIV	13	no	**Limestone Ruin**
1268 & 1768	04-06-43	PIII/PIV	70	yes	**Cornville Ruin**; central plaza
7327 & 9467	04-06-160	PIV	30+	yes	**Sheepshead Ruin**
—	04-06-341	PIV	20	no	**Oak Creek Valley Pueblo**
4645 & 5223	04-06-87 & 04-06-392	PIII/PIV	57	yes	**Spring Creek Ruin**; 2 room blocks; 3 Gila Poly
4160	04-06-85	PIV	8–12	yes	Fort; N of Red Rock
3470	04-06-86	PIV?	13	yes	Fort; SE of Red Rock
21,979	04-06-354	PIV	10–12	no	
11,297	04-06-153	PIII?	8–10	yes	Fort; NE of Little Horse Park
1255 & 3205–6	04-06-58	PIII/PIV	30	yes	**Honanki**; cliff dwelling; Jeddito B/y; tree-ring date: 1271rB
1251 & 3209	04-06-54	PIII/PIV	18	yes	**Palatki**; cliff dwelling; Jeddito B/y

Bridgeport to Perkinsville Subsystem (568+ rooms)

NA No.	Other No.	Age	No. of Rooms	Defensive?	Comments
979 & 1258	04-06-74	PIII/PIV	237	yes	**Bridgeport Site**; 2 room blocks
1260	—	PIV	10	yes	**Stone House Flat No. 2**
1259	—	PIV	13	yes	**Stone House Flat No. 1**; fort
1261 & 2733	—	PIII/PIV	93+	yes	**Tuzigoot**; partly burned; 6 Gila Poly (tree-ring dating: 1137–1221; 1314vv–1386)
—	N:4:26 (ASM)	PIV	20	yes	**Tuzigoot Extension**
1263 & 5225	—	PIII/PIV	125	yes	**Hatalacva**; enclosed plaza; tower room burned
3501	04-06-05	PIV	30–45	no	**Packard Ranch Ruin**
2487	—	PIII	8	yes	**Fort/Lookout**; SW tip of Packard Mesa; PIII
2440	N:4:2 (ASU)	PIV	85	yes	**Perkinsville Ruin**; central plaza; tree-ring date: 1387
5704		?	5+	yes	**Perkins Ruin (aka Precipice House)**; fort; N end Packard Mesa

Chavez Pass System

NA No.	Other No.	Age	No. of Rooms	Defensive?	Comments
659	04-07-21	PIV	685	yes	**Chavez Pass Pueblo 1**; tree-ring date: 1371
659	04-07-21	PIV	252	yes	**Chavez Pass Pueblo 2**
	04-07-20	late PIII	100	yes	**Chavez Pass Pueblo 3**; tree-ring date: 1264
1629	04-05-25	PIV	88+	yes	**Kinnikinnick**; burned; tree-ring dates: 1288rB, 1308r, 1310rB, 1374vv
2803	04-07-01	PIV	45	yes	**Grapevine Pueblo**
4315 & 19,692	04-05-210	1150–1250	38+	no	**Piglet**
39909	04004-456	PIII	7	yes	**Anderson Canyon Fort**
4317	04-07-48	late PIII	40–70	no	**Pollack Ruin**; tree-ring dates: 1280s–1303vv
9035	04-07-106	?	ca. 5	yes	Fort on Jack's Canyon
9055	04-07-107	PIII	10+	yes	**Jack's Canyon Fort**

Sources: Peter J. Pilles Jr.; MNA site files.

APPENDIX 7.2B. PUEBLO IV SITES ALONG THE UPPER LOWER VERDE RIVER AND SIDE DRAINAGES.

Davenport Wash to Fossil Creek Subsystem (1,208+ rooms)

Tonto Site No.: AR-03-12-	Other No.	No. of Rooms	Defensive?	Comments
01-640		65–100	yes	**Davenport Ruin**
01-24		20+	yes	**KA Ranch Site**

Davenport Wash to Fossil Creek Subsystem (1,208+ rooms), continued

Tonto Site No.: AR-03-12-	Other No.	No. of Rooms	Defensive?	Comments
01-188		30+	yes	**The Citadel**; PIII/PIV
01-187	U:2:27 (ASM)	none	—	Ceremonial hilltop?
01-17		40	no	**Howard Site**
01-04	NA3509; O:14:1 (ASM)	225-300	no	**Mercer Ruin**; 5 internal plazas; platform mound embedded in two-story room block
01-59		2	yes	Lookout; on Lime Creek
01-633	Verde 14:1 (GP)	20	no	
01-577/01-581	Verde 14;7 (GP); Verde 14:6 (GP)	40+, 30	no, no	**Ister Pueblo**
01-48	NA4650	20–30	no	**Sheep Bridge Ruin**
01-642	O:14:152 (ASU)	none	yes	**Tangle Fort**; compound; entry
01-583		50+	no	End of Tangle Creek
01-643	Verde 14:11 (GP)	40+	no	**Dry Creek Ruin**
01-644		c. 30	no	
unrecorded		?	yes	Fort/Lookout; PIII?
01-645		20+	no	
01-625	Verde 14:13 (GP)	20	no	**Alkali Seep Ruin**
01-58	Verde 14:14 (GP)	40+	no	**Red Creek Ruin**
01-669	NA1749?	95+	no	**Mule Shoe Ruin**
01-670		40+	no	
01-628	Verde 14:17 (GP)	50+	no	**Pete's Cabin Ruin**
01-646		20–30	no	
01-47	NA3512	small (13–20?)	yes	Not PIV?
01-590	Verde 14:18 (GP)	ca. 25	no	**Warm Springs Ruin**
01-296		ca. 40		**Squaw Butte Ruin**
04-589		30+	yes	**Cedar Bench Ruin**
04-45	NA3514	24+	no	**East Verde Ruin**; PIII/PIV
04-130	NA6345	21–30	yes	Cliff dwelling
04-598		big (40?)	yes	**Cedar Bench Ruin**
01-1486		45+	no	**Racetrack Ruin**; but no race track

Polles Mesa Subsystem (313+ rooms)

Tonto Site No.: AR-03-12-	Other No.	No. of Rooms	Defensive?	Comments
04-324		13–20	yes	
04-325	NA969	20	yes	**Cane Springs Ruin**

Polles Mesa Subsystem (313+ rooms), continued

Tonto Site No.: AR-03-12-	Other No.	No. of Rooms	Defensive?	Comments
04-39	NA6362	36	no	**Judge's Stand**; Peck's No. 25; PIII/V: racetrack (several 100 yds. long, 20 ft. wide); Homolovi Poly; Chavez Pass Poly; Jeddito B/y; Gila Poly; Tuwiuca O
04-122	O:10:13 (ASM)	184+	no	**Polles Pueblo**; central plaza; Homolovi Poly; Chavez Pass Poly; Jeddito B/y; Gila Poly; Tuwiuca O
unrecorded		20–30	no	PIII/PIV
04-484		10–16	yes	Cliff dwelling
04-485		8–12	yes	
—		c. 40	yes	J. T. Russell's No. 4; V-shaped pueblo on mesa tip; maze entry
—	"Ruins"		?	
—	"Ruins"		no	
04-83	NA6357		yes	Peck's No. 20; J. T. Russell's No. 8; fort/lookout; walled-enclosure; few artifacts; line of sight to NA6363
04-84	NA6363		yes	Peck's No. 26; fort/lookout

Bloody Basin and South Subsystem (368 + rooms)

Tonto Site No.: AR-03-12-	Other No.	No. of Rooms	Defensive?	Comments
01-01	NA1721	ca. 50	yes	**Lookout Ruin**
01-02	NA1722	ca. 50	no	**Dugan Ruin**
unrecorded		30–50	no	**South Fork Ruin**
01-64	NA1720	50–60	no	**Mud Springs Ruin**
01-649		20+	no	
unrecorded			yes	Fort/lookout; probably PIII
01-345		40+	no	
01-650		25	no	Racetrack
01-596		20+	no	**Rugged Mesa Ruin**
—	NA26,009	ca. 30	yes	**Holmes Canyon**
01-560		20+		**Stone Camp Spring Ruin**
01-630	Verde 13:3	18+	no	
01-629	Verde 13:2	ca. 40	no	**51 Ranch Site**
01-654		30	no	**Long Canyon Ruin**
01-1116	NA26,008	ca. 50-60	yes	**Cottonwood Springs Ruin**
01-1289		13+		PIII lookout
—		25		**Indian Ruin Tank**

Upper Camp Creek Subsystem (90 + rooms)

Tonto Site No.: AR-03-12-	Other No.	No. of Rooms	Defensive?	Comments
01-87		40–50	no	**Sycamore Camp Ruin**
01-706		50	no	**Humboldt House**

Sources: J. Scott Wood; MNA site files.

APPENDIX 7.3. CONSTITUENT SUBSYSTEMS OF THE VERDE CONFEDERACY

Most broadly, the settlement array along the Verde can be partitioned into two parts by virtue of the absence of Salado polychromes north of Fossil Creek (Pilles 1976, 1996) and the absence of "racetracks" north of the Hackberry Basin subsystem (see Appendices 7.2A and 7.2B). Salado polychromes and "racetracks" occur on Polles Mesa, in Bloody Basin, and frequently on Perry Mesa; no "racetracks" are currently known on Lower Verde sites. *Racetracks* is what ranchers have called these linear features, and that appears to us the best inference so far available. The one in Hackberry Basin is a magnificent example; it is 450 m long, has embankments like those of a Chaco road, and has small pueblo structures at either end.

The 20-mile spacing of the largest sites previously reported by Pilles (1996) is confirmed, and Figure 7.12 shows that this pattern extends into the northern Tonto Basin, where Rye Creek Ruin is the largest site. Chavez Pass, with 1,000+ rooms, is more than three to four times the size of any single Verde River site and, interestingly, is about 43 miles (two days' travel) away from the largest of the latter. Here there is a wide buffer zone comparable to the one separating the Perry Mesa/Verde sites from the Phoenix Basin.

The largest sites in the Verde settlement array are placed near boundaries rather than in the middle of the sets we identify as subsystems. Each of these cases merits separate discussion. Mercer Ruin, which Mindeleff (1896) first reported and Byron Cummings excavated in 1932, has been estimated to have 300 rooms in two stories (Jackson 1933:58). Joe Crary's (1991) sketch map, however, implies it is much smaller. Even so, with a platform mound embedded in it, a Casa Grande-like structure, and five enclosed plazas, it still is a major site. Significantly, it is located near the end of the Lower Verde subsystem and has the only platform mound known in the Verde Confederacy sites. The sites below it are all defensive, whereas it and those above it to the mouth of the East Verde are classified as not defensive (Appendix 7.2A). Like the Perry Mesa castle, the Horseshoe sites thus present a defensive perimeter *on behalf of the whole confederacy* toward the Phoenix Basin.

On Polles Mesa, Polles Pueblo (Figure 7.13) is estimated to have 184 to 200 rooms (Russell 1930; Olson 1954). Southeast of it down Rye Creek, across a day-wide buffer zone, is Rye Creek Ruin, the largest site in the northern Tonto Basin; it too has 200 rooms (Gregory 1995a). A day out from Rye Creek Ruin across rugged mountains is the whole line of the Lower Verde, from the mouth of the East Verde south to the mouth of Davenport Wash. Northeast of Polles Pueblo, up the East Verde or Pine Creek and beyond the Mogollon Rim, across a two-day buffer zone, is the Chavez Pass site, two huge pueblos that are most closely related to sites farther north and east in the Little Colorado Valley. The triangular relationship between these three large sites suggests that they are gateways connecting their different settlement systems in exchange relationships. Chavez Pass is an obvious conduit for yellowwares from the Little Colorado polities into those south and west of the Mogollon Rim. An alternative northeastern route for yellowwares into Tonto Basin, via Grasshopper or Q Ranch, is unlikely, given their complete absence in the Sierra Ancha/Granite Basin area (Ciolek-Torrello and Lange 1990:149). This may also mean, however, that the Sierra Ancha sites were abandoned shortly after A.D. 1325, when yellowware production began. Salado polychromes may have entered the Lower Verde settlements via Polles Pueblo, and these ceramics thus somehow crossed wide buffer zones.

North of the large sites of Brown Springs and Doran Castle is Sycamore Creek, where a string of "fort" (lookout) sites is known, possibly including four reported by Mindeleff (1896:213–217). This supposes that Mindeleff (1896) turned off the Verde River and up Sycamore Creek before proceeding to the famous Cavate Lodges. His sketch maps should make it possible to test this hypothesis once these "forts" are fully recorded. Either way, a boundary is thus indicated, and it is most interesting that Mindeleff's large Cavate Lodges site (NA1511) lies immediately north of this boundary. The Cavate Lodges are in the middle of the Verde Confederacy, being about 1.5 days away from the most distant allied sites; Rye Creek Ruin and Chavez Pass are outside the arc of that 1.5-day circle. One-day circles around the largest Verde sites and Chavez Pass meet in a narrow zone that includes Apache Maid Mountain.

Bridgeport is the other very large site in the Verde system, and it may be an exception to the boundary pattern. It is near the vertex of the Oak Creek sites and those above it on the Verde, however, making it both in the middle and at a boundary. We suggest that all the sites in the V-array were part of a single subsystem.

Talbot Ranch Ruin is the next site farther south, and though a bit smaller than the "largest site" class, it and Bridgeport may lie on either side of a political boundary. Alternatively, as we found on Perry Mesa, these villages may have been prepared to protect one another's backs. To test these ideas, Robertson and Wilcox visited Talbot Ranch in July and August 1998. They found that the cliffs around its two pueblos are vertical to the south and north but between them is an easy access from the river. The pueblo, which was three stories high (Mearns 1890), is set off on an island-like ridge spur and thus was defensible from attack from the east as well. The estimate of about 150 room spaces for these pueblos seems accurate. Wilcox and Robertson then searched for a lookout on a high ridge north of the site, where Robertson predicted there should be one, and found that the ridge has magnificent views of Bridgeport and over 270 degrees of the valley but that there was no physical evidence it had ever been used that way. Subsequent checking confirmed a "gap," and thus the hypothesis of political autonomy for the Bridgeport/Oak Creek system appears well founded. A lookout positioned on the west side of the valley remains a possibility, however.

Talbot Ranch is also about halfway (half a day) between Bridgeport and Mindeleff's Cavate Lodges. Verde Hot Springs (NA7187) is about halfway between the latter and Polles Pueblo, and Mule Shoe Ruin (AR 03-12-01-669) is half a day between Polles Pueblo and Mercer Ruin. Mercer is about half a day from Lookout Ruin (NA1721), the only site felt to be defensive in Bloody Basin, and Lookout is about half a day from Squaw Creek Pueblo. In this series only NA7178 and NA1721 are not particularly large sites. To see these distance relationships more easily, the reader may photo-enlarge Figure 7.12 and use a compass to draw whatever circles are desired. The more ambitious may wish to put together a digitized database of these sites and apply a variety of GIS studies to it.

Near Polles Mesa and in the Middle Verde the distribution of forts/lookouts extends eastward beyond the zones of pueblo sites, implying that each subsystem had its own early warning system against threats emanating across buffer zones from Chavez Pass or Tonto Basin. Systematic examination of line-of-sight relationships, however, remains to be done in all these areas.

APPENDIX 7.4. PUEBLO IV SITES IN THE GREATER TONTO BASIN/GLOBE-MIAMI
AND Q RANCH–GRASSHOPPER AREAS.

Payson (Redman 1993); Pueblo III

Tonto Site No.: AR-03-12-	Other No.	No. of Rooms	Defensive?	Comments
04-20	NA9753; Verde 15:21 (GP)	ca. 70	yes	**Shoofly Ruin**; early PIII; compound wall
04-12		ca. 30	yes	**Risser Ranch Ruin**; late PIII; Pinto Poly
04-89	NA9766	walls	yes	**Yerba Senta Butte Fort**
04-22		ca. 20	no	**Mayfield Canyon Ruin**; middle PIII
04-106		ca. 60-80	yes	**Round Valley Ruin**; middle PIII
05-974			yes	On Gibson Peak; lookout
—	NA9756	2+	Yes	Lookout

Upper Tonto Creek

Tonto Site No.: AR-03-12-	Other No.	No. of Rooms	Defensive?	Comments
06-54	NA9584; Verde 15:30 (GP)	200	yes	**Rye Creek Ruin**; late PIII/PIV; enclosed plaza; platform mound; tower
06-705		50+		**Lower Barnhardt Ruin**; late PIII
04-408		ca. 20		**Upper Barnhardt Ruin**; late PIII
04-127		ca. 40		**Rock and Rye Ruin**; early PIII
04-685		none	yes	On Table Mountain; 10x16-m walled area; few artifacts; lookout; 4,130 ft.
06-2525	Verde 15:20 (GP)	30–50	no	**C. C. Griffin Ruin**
06-529		2	yes	**The Box**; fort; compound, entry; no date
06-528		18	yes	**Black Mountain Ruin**; fort; no date; 3,971 ft.
06-541			yes	On Cottonwood Mountain; lookout; 4,497 ft.
04-105		75+	no	**Gisela Platform Mound**; PIV
04-192		25+	yes	**Gisela Schoolhouse Platform Mounda**; PIII
04-103		35–40	yes	**Houston Pocket Ruin**; late PIII/PIV
04-804	Verde 15:6 (GP)	walls	yes	Fort on Haycox Mtn; no ceramics
—	NA9747	ca. 30+	Yes	PIV

Lower Tonto Creek

Tonto Site No.: AR-03-12-	Other No.	No. of Rooms	Defensive?	Comments
06-42	Roos. 5:7 (GP)	ca. 30		**Horse Pasture Platform Mound**; late PIII/early PIV?
06-296		80	no	**Indian Point Ruin**; late PIII/PIV; burned
06-295		ca. 50		Late PIII/PIV; some burning
06-132		36	yes	**Cline Terrace Platform Mound**; late PIII/PIV; tower; burned; massive compound wall with parapet
06-811		50		**Casa Bandolero**; late PIII/PIV
06-809		80		PIII
06-810		14		PIII
06-769		45		Late PIII/PIV
06-763		70–80	no	**Dresden Ruin**[a]; late PIII/PIV
06-714		80	no	**Oak Creek Platform Mound**[a]; PIV
06-559		?	yes	**Chalk Springs Ruin**; late PIII/early PIV; fort; west side
06-357		70–80	no	**Trinity Ruin**[b]
06-128		13+	yes	**Haystack Butte Fort**; late PIII
06-1050		80+	no	**Hamburg Ruin**[b]
06-2114		20+	yes	Fort; late PIII/PIV; compound wall and two defense walls
06-549		16+	yes	**Hackberry Basin Ruin**; late PIII/early PIV
06-1044		ca. 50		**Park Creek Platform Mound**; late PIII?
06-17		ca. 50	no	**VIV Platform Mound**[a]; PIII/PIV; burned
—		?	yes	Fort
06-581		ca. 10	yes	Fort; compound wall
06-576		20–40	yes	PIV
06-550		48	yes	**Kayler Butte**; fortfied village; PIII

[a] Partially destroyed by machine work.
[b] Very heavily disturbed by pothunting.

Eastern Tonto Basin

Tonto Site No.: AR-03-12-	Other No.	No. of Rooms	Defensive?	Comments
06-1037		ca. 25?		**Bourke's Teocalli**; late PIII/PIV
06-55		50+		**Hotel Ruin**; PIV
	U:8:47 (ASM)	66	yes	**Lower Ruin, Tonto Cliff Dwellings**; late PIII/PIV
	U:8:48 (ASM)		yes	**Upper Ruin, Tonto Cliff Dwellings**; late PIII/PIV
06-2020		20+	yes	Fort; late PIII/early PIV
06-91	U:8:39 (ASM)	3	yes	Circular compound; 2 gates; 3,314 ft.
06-86	U:8:34 (ASM)	30-40	yes	**Valentine Butte Ruin**; circular compound; 2,880 ft.; PIV?
—		14		**Las Sierras**; central plaza; late PIII

Eastern Tonto Basin, continued

Tonto Site No.: AR-03-12-	Other No.	No. of Rooms	Defensive?	Comments
06-102		ca. 25	no	**Rock Island Platform Mound**; late PIII/early PIV; compound wall
06-177	U:8:23 (ASU)	15+		**Bass Point Platform Mound**; late PIII/early PIV
06-59 06-03 &		50+		**Porter Springs**; PIII/PIV
06-744		40+		**Windy Hill Ruin**; early PIV
06-44		20-30		**Grapevine Ruin**; PIV
06-346		ca. 80	yes	**Armer Ranch Ruin**; late PIII/early PIV; 2 plazas
06-13	U:8:24 (ASU)	100+		**Schoolhouse Point**; late PIII/PIV
06-15	V:5:1 (ASU)			**Pinto Point Platform Mound**; late PIII/early PIV
06-26	V:5:4 (ASM)	15+		**Meddler Platform Mound**; late PIII/early PIV
06-25	V:5:1 (ASM)	16		**Pyramid Point Ruin**; late PIII; tower
06-96	V:5:90 (ASM)	45+27		**Griffin Wash**; late PIII
06-689		50+	yes	**Pueblo Dinero Alta**; late PIII/early PIV
06-103		100+	yes	**Tuzigoot on Salome**; late PIII/PIV
06-121		ca. 20	yes	**Thompson Mesa Ruin**; late PIII/early PIV
05-514		13	yes	Late PIII; compound wall
06-137	Roos. 6:24	36	yes	**Tucker Box Ruin**; late PIII
06-135	Roos. 6:30	62	yes	**Conner Creek Ruin**; late PIII/early PIV
06-106	U:8:530 (ASU)	34		**Armer Gulch Ruin**; late PIII/PIV; burned (Oliver 1997:29)
06-2256	U:8:591	25	no	Late PIII/early PIV?

Granite Basin/Cherry Creek/Sierra Ancha System

ASM No.	Other No.	No. of Rooms	Defensive?	Comments
V:1:26	C:1:28 (GP); 12-06-70	140-150	yes	**Granite Basin Ruin (aka Banning Wash)**; PIV; 2 enclosed plazas
—	C:2:12 (GP); 12-05-08	5+	yes	Fort; PIV
—	C:1:7 (GP)	40-50		PIII/PIV; central plaza
V:1:130-132	C:1:16 (GP)	60-75	yes	Cliff dwelling; early PIV; 1288-1331; burned
V:1:133	C:1:21 (GP)	ca. 15		Cliff dwelling; early PIV; 1292vv-1320rL; burned
V:1:166	C:1:31(GP)	ca. 30	yes	**Pottery Point Ruin**; PIV
V:1:155		ca. 12	yes	**Knife Ridge Site**; PIII
—	C:1:32 (GP)	ca. 15		PIII/PIV
—	C:1:33 (GP)	ca. 60		PIII/PIV
V:1:177	C:1:37 (GP)	30-50	yes	PIV; on large knob; great view
V:1:135	C:1:40 (GP)	20		Late PIII?; burned; tree-ring date: 1304
V:1:167	C:1:44 (GP)	15-18		Cliff dwelling; early PIV; 1310r-1330rB; burned

Granite Basin/Cherry Creek/Sierra Ancha System, continued

ASM No.	Other No.	No. of Rooms	Defensive?	Comments
—	C:1:48 (GP)	50		PIII/PIV
—	C:1:49 (GP)	30		Pueblo
—	C:1:50 (GP)	18	yes	Cliff dwelling
—	C:1:51	50		
—	C:1:54 (GP)	40	no	Pueblo
V:1:192	C:1:55 (GP); 12-05-54	30	yes	**Bronko Canyon Castle**; PIV
—	C:1:56 (GP)	60	no	Pueblo
—	C:1:57 (GP)	25	no	Pueblo
—	C:1:59	16	no	Pueblo
—	C:1:61 (GP)	75	no	Pueblo
V:1:170	C:2:4 (GP)	25		**Upper Coon Creek Cliff Dwelling**; early PIV
V:1:145		15–20		**Cock's Comb Ridge Site**; PIV
V:1:160		—	yes	**Elephant Rock Fortress**; walls; PIII
V:1:185	C:1:64?	60–80	no	PIII; plaza?
V:1:186		20–30	no	**Site AA**; PIII
V:1:195	C:1:10?	30–50		Wall on W & S; PIII
—	—	ca. 100	yes	**Coon Creek Fort** (D. Gregory, p. c.)

Late Pueblo III Sites, Lower Cherry Creek (data from ASU Site Files)

ASU No.	Other No.	Elevation (ft.)	Compound Area (m²)	No. of Rooms	Comments
V:5:13					Fort?
V:5:37			181.5	ca. 7	
V:5:44				15–20	Wall on cliff edge
V:5:43				ca. 12	
V:5:42			x	ca. 12	
V:5:28	12-06-320	2150	x		
V:5:29	12-06-253		x	60–80	Lasts into middle PIV
V:5:26				20	Vertical cliffs 3 sides
V:5:27			324	10	
V:5:12			182.3		
V:5:30			x	10–12	
V:5:20			x	30–40	
V:5:15			672		
V:5:45			x	80	
V:5:48			342–3	10–12	

Q Ranch

ASM No.	Other No.	No. of Rooms	Defensive?	Comments
P:13:13	Holb. 13:6 (GP); 12-05-245	ca. 200+	yes	**Q Ranch Ruin**; late PIII/PIV; 2 room blocks; 2 enclosed plazas; Pueblo I 90% burned
—		ca. 20	yes	**Vosburg Fort**; late PIII

Q Ranch, continued

ASM No.	Other No.	No. of Rooms	Defensive?	Comments
05-87	12-05-87	ca. 20+	yes	Late PIII/early PIV
P:13:2	Holb. 13:5 (GP)	40	no	**Antlers Site**; PIV
P:13:14		30		**Pine Springs Pueblo**; PIV; plaza
P:13:15		6	yes	Fort; PIV
—	Verde 16:2 (GP); 12-05-312	ca. 20	yes	**Potato Butte Fort**; late PIII?; compound wall
V:2:99		5	yes	Fort
V:1:32	C:2:2 (GP)	21–29	yes	**Asbestos Springs Pueblo**; PIV; plaza
V:1:33		35–50	no	**Rock House Pueblo**; PIV; plaza
V:1:34		24–37	yes	**Castle Peak Fort**; PIV
V:1:41		2	yes	Fort; square compound; PIV
V:1:74		4	yes	**Gunsight Butte Fort**
V:1:76		5	yes	Lookout
V:1:49	C:2:1 (GP)	28	yes	**Horse Canyon**; early PIV
V:1:72		25	yes	**Double Buttes Fort**; PIV
V:2:98			yes	Fort/Lookout
V:2:64		16	yes	**Willow Canyon**; early PIV

Grasshopper Region

ASM No.	Other No.	No. of Rooms	Defensive?	Comments
P:14:8	GFS-76-65; Spier 275	15	no	**Grasshopper Spring Pueblo**; late PIII; burned
P:14:24		18		**Chodistaas**; late PIII; burned
P:14:69		24		**Glennbikii**; late PIII
P:14:69		24		**Cibecue Snowflake Site**; late PIII
P:14:12		65	yes	**Hilltop Pueblo**; PIV; plaza
P:14:1		500		**Grasshopper Pueblo**; PIV; enclosed plaza; great kiva; 1300v–1373vv
P:14:71		10	yes	**Pinnacle Pueblo**; fort
P:14:273		15		PIV
—	GFS 76-162	24		PIV
V:2:79	GFS 79-18	13–15		**Double Springs Cliff Dwelling**; PIV
V:2:83		18		PIV
V:2:87	GFS 79-31	14	yes	Fort; PIV
—	GFS 81-87	11	yes	**Masada**; PIV
—	GFS 81-79	19		**Lost Pueblo**; PIV
—	GFS 81-95	16		PIV
—	GFS 81-97	20		PIV
—	GFS 81-131	16		PIV
—	GFS 82-15	15	yes	**Masada II**; PIV
—	GFS 82-16	13		PIV
—	GFS 82-38	14		PIV
P:15:13 & 15	Holb. 15:1 (GP)	ca. 100		**Cibecue Creek Ruin**; 2 stories; middle/late PIV; Spier's 267
P:14:25		45		**Red Canyon Pueblo**; PIV; plaza
V:2:13	Spier 274	140		**Blue House Pueblo**; PIV; plaza; massive wall

Grasshopper Region, continued

ASM No.	Other No.	No. of Rooms	Defensive?	Comments
V:2:5		19		**Hole Canyon Cliff Dwelling**; PIV
V:2:7		100		**Ruins Tank Pueblo**; PIV; enclosed plaza; 2–3 stories
—	GFS 89-6	25	no	**Sanrace Cliff Dwelling**; PIV
V:2:3		85	yes	**Spotted Mountain Pueblo**; PIV
V:2:12		12–20		PIV
V:2:23		19		**Salt Draw Pueblo**; PIV
V:2:49	GFS-77-202	65	yes	**Canyon Butte Pueblo**; PIV; plaza
—	GFS 863	70		**Black Mountain Pueblo**; PIV
P:14:13		150		**Brush Mountain Pueblo**; PIV
P:14:14		30		**Red Rock House**; cliff dwelling; PIV: 1342–72
P:14:15		35	yes	**Oak Creek Pueblo**; middle/late PIV
P:14:281	GFS-77-224	31		PIV; no plaza
V:2:1	C:2:8 & C:2:11 (GP)	58+ 30+		**Canyon Creek**; mid PIV: 1324–46+

The Thumb Area

Tonto Forest No.	Other No.	No. of Rooms	Defensive?	Comments
12-02-219	—	36–40	no	**Ash Mountain Ruin**; plaza

Greater Globe-Miami Area

ASM No.	Other No.	No. of Rooms	Defensive?	Comments
—	12-02-376	100+	yes	**Murphy Mesa Ruin**; late PIII/PIV
—	12-02-225	132+	no	**Wheatfields**; late PIII/PIV; compound wall; platform mound
—	Globe 1:6	25+		
—	Globe 1:5	110+		
V:9:51	Globe 1:3	65+		**Horrel Ranch Ruin**; PIV
—	Globe 1:2	19		
V:9:20		30		5 plazas, compound wall: 3,500 m²; late PIII? 4,100 ft.
V:9:35		1+	yes	Fort/Lookout
V:9:174		115–120		**Togetzoge**; PIV; compound wall; 4,470 ft.
V:9:92	Globe 2:2	15–20	yes	PIII; 3,375 ft.
V:9:91	Globe 2:3	20–25	yes	PIII; 3,250 ft.
V:9:93	Globe 2:4	30–40	yes	PIII; 3,475 ft.
V:9:68		ca. 110	yes	**Hilltop House**; late PIII; compound wall; 3,700 ft.
V:9:67		ca. 88	yes	**Bead Mountain House**; PIV; 3+ plazas; compound wall; 3,700 ft.
V:9:70		ca. 15		3,600 ft.
V:9:89		15–20		
V:9:86		25–35		
V:9:98		ca. 30		**Ramboz Ruin**; PIV; 4,500 ft.

Greater Globe-Miami Area, continued

ASM No.	Other No.	No. of Rooms	Defensive?	Comments
V:9:97		ca. 27		**Ramboz Spring Ruin**; PIV; 4,000 ft.
V:9:95		ca. 30		PIV; compound wall; 4,000 ft.
V:9:94		ca. 20		PIV; 4,000 ft.
—	Globe 2:8	25+	yes	
—	Globe 2:11	25+		Compound wall
V:9:10	Globe 6:9	12–15		**Central Heights Ruin**; late PIII/PIV; compound wall
—	Globe 6:12	20+	yes	Compound wall
V:9:11	Globe 6:8	250+	yes	**Besh-Ba-Gowah**; PIV; central plaza with roofed access corridor; 2–3 stories; burned several times
—	Globe 6:10	50+	yes	**Pinal Pueblo**; PIV; compound wall
V:9:52	Globe 6:1	225+	yes	**Gila Pueblo**; PIV; 1345r; 1385r; 3,800 ft.; burned 3 times
—	Globe 6:2	ca. 20		
—	Globe 6:4	14		
—	Globe 6:7	ca. 14		
—	Globe 6:13	25+	yes	
V:10:54		50–100		**Hayes Tank Ruin**; late PIII/PIV; adobe construction
—		130+		**The Gap No. 2**; late PIII/PIV
—		150		**Bar F Bar Ruin**; late PIII/PIV
V:10:4		75–100		**Cutter (aka Ranch Creek) Ruin**; Brandes's No. 59; late PIII/PIV

Silver Creek System (Adler 1996:260; Mills 1998; MNA and ASM site files)

MNA No.	Other No.	No. of Rooms	Defensive?	Comments
NA1715	P:11:1 (ASM)	200–250	yes	**Bailey Ruin**; late PIII/early PIV
—	Holb. 11:10 (GP)	10	yes	**Rattlesnake Point**; PIII
NA1006	P:12:2 (ASM); Spier 221	200	no	**Pindale Ruin**; 2 stories; late PIII/ PIV; 1305, 1378vv
NA1007	Holb. 12:12 (GP)	60	no	PIV; SW of Pindale Ruin; central plaza
NA1066	—	20–40	yes	**Ranger Site**; late PIII
NA1013	P:12:12 (ASM); Spier 219	60	yes	**Pottery Hill**; late PIII
NA1005	—	30–40		**Roundy Ruin (aka Bagnal Hollow Ruin)**; PIII
NA1004	—	100		**Fool Hollow Ruin**; PIII; 2 stories; compound; 3 mi. W of Showlow
—	Holb. 12:7 (GP)	?	yes	**Adair Fort**; 2 mi. NW of Showlow
NA1003	P:12:3 (ASM); Spier 217	200	yes	**Showlow Ruin**; late PIII/PIV; 3 plazas (see also Holb. 12:2 [GP])
NA1012	P:16:3 (ASM); Spier 261	300	yes	**Tundustusa**; late PIII/early PIV; combo circular and rect pueblo
—	P:16:9 (ASM)	40	no	PIII
NA1010	—	40–50		PIII; 2 stories; E side of Silver Creek
NA1011 & 4567 & 5738	P:12:6 (ASM); Spier 214	54+	yes	**Shumway Ruin**; 2 stories; late PIII/PIV (Levine survey S5)

Silver Creek System (Adler 1996:260; Mills 1998; MNA and ASM site files), continued

MNA No.	Other No.	No. of Rooms	Defensive?	Comments
NA4572	—	ca. 50–70		PIII (Levine survey S10)
NA4579	—	ca. 20–35		PIII (Levine survey S17)
NA1055 & 4568	P:12:4 (ASM); Spier 213	400		**Fourmile Ruin**; late PIII/PIV
NA4580	—	ca. 50–75		late PIII/PIV (Levine survey S18)
NA4566	Spier 212	52		late PIII/early PIV (Levine survey S4)
NA4569	P:8:1 (ASM); Spier 209	50		**Flake Ruin**; PIII/early PIV (Levine survey S7)
—	P:11:133 (ASU)	ca. 40		PIV

Carrizo Creek System

ASM No.	Hough 1907	Spier 1919	No. of Rooms	Comments
—	GFS 88–9?	264	ca. 45	**Carrizo Ruin**; L-shaped; central plaza; PIV
P:15:4			15	Late PIII/PIV (see also Holb. 15:2 [GP])
P:15:5			12–15+	PIII
P:15:6 & 7			30+	Defensive; PIII
P:15:12	GFS 88–10		20+	**Blue Springs Ruin**; late PIII/early PIV
—			ca. 45	L-shaped; Reagan's (1930) RC; PIII?

Kinishba System

ASM No.	Hough 1907	Spier 1919	No. of Rooms	Comments
		225	40	Late PIII
—	132	229	ca. 50	**Sevenmile Ruin**; central plaza; PIV
—	133	228	ca. 135	Central plaza; PIV
—	—	237	15–25	Bracket-shaped; PIII? (see NA14368)
(48-33)			110	PIII
W:5:2	136	—	100+	PIII; see also AZ D:5:2 (GP)
W:5:1		246	40	Defensive; PIII
		245	ca. 20+	Fort
V:4:10			20	Fort; late PIII
		247	ca. 35	**Kelley's Butte Fort**; PIII?
V:11:4; NA3348	134	—	800	**Kinishba Pueblo**; late PIII/PIV
—		249	ca. 30	L-shaped fort; PIII?
V:4:4		250	100+	Circular, L-shaped, & 2–3 others; middle PIV
—			?	**Silver Butte Fort** (Reagan 1930)
		251	ca. 75+	2 stories, central plaza: PIV
V:4:25		253	ca. 50	L-shaped & plaza; 2 stories; defensive; PIV
		259	50–80	Rectangular & L-shaped blocks

Point of Pines System

ASM No.	Other No.	No. of Rooms	Comments
W:10:4		30	Late PIV
W:10:8		50	Late PIII/PIV
W:10:10		150	PIV
W:10:12		12	PIV

Point of Pines System, continued

ASM No.	Other No.	No. of Rooms	Comments
W:10:47	NA15872	100	Late PIV
W:10:50	NA4428; NA15,873	800	**Point of Pines Ruin**; late PIII/PIV
W:10:52		100	PIV
—	NA15,871	15	PIII/IV
W:10:65	NA15,870	70–100	Bracket-shaped; 2 stories; PIII/PIV?
W:10:68		50+	Late PIV
W:10:75		25+	Late PIII/PIV
W:10:76		30	PIII
W:10:78			**Turkey Creek Ruin**; late PIII
W:10:81		14	Late PIV
W:10:83	NA15,874	50+	Late PIV
W:10:90		25+	Late PIV
W:10:94		15+	Late PIV
W:10:105		75+	PIV
W:11:7		20+	PIII
W:11:12		150+	Central plaza; PIV
W:9:31		25+	Late PIII/PIV
W:9:52		60+	Late PIV
W:9:64		12–15	Cliff dwelling; late PIV
W:9:131		12–15	**Ash Flat Cliff Dwelling**; late PIII/PIV

San Carlos System (see Black and Green 1995)

ASM No.	Other No.	No. of Rooms	Comments
V:11:6	Hough 22	22+	**Rice Ruin**; late PIII/PIV; platform mound? Hough 1907:39–40; Hohmann and Kelley 1988)
V:11:4B			Late PIII/PIV
V:15:93			PIII/early PIV
V:15:15	Hough 21		**San Carlos Agency Ruin**; late PIII/PIV; plat- form mound? (Bandelier 1892:412–413)
V:15:14			**Old San Carlos Ruins** (under water); PIII/PIV: "a large village of small houses" (Lange and Riley 1970:97)
V:15:5			Late PIII/PIV
—	Hough 19		PIII? (Bandelier 1892:413)
V:15:18	NA1581; NA15819	200+ 50–75	**Dewey Flat Ruins**; 5+ room blocks; PIII/PIV
V:16:6		ca. 30	
V:16:7		ca. 50	Compound
V:16:8		20–40	Compound; PIII
V:16:9		20	
V:16:10		ca. 30	Bylas Ruin; PIII
V: 16:17		12–15	PIII
V: 16:20			3 compounds, 4 room blocks; PIII
V:16:63			PIII

Sources: J. Scott Wood; Stephen Germick; ASM and ASU site files; published sources.

CHAPTER EIGHT

Warfare in Tonto Basin

Theodore J. Oliver

Prehistoric acts of warfare in the American Southwest varied greatly in scale and level of violence. Only the most extreme events, such as village-wide massacres, are likely to leave incontrovertible evidence, and then only if postabandonment processes leave the evidence intact. Identifying less obvious expressions of prehistoric warfare requires consideration of a broader range of data reflecting incidents of warfare or violence (trauma pathology and burned sites) or indications that people feared or anticipated conflict (settlement pattern shifts, fortification of sites, aggregation). In this chapter I draw on data from Middle and Late Classic period Salado settlement systems in central Arizona's Tonto Basin to present a case study. Evidence of violence is present in both time periods, with dramatic increases in burned sites and settlement pattern changes during the Late Classic (Gila phase). I argue that an environment of increasing conflict and warfare is the best explanation for the observed data.

The online Merriam-Webster dictionary (http://www.m-w.com) provides two definitions of warfare: (1) military operations between enemies and (2) struggle between competing entities. Given these definitions, it is clear that warfare can include a broad range of expressions. In the American Southwest it may have included simple raids and crop vandalism, threatening shows of force, and killing individuals from enemy settlements, as well as massacres and burned settlements. All these acts reflect the decision of a group to use violence as a political strategy, with varying scales, acceptable methods, and goals. Different manifestations of warfare left different signatures on the archaeological record and in some cases may have left little or no evidence.

Incontrovertible evidence of warfare—burned sites with the remains of the dead lying in situ—is rare in the Southwest. If this is the only acceptable evidence of warfare, then only one kind of warfare—village massacres—can be considered. Such events likely are the culmination of escalating hostilities, many of which may have left a faint mark on the archaeological record. Battles probably resulted in relatively few casualties, treatment for the wounded, and burial of the dead. In other cases the goal of warfare may have been simply to force another group to abandon its settlement by burning it down—or convincing the inhabitants it was in their best interest to leave. Simply put, most forms of warfare that occurred in the past are not likely to have left unequivocal evidence in the archaeological record; these less extreme acts almost certainly occurred with much greater frequency than village-scale massacres.

Previous researchers have identified a number of different sources of evidence of prehistoric warfare. LeBlanc (1999) groups the archaeological evidence into three main categories: (1) settlement patterns (including changes in site size, site layout, and site locations relative to other sites; line-of-sight communication; or defensive attributes of the location), (2) burned sites or structures, and (3) deaths from violent causes. Haas and Creamer's (1993) study of warfare among the Kayenta Anasazi identified similar kinds of evidence: defensive site architecture, defensible site locations, settlement pattern changes, burned rooms (especially storage rooms), and evidence of physical trauma such as parry fractures or skull injuries. Not surprisingly, similar evidence is cited by Haas (1990) in an earlier consideration of southwestern warfare. Wilcox and Haas (1994) not only focus on architectural evidence of fortification and defensive locations for sites, or for sites within multisite communities, but also identify additional sources of evidence: "weapon" artifacts, burned sites, trauma pathology, rock art imagery, and the appearance of "no-man's-lands" between site clusters. Spoerl's (1984) early discussion focuses primarily on architectural data, such as evidence of fortification and selection of defensible site locations, but mentions other evidence such as mutilated bodies or destroyed settlements. It is clear that the three categories of warfare evidence described by LeBlanc (1999) represent an emerging consensus on evidence of prehistoric southwestern warfare.

The present study examines several of these lines of evidence, focusing on evidence of violence, including trauma pathology or unusual mortuary treatments; evidence of aggregation, settlement shifts, and fortification; and evidence of burned rooms and sites. It should be stressed that alternative explanations are clearly possible for some of the lines of evidence presented and that support for the posited model of increasing

Figure 8.1. Location of study area within Arizona. Small blocks represent locations of Figures 8.2 to 8.5.

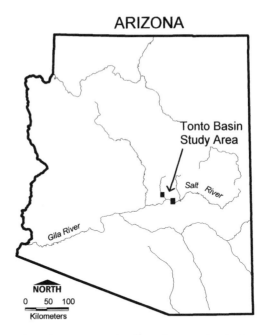

warfare during the Classic period is based on multiple lines of evidence. In the following paragraphs each line of evidence is considered in light of the Tonto Basin data to evaluate the first question posed: Did warfare occur in Tonto Basin? Where possible, the data are also examined from a diachronic perspective to address the second question: Did the incidence of warfare increase or decrease over time?

THE CASE STUDY

The current study examines multiple lines of evidence to evaluate the past occurrence of warfare in the northeastern periphery of the Hohokam culture area (Figure 8.1). Specifically, I examine data from the so-called Heartland of the Salado, primarily focusing on Tonto Basin during the Middle and Late Classic period (ca. A.D. 1250–early 1400s). This time period is traditionally divided into the Roosevelt and Gila phases (Elson and Gregory 1995); the Gila phase is marked by the dominance of later Salado polychrome ceramics, specifically Gila and Tonto Polychrome. These phases generally coincide with the Soho and Civano phases of the Hohokam core area.

The case study explores the question of warfare in Tonto Basin by examining multiple lines of evidence. Evidence of violent deaths and trauma pathology was considered by reviewing descriptive information drawn from a variety of previous research projects in Tonto Basin, including the Ash Creek project (Hohmann 1985) and the Roosevelt Rural Sites Study (Ciolek-Torrello et al. 1994) as well as the projects cited below. Quantitative analyses of room abandonment and burning are based on a data base of 62 sites and site components from which room excavation data are available, drawn from the published reports of the Roosevelt Platform Mound Study (Jacobs 1994, 1997; Lindauer 1995, 1996, 1997; Oliver 1997; Oliver and Jacobs 1997) and the Roosevelt Community Development Study (Elson et al. 1994; Elson and Swartz 1994). The sites represent components of several multisite communities, including those in the vicinity of the Meddler, Pinto Point, Bass Point, Pyramid Point, and Cline Terrace platform mounds and the Schoolhouse Point and Griffin Wash room blocks. Settlement pattern maps and data are based on a second, larger, GIS database of 143 sites or site components for which phase-level temporal assignments could be made and for which reliable information about site size is available. Information in this second data base was coded by the author, based on extant survey records and new data from the previously cited Roosevelt project reports. Data regarding the recovery of fragmentary human remains from domestic contexts are drawn solely from the Roosevelt Platform Mound Study data base, available on the World Wide Web (http://archaeology. asu.edu).

Evidence of Violent Death or Injury

Evidence of specific acts of violence against individuals is primarily in the form of mortuary data, specifically contextual or pathological indications of traumatic death by human-crafted weapons. Also included in this category is evidence of nonstandard treatment of human remains, including perimortem dismemberment, informal interment in nonmortuary contexts, and indications of possible "trophy" body parts such as limbs or skulls. Although it is generally not possible to infer whether these acts reflect actions of the community against one of its own or the results of violent conflict with an opposing group, they establish that mortal violence was considered by some members or segments of prehistoric Tonto Basin society to be a viable strategy for conflict resolution. If violence against individuals, perhaps even community members, is condoned in certain contexts, it seems reasonable that violence against opposing political groups or outsider villages might also be condoned.

Table 8.1 lists and briefly describes examples of violence against individuals from the Roosevelt projects. The examples include informal burial of dismembered but still articulated sections of bodies, burials of individuals with embedded projectile points or bone tools, and bodies recovered from the floors of burned rooms. It is clear from Table 8.1 that incidents of violence occurred during both the Roosevelt and Gila phases, but it is problematic to determine whether there is a change in frequency of such events in the two phases. Preservation of human remains in Tonto Basin is often poor, a fact compounded by the extensive vandalism that has occurred to sites (especially cemetery areas) in this area. Additionally, most of the examples in Table 8.1 are from one of several extensively excavated sites, suggesting the possibility that sampling bias is understating the occurrence of such data at smaller, less intensively excavated sites. Absence of evidence may also reflect poor preservation or limited excavation; presence of evidence demonstrates that violence occurred.

Several clear examples of violence bear further description. Perhaps most compelling is a room at a small Roosevelt phase compound excavated as part of the Roosevelt Rural Sites Study (Ciolek-Torrello et al. 1994). Feature 2 at site AZ-U:8:221 (ASM) is a typical cobble-and-adobe masonry room that burned at the time of abandonment; what is not typical are the three male skeletons lying on the floor, pinned under burned roof beams (Shelley and Ciolek-Torrello 1994:254–256). The first individual was a subadult, found with the lower portion of his torso intact and lying face down. Other skeletal elements were present but apparently had been disturbed by rodents or other scavengers. One of the cranial fragments from this individual had a well-defined depressed fracture that occurred around the time of death (Turner et al. 1994). The lack of any reflex action led Turner to suggest that the individual was either dead or unconscious when the roof collapsed. The second individual was an adult and consisted of a nearly complete skeleton, found lying face down on the floor with his arms outstretched beside his head. This nondefensive posture was also interpreted as evidence that the individual was either dead or unconscious when the roof collapsed, leaving a fallen beam

Table 8.1. Examples of Violence from Tonto Basin.

Example	Site	Roosevelt Phase	Gila Phase	Reference
Dismembered informal burial(s)	Cline Mesa, U:4:32, F14 and F29	X		Loendorf 1997a
Bodies in burned room	Grapevine Springs, U:8:221, F2	X		Shelley and Ciolek-Torrello 1994
Bodies in burned room	Schoolhouse Mesa, U:8:25	X		Lindauer 1997
Bone tool in vertebra	Schoolhouse Point, U:8:24, F390	X		Loendorf 1996
Dismembered informal burial	Uplands Unit 3, U:3:214, F5	X		Oliver 1997
Bodies in burned room	Ash Creek, U:3:96		X	Hohmann 1985
Dismembered informal burial	Cline Mesa, U:4:11, F13		X	Oliver and Jacobs 1997
Projectile point in vertebra	Cline Mesa, U:4:9		X	Regan 1997
Dismembered informal burial(s)	Cline Terrace Mound, U:4:33, F26 and F41		X	Loendorf 1997b
Dismembered informal burial(s)	Schoolhouse Point		X	Loendorf 1996
Bodies in burned room	Schoolhouse Point, U:8:24, F175		X	Lindauer 1996

lying across his back. Because only those skeletal elements with little flesh covering showed signs of burning, it appears the body was still fleshed when the roof burned. Elements from a third adult male skeleton were also recovered below the burned roof but had been disturbed by scavengers. Based on patterns of burning, Turner suggests this individual was lying on his side or face up when the room burned.

Generally similar examples of bodies or partial bodies found on the floors of burned rooms were recorded at the Schoolhouse Point site (AZ-U:8:24 [ASM]; Lindauer 1996), at a nearby compound (AZ-U:8:25 [ASM]; Lindauer 1997) and in a Gila phase room investigated during the Ash Creek project (Hohmann 1985).

Evidence of more traditional trauma pathologies cited as an indication of prehistoric warfare, such as parry fractures of the forearm bones or skull fractures or scalping marks (Haas and Creamer 1993:27), was not noted in the review of available descriptive reports. This lack may reflect the poor bone preservation that was present in many excavated inhumations (Loendorf 1996, 1997a, 1997b) or a failure on the part of the analysis to identify such evidence.

Unburied or hastily buried bodies are considered a good signature of warfare (LeBlanc 1999:85). Most individuals during the Classic period were buried in an extended supine position in formal burial pits, but a few individuals were treated much less formally. In several cases these individuals appear to have been dismembered at a time when flesh was still present and then buried informally in midden areas or shallow pits, in some cases with large rocks placed above the skeletal material (see Table 8.1 for references). The inference is based on the condition of the human remains, which generally consist of separate but articulated sections of skeletal material from a single individual. The position of the sections in relation to one another, the particular elements that remain articulated, and the occurrence of multiple, separate articulated sections of the skeleton indicate these disturbances are unlikely to have resulted from scavenger animals (Oliver 1997).

A potentially related pattern of uncertain meaning is the recovery of fragmentary human bone from rooms and other nonmortuary contexts. If these remains reflect the redeposition of materials originally in mortuary contexts as a result of erosion, bioturbation, or historic vandalism, such redeposition should occur in generally similar frequencies in all time periods. They may represent the remains of unburied battle casualties, ravaged by scavenger animals and other postabandonment processes. Alternatively, they may represent materials incidentally deposited during construction of structures atop previously occupied sites or cemeteries, or they may be the product of other disturbance factors.

These fragmentary remains were not a primary focus of the physical anthropology research conducted as part of the Roosevelt Platform Mound Study and have not been reported. Original analysis forms were examined by the author, and information including elements present, age estimates, and other analyst observations was entered into a computer data base. A total of 133 assigned specimen numbers, representing at least 149 individuals, was entered into the data base. Only specimens from undisturbed contexts associated with rooms were included (such as floors, roof fall, and undisturbed erosional deposition within rooms). Other contexts, such as plaza areas, burials, mixed strata, historic disturbances, and the modern ground surface, were excluded to minimize the impact of human remains disturbed by historic looters. To allow standardization to account for different levels of excavation, the sample was reduced further to 129 individuals recovered from screened excavation units (the remaining 20 individuals were from unscreened excavations).

Nearly 90 percent of the individuals identified from nonburial human remains (116 of 129) were recovered from Gila phase sites (Table 8.2), with the remainder from Roosevelt phase sites. To standardize for differences in excavation level, the counts of individuals are compared with the recorded screened excavation volumes from the same subset of undisturbed, domestic contexts described previously. Table 8.2 shows both standard density (individuals per cubic meter) and the inverse, the average number of cubic meters of excavation per individual. The overwhelming concentration of nonburial human remains at Gila phase sites is not a function of excavation volume, as the density of these materials is approximately five times as high at Gila phase sites as at Roosevelt phase sites. The highest Roosevelt phase site density value (U:8:458) is exceeded by all but two of the six Gila phase sites and is likely somewhat inflated because of the limited excavation volume and single specimen of nonburial human remains from that site.

Although the association with Gila phase sites is clear, it is less clear whether these individuals reflect the remains of individuals fallen in battle and left unburied. Table 8.3 summarizes the distribution of the age estimates for the 129 specimens listed in Table 8.2. Nearly 50 percent of the individuals are less than 2 years old, ranging from newborns and late-term fetuses up to 2 years of age. It seems unlikely that they represent the casualties of battle, particularly in view of the fact that subfloor infant burial was a common practice during the Gila phase (Loendorf 1996, 1997a, 1997b). Another 10 percent are either children (less than 14 years of age) or were not assigned an age estimate. The remaining 54 individuals were classified as adults.

Information about the elements present was also coded. For each individual, the presence or absence of elements was coded for the following categories derived from the original analysis forms: cranial bones, facial bones, carpals and tarsals, postcranial bones, and vertebrae. Of the 54 adults, 41 included bones from only one of these categories, and only 2 individuals included bones from three categories. No specimen included materials from more than three categories. Although count information was not consistently recorded during the original analysis of these materials, a minimum number of bone counts was recorded (based on assign-

Table 8.2. Counts and Standardized Values for the Number of Individuals Identified from Human-Remains Specimens Recovered from Screened Excavations in Undisturbed Domestic Contexts from Sites Dating to the Roosevelt and Gila Phases.

Phase Site	Count of Individuals	Excavation Volume (m³)	Density (count per m³)	m³ per individual
Roosevelt				
U:4:077	1	9.2	0.11	9.2
U:8:023	1	69.8	0.01	69.8
U:8:025	5	49.0	0.10	9.8
U:8:450 [early]	1	14.4	0.07	14.4
U:8:458	1	3.2	0.31	3.2
V:5:066	4	56.6	0.07	14.2
Roosevelt phase	13	202.2	0.06	15.6
Gila				
U:4:009	7	25.6	0.27	3.7
U:4:010	17	45.4	0.37	2.7
U:4:011	1	1.9	0.52	1.9
U:4:033	30	143.0	0.21	4.8
U:8:024	59	165.4	0.36	2.8
U:8:450 [late]	2	5.3	0.38	2.7
Gila phase	116	386.7	0.30	3.3
TOTAL	129	588.9	0.22	4.6

ing a count of 1 for each present element unless comments indicated a specific, higher count). The minimum number of bones recorded for all 54 adults was only 129, an average of about 2.4 bones per individual. Eight of the 41 adults with bones from a single category are represented by single teeth, and another 10 are represented by a single, intact phalange, metacarpal or metatarsal.

Several lines of reasoning suggest these remains do not reflect unburied casualties of a massacre. First, most are children, not adults. Second, the specific remains in question are extremely limited, consisting of very few bones from any particular individual. Third, some of the adults are represented by teeth, which may not even reflect the death of the individuals. Although some of these nonburied human remains may represent fallen battle casualties, other explanations may be more parsimonious. The concentration of these materials at Gila phase sites may simply reflect the fact that later-occupied sites are often built over the remains of earlier settlements and that prehistoric activities such as construction may have disturbed earlier cemeteries.

Table 8.3. Age Estimates for Individuals Identified from Human-Remains Specimens Recovered from Screened Excavations in Undisturbed Domestic Contests from Sites Dating to the Roosevelt and Gila Phases.

Phase ASM	Unknown	Infant (0-2 years)	Child (2-14 years)	Adult (14+)	Grand Total
Roosevelt					
U:4:077				1	1
U:8:023			1		1
U:8:025		2		3	5
U:8:450 [early]				1	1
U:8:458		1			1
V:5:066	2			2	4
Roosevelt phase	2	3	1	7	13
%	15	23	8	54	100
Gila					
U:4:009		2	1	4	7
U:4:010	2	7	1	7	17
U:4:011		1			1
U:4:033	2	5	2	21	30
U:8:024	1	42	3	13	59
U:8:450 [late]				2	2
Gila phase	5	57	7	47	116
%	4	49	6	41	100
Totals	7	60	8	54	129
%	5	47	6	42	100

Settlement Pattern Changes

Settlement pattern changes are one of the most obvious and frequently mentioned lines of evidence for southwestern warfare (LeBlanc 1999: 55). LeBlanc notes four major subcategories: (1) site configurations (including planned defensible layouts, planned growth, the abandonment of smaller sites before larger, and evidence of rapid construction), (2) sites on defensible landforms (or near a defendable water supply); (3) site distributions (evidence for clustering and "no-man's-lands"), and (4) sites located for line-of-sight communication. The present study focuses primarily on the first subcategory and does not explicitly consider the others. Within the first category, discussion centers on aggregation and the use of defensive architecture such as fortifications.

Aggregation may indicate anticipation of or fear of conflict with other groups, as reflected in changes to the layout of sites and multisite communities. A large enough site may not even require fortification if it can field more defenders than any attacker is likely to be able to raise (LeBlanc 1999:62). A dispersed community of many small sites, such as is typical in the Roosevelt phase, is difficult to defend because of the low population density and relatively large area to be protected. Relatively few potential warriors are likely to live at each dispersed compound, making these settlements vulnerable to attack by fairly small raiding parties. Assistance from neighboring compounds may arrive too late to help, because of communication failure or excessive travel time. Further, each neighboring compound is likely to be similar in size (to the one under attack) and may not be able to provide enough additional warriors to make a difference.

When a population aggregates into a smaller number of larger settlements, these difficulties are alleviated, for several reasons. First of all, the number of potential warriors at each settlement is much larger, reducing or removing the threat of small raiding parties and forcing opponents to raise considerably larger groups of warriors before any attack. Second, the geographic area being protected is much smaller, making it much easier to defend. Because most of the potential warriors presumably live in the larger, aggregated sites, problems of communication and travel are reduced. Simply stated, larger, aggregated settlements are much easier to defend, from both tactical and strategic perspectives, than are dispersed communities of smaller settlements.

Aggregation is not only defensive: it puts a larger number of people in more frequent contact with one another, creating opportunities for individuals to build political power at a larger scale than before. As an ironic result, the defensive response of aggregation may ultimately result in village leaders with the power and population to attack other communities. Aggregation puts other stresses on the new communities as well, such as requiring greater labor investment to raise sufficient food as fields farther from the settlement are brought under cultivation.

In Tonto Basin there is clear evidence of aggregation during the Middle to Late Classic period. This portion of the study draws on a data base derived from survey and excavation of 143 sites with phase-level chronological assignment. Figure 8.2 shows the Cline Terrace community settlement patterns during the Roosevelt phase, and Figure 8.3 shows the Gila phase. Twenty Roosevelt phase compounds, typically consisting of fewer than 10 rooms, evolve into 5 large Gila phase room blocks and several isolated habitations and roasting sites, with average spacing between settlements roughly tripling. The pattern is even more dramatic along the Salt River, at the other end of Tonto Basin. Figure 8.4 shows a broadly dispersed Roosevelt phase settlement pattern of 61 compounds and other sites largely abandoned by the Gila phase (Figure 8.5), leaving only a single, very large room block at Schoolhouse Point and four isolated rooms and roasting sites. Areas adjacent to the Salt River floodplain were left unoccupied after having been settled since the Preclassic period. These patterns are generally replicated across Tonto Basin within the settlement pattern data base: 98 Roosevelt phase residential sites, averaging fewer than 10 rooms each, developed into only 13 Gila phase sites, most with 26 to 60 rooms each. The median room count for Gila phase sites is higher than the room counts for all but a single outlying Roosevelt phase site. Thus the data fairly conclusively

Figure 8.2.
Roosevelt phase set-
tlement pattern in
the Tonto
Creek–Cline Mesa
area.

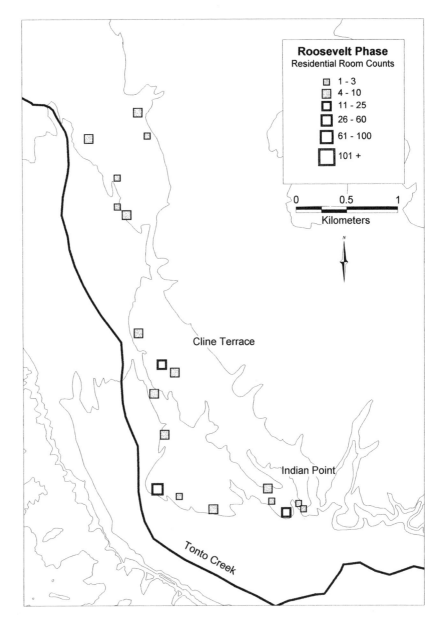

demonstrate a pattern of aggregation during the Middle to Late Classic periods in Tonto Basin, culminating in the Gila phase.

A second dimension of settlement pattern changes potentially indicative of warfare is the fortification of sites. Fortification increases the defensibility of a site through the construction of surrounding walls or the selection of geographic locations for sites that are difficult to approach (such as hilltops or caves). Like aggregation, fortification provides clear tactical and strategic advantages in warfare at the technological level of the Hohokam. Clear examples of fortification exist in Tonto Basin, including hilltop room blocks (Oliver 1997), terracing and wall augmenta-

Figure 8.3. Gila
phase settlement pat-
tern in the Tonto
Creek–Cline Mesa
area.

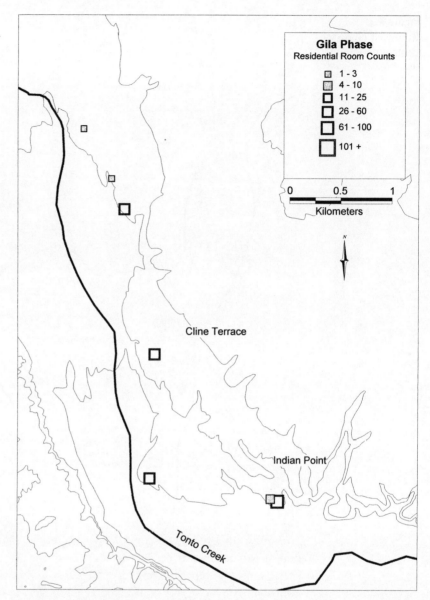

tion, cliff dwellings, sites built adjacent to steep slopes or washes, and en-
larged compound walls, such as the massive, 3-m-wide cobble-and-
adobe wall enclosing the Cline Terrace Mound (Jacobs 1997).

Less obvious forms of fortification may include the general shift to
compact room blocks from compound-style architecture. Although these
sites generally lack the large, walled plaza spaces of compounds, they
may have been easier to defend, as the exterior walls of the site are also
the walls of rooms. Room walls may have been taller than plaza walls,
were probably stronger (owing to their need to support the weight of
roof members), and provided a surface (the roof) where defenders could
stand and strike down at attackers climbing the wall. Roofs on contigu-

Figure 8.4.
Roosevelt phase set-
tlement pattern in
the Salt River–Pinto
Creek area.

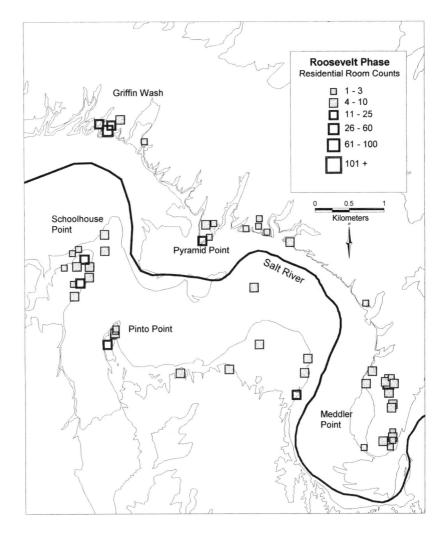

ous rooms offered a way for defenders to move rapidly from one area of
the site to another as needed. In some cases the use of cultural fill or the
selection of sloping locations for site construction may have resulted in
unusually high exterior walls or forced attackers to approach on uneven
or sloping ground.

Most Gila phase sites exhibit a compact room-block architectural layout, and the selection of this architectural style may reflect in part its advantages in defensibility. Other, more traditional forms of fortification
appear to occur in both the Roosevelt and Gila phases, however. With
the exception of the Cline Terrace platform mound site (Jacobs 1997)
and its massive defensive wall, and a Gila phase room block along Armer
Wash (AZ-U:8:530 [ASM]); Oliver 1997) with its substantial, double-
course walls, Gila phase settlements do not appear to have invested substantial amounts of labor in purely defensive architecture.

It appears that at least some groups feared the possibility of warfare
enough to invest labor in the construction of fortifications or the reloca-

Figure 8.5. Gila phase settlement pattern in the Salt River–Pinto Creek area.

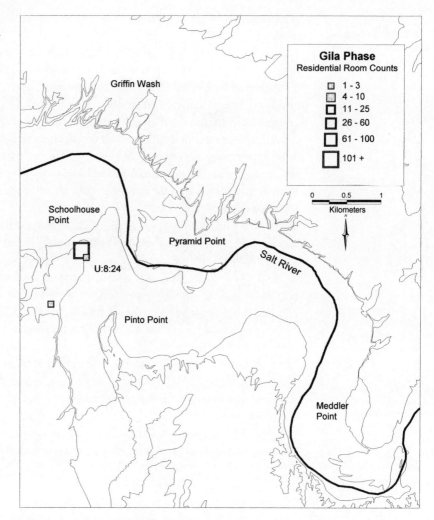

tion of sites to defensible settings such as hilltops. Sites located on hilltops or similar landforms incur additional labor costs because of the increased effort needed to haul water and other supplies to a remote location. This supports the notion that warfare was at least a concern of people in Tonto Basin during the Classic period. Whether or not this concern increased or decreased over time is less clear, in part because of the possibility that compact room blocks may have offered their own defensive advantages and reduced the need for more traditional and labor-intensive forms of fortification.

Burned Rooms

Burned rooms are the final line of evidence identified by LeBlanc (1999: 74). This chapter focuses not only on burned rooms but also on other aspects of abandonment patterns, specifically rooms with large de facto assemblages (Schiffer 1987). In this respect, two main assumptions are made.

The first assumption is that burning cobble-and-adobe masonry structures was a difficult process, unlikely to occur unintentionally. This view is supported by a consideration of the materials used (cobbles and adobe, and roof beams encased in adobe), which provide little in the way of combustible materials. Even the combustible roof materials appear to have been encased in adobe, which constrains the supply of oxygen and inhibits ignition or continued burning. The interpretation that adobe structures such as pueblo-like room blocks or pithouses are difficult to burn is supported by ethnographic data (Voth 1905) and experimental studies (Glennie and Lipe 1984; Wilshusen 1986). LeBlanc (1999:75) raises two important implications of these observations: accidental fires should not be very common, and they should occur in a generally random pattern over time, across a region, or within a site.

A secondary assumption is that abandonment of structures along with largely complete artifact assemblages is likely to indicate either unplanned abandonment or abandonment before a long-distance move. This is based on ideas first presented by Stevenson (1982) based on his research in the Yukon on historic mining camps, ideas that have in turn been embraced by southwestern researchers (Schlanger and Wilshusen 1993; Lightfoot 1993). If burning is also associated and there is little indication of erosional filling of rooms before burning, it is likely abandonment and burning occurred within a short period of time. A lack of evidence of postabandonment scavenging of useful artifacts may indicate that the burning occurred very shortly, possibly immediately, after abandonment. As it is considered unlikely that rooms or settlements burned unintentionally, either the inhabitants or outsiders must be responsible for the burning.

Although it is generally not possible to determine who may have caused the burning of a site, it may not be that relevant. In a social setting where warfare is occurring, it may not be important whether a victorious group burned a site or whether the inhabitants were motivated to burn it themselves as they left.

A data base of 62 Roosevelt and Gila phase sites or site components with room excavations was compiled, based on published data from the various Roosevelt projects (Table 8.4), to study patterns of room and site abandonment. Sixty-two Roosevelt and Gila phase sites are represented, each with data from 1 to 35 rooms, for a total of 345 rooms. For each site, the total number of excavated rooms and the total number of pottery vessels in place was recorded, as was the count of rooms that burned around the time of abandonment. These variables are used to calculate two basic measures: the average number of in-place vessels per excavated room (vessels per room) at each site and the proportion of rooms at each site that showed evidence of burning at or near abandonment (burned-

Table 8.4. Room Abandonment Data, by Site.

ASM	Phase	Tested Rooms	Burned Rooms	No. of In-Place Vessels	Vessels per Room	% Burned
U:3:121	Roosevelt	2	1	2	1.0	0.50
U:3:128	Roosevelt	4	2	9	2.3	0.50
U:3:128 [Late]	Gila	2	2	13	6.5	1.00
U:3:137	Roosevelt	1	0	4	4.0	0.00
U:3:140	Roosevelt	1	1	4	4.0	1.00
U:3:198	Roosevelt	3	3	13	4.3	1.00
U:3:199	Roosevelt	3	3	10	3.3	1.00
U:4:007	Roosevelt	6	2	6	1.0	0.33
U:4:008	Roosevelt	2	2	3	1.5	1.00
U:4:009	Gila	12	11	50	4.2	0.92
U:4:010	Gila	22	19	166	7.5	0.86
U:4:011	Roosevelt	4	0	0	0.0	0.00
U:4:012	Roosevelt	3	0	0	0.0	0.00
U:4:029	Roosevelt	4	3	7	1.8	0.75
U:4:032	Roosevelt	1	1	0	0.0	1.00
U:4:033	Gila	33	22	179	5.4	0.67
U:4:052	Roosevelt	1	0	0	0.0	0.00
U:4:060	Roosevelt	2	2	4	2.0	1.00
U:4:075	Roosevelt	2	1	0	0.0	0.50
U:4:077	Roosevelt	4	3	3	0.8	0.75
U:8:023	Roosevelt	19	5	28	1.5	0.26
U:8:024	Gila	35	11	187	5.3	0.31
U:8:025	Roosevelt	12	7	19	1.6	0.58
U:8:159	Roosevelt	4	1	10	2.5	0.25
U:8:291	Roosevelt	2	0	0	0.0	0.00
U:8:304	Roosevelt	3	0	1	0.3	0.00
U:8:318	Roosevelt	1	0	2	2.0	0.00
U:8:385	Roosevelt	3	0	1	0.3	0.00
U:8:450	Roosevelt	4	1	1	0.3	0.25
U:8:450 [Late]	Gila	2	2	15	7.5	1.00
U:8:451	Roosevelt	3	1	3	1.0	0.33
U:8:452	Roosevelt	1	0	1	1.0	0.00
U:8:454	Roosevelt	9	1	16	1.8	0.11
U:8:456	Roosevelt	2	0	1	0.5	0.00
U:8:458	Roosevelt	1	1	0	0.0	1.00
U:8:530	Gila	6	6	38	6.3	1.00
V:5:001.1	Roosevelt	1	1	0	0.0	1.00

Table 8.4. Room Abandonment Data, by Site, continued.

ASM	Phase	Tested Rooms	Burned Rooms	No. of In-Place Vessels	Vessels per Room	% Burned
V:5:001.1	Roosevelt	17	0	11	0.6	0.00
V:5:001.4	Roosevelt	1	0	0	0.0	0.00
V:5:001.3	Roosevelt	1	0	0	0.0	0.00
V:5:004.1	Roosevelt	2	0	0	0.0	0.00
V:5:004.2	Roosevelt	5	0	0	0.0	0.00
V:5:004.4	Roosevelt	2	0	0	0.0	0.00
V:5:004.7	Roosevelt	3	3	16	5.3	1.00
V:5:066	Roosevelt	8	2	11	1.4	0.25
V:5:076	Roosevelt	10	2	4	0.4	0.20
V:5:090a	Roosevelt	18	13	89	4.9	0.72
V:5:090b	Roosevelt	9	0	0	0.0	0.00
V:5:091	Roosevelt	1	1	0	0.0	1.00
V:5:096	Roosevelt	1	0	0	0.0	0.00
V:5:100	Roosevelt	1	0	0	0.0	0.00
V:5:106	Roosevelt	3	0	27	9.0	0.00
V:5:112	Roosevelt	9	2	11	1.2	0.22
V:5:119	Roosevelt	3	1	2	0.7	0.33
V:5:121	Roosevelt	5	3	17	3.4	0.60
V:5:128	Roosevelt	9	3	67	7.4	0.33
V:5:130	Roosevelt	5	0	9	1.8	0.00
V:5:137	Roosevelt	2	1	1	0.5	0.50
V:5:138	Roosevelt	3	1	11	3.7	0.33
V:5:139	Roosevelt	3	2	8	2.7	0.67
V:5:141	Roosevelt	1	0	0	0.0	0.00
TOTAL		345	151	1,082	3.1	0.44

room proportion). The vessel-per-room ratio is calculated by dividing the total number of in-place vessels from rooms by the total number of excavated rooms for each site, and it ranges from 0 to about 9.0. Vessel-per-room is used as a simple proxy to measure the presence and extent of de facto assemblages.

A total of 1,082 pots described as in-place vessels was recovered from the 345 rooms in the data base, or an average vessel-per-room score of about 3.14. Only 17 of the 62 site components have higher scores, indicating that most of the rooms with large numbers of in-place vessels are located in relatively few sites. A single site with a relatively small sample size (3 rooms) exhibited an average of 9.0 vessels per room; other, more extensively sampled sites had vessel-per-room scores ranging from 5.4 to

Figure 8.6. Average
number of in-place
vessels per excavated
room at sites dating
to the Roosevelt and
Gila phases.

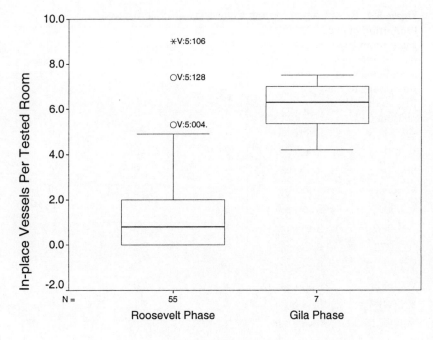

Excavated Sites

7.5. Rooms at 18 of the 62 site components did not contain any in-place vessels. These data suggest that there is considerable variability in the way different sites were abandoned; some sites were apparently largely cleared of in-use vessels (and presumably other objects), whereas others were abandoned with large numbers of useful vessels left where they were last stored or used.

Figure 8.6 shows that there is strong temporal patterning related to abandonment, at least as indicated by the vessel-per-room proxy measurement. The box plot compares the vessel-per-room scores for sites based on the temporal phase they have been assigned. High vessel-per-room scores are much more common in the Gila phase than in the Roosevelt phase. The median score for Gila phase sites (6.12) is four times as large as the median score for Roosevelt phase sites (1.50). The lowest-scoring Gila phase site, with only 4.2 vessels per room, has a higher score than all but 5 of the 55 Roosevelt phase sites. The presence of outlier values for several Roosevelt phase sites indicates that some earlier sites were abandoned in a similar manner to the Gila phase sites, but it is clear that Gila phase sites were consistently abandoned with much larger de facto assemblages than those typically seen in earlier sites.

The second aspect of abandonment to be considered is the occurrence of burning near the time of abandonment. Evidence of burning recorded during excavation includes the presence of ash lensing on the floor, oxidation of floor and wall surfaces, thermal deformation or fracturing of artifacts, burned artifacts, burned roof materials, and oxidized roof daub. Burning is generally assumed to have occurred near the time of

Figure 8.7.
Proportion of exca-
vated rooms that
burned at or near
abandonment at
sites dating to the
Roosevelt and Gila
phases.

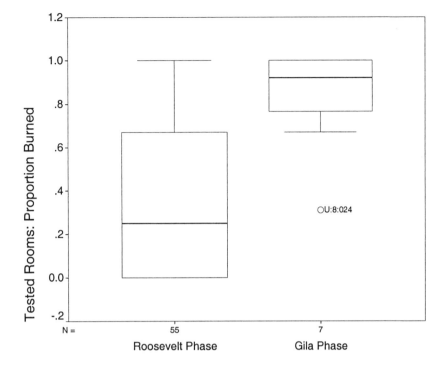

abandonment if there is little sign of wind- or waterborne silts between
the floor and burned fill deposits. This question was addressed by calcu-
lating the proportion of tested rooms at each site showing evidence of
burning at around the time of abandonment, resulting in a "percentage
burned" score for each site. Not surprisingly, there is considerable variability in the data set, with individual site proportions ranging from 0 to
1; the average for the entire data set is about 44 percent. Twenty-two of
the 62 sites did not contain any burned rooms among those tested, and
13 did not contain any unburned rooms (however, all but 1 of these had
3 or fewer tested rooms). When we consider only sites with at least 10
tested rooms, the range is nearly as wide, extending from 0 to 0.92. As
shown with the vessel-per-room data, it is clear that there are substantial
differences concerning the burning of settlements at the time of abandonment: no rooms were burned at many sites, whereas nearly all rooms
were burned at others.

The incidence of burned rooms also shows strong temporal patterning
(Figure 8.7). The median proportion of tested rooms with evidence of
burning was 82 percent at Gila phase sites but only 36 percent at Roosevelt phase sites. A single Gila phase site is an outlier, with only about 31
percent burned rooms; at least two-thirds (67 percent) of tested rooms
were burned at all other Gila phase sites. More than half the Roosevelt
phase sites exhibited evidence of burning in less than 25 percent of excavated rooms. Although a few Roosevelt phase sites have high proportions of burned rooms, the general trends for the two phases are quite
different. As seen with the vessel-per-room scores, these proportions sug-

gest that similar events (burning of settlements) occurred during both Roosevelt and Gila phases but may have been dramatically more common during the later time period.

Only rarely is there compelling evidence that a settlement burned as a single event. Site AZ U:4:7 (ASM) is one such example (Oliver and Jacobs 1997). This site is an unusually large Roosevelt phase compound with relatively few rooms located in an architecturally elaborated courtyard and with an unusually large pithouse incorporated into its central plaza. Excavations revealed a ramada-like structure along one wall filled with burned and even vitrified corn kernels, many of which had fused together. The condition of this corn was exceptional; it was not seen at other sites during the project. Corn in the same condition was also recovered from pits in the architecturally elaborated courtyard and adhered to a partial vessel interred with a comparatively shallow burial, suggesting that all three events (burning of corn in the ramada and in pits in the courtyard, and the burial of an individual) were part of a single episode. Similarly, refittable pieces of a Tonto Polychrome effigy vessel, an object generally assumed (on the basis of its rareness) to have been ritually important, were recovered from three burned rooms adjacent to a courtyard at site AZ U:4:10 (ASM).

It is unusual to find such evidence of synchronicity, however. Other sites with a high proportion of burned rooms may also have been burned in a single event. If the high percentage is a reflection of a series of smaller burning events, evidence of the remodeling of burned rooms or the construction of new rooms should be present. Similar patterns of de facto refuse across burned rooms may also suggest a single burning event: if the burnings resulted from multiple events, useful objects would probably be collected and reused, or at least disturbed, in rooms that had burned earlier in the sequence. In short, homogeneity of room abandonment is generally interpreted as an indication that the site was abandoned as part of a single event or short-term chain of events.

It has been shown that Gila phase sites are more commonly abandoned with large de facto assemblages and that rooms at Gila phase sites are much more likely to be burned. Figure 8.8 compares vessel-per-room scores and burned-room proportion scores. The Gila phase sites are clearly clustered in the upper right portion of the plot whereas the Roosevelt phase sites show a much wider range of variation along both axes. Of particular note are the Roosevelt phase sites showing high burning percentages. Unlike the Gila phase burned sites, which also have relatively high vessel-per-room scores, a full range of vessel-per-room scores is associated with burned Roosevelt phase sites. This difference suggests additional variability in how and why burned sites were abandoned in the two time periods, variability that is not explained by this analysis.

If the burning of rooms with extensive de facto assemblages is an indication of warfare, then the data suggest that it occurred in both the

Figure 8.8. Average number of in-place vessels per excavated room and proportion of excavated rooms that burned at or near abandonment at sites dating to the Roosevelt and Gila phases.

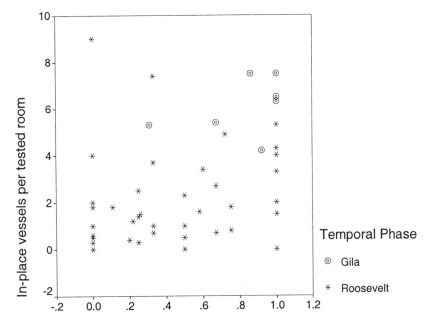

Roosevelt and Gila phases but apparently increased and was much more common during the Gila phase.

CONCLUSIONS

This case study of warfare examined several lines of evidence. Direct pathological and contextual evidence of mortal violence in Salado society indicates that violence was acceptable in some contexts. Examples of site fortification, coupled with a clear pattern of aggregation from the Roosevelt to Gila phases, suggest that the occupants of many settlements may have anticipated or feared warfare with other villages or groups. Sharply different patterns of site and room abandonment were documented for the two phases, suggesting that conflict and burned settlements were increasingly common near the end of the Classic period. The incidence of fragmentary human remains from nonmortuary, domestic-only contexts also rises during the Gila phase but may not be very compelling evidence of warfare. The Tonto Basin data support, to varying degrees, each line of evidence cited as a potential indicator of prehistoric warfare. Although none of the lines of evidence incontrovertibly demonstrates the past occurrence of warfare, taken together they provide a strong circumstantial case for this interpretation. This case is particularly strong for the Gila phase, in which a high frequency of burned rooms with large de facto assemblages was observed. It is particularly telling that during this phase, people were moving to fewer, larger, and probably more defensible sites. Although this pattern may indicate that people anticipated warfare during the Gila phase, it appears that ultimately nearly all communities succumbed to conflict or left Tonto Basin by the middle of the fifteenth century.

Alternative explanations for burned sites such as ritual abandonment (of rooms occupied by the sick or dying or used by those accused of witchcraft) focus on scenarios that would likely entail single rooms or groups of rooms, not entire sites. Even if we consider the "ritual" abandonment of whole settlements, the primary difference between this explanation and the warfare explanation is simply who made the decision to abandon a settlement. Ritual abandonment implies a decision reached by the inhabitants of a site, whereas abandonment or burning due to warfare reflects a decision forced by outside groups through violence or threat of violence. A period of increasing stress due to conflict and warfare would almost certainly be a factor in a group decision to abandon a settlement. It would also likely affect other explanations for violence, such as sanctions resulting from witchcraft accusations, which are prone to increase during times of stress. In other words, alternative explanations for the Tonto Basin data presented in this chapter such as ritual abandonment and witchcraft accusations are not mutually exclusive with a model of warfare and intersite conflict and in fact may be correlated with increased conflict.

The warfare hypothesis provides a logical explanation for burning sites: it is a strategy designed to force the abandonment of the settlement and the relocation of the people who lived there. Alternative explanations for burned rooms and settlements such as ritual abandonment do not provide logical reasons why people chose to burn rooms and settlements. They do not address obvious differences in making a decision to burn an isolated structure and making a decision to burn a room surrounded on all sides and sharing walls with other occupied rooms. These explanations do not explain why there is so much variation in the evidence across time and space. This is not to argue that ritualized structure burnings and witchcraft accusations did not occur but is simply to say that they are not the best explanation for all the available data for the Salado of Tonto Basin.

It is argued here that the most parsimonious explanation for the data presented is that occasional acts of war occurring during the Roosevelt phase (and probably earlier) became much more intense during the Gila phase, ultimately driving a basinwide pattern of community aggregation. Such warfare may be a causal factor in the regional abandonment of Tonto Basin by sedentary groups during the fifteenth century.

If the warfare interpretation is accepted for the Salado area, major questions remain unanswered: Who were the victors? If there was an outside, conquering group, why did it not reoccupy Salado sites or construct new settlements? The absence of pre-Apache, post-Salado sites suggests that conflict was internal to Tonto Basin, perhaps occurring between multisite communities in different areas of the basin. If so, it does not appear that a single dominant community emerged: no Gila phase settlement clearly postdates others, and nearly all Gila phase sites experienced a similar pattern of abandonment.

CHAPTER NINE

Conflict and Exchange among the Salado of Tonto Basin

Warfare Motivation or Alleviation?

Arleyn W. Simon and Dennis C. Gosser

Southwestern prehistory was punctuated by episodes of population movement and associated readjustment that produced strife and social change in various forms (Adams 1991; Martin and Plog 1973; Morris 1970; Upham 1982). Strong physical and circumstantial evidence of violence and conflict has been documented at many prehistoric southwestern settlements (LeBlanc 1999; Rice 1998a; Turner and Turner 1999). Nevertheless, explanations of the motivations for conflict and warfare, such as disputes over access to land and resources, are often drawn from ethnographic analogy rather than demonstrated from archaeological material evidence.

In this chapter we examine the role of exchange in provoking or redressing social tensions leading to warfare (Wolf 1982; Ferguson 1997:334–336; Naroll 1966; Otterbein 1970, 2000). The intersite distributions of obsidian, turquoise, shell, and intrusive and local ceramics at Salado platform mound sites in central Arizona's Tonto Basin are examined as a case in point: competition for these items is symptomatic of competition in the wider arenas of access to and control of both supporters and subsistence-related resources. The distributions of artifacts, especially rare and precious items as well as decorated ceramics, are compared to test whether the various platform mound communities shared access or whether access to these items was restricted or preferential. These items are often intrusive, brought in from adjacent areas, indicating either travel for direct procurement or the use of social networks for obtaining trade items.

Multiple lines of evidence demonstrate unequal distributions of these artifacts and provide compelling support for a schism between the major platform mound communities at opposite ends of Tonto Basin (Figure 9.1). Competition, as expressed in uneven distributions of fine goods and decorated ceramics, initially promoted the development of these multivillage communities but then exceeded the sociopolitical mechanisms that bound them together (Ferguson 1997:334–336; Otterbein 1970, 2000; Keeley 1996:113–116). The evidence supports the hypothesis that competition among platform mounds led to conflict and contributed to the final dissolution and dispersal of the allied settlements, corroborating the physical evidence of strife and related burning of villages (documented by Oliver this volume; Turner and Turner 1999:257–263, 291–293).

THEORETICAL BACKGROUND

The role of exchange in prehistoric social developments of the desert Southwest has been hotly debated in recent decades. Exchange of goods has several aspects that are intertwined in community and regional relationships: economic, ideological, and political (Wolf 1982:ix–x; Otterbein 1970, 2000:799–800; Ferguson 1997:337–340). We assert that all aspects are equally important and essentially inseparable but that recent archaeological discussions have greatly emphasized the first two, giving only narrow consideration to the last. In nonhierarchical societies political aspects of social organization permeate interactions within and among communities (Ferguson 1997:337–340; Otterbein 1970; Wolf 1982: 386–387). Further economic and ideological models in isolation do not fully explain exchange-related behaviors and patterned distributions of goods. When political analysis of exchange is included in interpretations of the archaeological record (Ferguson 1997:341; LeBlanc 1999:307–309: Otterbein 2000:801), it is possible to more fully explore past social processes and organizational changes.

A number of researchers have contributed to the economic-based managerial model,[1] proposing that the platform mounds were residences of elites who actively managed some combination of long-distance exchange, craft production, massing and redistribution of subsistence-related goods, and allocation of irrigation water. The managerial model assumed a high degree of centralized complexity through which the elites restricted access to fine goods and craft items. Recent excavations (Rice 1998a, 1998b), however, have not found evidence of massed surplus

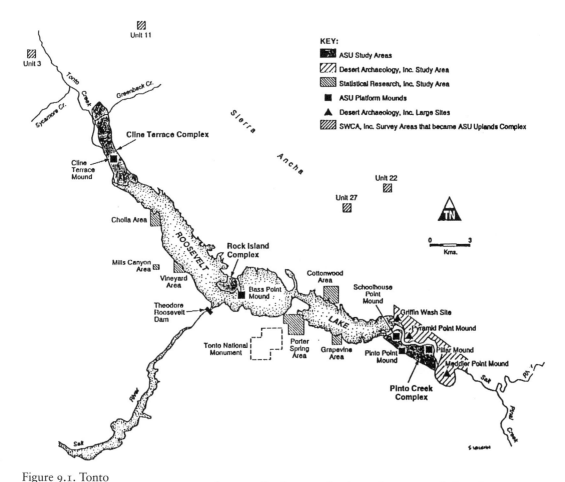

Figure 9.1. Tonto Basin with locations of the Roosevelt Archaeology Projects. The Cline Terrace Mound at the west end and the Schoolhouse Point Mound at the east end are Gila phase platform mounds and were investigated as part of the ASU Roosevelt Platform Mound Study. The Bass Point Mound, Pinto Point Mound, Pillar Mound, Pyramid Point Mound, and Meddler Mound are Roosevelt phase; the last two are part of Desert Archaeology's Roosevelt Community Development Study.

property and centralized control of production and distribution, thus casting doubt on the economic model of a managerial elite who commanded trade on a regional scale from centralized redistribution centers.

Ideological interpretations of Classic period iconography, including ceramic design, by Adams (1991) and Crown (1994) provide explanatory frameworks for the religious cults that developed and flourished throughout much of the Southwest. Some fine goods, including locally produced and exchanged items as well as Salado polychrome ceramics, were likely used in religious rites, but these are not exclusively found in ritual contexts. Indeed, Crown (1994) notes that Salado polychromes were recovered from a wide range of domestic and other contexts. Religious movements were undoubtedly major components of prehistoric life, participated in by many settlements, but the ideological framework does not fully explain the social development and dynamics of platform mound communities, including warfare. Rather, the presence and intensity of competition and conflict likely contributed to the adoption of such religious cults (LeBlanc 1999:285, 301–302).

Our perspective focuses on the political aspect but incorporates some elements of both economic and ideological explanations. Our emphasis is on social processes and organizational changes. It is generally recognized that prestige and status-marking items, preciosities, circulate within and between kin-based societies along various sociopolitical vectors (Wolf 1982:390–391; Ferguson 1997:335–337). Often the driving force behind the distribution of prestige goods is a network of aggrandizing individuals who attempt to maintain and elaborate their social status and political control (Clark and Blake 1994; Ferguson 1997; Keeley 1996; Otterbein 2000; Wolf 1982). Political and economic aspects of exchange are consistent with the development of complexity, the role of elites, and the mechanisms they use to maintain their privileges and authority (e.g., Sahlins 1968; Service 1962; Adams 1966; Johnson 1989; Redman 1978).

Nevertheless, exchange may be an integral part of competition and social process without centralization of authority and hierarchical structure (Swartz et al. 1966:6; Rice 1998a, 1998b, 2000). It is our hypothesis that exchange items are evidence of social networks operative in the platform mound communities and that these items served ritual and social roles signifying identity and support of organizational networks (Rice et al. 1998; Simon et al. 1997; Simon and Ravesloot 1995). Accordingly, masses of surplus materials are not expected as in the economic-based managerial model. Further, fine goods and decorated pottery are symbols not only of shared participation in religious movements but also of kin-based and other social obligations among members of the community (Simon and Ravesloot 1995; Simon and Jacobs 2000; Rice et al. 1992).

As stressed by Bradley (1996:116–133), gift-giving intimates obligations and is maintained by a constant flow of goods through the social system (Maus 1967). Success is accomplished by giving and invoking debts of reciprocity among the recipients, resulting in social inequity (Gosden 1989:361). Participation in social networks, kin-based and otherwise, holds communities together with mutually attendant obligations (Zedeño 1998). Boundaries are fluid; they expand and contract with participation and realign in response to shifts in support and opposition (Swartz et al. 1966:247–250, 252). The local descent group is the most stable of these networks, focused on localized economic activities (Swartz et al. 1966:252–253; Tuden 1966) but affected by large-scale disputes stemming from competition for land and supporters among people sharing common territory.

Whereas the managerial model expects rational economic behavior and the ideological model expects shared religious belief to enhance cooperation, the archaeological record indicates that platform mound communities were strongly competitive with respect to exchange and influence of supporters and that this competition coincides with conflict (Oliver this volume, Turner and Turner 1999:257–263, 291–293). Further, there is no subsistence-related reason to expect active cooperation between settlements at opposite ends of the basin on different drainages (Rice 1998b; Spielmann 1998).

Through exchange-related activities, platform mound complexes likely recruited additional members as supporters to balance the growth of neighboring settlements. The distributions of trade items on an intraregional and interregional scale identifies past exchange networks, associated alliances, and territories among these prehistoric communities. Thus trade items are physical evidence of these past social networks and territories. Possession and exchange of these items functioned to signify participation in the social sphere of a particular extended platform mound community. Trade items were not amassed or highly restricted in an economic sense, nor were they exclusively used in religious ceremony. Among Tonto Basin platform mound communities, trade items and decorated ceramics were found in varied contexts, signifying the affiliation of members with the community at large as well as social and kin-based networks (Simon and Ravesloot 1995; Simon 1998).

PLATFORM MOUND COMMUNITIES

At the localized level, platform mound communities are multivillage alliances in which the mound is the locus of communal integrative activities (Lindauer and Bliss 1997; Rice 1998a, 1998b; Simon and Jacobs 2000), supported by large residential secondary villages and buffering tertiary villages. The privileged few who resided at the platform mounds are likely the founding residents and define participation in calendrical rites as well as access to land and resources. The inhabitants of the secondary villages provide the labor and resources necessary for the successful completion of rituals and attendant feasting. At the tertiary villages immigrant or other ethnic groups are permitted to participate in community activities and gain access to resources in exchange for defense against outsiders.

When the tiers of the settlement system are allied, the local social network prospers, but this balance is tenuous at best (Rice 1998a; Simon and Jacobs 2000). The secondary and tertiary villages must be kept at appropriate physical and social distances for the primary village to maintain its control over participation in ritual activities and access to resources. If these villages become too strong, they will seize the decision-making power of the primary village. If the primary village becomes too powerful, the alliance system will collapse.

On a larger scale, alliances among platform mound communities ensure a level of cooperation and mutual coexistence: that is, protection from conflict (Simon and Jacobs 2000). These alliances may be extended on an even larger scale to encompass much of the region and neighboring areas (Upham 1982; LeBlanc 1999). Alliances are affirmed through the exchange of goods and social favors.

An equal distribution of goods, or one that follows a simple linear fall-off explainable by distance from source, would indicate that all settlements have equal access to goods. Those villages that have mutual ac-

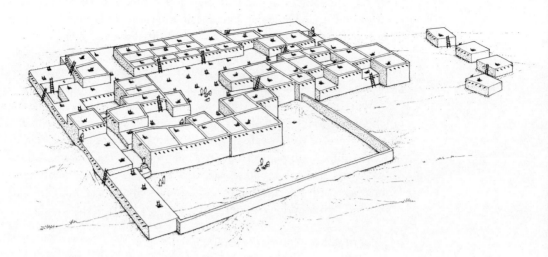

Figure 9.2. The Schoolhouse Point Mound (AZ U:8:24/13a) (artist's reconstruction), looking southwest. The central plaza is made of the roofs of storage rooms and is surrounded by compact blocks of contiguous residential rooms. A walled ground-level plaza adjoins the north side of the mound.

cess to certain goods not found in similar proportions among other contemporaneous villages are evidence of selective distributional networks and competitive opposition (Rice 1998a, this volume; Rice et al. 1998; Simon et al. 1997).

Many exchange items in Tonto Basin were likely procured through long-distance exchange, but these items were recovered in small frequencies from a variety of site types and contexts. The Roosevelt phase (A.D. 1280–1320) includes several small-scale platform mound communities dispersed throughout Tonto Basin (Figure 9.1), including several on either side of the Salt River at the eastern end (Heidke and Stark 1995). The Schoolhouse Point Mound (Lindauer 1996) was relatively small during this phase but included at least one large ceremonial room with assemblages of shell trumpets, elongated stone batons, turquoise pendants, and traces of unusual plants such as tobacco. The Bass Point Mound (Lindauer 1995), overlooking the confluence of Tonto Creek and the Salt River at the center of the basin, had collections of manuports, unusual stones, among other fine goods, located in ceremonial structures on top of the platform mound. At the western end, sites such as U:4:7 (Oliver and Jacobs 1997) exhibited ceremonial structures indicating extended community organizations as well.

By the Gila phase (A.D. 1320–1450), many of the smaller sites had been abandoned and two large aggregated platform mound communities (Figure 9.1), separated by 25 km, had developed: the Schoolhouse Point complex located along the Salt River at the east end and the Cline Terrace complex located at the west end. A few smaller mound complexes were present in the uplands.

The Schoolhouse Point Mound (Figure 9.2) represents the aggregation of the earlier multisite settlement pattern into a single mounded settle-

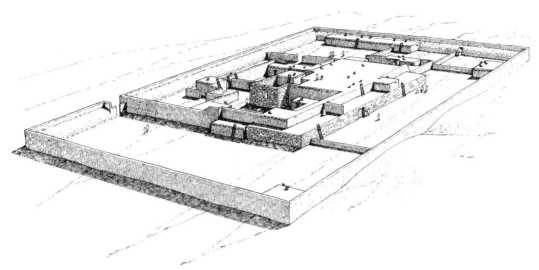

Figure 9.3. The Cline Terrace Mound (AZ U:4:33/132) (artist's reconstruction), looking south. The high boundary wall with interior berm and raised walkway surrounds the mound on all sides, enclosing large areas of public space. The unroofed tower doorway faces the secluded interior plaza, the focus of ceremonial activities.

ment (Lindauer 2000; Lindauer 1996). The resident population of the mound was sufficient to have constructed the architecture. The architecture exhibits the contiguous room blocks and inward-facing design of many puebloan sites.

In contrast, the Cline Terrace Mound (Jacobs 1997) (Figure 9.3) is primarily a structure of public architecture, with few residential rooms, surrounded by large public plazas. This mound has specialized storage rooms containing ceremonial objects surrounding a unique tower that faces an enclosed ceremonial plaza. There were several large residential sites near the Cline Terrace Mound that would have supplied the labor necessary to construct the platform mound and boundary wall.

METHOD AND RESULTS

To address the question whether the Tonto Basin platform mound communities shared equally in access to fine goods and decorated pottery, we examined the distributions of obsidian, turquoise and malachite, shell, and ceramics. As a control, the distributions of these artifacts were compared to normal fall-off curves to determine whether distance from source was solely responsible for different quantities and proportions. Uneven distributions of these classes of artifacts, beyond that expected due to distance from source, are evidence of differing procurement networks and related social connections. LeBlanc (1999) demonstrates that exchange networks may bypass villages that are not part of the same alliance, resulting in uneven distributions of goods.

The following sections summarize results of specialist studies of Gila phase site assemblages which address the particular question whether the platform mound communities at either end of Tonto Basin (Cline Terrace

Figure 9.4. Obsidian source locations, as identified by Shackley (1995, 1988) for the Roosevelt Platform Mound Study collection relative to the Tonto Basin study area.

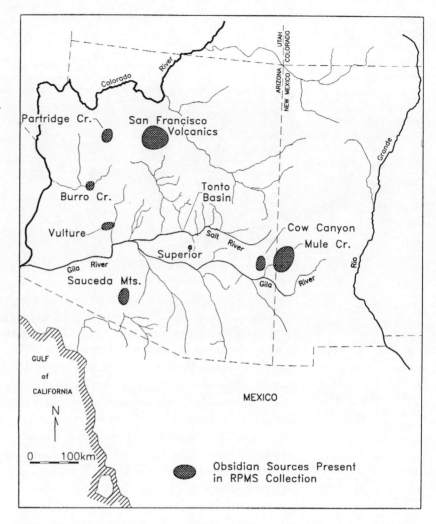

on the west and Schoolhouse Point on the east) had dissimilar trade networks.

OBSIDIAN

There is an increase in the use of obsidian artifacts in the Classic period (Figure 9.4; Shackley 1988, 1995, 1998; Simon et al. 1997); higher densities of obsidian artifacts were recovered in Gila phase contexts than in earlier Roosevelt phase contexts. Rice (1997a) compared proportions of obsidian recovered from burned-floor contexts and found that obsidian was more abundant during the later Gila phase occupations. Further, results of an XRF provenance study of obsidian (Shackley 1988, 1995, 1998) indicate that obsidian distribution is uneven in Tonto Basin and that there are both temporal and spatial trends.

The results of the XRF analysis were tallied separately for Roosevelt and Gila phase sites located along the Salt River (Schoolhouse Point and

Figure 9.5.
Proportions of ob-
sidian sources com-
pared for the
Roosevelt phase sites
located on Cline
Mesa (west end) and
Schoolhouse Point
Mesa (east end).
Sources of obsidian
are arranged from
west to east by dis-
tance from Tonto
Basin (refer to Figure
9.4).

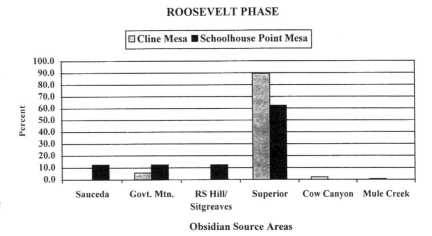

Livingston sites) and those along Tonto Creek (Cline Mesa sites) (Figures
9.5 and 9.6). A weighting for each of the major obsidian sources was determined from these tallies based on the sampling strategy for the XRF
study (Simon et al. 1997; Rice et al. 1998). During the Roosevelt phase
the Superior source (Figure 9.5), which is located closest to the study
area, about 45 km to the south, was heavily exploited by all sites, indicating the predominance of local procurement networks. This result
(Figures 9.4 and 9.5) is consistent with that from the Roosevelt Community Development Study (Stark 1995a:322–323) on sites located on
the opposite bank of the Salt River. Lesser proportions of obsidian
(Figure 9.5) from Government Mountain, Sauceda, and RS Hill sources,
located 180 to 200 km distant (Rice et al. 1998), are also present, but
such variety is more common at the Schoolhouse Point Mesa sites than
among the Cline Mesa sites.

In contrast, during the Gila phase the popularity of the Superior obsidian in Tonto Basin notably decreased (Figure 9.6). Five sources are
represented in the Gila phase obsidian collection as identified by XRF

Figure 9.6.
Proportions of ob-
sidian sources com-
pared for the Gila
phase sites located
on Cline Mesa (west
end) and
Schoolhouse Point
Mesa (east end).
Sources of obsidian
are arranged from
west to east by dis-
tance from Tonto
Basin (refer to Figure
9.4).

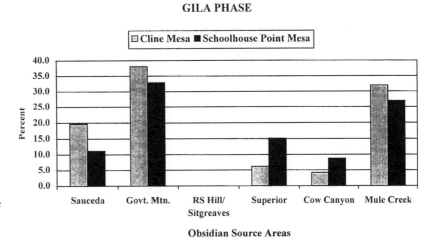

analysis (Shackley 1998; Simon et al. 1997; Rice et al. 1998). *Government Mountain*, located near Flagstaff, Arizona, about 185 to 200 km northwest of the study area, was the most abundant but was more common at the Cline Mesa sites. *Mule Creek*, located in New Mexico about 220 to 225 km east of the study sites, was also preferred but was more commonly represented among the Cline Mesa sites. *Sauceda*, located in the Arizona Sonoran Desert about 185 to 195 km southwest of the study sites, is also represented in fairly high proportions, especially at the Cline Mesa sites. *Superior*, located 45 to 55 km south of the sites, has relatively low proportions but is more abundant at the Schoolhouse Point Mesa sites. *Cow Canyon*, 170 to 200 km east of the sites, is the least abundant category but is more common at Schoolhouse Point Mesa sites than among the Cline Terrace sites.

This uneven distribution of obsidian, which becomes more pronounced during the Gila phase, is evidence of active avoidance or restriction of access to sources favored by the opposite group. Pueblos located on Anderson Mesa about 100 km north of Tonto Basin were active in procuring and trading Government Mountain obsidian (Brown 1991: 380–381) and may have provided this material to the Cline Mesa sites. The decline in the Superior source may have been due to depletion or to control of the source by local settlements (Rice et al 1998; Shackley 1988, 1995:547, 1998); further research in the area of the source is necessary to resolve this problem.

The comparison of obsidian source distributions illustrates different trade networks that were active at the Schoolhouse Point Mesa and the Cline Mesa platform mound communities during the Gila phase (Rice et al. 1998; Shackley 1998; Simon et al. 1997). The short distance of 25 km between the major site groups was a fraction of the distance to the sources (most were 150–200 km away). One would expect a higher level of intraregional exchange resulting in a more homogeneous distribution of source materials. We conclude that platform mound communities at opposite ends of the basin procured obsidian from preferred sources through trade networks and either avoided or were discouraged from using sources of the competing settlements. These differences became more pronounced during the Gila phase.

TURQUOISE AND MALACHITE

Turquoise trade was of minor importance until the Sacaton/Ash Creek phase and became increasingly important in the Miami and Roosevelt phases (Rice et al. 1998; Stark 1995a:326–328), a trend that continued into the Gila phase. Turquoise, malachite, and azurite have been recorded along Cherry Creek and Canyon Creek and on the Pinal drainage near Miami, Arizona (Stark 1995a; Welch and Triadan 1991). The Canyon Creek mine was a major source of these materials for the Mogollon settlements in the vicinity of Grasshopper Pueblo. Other sources of turquoise and malachite are present at greater distances in southern Arizona and New Mexico.

It is not possible to distinguish turquoise and malachite from these sources with a high degree of accuracy given the wide range of variation within single source areas and the compositional overlap among sources. Further, it is likely that some prehistoric mines have been obliterated by historic and modern copper-mining activities. Many Tonto Basin artifacts are from burial contexts and consequently were not candidates for destructive analyses. Therefore, our discussion focuses on the distributions of these artifacts within the sites and for the purposes of this study considers the Cherry Creek, Canyon Creek, and Pinal drainage locations the most likely sources of these artifacts from sites in Tonto Basin.

Turquoise and related copper minerals, such as malachite, azurite, and bornite (peacock rock), constitute less than 1 percent of the lithic assemblages in the Tonto Basin settlements (Rice et al. 1998). Distribution patterns of turquoise and malachite are presented with the caution that these collections represent small counts, a fact that may influence comparisons between sites and groups of sites. These stone artifacts show little tendency to drop off in frequency with distance from source, however (Rice et al. 1998), presumed for the purposes of this study to have been in the Sierra Ancha and the Globe/Miami, Arizona, areas.

Turquoise and malachite are more plentiful in the Gila phase sites than in the earlier Roosevelt phase sites (Rice et al. 1998); turquoise and malachite were present in the lithic assemblages of the platform mound communities on the basin floor, but sites located in the uplands had none. The Schoolhouse Point Mound (U:8:24/13a) had the highest frequencies of turquoise, appropriate to its relatively close distance from the assumed source areas to the east. The Cline Terrace Mound (U:4:33/ 132), located at the western end of Tonto Basin, had less turquoise but more malachite. The Cline Terrace complex may have obtained malachite from the Globe/Miami area through settlements located along Pinto Creek, whereas the Schoolhouse complex may have obtained turquoise from mines in the Sierra Ancha through communities located along Cherry Creek.

The fact that malachite is more common at the Tonto end and turquoise is more common at the Salt end of Tonto Basin is not consistent with expectations if distance from source was the primary explanation: that is, all related materials would drop off in equal proportions. It is apparent that the cultural preferences of each platform mound community prescribed stones of different colors and characteristics. The distributions in turquoise and malachite indicate different networks of procurement for platform mounds at either end of Tonto Basin.

SHELL

A stylistic and chemical analysis of shell artifacts by Bradley (1996) found that a boundary between two regional trade networks bisects Tonto Basin

(Figure 9.7), indicating that the various platform mound communities did not share shell procurement networks. Shell artifacts, particularly those of marine shell, have an uneven distribution in the platform mound communities (Rice et al. 1998). A few distinctive pendants of the local freshwater *Anadona* sp. shell were recovered, but most of the freshwater shell in the assemblages was unworked fragments that may have been the result of some purpose other than jewelry production.

Marine shell artifacts were found in the Classic period, Gila phase, Tonto Basin site assemblages but in lesser quantities than during the Preclassic (Rice et al. 1998). Trade in marine shell and decorated vessels was well established by the Colonial period (A.D. 800) (Stark 1995a:328) but declined during the Sacaton/Ash Creek phases, with a resurgence in the Roosevelt phase (Rice et al. 1998). The drop in the intensity of the shell trade at the Classic period transition suggests a temporary interruption of trade with the Gulf of California or with the intervening Hohokam region. The shift in the character of the shell assemblage did not occur to the same extent in all parts of Tonto Basin, however.

In general, marine shell artifacts are concentrated at the platform mounds and surrounding residential sites located along the valley and are sparse or absent in settlements in the upland bajadas. Bracelets declined in importance during the Roosevelt phase (*Glycymeris* bracelets were only one-fifth the Roosevelt phase shell assemblage, compared with half in the earlier Gila Butte phase), but shell tinklers and beads increased in frequency (Vokes 1995:209). Tinklers, *Olivella* shell beads, and broken shell (possibly container fragments) were recovered from public ceremonial rooms at two of the platform mounds, but shell bracelets were nearly excluded from these contexts (Bradley and Rice 1997; Rice 1995:209). Shell trumpets were found exclusively at platform mounds, indicating the specialized ceremonial use of these instruments.

The density of shell in the site deposits, expressed in terms of the number of pieces per cubic meter of excavated and screened deposits, is not explained by distance from the source (Rice et al. 1998). The distribution is likely the result of the procurement of shell artifacts through several intermediary sources. Social networks instrumental in obtaining these rare artifacts were probably active in different parts of the Hohokam region, as demonstrated in Bradley's 1996 regional study of shell exchange.

Bradley's (1996:116–122, Figure 17) study of shell exchange networks identified a network of Hohokam, Sinagua, and Anasazi sites to the west, and another network associated with Casas Grandes, Mogollon, and late Anasazi traditions to the east. The two distribution networks are supported by stylistic analysis and the chemical data derived from ICP-MS (Bradley 1996:127–133, Figure 19).

These two shell exchange networks indicate east-west distinctions rather than north-south (desert vs. plateau) distinctions across the study area. The Tonto cliff dwellings are part of the western Hohokam net-

Figure 9.7.
Hohokam and Casas Grandes marine shell exchange networks identified by Bradley (1996:Figure 17). Tonto Basin is located at the left center of the map, including the VIV Ruin located in the extreme west end of Tonto Basin and the Tonto Cliff Dwellings located at the center. It is notable that the boundary between the two exchange networks bisects the Tonto Basin study area.

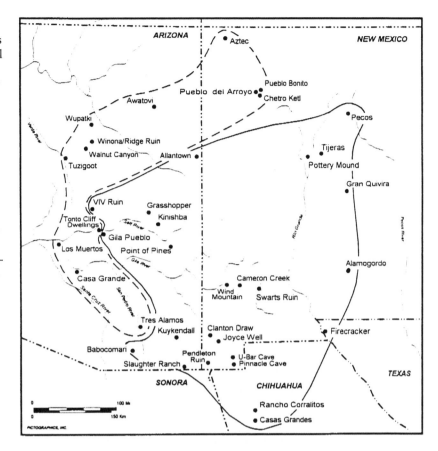

work, while VIV Ruin and Gila Pueblo are part of the eastern Casas Grandes network, which includes Grasshopper, Kinishba, and Point of Pines. The Cline Terrace complex likely obtained shell artifacts from desert networks to the southwest, whereas the Schoolhouse Point complex obtained shell artifacts from areas shared with other sites to the east. The uneven distribution of shell artifacts is not explainable by distance from source but is an artifact of the different social networks instrumental in obtaining these rare artifacts.

CERAMICS

Ceramic distributions at Classic period sites in Tonto Basin (Simon 1998) indicate that different networks of intraregional and regional exchange existed among contemporaneous platform mound communities. The production locations of various local wares during the Roosevelt phase shifted during the Gila phase. Undecorated pottery, as well as corrugated and decorated vessels, were brought to settlements at some distance across the basin, indicating movement of goods along social networks and in some cases probably associated with group relocations.

Frequencies of various ceramic classes in the site ceramic collections indicate both shared and disparate traditions (Simon 1996, 1998; Simon et al. 1998). Some of the contrasting ceramic distributions that illustrate the presence of different social networks within Tonto Basin are summarized below.

Undecorated Ceramics

Mineral temper in locally produced pottery has been used to identify production locations within the study area (Simon et al. 1998; Heidke and Stark 1995); for example, granite-tempered ceramics were made in the vicinity of Ash Creek on the Tonto arm but occur in relatively high frequencies at certain sites on the Salt arm of the basin. A distinctive granite-and-diabase combination was used to make large numbers of undecorated vessels at the Cline Mesa sites (Richardson 1994). Other combinations of granite-and-diabase temper distinguished pottery made at villages located along Pinto Creek and its tributaries (Simon et al. 1998; Heidke and Stark 1995), and diabase was the primary temper of certain plain and corrugated ceramic production locations along the slopes of the Sierra Ancha.

During the Roosevelt phase there was intrabasin exchange of undecorated ceramics from several production locations. In contrast, plain corrugated wares produced at the east end of Tonto Basin were more restricted in distribution. Plain corrugated ceramics occur in the highest frequencies at specific sites that exhibit linear block architecture, evidence of migrant populations settling among indigenous extended communities (Simon 1998). At the end of the Roosevelt phase numerous sites on the east end were abandoned. It is likely that many of these villagers joined the aggregated community at the Schoolhouse Point Mound (Lindauer 2000), where plain corrugated ceramics continued as a subset of the vessel assemblage. Productive specialization of smooth finished plainware ceramics continued throughout the Gila phase, especially at the Cline Terrace complex.

Salado Red

Salado Red ceramics, distinguished by their obliterated corrugated texture, raspberry-red slipped exteriors, and black smudged interiors, were primarily produced at upland sites along the Sierra Ancha, northwest of the Cline Terrace complex, and were traded extensively throughout the basin through both the Roosevelt and Gila phases (Simon 1998; Heidke and Stark 1995). Salado Red vessels are an integral part of the ceramic assemblages, both in residential areas and as burial accompaniments throughout the Roosevelt and Gila phases (Simon 1998; Simon and Ravesloot 1995).

A shift to local production of Salado Red has been documented in the

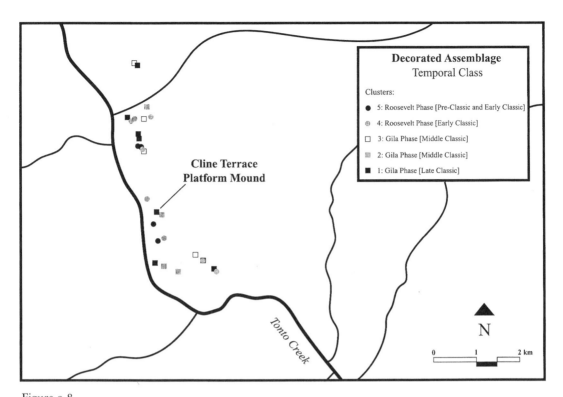

Figure 9.8.
Excavated sites at
the west end of
Tonto Basin along
Tonto Creek and the
Cline Terrace Mesa.
Sites are coded by a
cluster seriation of
decorated wares
(Simon 1998);
Clusters 4 and 5
were abandoned by
the end of the
Roosevelt phase;
Clusters 1, 2, and 3
denote the Gila
phase sites. The
Cline Terrace
Mound and only a
few other residential
sites are contempo-
raneous at the termi-
nal Gila phase
(Cluster 1).

Gila phase for both ends of the basin, but its highest concentration remained at the western end (Simon 1998), near present-day Tonto Basin,
Arizona. The high frequencies of Salado Red ceramics in sites at the west
end of Tonto Basin indicate social ties among the neighboring upland settlements and the Cline Terrace sites.

Salado Polychromes

An intraregional compositional study of Salado polychromes by Simon,
Burton, and Abbott (1998), found that exchange networks were extensive during the Roosevelt phase, including sites in the mountains to the
north and east. During the Gila phase, however, connections to other
riverine settlements to the east and south were strengthened. Differential
circulation of Salado polychromes is indicated for the eastern and western Tonto Basin; the Pueblo Grande platform mound likely obtained its
Salado polychromes from the Cline Terrace complex (Figure 9.8), whereas
Casa Grande on the Gila River obtained Salado polychromes from the
Schoolhouse complex (Figure 9.9). These differences in compositional
group distributions are evidence of separate spheres of exchange for each
of the large platform mound communities.

Salado polychrome paint, primarily carbon-based in the later Gila and
Tonto Polychromes, is influenced by ceramic paint traditions from the
north and northwest rather than the northeast and east (Simon 1996,

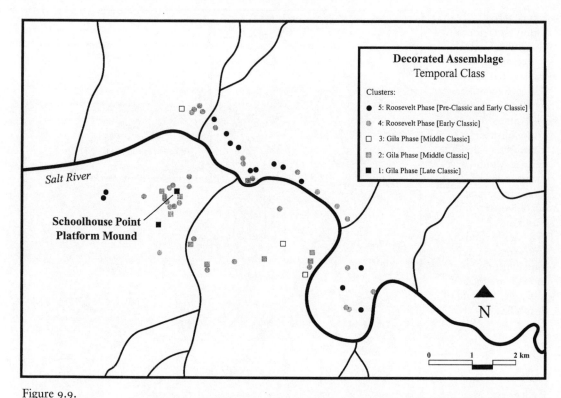

Figure 9.9.
Excavated sites at the east end of Tonto Basin along the Salt River. Sites are coded by a cluster seriation of decorated wares (Simon 1998); Clusters 4 and 5 were abandoned by the end of the Roosevelt phase; Clusters 1, 2, and 3 denote the Gila phase. The Schoolhouse Point Mound and only a few other sites are contemporaneous at the terminal Gila phase (Cluster 1).

1998). Tusayan White Ware and Little Colorado White Ware emphasized the use of carbon paint and have the most in common with Salado polychrome ceramics of Tonto Basin (Hensler 1993). Carbon paint was also used on occasion by desert peoples to the south (Wallace 1995b). In contrast, the Cibola White Ware and White Mountain Red Ware traditions, originating to the east and northeast, made use of mineral paint. The boundary between the use of mineral paint vs. carbon paint appears to have had an east vs. west distinction, rather than a north vs. south, or plateau vs. desert, distinction.

Intrusive Wares

Two primary cultural corridors by which intrusive decorated wares entered Tonto Basin have been identified by Hensler (1998). The western corridor connected the Hopi Mesas with Rye Creek Ruin and the Cline Terrace complex, as well as U:8:530/106, an upland platform mound located along Armer Gulch (Figure 9.10). The eastern corridor connected the Schoolhouse Point Mound with sites along Cherry Creek and settlements farther north. Salado Red was more common on the Cline Terrace end, as were Hopi yellowware, Hohokam buff- and brownware, and early intrusive Pinto Black-on-red and Pinto Polychrome types. Cibola White Ware and White Mountain Red Ware, as well as Mogollon corru-

Figure 9.10.
Cultural corridors
along which intru-
sive ceramics were
transported to Tonto
Basin, as identified
by Hensler (1998).
The Cline Mesa
group of sites
includes the Cline
Terrace Mound at
the west end of
Tonto Basin; the
Schoolhouse Point
Mound (AZ
U:8:24/13a) and AZ
U:8:530/106, an up-
land platform
mound, are located
along the east end of
Tonto Basin.

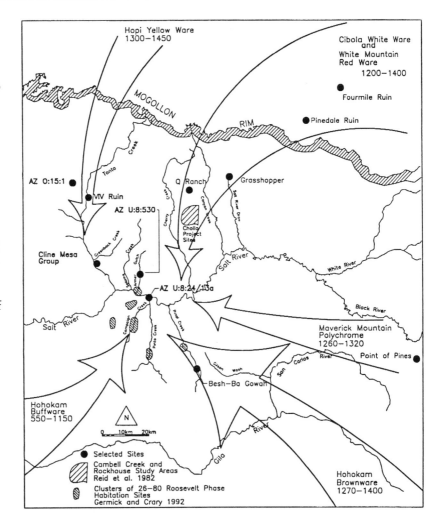

gated types, were more common at the east end, including the Schoolhouse Point complex.

Schoolhouse Point and Cline Terrace are equidistant from the source
areas for the various intrusive decorated wares, so distance from source
does not explain the differential distributions of these wares (Hensler
1998). Hopi yellowware exhibits declining frequencies along the western
corridor sites into Tonto Basin. Fourmile Polychrome was preferentially
distributed along the eastern corridor to the Schoolhouse Point Mound,
where densely populated settlements participated in down-the-line exchange. Inequities in the distribution of the Cibola White Ware and
White Mountain Red Ware occur most markedly in the late types:
Pinedale Black-on-white and Fourmile Polychrome (Hensler 1998). This
difference in access and distribution indicates that a major division in
trade connections and associated social contacts developed in the Gila
phase, evidence of intense competition among the large platform mound

communities at either end of Tonto Basin. The tradeware imbalance at the end of the Gila phase has further implications for the division and dispersal of social groups when the platform mound system collapsed in the fifteenth century (Hensler 1998; Simon 1996, 1998; Simon et al. 1998).

CONCLUSIONS

The distributions of obsidian, turquoise and malachite, shell, intrusive ceramics, and locally produced ceramics all indicate that differential access was present during the Roosevelt phase and that during the Gila phase these distributions were polarized at either end of Tonto Basin between the two remaining large platform mound communities, Cline Terrace and Schoolhouse Point. The abandonment of much of the intermediary territory indicates that a schism had developed in the social alliances of the region. The Schoolhouse Point Mound, exhibiting many Mogollon-influenced architectural features and ceramic traditions, did not have the same cultural corridors and access privileges as the Cline Terrace Mound and allied communities located in the uplands and along Tonto Creek.

This study illustrates the advantage of examining multiple lines of evidence based on the distributions of fine goods and classes of undecorated and decorated pottery, locally and nonlocally produced, to provide empirical evidence of social networks and boundaries within a study area. The platform mound communities are located in a geographically restricted area, in similar environmental settings, within 25 km of each other. Yet each group of settlements participated in widespread social and trade networks that extended well beyond Tonto Basin. This material evidence corroborates the evidence of conflict and violence presented elsewhere by Oliver (this volume) and Turner and Turner (1999:257–263, 291–293).

In this study and others (Rice et al. 1998; Simon et al. 1997; Simon et al. 1998) we found no centralization of platform mounds into a basin-wide cooperative organization. Rather, the distributions of trade items indicate differential exchange networks at east and west ends of the basin. These patterns began in the Roosevelt phase (A.D. 1280–1320), when there were multiple small platform mound communities, but during the Gila phase (1320–1450) these communities became polarized into two opposing aggregated polities, centered at the Cline Terrace Mound on the west and at the Schoolhouse Point Mound on the east.

Some materials were apparently procured from different sources, indicating the importance of cultural requirements or preferences rather than simply proximity to the source. Fine goods and decorated pottery were obtained in greater quantities by populations living near the valley bottom than by those occupying the upland bajadas (Oliver 1997; Rice et al.

1998). Such materials included marine shell, turquoise, azurite, malachite, iron-based pigments, and Cibola White Ware (Rice et al. 1998). Settlements on the valley floor would have used the well-watered river terraces as farm fields and may have had greater food surpluses to devote to the procurement of foreign commodities than populations on the pediments.

The platform mound communities of Tonto Basin experienced episodes of stability and conflict that resulted in the realignment of alliances and the aggregation of populations and social power into fewer, larger settlements. The ideology of the platform mounds and attendant communal integrative activities were able to integrate and redress conflicting value systems of the multiethnic communities to a large degree but ultimately could not quell the competition between the aggregated platform mounds. Evidence of conflict and violence throughout the Classic period (Oliver this volume; Turner and Turner 1999:257–263, 291–293) indicates that conflict between competing Gila phase polities was not resolved and that internal stress and competition for resources within a geographically bounded area led to the demise of the platform mound communities.

Competition for exchange items is a double-edged issue, on the one side fostering alliances and cooperation that alleviate tension and conflict but on the other side provoking intense disputes over acquiring and maintaining supporters, resources, and territory. The social and political processes necessary to contain the elevated intensity of competition between the terminal Gila phase platform mound communities were not successful, and the result was the collapse of the social system and dispersal of the population.

ACKNOWLEDGMENTS

Much of the research for this chapter was conducted as part of the Roosevelt Platform Mound Study under contract with the Bureau of Reclamation and under permit from the Tonto National Forest. The opinions expressed in this chapter are the authors' and synthesize some of the findings reported in the three Roosevelt Platform Mound Study final volumes (Rice 1998b; Simon 1998; Spielmann 1998) and related specialist studies. We thank Glen Rice and Steven LeBlanc for asking us to participate in the SAA Warfare Symposium and this volume. We thank our colleagues Ted Oliver, Ronna Jane Bradley, Steve Shackley, Kathy Niles Hensler, Chris Loendorf, Vern Hensler, Jim Burton, and Dave Abbott for the contributions of their specialist studies. Figure 9.1 was drafted by Shearon Vaughn, the artist's reconstructions (Figures 9.2 and 9.3) were drawn by Glena Cain, Lynn Simon prepared Figures 9.4 and 9.10, and Figures 9.8 and 9.9 were drafted by Dennis Gosser and Christian Wells. Further information on the Roosevelt Archaeology

Projects is available at the Arizona State University Archaeological Research Institute website: http://archaeology.asu.edu.

NOTE

1. On the "managerial model," see Doyel 1981, 1991; Fish and Fish 1992; Grebinger 1976; Gregory 1987; Howard 1987; McGuire 1985; Martin and Plog 1973; Neitzel 1991; Teague 1984; Upham and Rice 1980; and Rice 1990.

CHAPTER TEN

Classic Period Warfare in Southern Arizona

Henry D. Wallace and William H. Doelle

Warfare is commonplace and frequent among investigated cultures worldwide (Ember and Ember 1992; Keeley 1996). Between 90 and 95 percent of known societies engaged in war, and the remaining 5 to 10 percent tended to be isolated with no one to fight or were incapable of developing a fighting force (Ember and Ember 1990; Jorgensen 1980; Keeley 1996; Otterbein 1989). Although ubiquitous, warfare generally leaves few traces in the archaeological record (Vencl 1984), and the lack of such evidence is often interpreted by archaeologists as an indication of peaceful times. The difficulties in addressing prehistoric warfare led us to focus on areas in southern Arizona with particularly strong data sets. We present theoretical arguments and empirical evidence suggesting that areas of cultural, ethnic, and economic boundaries in the prehistory and history of southern Arizona are settings that promote conflict. We then apply insights from these frontier zones to panregional, larger-scale processes.

Following Ferguson (1984:5), we define war as "organized, purposeful group action, directed against another group that may or may not be organized for similar action, involving the actual or potential application of lethal force." There are two key points to consider here. First, war is social. Individual killings are homicides; only group actions against other groups constitute warfare. In kinbased societies individual violent actions often escalate to group-level reactions. It is the group responses

Figure 10.1.
Southern Arizona:
Tucson Basin, north-
ern Tucson Basin,
Picacho District, and
lower San Pedro
Valley.

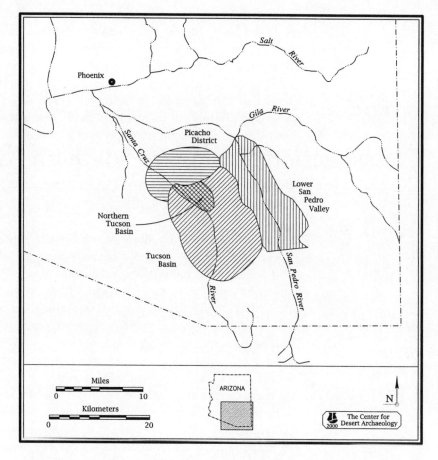

that we consider warfare. Second, war involves not only the application of deadly force but also the *potential* for such conflicts. It is not necessary to have been attacked to be fearful of attack. This distinction is important because the social responses to attack or the threat of attack can be equally dramatic and significant in cultural development.

We now turn to two data sets from southern Arizona that present clear evidence of prehistoric conflict: the northern Tucson Basin and the nearby lower San Pedro Valley (Figure 10.1). In the Classic period of the local Hohokam sequences, dated between A.D. 1150 and 1450, there were many large settlements in this region. Durable construction with highly visible masonry and adobe walls has facilitated site discovery and mapping, allowing for comparisons and documentation. Both regions of interest have been covered by large-scale survey and excavations (Di Peso 1958; Downum 1993; S. Fish et al. 1992; Franklin 1980; Henderson 1987; Rice 1987; Wallace 1995a; Wallace and Doelle 1997; Wallace et al. 2000). The northern Tucson Basin case directs attention to a long-term cultural and economic boundary that becomes a zone of conflict and ultimately a large-scale depopulated zone. Environmental and social factors are seen as key components of the local process that ultimately leads to abandonment and aggregation. The San Pedro case also considers a long-lived cultural and probably economic boundary, this time in relationship to long-distance migrations into the area that stimulated or accentuated conflict. Long-distance migrations into the lower San Pedro and eastern Tucson Basin are also considered indirect contributors to the events that transpired in the northern Tucson Basin. Platform mounds signal related processes in both regions. By concentrating power and authority, the social institutions represented by platform mounds provided a context in which warfare was propagated or promoted.

SOME INSIGHTS FROM DOCUMENTARY AND ETHNOGRAPHIC SOURCES

It is recognized that conditions in the Greater Southwest from around 1690 to the late 1800s were constantly changing and are not directly comparable to conditions in prehistoric times. Nevertheless, these sources link specific human behaviors whose causes are reasonably well documented with material patterns that should be detectable in the archaeological record. Of particular importance to this study are such broad-scale responses as aggregation, territorial abandonment that creates a depopulated zone, and the presence or absence of defensive features. This brief review is intended to provide examples of such behaviors; it is not meant to be an exhaustive methodological study.

Early historic documents are a good source of insight into potential responses to warfare. The richest early documents pertaining to the lower San Pedro come from the November 1697 journey of Father Kino and military captains Manje and Bernal (Burrus 1971; Smith et al. 1966). There were two supra village leaders in the valley, Humari (= Humaric), residing at La Victoria de Ojo near the mouth of Aravaipa Creek, and Coro, initially residing at San Salvador Baicatcan, not far south of Redington (Figure 10.2). In the year before Kino and Manje's arrival in the valley, hostilities broke out when one of Coro's relatives was killed by Pimans who lived on the northern San Pedro. The result was establishment of a 50-mile-wide unoccupied zone between these two groups and the relocation of Chief Coro's seat of power to Quíburi. The distance between the two political centers of the valley went from 30 or 40 miles to nearly 80 miles. In a separate but contemporaneous set of events two small settlements at the far northern end of the San Pedro were abandoned because of hostilities with Apaches. These villages joined the settlement of the northern headman, at least doubling its population. These accounts offer clear documentation of a process of aggregation and the development of a depopulated zone, something echoed in the prehistoric record of the region.

Father Kino's account (Smith et al. 1966:48–49) of the 1698 battle between the Sobaipuri of the upper San Pedro and their enemies the Jocomes, Janos, Sumas, and Apaches is instructive on several counts.

Figure 10.2. The San
Pedro Valley in the
1690s.

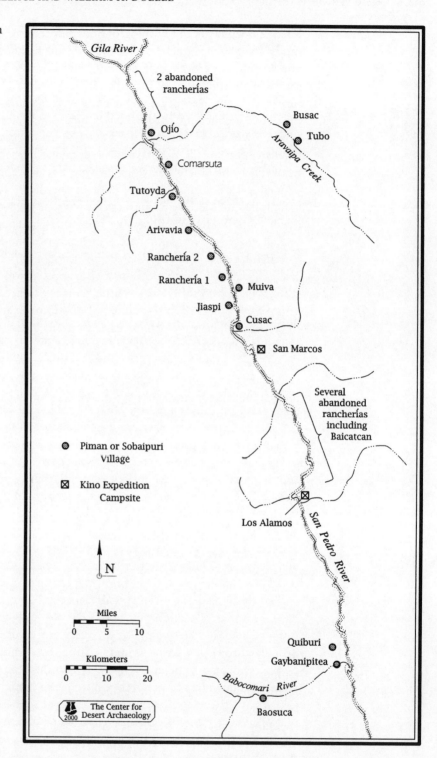

First, it documents the burning of Sobaipuri houses as a specific action undertaken by the attackers after the residents had fled. Furthermore, the attackers began processing and consuming stored foodstuffs right within the village setting. Third, the villagers had fled to a small adobe structure. This Spanish-inspired architecture was much more substantial than the native architecture of small brush huts. Kino refers to it as a "fortification," and its use as such by the Sobaipuri underscores the fact that defensive features do not have to be dramatic in their efficiency and effectiveness; they merely have to provide a relative improvement or advantage over an alternative option. In this light, the introduction of compound architecture to southern Arizona clearly would have provided a substantial defensive advantage over the open courtyard groups that had characterized residential areas for some five hundred years.

Finally, descriptions by Russell (1975:200–202) indicate that the absence of defensible site locations or fortifications in the archaeological record is not necessarily a sign of the absence of warfare. In the relatively difficult-to-protect open setting of villages of the Gila River Pima during the nineteenth century, defensive measures included positioning sentries to guard field workers and villages and the establishment of intervillage cooperative war parties to repel Apache raiders (Russell 1975:201). These organizational responses would be archaeologically invisible, though the abandonment of outlying villages and aggregation into larger villages might be detectable.

TRINCHERAS: DEFENSE OR AGRICULTURE AND RITUAL?

Throughout southern and central Arizona are mountain slopes and summits with masonry walls, terraces, and structures that have been called *cerros de trincheras* or simply *trincheras* sites. These sites have commonly been interpreted as defensive fortifications (e.g., Huntington 1914; Sauer and Brand 1931; Fontana et al. 1959; Spoerl 1984; Stacy 1974; Wilcox 1979b, 1989; Wallace 1995a); some authors, however, have promoted alternative explanations centered on agricultural diversification (Downum 1993; Downum et al. 1993, 1994; Fish and Fish 1989) and ceremonialism (Downum 1993).

We prefer to avoid the use of the term *trincheras* because it has been loosely applied to potentially dissimilar sites in different cultural and temporal settings. The sites discussed here are believed to have functional relationships related to defense and are therefore discussed with appropriate descriptive terminology. We focus on the sites of Black Mountain (Fontana et al. 1959; Martynec 1987), Tumamoc Hill (Wilcox 1979b; Wilcox et al. 1979), Linda Vista (Downum 1986, 1995; Wallace 1995a), Rillito Peak (Wallace 1983), and Cerro Prieto (Downum et al. 1993, 1994). Significant numbers of additional sites are reported from surrounding regions (Tanner 1936; Sauer and Brand 1931; Stacy 1974). Most if not all of these sites appear to have components dating to the

244 HENRY D. WALLACE AND WILLIAM H. DOELLE

Classic period, and those with sufficient data, including all those considered in the Tucson area, have components dated to the Early Classic period (A.D. 1150–1300) (Fontana et al. 1959; Hartmann and Hartmann
1979; Downum 1986, 1995; Downum et al. 1993; Wallace 1983).
According to recent work by Robert Hard and John Roney (1998) in
northern Chihuahua and Suzanne Fish on Tumamoc Hill in the Tucson
Basin (Suzanne Fish, personal communication 1998), some hilltop sites
in the region also have components dating earlier than A.D. 700.

Tucson Basin Fortifications

The most detailed and well-reasoned investigation of the defensive character of these sites is that of Wilcox (1979b), who focused on Tumamoc
Hill. After carefully mapping and documenting the walls on Tumamoc,
he found that a defensive explanation was the only one that fit the evidence observed. The summit of Tumamoc Hill is surrounded by massive
masonry revetment-like walls. Within the relatively level "protected"
summit area, there are 125 rock circles averaging 3.3 m in diameter in
addition to dozens of mortars, cupules, a moderate density of pottery
sherds (Larson 1979), and abundant petroglyphs (Ferg 1979). A major
prehistoric trail extends from the base of the hill to the summit on the
north slope (Hartmann and Hartmann 1979). Wilcox's interpretation of
the massive walls surrounding the Tumamoc summit as defensive fortifications was based on several key facts. First, the walls were situated at
upper slope inflection points that maximize their defensive qualities.
Second, they are most continuous and numerous on the gentlest slopes in
the areas most difficult to defend. Finally, although soil buildup was present along some portions of the walls, many areas entirely lacked any soil
and could not be viewed as agricultural constructions.

Wilcox's work on Tumamoc is echoed in the studies by Fontana et al.
(1959) and Martynec (1987) on Black Mountain. The massive walls surrounding the only ready access points to the summit of Black Mountain
are similar to those of Tumamoc Hill, and as pointed out by Martynec,
none has significant soil development and there are no identifiable terraces on the mountain. Neither Tumamoc nor Black Mountain offers
convincing evidence of long-term on-site residence. The paucity of artifacts indicates that if people did live on these mountains, it was for only
short spans of time.

Recently, Suzanne Fish, of the Arizona State Museum, conducted excavations atop Tumamoc Hill, determining that at least some of the
small rock enclosures marked pit structures dating to the Early Ceramic
period (A.D. 150–700) (Suzanne Fish, personal communication 1998).
Similar rock enclosures are found atop Cerro Prieto, Black Mountain,
Martinez Hill, Blackstone Ruin, and other sites in the region to the west.
For Tumamoc, Black Mountain, and Martinez Hill, where later use of
the hill summits is indicated by artifact data, it is difficult to determine

which defensive constructions were built when. For Cerro Prieto, these constructions are limited to a small portion of the hill summit away from other constructions dating to the Classic period, and there is little doubt which component is which.

In our northern Tucson Basin study area there are three large mountain slope/summit sites: Linda Vista and Rillito Peak adjoin the large lower-terrace communities of Los Morteros (Figure 10.3) and Huntington at the northern tip of the Tucson Mountains, and Cerro Prieto is found in the Los Robles area to the northwest. Linda Vista (Figure 10.4) is a hillside village dating to the thirteenth century. At least 80 pit structures were constructed on the rocky slope, accompanied by terraces and possible ramadas and storehouses (Downum 1986, 1993, 1995). Quantities of trash and burials and the nature of the architectural remains suggest that the site was occupied for a period of years rather than being a limited defensive retreat used only in times of danger. Near the mountain summit is a small walled compound with one or more interior surface adobe structures. Rillito Peak has similar features, though fewer in number, and there is less trash (Wallace 1983).

Both Linda Vista and Rillito Peak are sites built with defense in mind. The structures on Rillito Peak are on a rugged mountaintop (Figure 10.5), surrounded by cliffs on three sides and precipitous slopes on the fourth. Linda Vista was built on the portion of the northern Tucson Mountains with sheer cliffs on the west side. The only ready access from the west side is through a small pass, and a massive masonry wall, still up to a meter in height, seals off this approach (Figures 10.4 and 10.6). Secondary access points through the pass flanking the wall were fortified with loose rock talus and low walls. Low cliffs above the saddle would have provided a secure post for guards to repel intruders. A small structure located just inside the main wall may represent a sentry's house. Access to the lower portions of the site from the east slope adjacent to the by-then abandoned Preclassic portion of Los Morteros was not difficult, and if defense was a concern, protective strategies would have been required. Note that this would have been the case only for the lower slope, however, because once one reaches the steeper upper third of the slope, mountain slope talus and vegetation make rapid ascent difficult. Furthermore, access to the summit compound at the site was possible only through two narrow lateral routes, as it is flanked by cliffs to the east and west. For residents of Linda Vista familiar with trails and access routes, the village setting provided a series of secure fall-back positions if retreat from attack was required.

Cerro Prieto is a partially terraced hillslope village focused on the lower north slope of a large boulder-strewn volcanic mountain. The summit of the mountain contains a discrete set of small rock enclosures, as mentioned earlier, similar to those seen on Tumamoc and Black Mountain, as well as a large tabular andesite quarry. The summit structures may not be coeval with other portions of the site. The village portion of

Figure 10.3.
Distribution of Early
Classic period
(Tanque Verde
phase) settlement at
Los Morteros and
the adjacent moun-
tain slopes, includ-
ing the fortified
Linda Vista and
Rillito Peak locali-
ties. Canal headings
taken from S. Fish et
al. (1992:23).

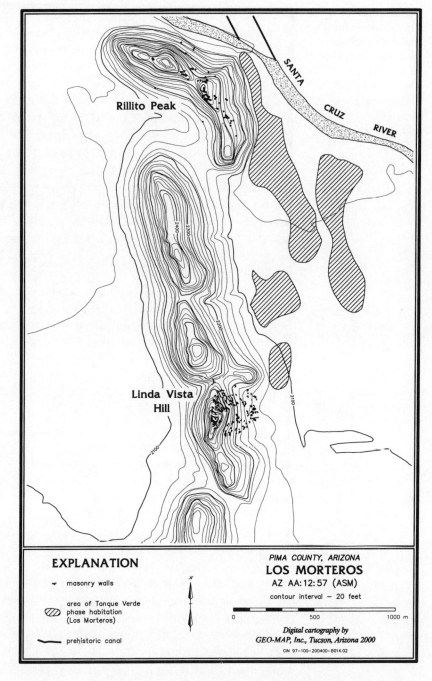

the site contains many masonry-walled compounds and at least 232
probable residential structures (Downum et al. 1993:69). Trails angle up
the hillslope connecting residential areas. Extensive trash deposits, evidence of cremation burials, and intensity of occupation point to long-
term settlement rather than temporary residence. Massive terraces, the
largest such constructions north of the famous Cerro de las Trincheras

Figure 10.4.
Distribution of walls
and rock enclosures
on Linda Vista Hill
(adapted from
Downum 1995),
including the wall
across the pass seen
in Figure 10.6.

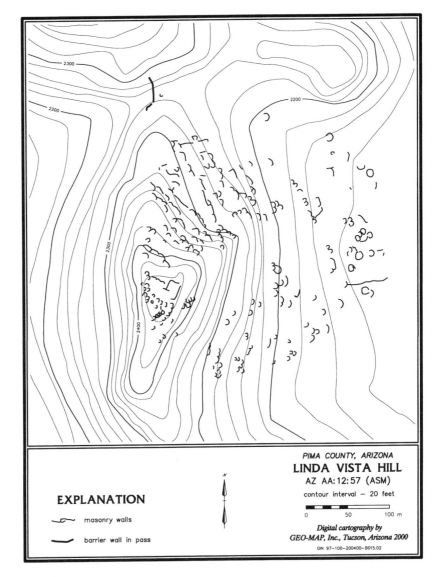

EXPLANATION

⌐ masonry walls

barrier wall in pass

PIMA COUNTY, ARIZONA
LINDA VISTA HILL
AZ AA:12:57 (ASM)
contour interval — 20 feet

0   50   100 m

Digital cartography by
GEO-MAP, Inc., Tucson, Arizona 2000
GIN 97-100-200400-B015.02

site in northern Sonora, were used for residential and probable agricultural and mortuary purposes at the site. Although the lower slope of Cerro Prieto is a gentle one, rapid vertical access is limited because of the boulder-strewn surface. Without an intimate knowledge of the trail system, one cannot move rapidly in any direction within the village. Access to the community is further restricted by the very large terraces and compound walls.

Peaceful Walls?

Some researchers (Downum 1986, 1995; Downum et al. 1993, 1994, Fish and Fish 1989; Katzer 1985, 1993) have countered the hypothesis that warfare was the motivation for wall and village construction at the

Figure 10.5.
Distribution of walls
and rock enclosures
on Rillito Peak.

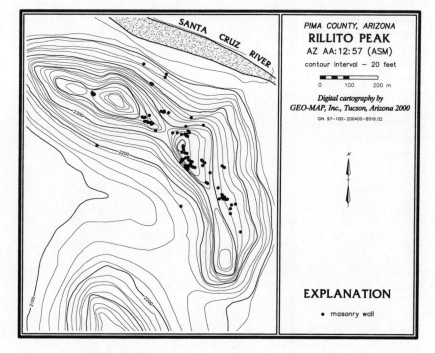

hillslope and summit sites discussed here, suggesting instead that they were placed and constructed for the purposes of agricultural diversification and/or that they were ceremonial constructions. Neither hypothesis accounts for the data now available from the sites, nor are these functions shown to be exclusive of a primary defensive motivation for site construction.

The agricultural hypothesis requires demonstration that the walls and other constructions are built with this goal in mind, that there is a cultural advantage to do so, and that there is not a better place to build than the spots selected. None of these requirements is met. Katzer's (1985, 1993) study of slope orientation for trincheras sites is used by Downum (1993), Downum et al. (1994), and Fish and Fish (1989) as the proof that the sites are oriented most often in a northward direction, the best orientation for agricultural purposes; however, large portions of the walls and structures at Black Mountain, Tumamoc Hill, Linda Vista, and Rillito Peak are on slopes facing directions other than north, northeast, or northwest. If agriculture was a prime motivation, then all the sites should be oriented in the optimal manner. Furthermore, one would expect construction of such sites on the best climatically suitable slopes that can be readily reached. Access and construction-potential arguments also apply if the sites were peaceful villages placed on hillslopes for ceremonial or aesthetic purposes. There are much more suitable locations than those chosen if these were the principal concerns for site placement. For example, in the Linda Vista/Rillito Peak area there is a well-suited north-facing gentle-sloped hill ideal for terracing located between the

Figure 10.6. Plan map of massive masonry wall blocking access across mountain pass north of the Linda Vista hillside village (contours and scale approximate; from Wallace 1995:817).

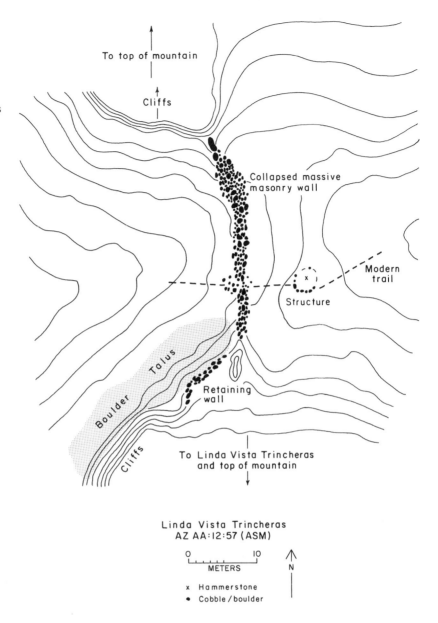

two sites; the location lacks natural barriers such as the cliffs present north and south, however, and it was never used. For Black Mountain and Tumamoc, the gentle lower slopes of the mountains *were* used for agricultural purposes (Masse 1979; Doelle and Wallace 1986), leading us to ask why such an argument would apply to the difficult-to-reach summits.

For the three hillslope sites in the northern Tucson Basin—Cerro Prieto, Rillito Peak, and Linda Vista—the agricultural hypothesis is particularly weak. Mapping and excavations at these sites (Downum 1986, 1993, 1995; Downum et al. 1993, 1994; Fish and Fish 1989; Wallace

1983) have demonstrated that considerable areas of the slopes where agriculture could have been practiced are the locations of residences and associated domestic work areas. Although some of the areas on these slopes may have been used for agricultural purposes, the kinds of optimizing behavior that Katzer considers in his study are clearly not supported by the archaeological evidence. Katzer (1985, 1993) posits that groups may have been employing rather refined strategies to use microenvironments with slightly different orientations or soil moisture conditions. If such a primary agricultural motivation was being implemented in the past, then the expectation would be for an exclusive agricultural use of hill space, not a yielding of most of the potential agricultural area for residential use. This is particularly the case when suitable residential space is available just a few hundred meters away and was used for centuries before the construction of these hillslope sites.

There is no reason to doubt that there were small garden plots related to individual households or corporate groups at mountainslope village sites such as Cerro Prieto and Linda Vista. But can one justify placing a village in such a setting for these small kitchen gardens? S. Fish and others (1984:69) acknowledge that "production from the terraces would have been relatively minor. Labor investment was substantial and acreage was very modest." Terrace crops would have provided a route toward agricultural diversification, but there were easier solutions unless one could not safely reside in other settings. S. Fish and others (1984:70) also recognize that "as less accessible, dispersed, and defensible targets, terrace crops also might have survived intentional destruction during conflict." By all measures, agriculture is unlikely to be the motivation for building these sites.

A key component of the argument that the hillslope sites were constructed with defense in mind is the presence of the masonry features called "walls" or "revetments" by Fontana and others (1959) and Wilcox (1979b). Downum and others (1994) suggest that these features represent agricultural terracing, overlooking the fact that significant portions of the features are built on bedrock or boulder talus where soil retention was unlikely in the past and is certainly not present today. The location tested by P. Fish and others (1986) on the summit of Tumamoc was situated in an area of maximum soil deposition unrelated to the perimeter wall and did not address the overall morphology and depositional character of the summit constructions. These test excavations revealed evidence of maize atop Tumamoc Hill during what is now referred to as the Cienega phase of the Early Agricultural period, which dates between 400 B.C. and A.D. 150. This material could be related to the contemporaneous Clearwater site that lies immediately below Tumamoc Hill adjacent to the floodplain of the Santa Cruz River, or it may represent a relatively early residential and/or agricultural adaptation. The more recent excavations by Suzanne Fish identified additional slightly later occupation on the Tumamoc summit. Current data cannot definitively place the revetment-like "walls" on Tumamoc in the Classic period; regardless of when they were constructed, however, we see defense as their most likely purpose.

Other "wall" characteristics, such as termination points and correlation with slope gradient, all of which were systematically measured and discussed by Wilcox on Tumamoc Hill, are overlooked by Downum et al. (1994). The massive wall at Linda Vista that blocks the only ready access from the west was also overlooked by these researchers and was shown for the first time in Wallace (1995a:814–817) and here in Figures 10.4 and 10.6. We doubt that anyone could interpret the Linda Vista wall as anything but an intentional physical barrier.

The second major hypothesis presented by Downum (1993) and Downum and others (1994) is that all or many of the sites in question were constructed as a result of new ideological and ritual belief systems initiated in the Early Classic period as part of a reorganization on the heels of the retraction from the ball-court system. To support such a claim, Downum points to petroglyphs that might suggest rituals on the mountains and ritual artifacts recovered from Linda Vista. This argument is a particularly weak one. Some ritual use of the mountains where these sites are located is expected whether warfare was involved or not. If the sites were purely ritually focused, repeated ritual behavior should be observed. Such behavior is archaeologically discerned at other types of sites, such as large petroglyph sites and platform mounds. No such consistency in behavior is noted for the sites in question. Furthermore, the theoretical underpinning of Downum's arguments rests on the decline of the ball-court system immediately prior to the construction of these sites. Current research in the Tucson area places these events significantly apart from one another, on the order of at least 150 years (Doelle and Wallace 1991; Wallace 1987, 1988).

In summary, a central problem of the previous research related to so-called trincheras in the Tucson Basin is that researchers have not adequately considered variability between and within these sites. Wilcox, for example, states: "The purpose of this paper is to show that *the defensive refuge hypothesis* is plausible and is supported by the results of a detailed study of one site" (1979b:16, emphasis added). Fish and Fish (1986:122, emphasis added) note, "Excavations at larger trincheras locations reveal complete villages rather than refuges, *a fact which is not necessarily at odds with a general defensive function.*" Even Katzer (1985:6, emphasis added) states: "It is also possible that some trincheras had multiple uses, *such as for both defense and agriculture.*" It seems very clear that it is necessary to consider defensive refuges and residential sites as two very distinct classes of sites—though previous discussions lump them casually under the label *trincheras.* Also, multiple functions that may include limited garden plots and ceremonial activities are in evidence at the residential sites that have been studied. Furthermore, the possibility of multiple or repeated uses of the hill summit areas at different points in prehistory has not been adequately considered or tested. Nevertheless, as the quotations above also show, for all these sites a defensive function is the single common theme regardless of time, site type, or site structure. We argue that it is a very compelling common theme. When the three residential sites of Cerro Prieto, Rillito Peak, and Linda Vista are put into a larger-scale temporal and settlement pattern framework in the section that follows, the case for warfare and defensive concerns becomes even stronger.

CASE STUDY: WARFARE IN THE NORTHERN TUCSON BASIN

The thirteenth- and fourteenth-century Tucson Basin is a broadly defined cultural and physiographic subarea centered on the Santa Cruz, Rillito, and Cañada del Oro drainages (Figure 10.1) and bounded by mountain ranges in nearly every direction. These major drainages supplied critical water and arable land in segments of the stream courses that became the foci of large prehistoric settlement systems. The northern and northwestern portions of this culture subarea, lying roughly between the Cañada del Oro Wash to the south and almost to Picacho Peak to the north, is commonly referred to as the northern Tucson Basin. Beyond this zone to the north is a large desert region characterized by very limited water resources and large tracts of land with no evidence of prehistoric occupation. Settlement occurs in areas around springs and on the drainages surrounding the Picacho Mountains and in the Santa Cruz Flats to the west where reservoirs could be constructed (see Bayman 1996; Bayman et al. 1997). This Picacho Mountain/Santa Cruz Flats area is referred to here as the Picacho District.

The Picacho District's relatively harsh desert environment and limited water and agricultural resources stand in sharp contrast to the northern Tucson Basin environment, which was enriched by permanent or seasonal water from the Santa Cruz River. Long histories of cultural development in both the northern Tucson Basin and the desert area to the north reveal a well-established cultural and economic boundary in this zone. Aside from the two regions' striking differences in subsistence economies, there is a boundary in ceramic commerce that has been used to define the limits of the Tucson Basin. Few Tucson Basin decorated vessels were acquired by settlements along the Picacho Mountains (Heacock and Callahan 1988). Before A.D. 1050, buffware vessels from the Middle Gila passed through this borderland, but the numbers were never very high and the mechanisms of transport are unknown. North of the Picacho District, settlement drops off until one reaches the rich and densely settled canal-irrigated southern terraces of the Middle Gila River valley. In the pre-1050 period this entire region, extending to the southern limits of the Tucson Basin and beyond, was integrated through the ball-court system and the religious ideology that accompanied it (Wallace et al. 1995; Wilcox 1991b; Wilcox and Sternberg 1983). After 1050 the Tucson Basin ball-court system may have dropped out of the regional network (Doelle and Wallace 1991), and long-established ties to the north may have been severed.

The twelfth and thirteenth centuries in the northern Tucson Basin around the northern point of the Tucson Mountains were the scene of dynamic settlement pattern shifts, seasonal population movements, and ultimately, large-scale abandonment. Warfare is seen as a major stimulus for the concluding chapters of this dramatic story. Our reconstruction of these events represents an alternative to the sequence presented by P. Fish, S. Fish, and their colleagues (Downum et al. 1994; P. Fish 1989; S. Fish 1996; Fish and Fish 1993, 1994; P. Fish et al. 1994; S. Fish et al. 1984, 1992). Some of the information incorporated here was not available for consideration in previous studies. A map (Figure 10.7) is provided to help place the sites discussed in context.

Settlement System Dynamics in the Northern Tucson Basin

By A.D. 1050, settlements in the Tucson area had shifted from being nucleated around ball courts and plazas to being dispersed, loosely integrated village segments, each segment representing two to four related households with their own communal cooking facilities and cemeteries. Similar settlement shifts are widespread in southern Arizona. It is possible they related to a particularly favorable climatic regime involving dependable rainfall and river runoff (see Dean et al. 1994), which would have promoted canal construction and agricultural expansion. The Marana canal system was constructed during this era of settlement expansion around 1075 (based on the earliest decorated ceramic styles present at villages excavated along its course). Heading on the east side of the Santa Cruz River opposite the large village of Los Morteros, it extended 7 km along the margin of the floodplain below the Tortolita Mountain bajada. This canal provided water for a string of small villages and opened up a large new area to cultivation. A short time later, about 1125, the southern half of Los Morteros was abandoned and new areas were settled at the north end of the site.

Across the river to the north a large settlement known as the Marana Mound site or Nelson's Desert Ranch site was founded at the terminus of the canal system (Figure 10.7). At some point in the thirteenth century a platform mound and surrounding compound enclosure were built at the site. Other compounds were also built, but none of them contained platform mounds. Large dry-farming field systems designed for the cultivation of agave were established on the bajada slopes on this side of the river (S. Fish et al. 1992:73–87). A strong link between the two sides of the river is evident. Multiple lines of evidence from excavated portions of Los Morteros suggest that the residents were seasonally mobile, traveling across the river to the Marana area to participate in the agave harvest and the probable feasting and social occasions associated with it (Wallace 1995a:809–810).

Figure 10.7.
Locations of sites
discussed in the text
in the northern
Tucson Basin and
Picacho District.

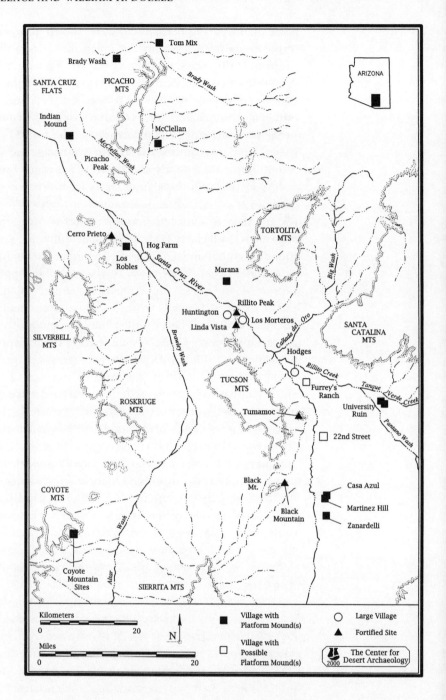

The possibility of seasonal mobility and other population movements suggests a much more dynamic system with much lower population levels than has been previously posited (Bayman 1994:17–18). It also calls into question the drastic population increase for the region suggested in previous studies (Fish and Fish 1994; P. Fish et al. 1994; S. Fish et al. 1992). We believe momentary population levels in the vicinity to be no more than 650 and perhaps closer to 300 or 400 persons, based on ex-trapolations from levels in the much more controlled Middle Rincon subphase (A.D. 1000 to 1100) data set (Wallace 1995a:805). The assumption of contemporaneous sedentary occupation in all Early Classic period settlements by previous researchers (Fish and Fish 1993, 1994; P. Fish et al. 1994; S. Fish et al. 1992:20–40; S. Fish 1996) drastically skews perceptions of settlement trajectories in the region, as it has population levels. Similarly, shifting settlement strategies and poor chronological resolution in the twelfth and thirteenth centuries may account for reported increases in population levels from Preclassic times to the Early Classic period (S. Fish et al. 1992:20–40), and we see no clear evidence for an influx of outsiders into the region as suggested by Fish and Fish (1993:105) and Harry (1997). Seasonal influxes of populations from surrounding communities such as Los Morteros to the Marana Mound area as suggested by Wallace (1995a:809–813) and supported by a range of excavated data at that site seriously undermine population increase models for the area. Harry (1997:248) argues that immigrant group(s) from outside the Tucson Basin settled the sites south of the Marana Mound along the Marana Canal System, basing her interpretation on the low frequencies of Tanque Verde Red-on-brown pottery. The evidence of large-scale production of plainware pottery at these sites (Kisselburg 1987) points to an alternative perspective: that specialist communities often have larger percentages of locally produced items than nonspecialist communities. Many prehistoric examples can be cited, such as shell at Shelltown (Howard 1993), turquoise at Redtail (Bernard-Shaw 1989), and perhaps most telling, the decorated ceramic production and importation data from the southern Tucson Basin focused on the zone around the West Branch community (Wallace 1987; Doelle and Wallace 1991).

The construction of the Marana Canal System and the establishment of the Marana Mound site at its terminus may have fostered a political schism in the area. On the one hand, there might have been competition between the old seat of power in the region at Huntington or Los Morteros and the new center at the Marana Mound; and on the other, there was a significant subsistence risk involved in the construction of a seat of power and authority on a canal established in a marginal area for dependable water. A few years of low crop yields could easily have strained the social mechanisms linking populations in the region.

The population centers around the Point of the Mountains and along the Marana Canal System continued to be occupied into the last half of the thirteenth century, when they were abruptly abandoned. Given the defensive character of the Linda Vista and Rillito Peak villages, we think it unlikely that they are contemporaneous with the adjacent Los Morteros and Huntington villages. Therefore, the most likely scenario places them at the terminus of the occupation in the region near the closing decades of the thirteenth century, a contention supported by a radio-carbon date obtained from one of the Linda Vista structures (Downum

1986:228). These fortified sites were occupied for at least a few years, based on the trash present at the sites, and then they too were abandoned.

The general sequence of events documented in the Marana area is replicated in the Los Robles area only a short distance to the west-northwest (Figure 10.7) at the northernmost limit of the Tucson Basin. There a Preclassic ball-court settlement known as the Hog Farm site continues to be inhabited into the Early Classic period, but a separate settlement is established in the Early Classic period about 5 km farther downstream with a platform mound, known as the Robles Mound (Downum 1993). As with the Marana Mound site, this separation of the "ancestral" seat of power or ritual from the new platform mound location could mark a process of political fragmentation. The large Cerro Prieto mountainslope village, dating to the late thirteenth century, is believed to be the terminal occupation in this area, a contention supported by architectural traits such as contiguous rooms and rectangular standing masonry-walled rooms (Downum et al. 1993).

The abandonment of the fortified villages of the Robles and Marana areas marks the termination of settlement in the northern Tucson Basin and a retraction to a series of aggregated communities in the central Tucson area. The closest one is Furrey's Ranch near the confluence of the Santa Cruz and Rillito Rivers. Others are found farther south and east. A similar phenomenon is reported in the Santa Cruz Flats (Henderson 1993).

Discussion

Our model of the sequence of events in the northern Tucson Basin is summarized in Figure 10.8. To recap, before A.D. 1050 ball-court communities were present throughout the northern Tucson Basin and region to the north (Figure 10.8a). In the Early Classic period large dispersed communities with platform mounds were established (Figure 10.8b). The platform mounds in the Santa Cruz Flats, Picacho, and Tucson areas may also have been established at this time. Sometime in the late 1200s social conditions deteriorated and large-scale warfare or the threat of large-scale warfare led to the establishment of fortified villages at Linda Vista, Rillito Peak, and Cerro Prieto (Figure 10.8c). In the Marana/Los Morteros zone most of the Early Classic period inhabitants left the region, presumably for the settlement concentrations farther south. Linda Vista and Rillito Peak are not large enough to have supported the entire population of the villages in the area. Cerro Prieto, however, is a large site and may well represent the aggregation of a significant portion of the residents from the surrounding settlements. The dividing wall noted by Downum (1986) at Linda Vista, the separate settlement on Rillito Peak, and a dramatic barrier in the center of the Cerro Prieto community (Downum et al. 1993) all support the idea that these fortified communities represent an amalgamation of residents from multiple villages. That they were not large enough to have housed all the region's Early Classic population is no surprise if there was a threat of imminent attack. Under such conditions, many families might have opted for more secure territory if it was possible for them to do so. Furthermore, if political control was already tenuous because of internal schisms in the regions, the pressures of war may well have been sufficient to fragment the communities.

The fortified villages of the northern Tucson Basin represented the last bastion of settlement in the region. Sometime in the decades preceding the introduction of Gila Polychrome to the region, they too were abandoned and a large unoccupied zone opened up (Figure 10.8d). Large-scale aggregation of populations on either side of the unoccupied zone is documented for the Late Classic period (Henderson 1993; Doelle and Wallace 1991; Wallace and Holmlund 1984).

The sequence of events in the northern Tucson Basin suggests that the likely adversaries are to be found at the northern margin of the unoccupied zone: populations in the Picacho District. Both regions had large Early Classic period settlements that continued to be occupied into the Late Classic period (Ciolek-Torrello et al. 1988; Downum and Madsen 1993; Henderson 1993; Skibo 1988). Populations in these nonriverine settings were highly dependent on favorable environmental conditions for floodwater farming and reservoir irrigation. During hard times they would have been unlikely to raid the large population centers along the Gila to the north because of fear of overwhelming reprisals; populations were nowhere near as large at the margins of the Tucson Basin, however, and settlements such as Los Morteros, Huntington, and the Marana and Robles mound sites might have been favored targets owing to their riverine settings, large mesquite bosques, and likelihood of food stores. The villages were in highly visible lowland settings, and their prime agricultural plots would have been consolidated in a limited and vulnerable zone along the Santa Cruz River and its floodplain. In contrast, even though the residents of the Picacho District had established villages, as did the people in the Marana area, they probably had farming plots scattered over a wide area to maximize their potential return (see Henderson 1993), thereby limiting the ability of an attacking force to damage the food supply significantly or gain access to it. Furthermore, it would have been difficult to wage an effective counterattack in the Santa Cruz Flats or Brady Wash areas because the large mesquite forests would have facilitated ambushes and the ability to escape. The initial response of the Picacho District populations to food and water shortages probably involved contact with settlements along the Casa Grande Canal System. We suspect relatively strong ties in this direction, based on the history of long-term interaction in the Preclassic and ongoing similarities in utilitarian wares in the Classic period. These social relations may have limited aggression in this direction.

That a significant decline in environmental conditions may have oc-

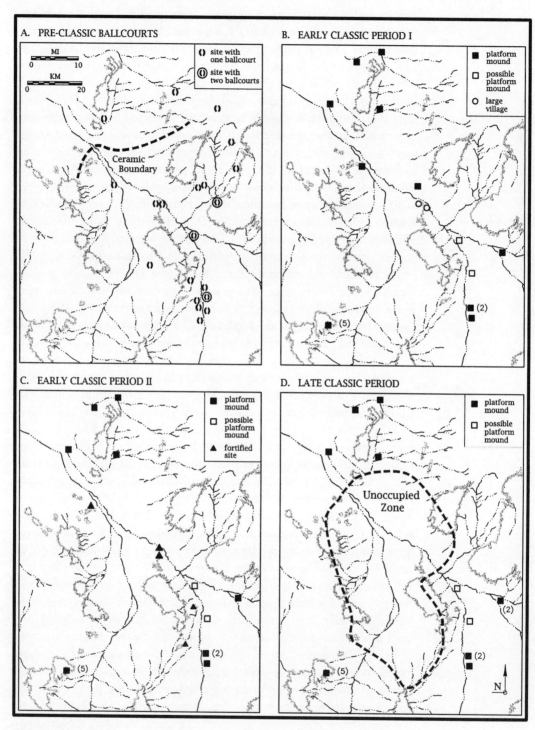

Figure 10.8.
Modeled sequence of
events in the north-
ern Tucson Basin
and Picacho District.
See Figure 10.7 for
site names.

curred, influencing the growing populations in the Picacho District, is supported by evidence of Early Classic period settlement in previously unoccupied parts of the Santa Cruz River floodplain in the Marana and San Xavier areas (Doelle and Wallace 1986; Wallace 1995a; Waters 1987, 1988) and by larger-scale environmental perturbations addressed below.

If these interpretations are correct, the escalated defensive strategies represented by the construction of fortified villages and defensive refuges is partly explicable. Before the late thirteenth century, conflicts in the regions were probably small in scale and perhaps somewhat ameliorated because of long-standing trade relations through the region. With sufficient population expansion into the nonriverine desert zone of the Picacho District, even moderate environmental perturbations could provide the stimulus for raiding by Picacho District populations targeted at food supplies and water resources in the northern Tucson Basin.

It may not have taken anything more than limited raiding and the threat of large-scale attack to have initiated a devastating chain of events in the northern Tucson Basin. A successful raid on the Marana Mound site, perhaps resulting in the death of the village leader or the destruction of crops along the river, could well have been enough to fragment the already politically unstable settlement system. Such an event or perhaps just the threat of such an event might have been sufficient to result in the dispersal of some families and the construction of the Linda Vista and Rillito Peak settlements by others.

The strongest support for this scenario comes from thirteenth- and fourteenth-century ceramic distributions and the abandonment processes evident in the region. In a previous study we pointed to discrete ceramic distributions in the fourteenth century that separate the Phoenix Basin from the Tucson Basin (Doelle and Wallace 1990). This trend is initiated in the Early Classic period. In the northern Tucson Basin sites discussed here the dominant decorated ceramic type is Tanque Verde Red-on-brown, occurring in proportions ranging from 18 to 25 percent of total sherd ceramic collections (Downum 1986; Downum et al. 1993; Bayman 1994; Heidke 1995). Sites with Early Classic period components in the Santa Cruz Flats areas have very low percentages of Tanque Verde Red-on-brown, and Casa Grande Red-on-buff is almost entirely missing from their inventories (Martynec 1993). In the Picacho Mountains area percentages of Tanque Verde Red-on-brown are limited to trace amounts and Casa Grande Red-on-buff is also quite rare (Heacock and Callahan 1988). Tanque Verde Red-on-brown is present on Gila River sites but is very rare. Studies of the type in the Phoenix area suggest local production in that region rather than importation from the Tucson Basin (Crown et al. 1988).

The distribution of decorated ceramic types is related to the locations of production centers and their distance in spatial and social terms from potential consumers. Distribution and consumption are also related to the popularity and acceptance of the products involved. For Tanque Verde Red-on-brown, a type of decorated pottery commonly used throughout the Tucson area, the near absence from sites in the Picacho District is suggestive of a social or ethnic barrier. Since Cerro Prieto has percentages of this ware close to that present in the Tucson Basin proper, it is unlikely that distance from a production center is the only factor involved. This decorative reticence is all the more curious when one considers the quantities of buffware pottery that passed through this region in earlier centuries. Sometime in the mid to late eleventh century A.D. that exchange or distribution network collapsed along with the ball-court system in the Tucson area (Doelle and Wallace 1991). The loss of that network and the increasing regional diversification evident in the Tucson area in the twelfth and thirteenth centuries (Doelle and Wallace 1991; Wallace and Holmlund 1984) are undoubtedly key pieces to this puzzle. The barriers to ceramic distribution may have been initiated at that time, but they became accentuated in the thirteenth century.

In summary, for the northern Tucson Basin, all lines of evidence point the finger of aggression to the north. For the central and southern Tucson Basin, where Tumamoc Hill and Black Mountain are located, the directions of concern are more likely to have been east or west, and this brings up a critical point: even though the case can be made for warfare in the northern Tucson Basin with populations in the Picacho District, this cannot be the full picture. Warfare of this sort is still a limited phenomenon and does not explain the construction of defensive facilities farther south in the Tucson Basin (or elsewhere), nor does it explain why warfare is evident over a much larger area at this time (Spoerl 1979, 1984; Wilcox and Haas 1994). If there was warfare of the sort proposed here, it is merely one symptom of larger-scale processes. With this thought in mind, we move one valley farther east.

CASE STUDY: WARFARE IN THE LOWER SAN PEDRO VALLEY

East of the Tucson Basin, the next valley across the Rincon and Catalina Mountains is the San Pedro. Still largely undeveloped, the portion of the valley considered here is the lower section between Benson and the town of Winkelman where it joins with the Gila (Figure 10.1). This part of the valley is flanked on either side by high mountain ranges topped with coniferous forests. The San Pedro River currently flows through a relatively narrow floodplain on a perennial basis along portions of the channel where springs occur and underlying impervious strata are near the surface. The present-day deeply downcut channel of the river is very different from that observed in the nineteenth century, when the river was a meandering stream with frequent cienegas or marshy areas. Many tributary drainages also have permanent water in mid-bajada and mountain flank zones, and one, Aravaipa Creek, has a significant perennial flow. Springs and seeps are also commonplace in secondary drainages near the river. The lower San Pedro Valley differs from many other desert valleys in southern and central Arizona in that for much of its length it is very narrow, the bajadas are relatively narrow and steep, and adjacent mountains drain considerable quantities of captured rainfall. A wide range of resources is available from a full complement of Sierra Madrean mountain and Sonoran desert ecological zones within a very short distance of the river.

The lower San Pedro Valley is a particularly interesting focus of archaeological study for several reasons. Prehistoric occupation in the valley was widespread and long-lived, and it is distributed in a well-bounded linear corridor, making an ideal setting to investigate interaction and exchange systems. Archaeological remains are still relatively intact in the valley, and it has not seen the urban expansion that has destroyed so many sites in Tucson and Phoenix.

From 1990 to 1995 the Center for Desert Archaeology in Tucson conducted a reconnaissance-level survey of the lower San Pedro Valley (Figure 10.9). The survey focused on habitable terrace tops adjacent to the San Pedro River and had as its goal the identification of all moderate to large prehistoric and historic sites in the valley located along the river. It was made possible through the efforts of more than 85 dedicated amateur and professional volunteer archaeologists. A total of 442 previously unrecorded archaeological sites was documented. One hundred seventeen additional sites with good locational information had been recorded previously in this portion of the valley. Forty-six of them were revisited as part of the survey. In addition, a long-term project is under way to map a series of the large sites. Most have been mapped at a preliminary level, and three of the sites have now been mapped using high-resolution photogrammetry (Doelle et al. 1995; Wallace and Doelle 1997; Wallace et al. 2000).

Settlement Overview: A.D. 800 to 1450(?)

The culture history of the San Pedro Valley spans the full sequence of North American prehistory. Emphasis is placed here on the post–A.D. 1200 portion of the sequence, but a brief consideration of earlier occupation places the areas of interest in context.

The focal points of settlement systems in the San Pedro Valley are zones of perennial flow in the river and tributary drainages, particularly large areas of floodplain that could be irrigated and sizable secondary drainages with Holocene fan deposits suited to ak chin farming. The two largest such areas, occupied intensively throughout prehistory, were near the mouth of Aravaipa Creek and near the small rural community of Redington where Redfield and Buehman Canyons empty into the river.

Ball courts first appeared on villages in the lower San Pedro around A.D. 800 at about the same time that they first show up elsewhere in Arizona (Figure 10.10). They occur in the San Pedro Valley as far south

Figure 10.9. The
lower San Pedro
Valley, with the
Center for Desert
Archaeology survey
area and all recorded
archaeological sites
indicated.

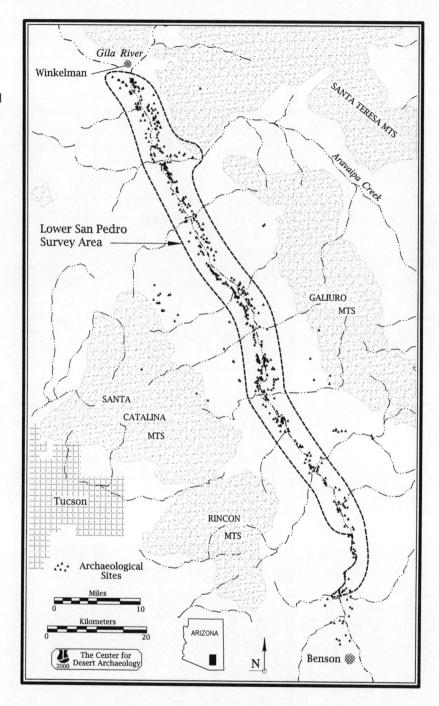

as Tres Alamos and as far north as the Gila River. Most of the early
courts are large, constructed at sites on low terrace settings near perenni-
ally flowing stretches of the river and the largest zones of arable land. In
the period from about 800 to 900 all large sites on the portion of the San
Pedro surveyed had ball courts and relatively few moderate-sized sites

Figure 10.10.
Settlement distribu-
tion in the lower San
Pedro Valley during
the A.D. 800–900,
900–1050,
1150–1275, and
1275–1400 time
periods.

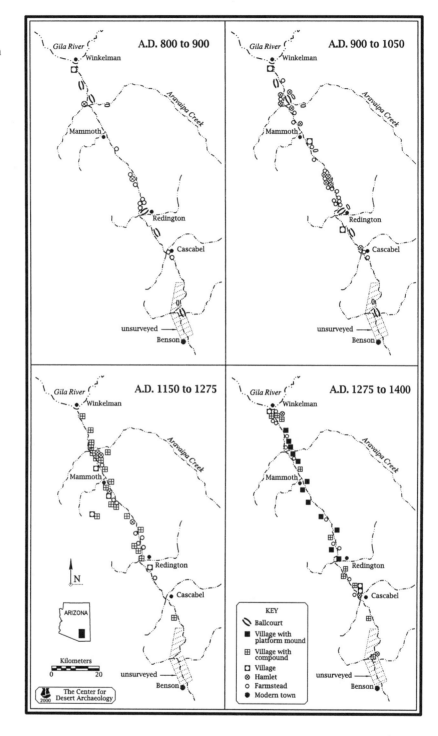

are known. Most non–ball-court sites appear to be minor occupations no more than a household in size; they were probably seasonally occupied limited-activity sites related to agricultural pursuits.

Smaller courts were present on five sites in the valley, including the two largest sites with large courts, Redington and Big Ditch. At least some of these courts were constructed after A.D. 900 at a time when many such courts were being built in neighboring areas (Debowski et al. 1976; Wasley and Benham 1968; Wilcox and Sternberg 1983:121). Sites of this time period are hierarchically organized in household and supra-household clusters of mud-coated pit dwellings surrounding a central plaza. At Redington and possibly at Big Ditch, trash mounds and artificially constructed mounds similar to the capped mounds discussed by Haury (1976) at Snaketown are integral parts of the village structure.

Large quantities of schist-tempered red-on-buff and plain pottery from the Middle Gila occur on sites dating to the period from A.D. 800 to 1050 throughout the lower San Pedro and to a lesser extent on sites farther south. There are two disparate and largely nonoverlapping traditions of locally produced decorated pottery at this time in the valley. North of Mammoth there is a close copy of Middle Gila buffware. A plainware also produced in this area mimics the Middle Gila plainware. With both technology and iconography duplicated in these locally produced wares, we suspect very close interaction and probably small-scale immigration or inmarriage of potters to the Big Ditch site, the most likely production center based on temper source areas and finds of tempering material scattered on the surface of the site.

Pottery of the San Simon series increases in frequency as one moves south of Mammoth, and it becomes the dominant decorated ware during the period of ball-court construction from Redington south. Some of this pottery appears to have been imported, but based on its abundance and distribution, most is thought to have been locally produced somewhere between Redington and Tres Alamos. While bearing some relationship to the designs seen on Middle Gila buffware, the San Simon pottery is most similar to poorly known ceramic styles seen across southeastern Arizona and as far north as the Safford Valley. The production of this pottery in the San Pedro Valley suggests contact in that direction.

After the second wave of ball courts was constructed in the lower San Pedro and elsewhere in southern Arizona between A.D. 900 and 1000, the organization of the settlement system began to shift (Figure 10.10). Where before there had been nucleation, by 1050, settlements became more dispersed and the central-plaza–ball-court focus of the communities was lost. This correlates with the collapse of the ball-court system in southern Arizona and a general process of localization (Milner 1991:36) that may have resulted from increased packing of local groups in the region and the development of closure mechanisms in social networks. This process probably stimulated the expansion of canal systems and increasingly exclusive systems of land tenure. Population increases and favorable climatic or hydrological regimes could also have played roles, as we noted above for the northern Tucson Basin. This expansion of agricultural systems facilitated the dispersal of settlement along them. After 1075 buffware pottery from the Middle Gila was no longer imported to any significant degree in the valley. In areas south of Mammoth, where San Simon wares were produced, styles of design became more and more similar to those seen on buffware and brownware from the Gila and Tucson areas.

By A.D. 1150 the settlement system in the lower San Pedro underwent a major transformation (Figure 10.10). Settlements remained in the same key locations in the valley where there were optimal land and water resources, but they moved to defendable higher terrace settings. Some settlements were established near springs at the flanks of the mountains as well, but little is known of this environmental zone in the valley. Masonry and adobe architecture appears in house construction and newly added compound walls. Settlements were still relatively dispersed, with no more than one to three households living together in a compound and not all households residing in compound enclosures. Up to this time the subsistence base for settlement in the valley had been focused on irrigation and ak chin agriculture in the river floodplain and the mouths of tributary drainages, with minor forays into dry-farming techniques on nearby terraces. After 1150 hundreds of large dry-farming field systems were established on the high terraces and lower bajadas of the valley. Thought to be focused on the cultivation of agave, they are an indication of diversification and their construction parallels a trend seen in other areas such as the Tucson Basin, Middle Gila, and Tonto Basin.

Sometime in the late thirteenth or early fourteenth century platform mounds were constructed on twelve sites in the lower San Pedro (Figures 10.10 and 10.11). Some of the sites have evidence of occupation in the 1200s preceding the construction of the mounds, and in one recently discovered case (Bayless Ruin) a possible platform mound may have been constructed and abandoned before the fourteenth century. The northernmost mound is found near Dudleyville, the southernmost at Bayless Ruin near Redington. Eleven of these sites remain at least partly intact, and preliminary maps have been prepared of 10 of them (Figure 10.11). The recently identified possible Bayless mound has not yet been mapped, and the Big Bell site was destroyed before it could be recorded.

The fourteenth-century platform mound compounds in the San Pedro system were the focal points of population aggregation, and most of the population in this portion of the valley lived in them. Compounds and room blocks dating to the Late Classic period are found near some of the platform mound sites; none is very large or contained sizable populations. In contrast, both north and south of the known mound sites there are concentrations of population residing in relatively dispersed groups of compounds that lack mounds (Figure 10.10). One such concentration is located just south of Winkelman. Another is the recently mapped

Figure 10.11.
Locations and pre-
liminary maps of
platform mound
compounds in the
lower San Pedro
Valley. Note that
most internal rooms
are not shown.

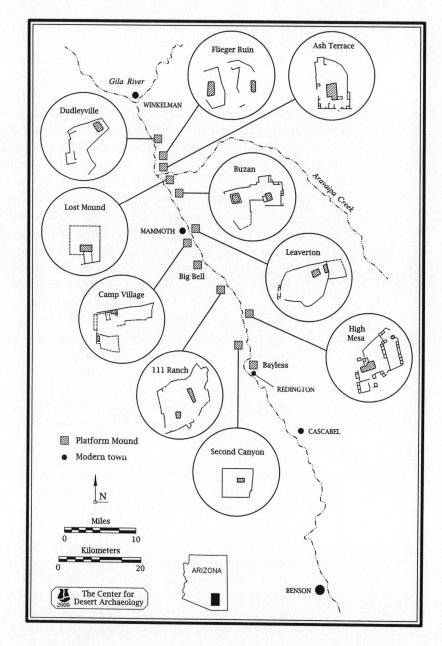

fourteenth-century portion of the Bayless Ruin and the nearby Davis and
Reeve ruins, which were excavated by the Amerind Foundation in the
1950s (Di Peso 1958). Several other concentrations of Late Classic period population residing in compounds are found between Redington and
Cascabel and farther south between Cascabel and Tres Alamos.

A great deal of architectural variability is evident in the thirteenth-
and fourteenth-century occupations in the valley. Much of this variability
has been attributed to an influx of migrants from the Safford or Point of
Pines area of eastern Arizona, a point further considered below.

Evidence of Warfare in the Lower San Pedro Valley

The settlement-pattern shifts in the lower San Pedro Valley north of Redington initiated in the twelfth or thirteenth century are indicative of a significant concern with defense and warfare. With the change from low riverine settings for the larger villages to high second-terrace settings, there is a concomitant appearance of compound enclosures and masonry construction. In the Redington area these new architectural forms and shifting village locations are coeval with the appearance of corrugated pottery.

The change in village locations is not a minor one. Examined in isolation in most areas, the settlement shifts might be attributed entirely to internal social processes. When the sum of the cases present in the valley is considered, however, a pattern emerges. Two examples are illustrative of the trend and its significance. The first is the area north of Aravaipa Creek. For at least four hundred years, people had been living in the large Big Ditch community on a large low terrace immediately above the floodplain of one of the richest portions of the San Pedro Valley. In addition to the large Big Ditch site, small villages were present in the eleventh century throughout the area near the river and along Aravaipa Creek. Sometime in the late twelfth century or early thirteenth century Big Ditch and most of the smaller nearby sites were abandoned and a set of residential compounds was constructed on the high second terraces. We suspect the largest of these ultimately developed into the Ash Terrace, Flieger, Lost Mound, and Buzan platform mound villages, all of which are known for their concentrated settlement in the fourteenth century. The second-terrace settings used by these communities were not fortress-like mountaintops. There are no such high, readily defended settings in this portion of the valley. Instead, we see two processes under way as lower terrace settings were abandoned. First, there was the construction of multiple residential areas on second-terrace settings. Second, there was a consolidation of populations into the vicinity of Aravaipa Creek and the richest arable land in the valley. Although these populations are scattered north and south of the creek, in the thirteenth century, by the time Gila Polychrome appears on the scene, populations had aggregated to the extent that virtually all residents lived within the walls of the platform mound compounds.

The second example provides the key to the processes under way. In the area north of Redington near the mouth of Kielberg Canyon and Alder Wash, populations in the eleventh and twelfth centuries lived in a set of small villages and hamlets strung out along the lowest habitable terraces above the river. Several of these settlements, including Alder Wash, Dos Bisnagas, and Una Cholla, have been excavated (Masse 1974; Masse et al. 1998). The east side of the river in this area has high precipitous cliffs and very high terraces that were shunned for habitation at that time in favor of lower settings on the west bank closer to fields and

Figure 10.12. Aerial view of the defensible high terrace where the High Mesa Ruin is located.

water. Sometime in the thirteenth century the High Mesa village was founded atop one of the highest terraces in the region (Figures 10.12 and 10.13). Recent test excavations indicate that several compound enclosures were built at the site, including Compound 3 at the northeast portion of the ruin and a portion of or predecessor to Compound 1. Sometime in the late 1200s or early 1300s a platform mound and possible tower were constructed in Compound 1 and the compound was rebuilt or expanded. We are currently unsure whether Compound 2 was constructed before 1300; it was certainly occupied after that date, however.

The terrace remnant on which High Mesa occurs rises 50 m above the modern San Pedro River floodplain. Shaped like a human foot with the "toes" fronting the river, the terrace narrows to a heel no more than 25 m across. All sides of the terrace other than the narrow heel are bordered by cliffs and precipitous slopes. The terrace top is relatively level. A probable prehistoric trail climbs from the mouth of Kielberg Canyon to the ruins on the terrace top, passing several areas with cultural remains on the way. At the base of the trail several possible masonry structures flank it, possibly controlling access. The natural topography of the High Mesa terrace provides excellent protection from attack, leaving only the narrow upslope end open to ready access and potential danger. At the narrowest point of the heel a masonry and adobe wall was constructed to seal off access (Figure 10.13). Because the wall was built at a high point immediately beyond which the elevation dropped off, its height was accentuated by the natural topography. Just inside the wall, rock rubble and dirt was removed to accentuate the wall's height, leaving a

Figure 10.13. The
High Mesa Ruin.

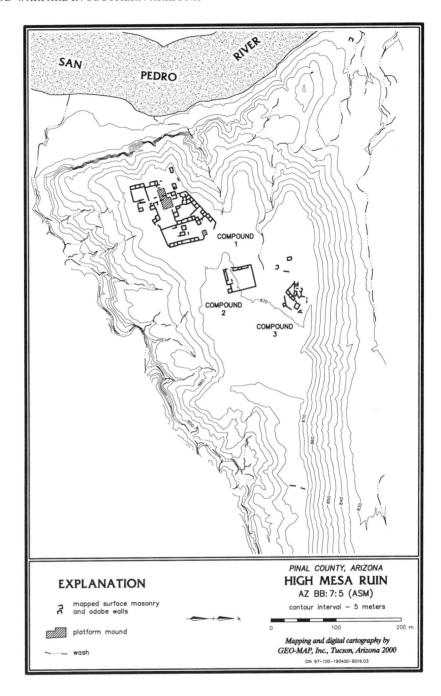

pile of rubble with the appearance of a secondary rampart. Overlooking
the High Mesa site immediately south of the ruin is an even higher mesa
that is the highest single point overlooking the river in this portion of the
valley. In the spot most suited for a lookout, there is a cleared area and
Classic period artifact scatter indicative of temporary residence. We suspect this was a sentry's lookout post. Given its dramatic view, the setting
would have been ideal for signaling to a large portion of the valley.

Figure 10.14. The Redington area in the fourteenth century with discussed site locations.

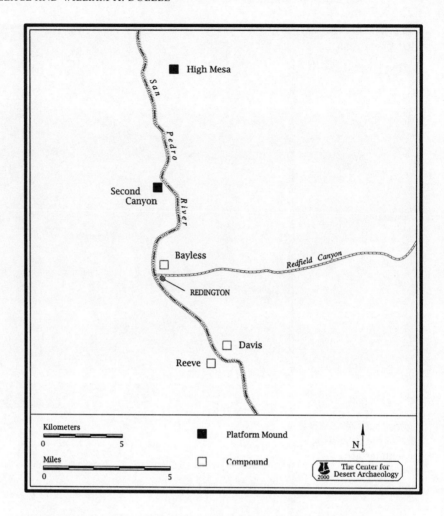

Even without the wall and possible lookout, High Mesa's setting is suggestive of defense, although one might conceivably argue that the location served a ritual or signaling role. When the sum of the evidence is considered, there can be little doubt that the ruin and related facilities were built with defense in mind.

Before we consider the implications of the High Mesa data, it is important to note that the site is not the only one in this portion of the valley to exhibit obvious fortifications. Figure 10.14 illustrates site locations in this part of the valley. Reeve Ruin, a small village constructed sometime very early in the fourteenth century, is comparably sited (Figure 10.15), with a massive wall sealing off the terrace on which it is located from upslope attack (Di Peso 1958). Just upslope from the site is a small conical hill that overlooks the ruin and surrounding territory. A moderate artifact scatter atop the hill bearing ceramics coeval with Reeve could indicate the presence of a sentry post similar to the one documented at High Mesa.

Taken together, High Mesa and Reeve Ruins offer compelling evi-

Figure 10.15. Aerial view of the defensible high terrace where the Reeve Ruin is located.

dence that conditions of warfare—either the threat of deadly force or actual attacks—were present in the lower San Pedro Valley. The sequence of events at High Mesa places the settlement shifts elsewhere in the lower San Pedro Valley in context. If the shift from lower terrace settings to the High Mesa terrace indicates a concern with defense, there is no reason to doubt that this was also the case in other areas such as the Aravaipa Creek region. We emphasize that this need not be the *only* reason to move to these areas. If the shift is accompanied by changes in social and community organization (as we suspect), village leaders may have couched the move in a ritual and organizational framework that also happened to offer increased protection. Also, it must be acknowledged that this process of settlement movement was not universal. Some Preclassic settlements are found on midlevel terraces, and there are a few late sites known from low terrace settings. We are warranted in generalizing, however, because the exceptions are all attributable to a lack of the favored settings in portions of the valley.

At the High Mesa and the Aravaipa Creek area the process of settlement movement was accompanied by aggregation. Dispersed populations joined together into large platform mound compounds. As noted earlier, this pattern of aggregation occurs throughout the investigated region.

If it is true that warfare on a regionwide scale motivated shifts in settlement, we would expect to see other responses to it in the lower San Pedro. There should be other dramatic high-terrace settlements founded in the Early Classic period. Massive defensive walls might be constructed to protect vulnerable settlements. Unoccupied zones might occur in adjoining regions. Ideally, we would find burned villages and bodies with trauma-related injuries. Some of these data are recorded for the region. Additional high-terrace settings occupied in the fourteenth century with known Early Classic period occupations include Leaverton, near the town of Mammoth, and Second Canyon (Franklin 1980), just south of High Mesa. Recent excavations by the Center for Desert Archaeology indicate that others exist at Dudleyville and 111 Ranch underlying the fourteenth-century compounds.

Massive perimeter walls are unknown from any of the definite thirteenth-century occupations in the valley, but they are present in key settings at fourteenth-century ruins. Leaverton, Buzan, and Flieger offer the best examples in this regard. Leaverton and Flieger are situated on narrow, high terraces and are enclosed by massive cobble masonry compound walls at the inflection points of the upper slope, thereby maximizing the effective wall height. This is the same strategy described by Wilcox (1979b:27–28) for wall construction on Tumamoc Hill in the Tucson Basin. Buzan is on a larger, more open terrace, but the walls are similarly positioned as much as was possible. The two Second Canyon sites (the excavated compound reported by Franklin [1980] and the Second Canyon platform mound site), Big Bell, and 111 Ranch may also be viewed in this light. One might expect that all late sites in the valley would be constructed with massive perimeter walls if defense was a concern. We can think of several reasons why such was not the case. First, some sites such as High Mesa and Reeve relied more on topography than on walls. At both these sites the unwalled portions of the village face the river where there were high cliffs. There was no reason to fear attack from this quarter. Had the perimeter walls that were present at these sites been constructed entirely for social purposes, these areas would not have been left open—the steep cliffs were a serious safety hazard for children. Second, it is the two innermost mound sites in the Aravaipa cluster of four, Lost Mound and Ash Terrace, that are set back from the edges of terraces and are more vulnerable. This is explicable if the four sites are viewed as a confederacy, with the central sites having the most warning and least likelihood of sudden attack. In the Redington area the large Bayless Ruin (Figure 10.16), sited in the center of a very large open terrace, is similar in some respects to the concentration of settlements at Aravaipa Creek in that it was undoubtedly the focus of a large population. Perhaps sheer numbers of people were defense enough in this location. The site is walled and in this respect does not differ from the others in the region.

As for unoccupied areas, there is such a zone that opens up in the Buttes district of the Gila River a short distance to the northwest, but it

Figure 10.16. The
Bayless Ruin.

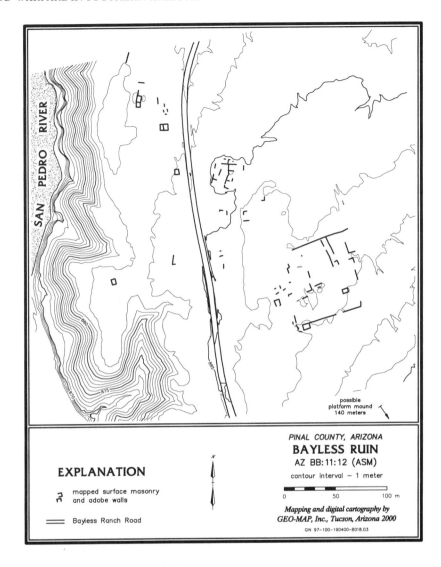

is unclear to us whether it is directly related to the events in question
here. Otherwise there are no large-scale abandonments in the valley until
the terminus of the Classic period. We return to this issue in the concluding discussion.

There is very little direct evidence of warfare in the form of mutilated
bodies and ransacked villages from the San Pedro, but it must be noted
that none of the platform mound sites has been excavated (other than
test pits in trash deposits), and few other Classic period sites have been
investigated. An eleventh- or early twelfth-century structure excavated at
the Big Ditch site produced a mutilated adult skeleton, potentially a result of violent behavior (Masse 1974; Masse et al. 1998). An earlier
eleventh-century pit structure at Alder Wash contained the remains of a
woman with an arrow point in her ribcage (Masse 1974; Masse et al.
1998). Neither of these contexts is definitive evidence of warfare. The

three largest Classic period excavations that have resulted in data sets available for inspection are the unpublished excavations at Ash Terrace, just north of Aravaipa Creek (Mike Bartlett, personal communication 1998; material stored in the Arizona State Museum archives), Reeve Ruin (Di Peso 1958), and the investigations at the Second Canyon compound (Franklin 1980). As only a few masonry rooms were excavated at Ash Terrace, little can be said concerning site abandonment processes; it is notable, however, that at least one of the structures excavated was burned and contained a large intact floor assemblage of household goods (ASM archives). Both Reeve Ruin and the Davis Ruin appear to have been deliberately abandoned and stripped of floor artifacts (Di Peso 1958; Allan McIntyre, personal communication 1997). Reeve Ruin also produced only limited quantities of trash, and it is uncertain whether the excavated contexts were screened, leaving us with little to evaluate and a level of uncertainty that precludes consideration for artifactual data. Data on artifacts from the Davis Ruin have not yet been published. There is no evidence of catastrophic abandonment at the Second Canyon compound.

In summary, the strongest evidence of warfare or the threat of attack in the lower San Pedro Valley consists of three lines of evidence: movement of settlements to defensible settings, construction of fortifications (barrier walls and some compound walls), and aggregation of populations into single large compounds or several closely spaced compounds. We turn now to the cultural backdrop and social processes that may have led to conflict in the area.

Migrations and Ethnic Boundaries

Evidence is accumulating that multiple waves of immigrants from the east or northeast moved into the lower San Pedro Valley during the thirteenth and fourteenth centuries (Doelle 1995; Lindsay 1987; Clark et al. 1998). The earliest evidence for this population influx, including such things as production of corrugated pottery and room-block architecture, is coincident with the shift in settlement to second-terrace settings. Corrugated pottery first appears in the San Pedro Valley sometime in the thirteenth century. It is most abundant in the portion of the valley south of Mammoth, with the densest concentrations noted in the stretch from the Big Bell to Bayless sites. Long viewed as an indication of Mogollon influences, corrugated wares follow very restricted and selective distributions on both a regional scale and within particular sites (Clark et al. 1998). This distinctive distribution, the fact that it is a utilitarian ware, and its co-occurrence with other material culture and architectural traits support its utility in documenting prehistoric population movements. Specialization in corrugated pottery production by immigrant households has been documented in a comparably dated settlement in the eastern Tonto Basin (Heidke and Stark 1995; Heidke 1998); this may have occurred in the Redington area as well.

Additional thirteenth-century indications of population movements into the San Pedro Valley are limited to architectural traits (especially room-block architecture as opposed to compound enclosures) observed at a set of compounds explored and mapped by Dudley Meade which have been recently reevaluated and analyzed by Clark and others (1998). These sites are located in an upland setting near Oracle, and it is unknown how representative they are of trends in the valley at large. It is important to note, however, that a significant immigration of populations from the Point of Pines area and beyond was under way in the Safford area by the late 1200s and that some of the sites in that area were built in defensible settings (see Clark et al. 1998; Woodson 1995). Furthermore, Clark et al. (1998) and Slaughter (1996) argue that some of the immigrants into the region spilled over Redington Pass and perhaps around the southern end of the Rincon Mountains into the eastern Tucson Basin.

The most dramatic evidence for immigration into the San Pedro Valley is seen at the southern margin of the platform mound distribution where a string of excavated fourteenth-century sites have unmistakable intrusive architectural features. These include a rectangular kiva at the Davis Ruin (Di Peso 1958:14), slab-lined hearths and mealing basins at Bayless and Second Canyon (Duffen 1936; Franklin 1980), and entry-box complexes at the Reeve and Davis Ruins (Lindsay et al. 1968:7–8, Figure 204; Di Peso 1958:36; Amerind Foundation archives). A map of the main compound at the Davis Ruin is provided in Figure 10.17. The kiva and some rooms with entry boxes are visible. A migration route originating in the Tusayan or Kayenta area and passing through the Point of Pines and Safford areas before heading to the San Pedro has been postulated (Clark et al. 1998; Doelle 1995; Duffen 1936; Lindsay 1987; Woodson 1995). The architectural and ceramic data indicate varying levels of immigration. In some cases it appears that one or two households moved into a previously occupied site (Second Canyon); at Reeve and Davis the entire population may have immigrated. Artifact data supporting this concept are perforated plates and Tucson and Maverick Mountain polychrome pottery. They are viewed as intrusive in form or design to the region but were produced in the area. These pottery types follow a distribution that includes most of the lower San Pedro and extends eastward where they are abundant in the Aravaipa drainage (Allan McIntyre, personal communication 1997), Safford Valley (Crary 2000; Woodson 1995), and Point of Pines area (Haury 1986; Lindsay 1987, 1992).

In addition to evidence of immigration, several lines of evidence point to an ethnic or social boundary in the Redington area. We alluded above to the mutually exclusive distributions of copies of Middle Gila pottery,

Figure 10.17. Main
compound at the
Davis Ruin (courtesy
of the Amerind
Foundation).

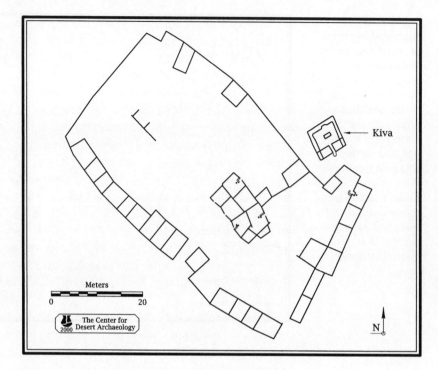

produced in the vicinity of Aravaipa Creek, and San Simon pottery, produced between Tres Alamos and Redington. Because the contrasts between these ceramic systems involve both the use of distinctive culturally
defined symbols and the employment of different technologies that reflect the learning process (see Sackett's [1985] and Stark's [1995b] discussion of emblemic and isochrestic stylistic variation), we suggest that
there may have been a social boundary in the valley somewhere between
Alder Wash and Redington (Figure 10.18). South of the suggested social
boundary line, ceramics suggest a southeastern Arizona tie with strong
links to the Tucson Basin. The ball-court system crosscuts this boundary,
and it is curious that one of the two most elaborate Middle Gila–like
sites in the valley, Redington, lies just south of the line. Why here? We
suggest that the presence of a social boundary adjacent to the second-
best place to live in the valley may have motivated the development of
this site. Tensions between social groups within the valley could have
been minimized by the wholesale adoption of the same ritual system and
establishment of direct contact with leaders in the Middle Gila and perhaps also in the Safford Valley.

The social boundary north of Redington persisted into the 1300s, as
seen in the distribution of platform mounds, which terminates in this
portion of the valley. The ceramic assemblage of the northern area was
noted to be essentially identical to that observed in the Middle Gila from
A.D. 800 to 1050, and it is therefore not surprising, if one assumes ongoing close interaction, that it is this zone that later adopts platform
mounds. The curious phenomenon of the Bayless site must be considered

Figure 10.18.
Suggested locations
of social boundaries
and immigrant
groups. A social
boundary is marked
by the distributions
of ceramics in the
period A.D. 800 to
900 and by the
southern terminus of
the platform mounds
in the 1300s. The
inferred social
boundary crosscuts
the Preclassic ball-
court distribution.

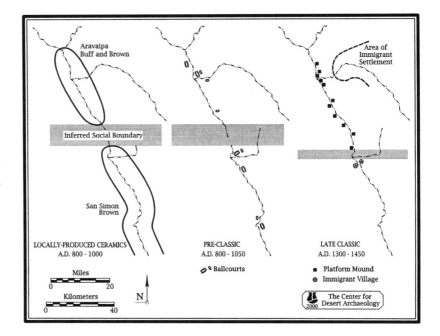

here. In a portion of the Bayless site that was soon to be abandoned, what appears to be a small platform mound was constructed (the feature requires testing to be certain). The level of effort put into this construction was probably minimal, as it seems to have used a Preclassic period trash-and-cobble mound as its core. Presumably dating to the late 1200s based on abundant corrugated pottery in its vicinity, the mound, including any population that may have been directly associated with it, was abandoned before the appearance of Gila Polychrome in the valley. Most of the Bayless Ruin is located slightly north of this possible platform mound, and it was occupied continuously well into the fourteenth century. This portion of the site definitely lacks a platform mound; therefore, after 1300 the southernmost mound was the Second Canyon site. This fleeting example of mound construction at the terminus of the mound distribution is curious. Were competing factions in the community fostering different approaches to political and religious power? Until testing confirms the status of this feature as a platform mound, further speculation is unwarranted.

Structurally, the platform mound sites in the San Pedro Valley are more similar to those in the Tucson Basin than to those of the Middle Gila (Hayden 1957; Wallace 1996; Wallace and Holmlund 1984). It may be that the Tucson and San Pedro areas were responding in similar ways to the pressures leading to aggregation and that these processes did not affect the larger populations of the Phoenix Basin in the same way. The stimulus for the adoption of platform mounds may well have originated in the Phoenix Basin, but the response is a local one that mirrored those of other outlying areas (Doelle et al. 1995).

Who Did They Fear?

Where is the enemy in the lower San Pedro Valley? The appearance of the unoccupied zone in the northern Tucson Basin provided strong clues for the direction to turn in that case, but no such zone opened up in the lower San Pedro Valley. The most striking data from the lower San Pedro are the concentrations of fortified sites in the Redington area, the evidence for large-scale immigration in this zone, and the existence of a long-term social or ethnic boundary here. Complementing these data and providing some context for potential defensive responses seen in the northern end of the valley are the tantalizing data from Aravaipa Canyon and the portion of the Aravaipa drainage above the canyon narrows. Both immigration and the construction of fortified villages are indicated in the limited data available from that region. During the Preclassic the upper Aravaipa area would have been similar in many respects to the Santa Cruz Flats, in that it is a borderland between the Middle Gila–tied population concentration in the northern portion of the lower San Pedro and the large concentration of settlement in the Safford Valley. In the Classic period the region acts as a conduit for immigration to points westward. Fortifications in the Aravaipa and the choice by some families to live in cliff dwellings within the canyon are a sign of strife.

For the San Pedro, tensions could have developed on several fronts. The social mechanisms that were in place during Preclassic times to mediate disputes across ethnic or social boundaries in the Redington and Aravaipa Canyon areas may have become increasingly strained as immigrants settled in the valley and allied themselves to populations in the borderlands. Social reorganization by populations in the northern valley involving the construction of platform mounds and population aggregation may have aggravated the situation. There is a strong possibility that alliances among villages shifted over time. We do not know who the protagonists were in this context and decline to attempt a specific identification. What can be suggested is that a general antagonism across the ethnic or tribal boundaries in the Redington and possibly the Aravaipa Canyon areas could easily have led to skirmishes in these directions.

An additional local system boundary had been proposed in the Benson area just south of Tres Alamos (Altschul and Jones 1990; Wilcox 1995a:284–285), but new data (Altschul et al. 1998; Wallace 1998) weaken aspects of the earlier argument, and additional research is needed in the portion of the valley between Benson and Charleston before this possibility is developed further. We do not view the limited distribution of Babocomari Polychrome as an indicator of social boundaries in this zone, contrary to Altschul and Jones (1990) and Altschul et al. (1998), instead regarding it as one of many local variants of a panregional style that crosscuts tribal boundariea

DISCUSSION

Data from two adjacent regions have been presented, and for each region the case has been made that there is strong evidence for prehistoric warfare. Additional information presented in this section supports these conclusions and considers points of similarity and contrast between the two cases. Of particular interest is the substantial difference between conditions in adjacent areas at the same period of time.

The Tools of War: Projectile Points

The primary data reviewed thus far have focused on architecture, settlement patterns, and evidence for the degree of interaction between settlements or geographic areas. One line of related evidence that ties directly with warfare is the frequency and distribution of projectile points. Evidence of warfare in the northern Tucson Basin is bolstered by mortuary and ritual data from Los Morteros and the Marana Mound site. Large numbers of small triangular obsidian and chalcedony arrow points were recovered from Early Classic period mortuary and midden deposits. At Los Morteros 6 of 17 undisturbed excavated cremation burials contained arrow points (Lange 1989; Wallace 1995a), and in one unusual cemetery area two cremations contained a total of 139 points in addition to a range of other unusual artifacts. This contrasts sharply with cremations from previous phases that lack projectile points. At the Marana Mound site across the river large numbers of small arrow points were recovered from midden contexts (Bayman 1994). Also of interest is Hackbarth's (1993:573–574) report of increasing frequencies of arrow points over time at the Santa Cruz Flat sites even though large game animal remains significantly decreased. They point out that the "higher frequency of projectile points at . . . [these] sites could signal an increase in the need for offensive/defensive tools."

For the San Pedro, excavations at the sites of Second Canyon and Ash Terrace yielded an abundance of small triangular arrow points made from obsidian and chalcedony. Fifteen or more of these points were recovered from two rooms and the adjoining extramural area at Ash Terrace. At Second Canyon a minimum of 62 of the 80 projectile points recovered date to the Classic period occupation; and as seen in the northern Tucson Basin, numerous examples were found associated with cremation burials (Franklin 1980:167–169). The frequencies of arrow points recovered from these limited Classic period excavations in the valley stand in sharp contrast to the small numbers of arrow points from Preclassic excavated contexts in the area (e.g., Franklin 1980; Masse 1974). The difference is an order of magnitude in scale and likely to be significant. The trend is consistent with that observed in the northern Tucson Basin and Santa Cruz Flats.

These finds from both study areas raise the possibility that war societies and special statuses related to warfare were present. Stone arrow points, particularly those made of obsidian as are many of those cited here, are cross-culturally favored for warfare (Ellis 1997). Support for this contention is seen in historic documentation. In an eighteenth-century document on Pimería Alta, Pfefferkorn (1949:202–203) describes in fair detail the process of manufacturing arrows by northern Pimans. He specifically reports that stone-tipped arrows were used in warfare. Brew and Huckell (1987) document an early Piman burial from the Tucson Basin with a complete arrow-maker's toolkit, and Russell (1975:200–204) and Underhill (1939:128–131) report on warrior societies for the Pima and the Tohono O'Odham, respectively. Continuing research in the northern Tucson Basin and the San Pedro Valley should add to our knowledge of the tools of war and their implications.

Keeping Close Company: The Aggregation Response

Large-scale population aggregation occurred in both the Tucson and San Pedro regions during the late thirteenth and perhaps early fourteenth centuries, but the process differs significantly between the two study areas. A clear process of aggregation is documented in the lower San Pedro Valley at sites where platform mounds were constructed. Architecture at these sites shows clear signs of accretionary growth. New rooms were added, suggesting that new domestic groups were joining the settlement. In numerous cases multiple compounds with separate platform mounds grew to form a single architectural unit. These consolidations of once distinct social groups and substantial populations into single settlements would have required effective functional integration to preserve internal order and maintain relations with other platform mound settlements undergoing similarly complex growth trajectories. Platform mounds in these aggregated communities undoubtedly functioned to help integrate populations and ameliorate internal disputes, and they likely played a role in organizing for and responding to warfare in the San Pedro area during the Late Classic period.

In the northern Tucson Basin, aggregation failed as a social response to conditions of warfare. Large portions of the northern Tucson Basin populations residing in the platform mound villages and other villages located nearby chose to flee rather than join forces. Instead of aggregating into a large lowland platform mound community, the people established fortified mountainslope villages. Linda Vista and Cerro Prieto probably represent a consolidation of population from multiple villages, given their size, evidence of contemporaneous occupation among habitation units, and the presence of village dividing walls (suggesting the presence of multiple social groups). A short occupation span at these sites and subsequent abandonment of the region around them point to the failure of this adaptive strategy.

Although the populations that abandoned the area between the Rillito–Santa Cruz junction and Picacho Peak cannot be traced to specific villages, it is likely that they contributed to a process of aggregation evident in the Late Classic period in the Tucson Basin. Population was concentrated in three areas: along the Santa Cruz from the Cañada del Oro south to modern Twenty-Second Street, along the Santa Cruz from Martinez Hill south four miles to the Zanardelli site, and around University Ruin at the juncture of the Pantano and Tanque Verde washes. Similarly, the large sites around the Picacho Mountains and in the Santa Cruz Flats represent the aggregation of multiple compounds around a platform mound center. Thus, we can say that aggregation occurred in the region, but it was effective only when a 29-mile-wide unoccupied zone was established. Those that attempted small-scale aggregation and fortification as a defensive strategy met with failure.

Keeping One's Distance: The Development of an Unoccupied Zone

Increasing the physical distance between adversaries raises the costs of implementing hostilities. It requires more time and consumes more supplies just to get within striking distance, and the likelihood of detection is greater. These factors raise the risk of failure, with its accompanying loss of prestige and, ultimately, loss of life. Different responses were noted in our two study areas: a substantial unoccupied zone opened up in the northern Tucson Basin but not in the San Pedro. Several ethnographic and documentary observations provide further perspective on these issues.

Compared with a historically documented buffer zone on the lower Gila River, the unoccupied zone in the northern Tucson Basin was not particularly wide. A long-term enmity relationship between groups resident on the lower Colorado River and the Pima and Maricopa of the middle Gila River is well documented (e.g., Kroeber and Fontana 1986; Russell 1975; Spier 1933). Over time, settlement relocations led to development of an uninhabited zone between these groups of at least 150 miles, which represents a travel time on foot of six days. Nevertheless, parties of 100 to 150 or more warriors were recruited to travel this great distance in order to engage the enemy. Both the historic records and the ethnographic information for these groups underscore the deep-seated nature of the hatreds that kept this warfare going despite the broad buffer zone (see Rice this volume). In the case of the 50-mile-wide unoccupied zone noted earlier for the historic Sobaipuri of the San Pedro Valley, there is insufficient documentary detail to know whether that distance was sufficient to curtail raiding altogether or whether it just reduced the frequency of raiding. These observations suggest that the unoccupied zone in the northern Tucson Basin might not have been an effective deterrent in and of itself. It may have been necessary to combine aggregation with the buffer zone to be effective.

The absence of any kind of unoccupied zone in the San Pedro during the Classic period merits further discussion. Two factors are considered particularly relevant. First, there is the likelihood that relatively high population density (significantly more than what was recorded in the 1690s) and relatively uniform population distribution created a situation of social circumscription (Carneiro 1970) that precluded the unoccupied zone option. The platform mound distribution map (Figure 10.11) shows the relatively even distribution of intensive settlement along the San Pedro River. In addition, extensive areas of nonriverine dry-farming systems occur along most of this settled zone and are indicative of some degree of agricultural intensification. Thus it is very likely that abandonment of any sizable area in order to create a buffer zone would have resulted in substantial reductions in subsistence productivity because it would have entailed giving up highly productive lands. The incentives to avoid this option would have been great.

Second, it is possible that the intensity of hostilities between groups in the San Pedro was less than that experienced in the northern Tucson Basin or that more effective mechanisms had been developed to regulate the intensity of their expression. More effective coping mechanisms are predicted in the San Pedro than in the northern Tucson Basin because the cultural boundary near Redington in the San Pedro was located within a zone of dense settlement and there had been extensive contact throughout prehistory in the area. This situation differs from the more dispersed character of settlement in the region north of the northern Tucson Basin. The defensive character of many of the San Pedro sites could indicate a degree of consciousness of the threat of aggression even if that threat was not imminent. It may have been an "insurance policy" for those times when the available coping mechanisms failed. The evidence of a planned abandonment of the Reeve Ruin, the fact that the kiva at Davis Ruin was filled and used as a cemetery—suggesting a process of local accommodation by the residents—and the fairly lengthy period of time that immigrants and local groups lived near one another all mark a reasonably successful strategy of coexistence. It remains unclear how to interpret the abandonment of Reeve and Davis. Perhaps it is simply evidence that the immigrants found it difficult to adjust to the social and environmental conditions in the San Pedro, conditions very different from those of their homeland. Alternatively, maybe social tensions were too great and eventually precipitated village abandonment. The apparently orderly, planned process of abandonment is an important factor to account for in future research.

Broader Context 1: Regional Environmental Factors

Given the coincident timing of events in the northern Tucson Basin and San Pedro Valley and the knowledge that similar events were occurring in the Classic period all across southern and central Arizona, it is reasonable to look to large-scale processes that may have fostered warfare.

Dean and others (1985, 1994) hypothesize and demonstrate that when severe environmental degradation and serious droughts coincide with areas and times in prehistory where there are high population densities, social responses are most pronounced. A long period of moderate environmental conditions that fostered stable population growth and expansion in the eleventh century across most of the American Southwest abruptly terminated around A.D. 1130 when conditions worsened throughout the region. "On the plateau and in the mountains, a secondary dip in alluvial groundwater levels and minor floodplain erosion were accompanied by severe drought. In the desert, the climatic downturn was reflected in reduced streamflow in the Salt and Verde rivers" (Dean et al. 1994:75–76). Stream courses such as the Santa Cruz and San Pedro may also have been affected; such depletions are unlikely to have been as widespread or severe as those experienced on the plateau, however, and dependable oases were certainly present. Reduced carrying capacities and changes in areas suitable for settlement would have had a significant impact on densely populated zones. These effects are reflected in large-scale settlement reorganizations across the Southwest in the late 1100s and early 1200s and the abandonment of some regions. It is during this span of time that we first see evidence of immigrant groups moving southward into the Point of Pines, Tonto, Safford, San Pedro, and Tucson areas. An important aspect to consider in the environmental history of the region is a fundamental difference between the mountain and plateau areas and the riverine desert areas of southern and central Arizona. Riverine desert environments offered a much more stable and rich biotic resource base than other areas, and this base could be supplemented by irrigation agriculture: "Other areas lacked the cushion provided by long-term subsistence stability and were more susceptible to environmental and sociocultural perturbations" (Dean et al. 1994:74). During hard times this would have made the riverine desert areas particularly attractive to peoples living in other areas.

Regional settlement reorganization in the early 1200s was followed by severe environmental perturbations and serious droughts (ca. A.D. 1275) across northern and central Arizona, resulting in settlement dislocation on a grand scale. The specific environmental effects of this event in southern Arizona are uncertain, but it is reasonable to assume that critical water and arable land resources continued to be available in the prime zones in the Tucson and San Pedro areas. The processes of settlement dislocation and migrations at the scale evident during this time period would have been communicated throughout the region. Tensions were high, and people residing in resource-rich zones would have been worried about protecting their claims to the land. Immigrants who may have already established footholds in the San Pedro area in the early 1200s may have invited their relatives and friends to join them as conditions deteriorated in the region. By the early 1300s entire immigrant villages were present in the Point of Pines, Tonto, Safford, and San Pedro areas. Platform mound systems developing at this time in the San Pedro Valley and other portions of central and southern Arizona may have been responding to the need to consolidate and temper the ethnic, social, economic, and religious tensions that ensued (Clark 1995; Doelle et al. 1995; Elson 1998). Evidence that the mounds in the San Pedro Valley were a response rather than a cause of the conflict in the region was seen in the sequence of events in that area.

We are not the first to have considered environmental deterioration in the late thirteenth century a factor leading to conflict in southern or central Arizona (e.g., Haury 1986), but we suggest that the implications of this large-scale event in the northern and central American Southwest on populations in southern and central Arizona may have been underestimated. Haury (1986:419), commenting on migration from the Tusayan to Point of Pines area, reported that there was a logical succession of events. These events would not have stopped at Point of Pines. Large-scale and even moderate-scale migrations have a ripple effect through regions as assimilation or dislocation occurs in target areas and some migrants or previous residents are pushed on into other regions. If most areas were already straining their carrying capacities, even small-scale migrations could result in major impacts (Jeffery Clark, personal communication 1998).

The first signs of a scalar increase in warfare and the threat of villagewide destruction in the Tucson and San Pedro areas correlate with large-scale settlement dislocations in northern and central Arizona and the first indications of immigration into the San Pedro Valley and the eastern Tucson Basin. There is little doubt in our minds that the signs of warfare and the concern with defense in the region are directly tied to the influx of newcomers. We suspect that some of the responses of the northern Tucson Basin populations may be a result of tensions rippling through the region ahead of the immigrant populations. The specific processes involved remain to be fully worked out. A likely scenario involves conflicts between groups with different cultural traditions over land and water rights that were exacerbated by alliances established with immigrants, but there are a number of equally plausible possibilities. Regardless of the specifics, many of which are likely to remain unknowable, the most important result of this investigation is the integration and interplay of a series of sociopolitical and social processes in the valley involving immigration, the establishment of new social, religious, and political systems, and the incorporation of the institutions and responses of large-scale warfare into daily lives.

Broader Context 2: Institutions and Information Flow

Platform mounds are very likely to have been associated with roles of power and authority in the Classic period communities in southern Arizona that adopted them. Key aspects of maintaining positions of power and authority are ensuring access to diverse types of information. Some of the most important information for community leaders under the social conditions outlined in this chapter would have been related to local and regional conditions that affected warfare. Therefore, a brief consideration of some documentary information provides another means for conceptualizing the rate and spatial scale of information flow in the past. Wilcox (1979b:21) states that in historic times "the communication and trade networks were extensive, allowing a fairly rapid dissemination of information and trade items (Riley 1976)." Two examples from early documents put a much sharper focus on Wilcox's generalization. First, in 1695, when Father Saeta was killed during an uprising of the Pimans of Caborca and nearby mission settlements in what is now northern Sonora, the information reached Father Kino some ninety miles away within 27 hours (Polzer 1971:76–77). Apparently, this feat was accomplished by native runners who covered the distance in some sort of relay fashion. It underscores how rapidly important information could be moved across large distances.

Another key insight is provided by a military document that also dates to 1695 (Polzer and Naylor 1986; Polzer 1971). Polzer (1971:313) summarizes events at the upper San Pedro River village of Quíburi: "At the banquet in the Quíburi fields that afternoon Coro explained to the generals that the Jocomes and Janos had been planning to ambush the Spaniards in the Sierra de Chiricahua. But Coro thought that there would be very little chance of that since the Spanish forces were so huge [approximately 320 to 350 troops]." The Chiricahuas are located to the east of Quíburi, roughly fifty miles away. This is of particular interest, for the relationship between Coro and the Jocomes and Janos was one of intermittent enmity and alliance. Thus, sensitive "military" information was able to flow across a physical distance of nearly fifty miles despite the fact that there was a substantial social distance that could have intervened to hinder it.

Conditions of warfare place a premium on information. With good information, threats of attack can be countered. Under some conditions those countermoves could result in an avoidance of armed conflict through a show of force or through peaceful negotiations. Alternatively, they might turn an attempted attack into a rout of the enemy. Similarly, without adequate information, a leader and the entire community is extremely vulnerable. Thus, although the specifics are not likely to be known, it is reasonable to infer that the leadership roles associated with the platform mound system involved maintenance of systems of communication between neighbors that allowed for the flow of important information about the behavior of potential enemies. Even barriers such as unoccupied zones and hostile relationships could probably be lessened or overcome with good organizational strategies.

CONCLUSIONS

Cross-cultural, historic, and prehistoric data confirm that warfare has been an integral part of human existence since at least the appearance of *Homo sapiens sapiens*. As reported by Keeley (1996), war is not a product of modern "civilized" or industrial societies. Between 70 and 90 percent of societies included in the Human Relations Area Files ranked as bands, tribes, or chiefdoms were at war at least every five years (Otterbein 1989; Murdock and Provost 1973; Ross 1983; Jorgensen 1980; Ember and Ember 1990:255; Keeley 1996:32, 185–187). Warfare in nonstate societies is often more deadly and of greater social consequence than that occurring between recent and modern state-level societies because of the often repetitive nature of skirmishes and the small sizes of social groups. Certain conditions are known to foster warfare, including cultural, ethnic, and economic boundaries or frontiers, hard times stemming from natural disasters such as droughts or floods, and the rise of belligerent charismatic leaders or social groups. Trade relations and marriage alliances often provide contexts *for* hostilities and do not of themselves preserve peace (Keeley 1996).

We can assume from cross-cultural evidence that warfare was an integral part of southern Arizona culture history before the thirteenth- and fourteenth-century events considered in this chapter, but there are few direct archaeological traces of it. We suspect that disputes were most often of limited duration, involved relatively small groups of individuals, and were probably either ritually staged in established fighting areas or limited to small-scale raiding. The events that transpired in the thirteenth and fourteenth centuries represent a scalar shift in the prominence and effects of warfare. Our evidence indicates that people in a large portion of southern Arizona had reason to fear for their personal safety as well as for the safety and integrity of their villages. How this came to be the case is a complex topic that we have only touched on here. By necessity, we have focused on local contexts and suggested regional events of relevance.

The lessons of the present and recent past tell us that peace is rare and fleeting and that we should be very cautious in proposing its presence from archaeological data. More often than not, we can expect to find conflict if we open our eyes to see it. It is time to face the dark side of the past and learn from its most painful lessons. There can be little doubt that warfare afflicted populations in the thirteenth and fourteenth centuries of southern Arizona. Perhaps we can better understand ourselves and the myths of warfare our own society promotes by learning from the past.

ACKNOWLEDGMENTS

We thank Glen Rice and Steve LeBlanc for their help and determination to see this volume to print, for their encouragement and scholarly discussion, and to Glen for asking us to join the effort in the first place at the Society for American Archaeology symposium in Nashville. This chapter grew from a paper we read at those 1998 meetings. Other than Glen and Steve, various researchers offered useful comments and critiques along the way. We especially want to acknowledge Jeff Clark, Dave Wilcox, Mike Diehl, Anne Woosley, and Allan McIntyre. Although we are at odds with Chris Downum, Suzanne Fish, and Paul Fish in our interpretations herein, we acknowledge their research and appreciate their scholarly debates! Thanks are also due Allan McIntyre, Jan Bell, and Arthur Vokes for helping the senior author track down and inspect important collections and maps, to Stephen Plog and three anonymous reviewers for their helpful comments, and to Kimberley Vivier, copyeditor, who made it all much more readable. This research would not have been possible without the efforts of a large cadre of volunteers at the Center for Desert Archaeology who contributed many long field days to complete the San Pedro survey. We apologize for not listing all your names, but know that your help is appreciated. We also thank Catherine Gilman at the Center for Desert Archaeology and Jim Holmlund at GeoMap, Inc., for their excellent maps. Mike Lindeman, Ellen Ruble, Jeff Clark, Sara Herr, Jim Holmlund, and other volunteers with the Center helped update the platform mound maps provided herein. Jessica Silvers helped in ways too numerous to mention. Finally, the senior author wishes to thank his wife, Cindy, and two daughters, Jenelle and Kristin, for keeping it all in perspective.

CHAPTER ELEVEN

Warfare and Massing in the Salt and Gila Basins of Central Arizona

Glen E. Rice

This chapter examines the role of warfare among historic and prehistoric irrigation agriculturalists on the Salt and Gila Rivers of central Arizona. The historic accounts are of the nineteenth-century Maricopa (Pee Posh) and Pima (Akimel O'Odham) tribes of the Gila River, and the archaeological data are from the Hohokam sites and canal systems of the Salt and Gila Rivers. The irrigation agriculturalists of the Sonoran Desert were capable of massing large military forces drawn from multiple settlements dispersed across territories that at times covered hundreds of square kilometers. In this ability the Hohokam and their O'Odham descendants differed from many other prehistoric and historic populations of the American Southwest who were accustomed to aggregating into large settlements to ensure the availability of large military forces.

Both the historic and prehistoric populations of the Arizona Sonoran Desert lived in dispersed settlements spread across the valley floor with little apparent concern for defense. The sprawling layout of houses in prehistoric sites is commonly cited as evidence that war was not an important factor among the Hohokam. Moreover, the Hohokam reliance on irrigation agriculture clearly necessitated cooperation among settlements, perhaps even management by some centralized authority, and the needs of an irrigation system seem to be antithetical to the instabilities associated with war (Hunt and Hunt 1974:117–118).

Pima and Maricopa settlements were at least as dispersed as those of the prehistoric Hohokam, yet historic accounts show that the Pima and Maricopa engaged in war on a nearly annual basis. Some of these engagements were skirmishes in which the Pima and Maricopa sought to repel raids by small groups of Apaches, but every few years these allies also met the Yuma or the Mohave in formal battles involving hundreds if not thousands of combatants. Their forces fought in disciplined ranks with archers providing cover for front-line warriors armed with clubs. And although they occupied only part of the area that had one time been covered by the Hohokam irrigation systems (the rest being unoccupied), they nonetheless had large areas of irrigated fields and constructed canals that were shared by the members of dispersed settlements.

Clearly, the historic record shows that people living in dispersed settlement systems and practicing irrigation agriculture could nonetheless also be well organized for war. There is also evidence of war during the Hohokam period, but it takes a form different from the aggregated villages, fortifications, and high frequencies of burned rooms that are commonly found as evidence of war in prehistoric Puebloan sites on the Colorado Plateau and in the central mountains (see LeBlanc 1997).

Two essentially different defensive strategies were used by the native peoples of the American Southwest. A considerable part of success in war has to do with the size of the military force that can be placed in the field, and getting a larger force than one's enemy is a problem that can be handled in different ways. The rainfall agriculturalists living on the Colorado Plateau and in the central mountains of the Southwest tended to ensure large fighting forces by *aggregating* into large settlements, and those settlements were frequently fortified or placed in defendable locations. The irrigation agriculturalists on the Salt and Gila Rivers, however, were capable of *massing* forces from multiple settlements in the defense of a common territory. Evidence for the differences between massing and aggregating can be seen in the archaeological record at least as early as the ninth century A.D. and as late as the nineteenth century, when intertribal warfare was suppressed by the U.S. military. This evidence of organizational differences in war among neighboring populations makes the study of warfare in the American Southwest of particular importance.

In the absence of central governments the operation of a large irrigation system may depend very much on the use of force. The Hohokam use of irrigation agriculture created an ecological form of complementary opposition. People on the same canal system fought (or at least argued forcibly) one another over the use of water but also joined together as a unit to oppose people from beyond their canal system (Rice 1998). Because the primary concern of the people living on a canal was to defend their common control of a headgate, it made little difference whether they lived in aggregated or dispersed settlements. At the first sign of a threat, people from all parts of the canal would mass to repel the attackers. The archaeological evidence of war is different for populations that lived in dispersed settlements and relied on territorial massing rather than aggregation into large settlements as their basic defensive strategy.

Four centuries after the end of the Hohokam Classic period the Pima and Maricopa were still massing to defend their joint territory, and the historic accounts of their organization in war provide useful details about how the process of massing operated among the Hohokam. The Pima and Maricopa also illustrate the use of allies as a buffer against enemy attacks. The numerically smaller Maricopa group served to buffer the Pima from the full force of the Yuman attacks; although this arrangement has the appearance of being one-sided, it very likely provided benefits to both groups. Historic descriptions of armament and battlefield tactics also provide an understanding of how the Hohokam might have dealt with such matters and offer us the necessary context for recognizing prehistoric fortifications.

For the purposes of this chapter, war is "a state or period of armed hostility existing between politically autonomous communities" in which each community sees its actions as "legitimate expressions of the sovereign policy of the community" (Meggitt 1977:10). Meggitt's definition does not link warfare to a particular scale of complexity, nor does it confuse the state of war with the tactics of engagement. Such distinctions are important in dealing with the variability found in nonstate societies and in the differences of scale that exist between tribes and more complex societies.

The definition can be applied in situations where the boundaries of political units are context-dependent and changeable in scale. Settlements within the same tribe may battle one another over a local issue and yet act as a single unit (or community) when engaging in armed conflict against members of a different tribe; the grievances between the settlements do not need to be resolved in order for them to act as a cohort in a different context. The definition also does not confuse warfare with tactics, which can include pitched battles between formally arrayed forces, raiding, or even a failure to engage by retreating in the face of an advancing enemy (LeBlanc 1999:7; Keeley 1996). This is important because different tactics can have similar outcomes when allowances are made for differences in scale. In a small society the occasional casualties incurred during raids can constitute a mortality rate proportionate to that sustained by modern nation-states engaged in pitched battles (Keeley 1996).

PIMA AND MARICOPA WARFARE

The first Spanish accounts of the Gila River date to the late seventeenth century and describe Pima settlements located on both sides of the Gila

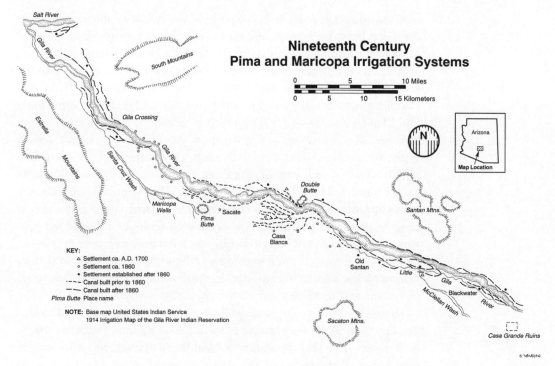

Nineteenth Century
Pima and Maricopa Irrigation Systems

KEY:
△ Settlement ca. A.D. 1700
○ Settlement ca. 1860
• Settlement established after 1860
--- Canal built prior to 1860
— Canal built after 1860
Pima Butte Place name

NOTE: Base map United States Indian Service
1914 Irrigation Map of the Gila River Indian Reservation

Figure 11.1.
Nineteenth-century
Pima and Maricopa
settlement patterns
on the Gila River.
Settlement informa-
tion from Spier
1933, Russell 1975,
and Hackenberg
1974a, b. Canal
dates from
Southward's 1914
report in
Hackenberg
1974b:9–64. Canal
map courtesy
Arizona State
Museum.

River from about one "league" west of the archaeological ruin of Casa
Grande downstream to approximately the vicinity of Gila Crossing
(Figure 11.1), but at that time the Maricopa had not yet become the
neighbors of the Pima (Hackenberg 1974a:100–105). They lived in the
vicinity of other Yuman-speaking tribes in the area near Gila Bend, well
downstream of the Pima (Spier 1933). Over the course of the next few
centuries the Maricopa gradually migrated up the Gila River, seeking escape from the attacks of their traditional enemies on the Colorado River.
By the middle of the eighteenth century the Maricopa occupied a series
of villages near the Salt and Gila confluence (upper left corner of the map
in Figure 11.1), and Pima settlements did not apparently extend west of
Pima Buttes. At the start of the nineteenth century, after gaining permission from the Pima, the Maricopa settled on the Gila River between Pima
Butte and Gila Crossing adjacent to the Pima villages (Hackenberg
1974a:63).

In the first half of the nineteenth century the settlements of these two
tribes extended in an unbroken line a distance of about 60 km along the
Gila River. The Pima settlements began at Blackwater, just slightly west
of the Hohokam site of Casa Grande, and extended downstream for
about 42 km to the vicinity of Pima Butte; the Maricopa settlements occurred in the next 16-km segment from Pima Butte to Gila Crossing.

Spier concludes that the Maricopa were driven from their original
homes on the lower Colorado River before the sixteenth century
(1933:14). If that was the case, the Maricopa may well have begun their
eastward movement up the Gila River during the Hohokam period.

There is in fact at least one archaeological example of immigrants from the Gila Bend or Lower Colorado River being incorporated into the Hohokam site of Las Colinas in the Phoenix Basin (Teague 1989:122–123). The ancestors of the Maricopa may have been in contact with the Hohokam as early as the thirteenth or fourteenth century. The Pima (and the closely related Tohono O'Odham) are among the descendants of the Hohokam, and their oral traditions describe Hohokam platform mounds, site locations, and geographic localities (e.g., Teague 1993).

By the middle of the nineteenth century, under the pressure of increasing attacks from the Apache, the Pima had abandoned their settlements on the north bank of the Gila and in the Blackwater area on the east; the Maricopa settlements had also contracted in number and were located in the proximity of Pima Butte. Within a matter of about a decade the east-to-west distribution of Pima and Maricopa settlements had been reduced from 60 to about 25 km. The pressure from Apache raids began to alleviate after the signing of the Gadsden Purchase agreement and the arrival of United States military and surveying crews along the Gila River. The lessening of tension, the introduction of metal tools, and the development of a market for wheat prompted the Pima and the Maricopa to build new canals and expand once again the range of their settlement locations (Hackenberg 1974a:48–50), as shown in Figure 11.1.

The Pima and Maricopa lived in round, jacal structures, and each family made use of several additional facilities such as ramadas, storehouses, and cooking areas surrounded by low brush windbreaks (Figure 11.2). Distances of 40 to 70 yards could separate one household's group of structures from the next, and a single village might sprawl in this manner over a distance of several miles (Hackenberg 1974a:145; Spier 1933: 22). Among the Pima a village was synonymous with the group of people who shared the use of an irrigation canal, and the houses of each family were located as close as possible to its particular set of fields (Hackenberg 1974a:139). (For purposes of clarity, the locations of villages in Figure 11.1 are shown as much more compact than the sizes of the actual villages; some of the settlements, especially those in the Casa Blanca area, were not contemporary occupations.)

In the early nineteenth century there were at least eight Piman canals providing water to about 12,670 acres of land, as shown in Figure 11.1 (Hackenberg 1974a:50). The Pima referred to their nineteenth-century locations as "gathered together" for defense against the Apache, and their territory had contracted from the early nineteenth century because of constant raiding and attacks from surrounding groups (Hackenberg 1974a:85), but individual settlements were clearly dispersed. A Pima village could not be described as a "formal geometric arrangement of houses" (Hackenberg 1974b:349).

Both the Pima and Maricopa had tribal chiefs. The Pima tribal chief was elected from a council formed of the village chiefs (Hackenberg 1974a:88); the Maricopa tribal chief was "in reality the chief of the

Figure 11.2. A nine-teenth-century Pima household in part of a dispersed settlement. In the eighteenth and for much of the nineteenth century, Pima as well as Maricopa settlements were made up of scattered arrangements of household units resembling this one. Photo courtesy of the Southwest Museum, Los Angeles. Photographer: C. S. Fly, in Arizona, between 1880 and 1889 (photo no. 20591, Braun Research Library).

strongest village" (Spier 1933:155). Other prominent leadership roles included shamans, orators, champions, and war leaders who were not necessarily the tribal chiefs (Spier 1933:164–166).

Although the Pima and Maricopa were separate tribes speaking different languages, they showed considerable solidarity when it came to matters of war against their common enemies, the Yuma, Mohave, Yavapai, and Apache. Engagements against the Yuma and Mohave involved groups of hundreds of combatants in formal battles whereas encounters with the Apache and Yavapai were usually in the form of raids launched against the Pima and Maricopa.

In the mid-nineteenth century, raids by Apache and Yavapai in small parties of five to ten individuals occurred every few days; raids by larger groups took place once or twice a month (Russell 1975:201). The reference to females and children among the small parties suggests that in at least some of the raids family groups attempted to steal food and other resources from agricultural fields. Nonetheless, even such encounters could result in deaths among Pima and Maricopa as well as Apache, and the intensity of the combined Apache forays, whether by families foraging for resources or by raiding parties composed solely of adult warriors, led to a 10-mile (16-km) contraction of the Piman territory in about one decade (Hackenberg 1974a, b). In previous centuries such constant raiding had forced the Sobaipuri completely out of the San Pedro Valley to the east of the Pima.

The Pima and Maricopa occasionally retaliated by sending forces of several hundred warriors into Apache and Yavapai territory, but they seldom succeeded in finding or engaging large numbers of the enemy. A successful attack by a war party of 200 Pima and Maricopa warriors might involve the slaying of fewer than a dozen Apache warriors and the taking prisoner of some two dozen women and children; less successful forays of several days' duration might encounter no more than a few solitary Apache or Yavapai (Hackenberg 1974a:189, 225–226; Russell 1975:34–66). The seasonally mobile and at times dispersed settlement system of the Apache and Yavapai may have contributed to the inability of the Pima and Maricopa to find them in large groups, or perhaps the Apache and Yavapai intentionally scattered on the approach of their enemy. Whether intended or not, the ability of the Apache and Yavapai to avoid large-scale engagements was an effective defense against the better-organized Pima and Maricopa.

Between 1833 and 1857 some seven to fifteen battles were fought by the Maricopa and Pima against the Yuma (Quechan) and Mohave (Russell 1975:38–66; Kroeber and Fontana 1986:193; Spier 1933). The encounters were recorded on native calendar sticks (Russell 1975; Shaw 1974; Kroeber and Fontana 1986), and the different numbers have to do with the location of the native observers; some of the encounters, for instance, were attacks that occurred during plant-gathering forays well away from the main villages. The calendar sticks that record these battles can be correlated to the modern calendar because the native records mention a heavy meteor shower that occurred in 1833 and because the 1857 battle was also witnessed by Anglo-Americans traveling through the area; descriptions of the event were published in newspapers of that year (Kroeber and Fontana 1986). During this 25-year period the Maricopa repulsed one Yuma attack on their own before the Pima had a chance to prepare for a counterattack, and in 1841 the Maricopa crossed the desert to the Little Colorado and attacked the Yuma villages without the assistance of their Pima allies although one Pima accompanied the group. Most frequently, however, the Pima and Maricopa joined forces in repelling Yuman and Mohave attacks.

The Pima preparedness for war was impressive. Male children were proficient hunters with the bow by the age of nine and received combat training in the use of the shield and club during puberty (Shaw 1974: 35–44). The "shield lessons" began with the use of mudballs as projectiles, but in later stages trainees were expected to practice dodging and shielding themselves from fired arrows (Shaw 1974:44). Adult warriors engaged in sham training battles against one another to keep fit (Russell 1975:204).

In 1852 the Pima and Maricopa numbered about 4,200 people, of which about 1,000 men were judged to be warriors; some 300 to 400 were constantly deployed in the field against the Apache, largely performing sentinel duty (Kroeber and Fontana 1986:85). That is, between 7 and 10 percent of the population was essentially on "active duty." Men with strung bows maintained watch while women worked in the fields. During times of danger sentinels were posted at night around the villages

(Russell 1975:200–201). One Anglo American reported seeing a party of 250 Pima women gathering wood in the desert while a line of warriors with bows in hand stood guard on a nearby ridge (Kroeber and Fontana 1986:86).

John Bartlett and some two dozen soldiers and surveyors were mistaken for Apaches in July 1852 when they approached the Pima villages early one morning in single file from the direction (north) normally used by the enemy. They were quickly observed by sentinels posted in trees, and the alarm "was sounded from one tree or house top to the other" throughout the Pima communities, extending "even to their allies the Maricopa." Within a few minutes mounted horsemen were galloping across the desert toward the party, and other armed warriors were following behind on foot (Kroeber and Fontana 1986:85; Hackenberg 1974b:264). The mistaken identity was treated by the Pima as a good joke, and forming an advance and rear guard for their guests, the assembled warriors accompanied the American troop back to its base camp on the Gila River.

Massing a Military Force from Multiple Settlements

The scale of the Pima response to attacks, and the immediacy of their response in coming to the aid of the Maricopa villages, is of particular interest. Yuman attacks were directed at the Maricopa villages because these were the first settlements the Yuma encountered in moving upstream from the Lower Colorado River. At the first sign of attack, the Maricopa would send word to the closest Pima village for assistance, and Pima runners would spread news of the attack to the other Pima villages. On such occasions the Pima were able to draw combatants from settlements that lay as far as 40 km from the scene of battle. The response to a Yuman attack was automatic; on hearing the news, each Piman warrior would gather his equipment and set out immediately for the location of the battle. No time was spent in village-level discussions to determine if members of the community should join in the counterattack. Given the distance involved, the better part of a day and night might be required for the combatants to gather at a common point, but this time was devoted solely to the logistics of getting combatants to a single location. During these intervals the Yuma would regroup, eat the food stores of the Maricopa, and hold their own war councils, or they might attempt to withdraw but were usually pursued by the Pima. Once assembled, the Pima and Maricopa forces could number in the high hundreds, and the counterattack against the Yuma could lead to considerable fatalities on both sides (Russell 1975:38–66). Faced with an external threat, the Pima population of about 4,000 people (Russell 1975:20–21), distributed among eight or more settlements in a territory 40 km in length, operated as a single unit.

The arrangement of Maricopa and Pima settlements on the Gila River was advantageous to both tribes in mounting a common defense against their Yuman enemies. The Maricopa essentially served as a buffer for the Pima against Yuman attacks, and the Maricopa aided the Pima in dealing with Apache raids and skirmishes (Hackenberg 1974a:94). Attacking Yuman war parties would encounter the Maricopa villages first, there would be a skirmish during which some Maricopa houses would almost inevitably be burned, and a messenger would be sent to the Pima villages for help. If pressed too hard, the Maricopa forces would scatter and retreat toward the Pima villages. Once the Pima forces had gathered, they would counterattack, forcing the Yuma and their allies to withdraw. On at least one occasion the Piman counterattack freed a large group of Maricopa women taken prisoners by the Yuma (Russell 1975:38). The Pima benefited considerably from all this because the only houses that were burned and looted were those of the Maricopa. The Maricopa were the early warning system for the Pima, and by coming to their defense, the Pima kept that system in place. The Maricopa suffered the loss of food and possessions and very likely incurred a greater number of casualties than the Pima. This may seem untenable from the perspective of the Maricopa, but the relationship actually benefited them considerably. They were a much smaller tribe than the Yuma (or Pima) and would have been easily destroyed by the Yuma without the help of the Pima. By living next to the Pima settlements, they had access to agriculturally productive lands on the Gila River and the Santa Cruz slough and the ability to fall back under attack and regroup with their Piman allies. The cost for this dependence on the Pima was the occasional loss of food, equipment, and houses, all of which were replaceable, and the prospect of fewer deaths among the warriors.

Intersettlement Feuding

Despite the Pima's solidarity in facing common external enemies, bitter feuds arose at times between neighboring Pima settlements on the Gila River, with the possibility of armed conflict and death. One of the most strident events occurred in 1879 and involved two factions living in the Santan and Blackwater settlements (Russell 1975:56–67). Although the antagonism existed primarily between one group at Santan and another at Blackwater, the Santan faction had a group of collaborators who lived in the Blackwater area. The hostilities stemmed from an argument that arose during the preceding year when people from both settlements attended a gathering held at a third village. In 1879 the group living at Santan developed a plan to attack their adversaries in the Blackwater area, and they enlisted the help of their collaborators at Blackwater. The opposing faction in Blackwater learned indirectly (through a man living at Casa Blanca) of the threat and sneaked out of their village. In a surprise move they marched downstream and at dawn the next day conducted a peremptory attack on the head family of the Santan faction.

The leader of the Santan faction was wounded in the arm by an arrow and in the abdomen by a bullet, but in the first encounter there were no deaths. Most of the members of his family were working in the fields and escaped the attack. Later in the day the Santan faction counterattacked the Blackwater group, which they met at the government school with firearms. Three people were killed, and at that point the two sides disengaged and withdrew.

This feud occurred between factions living in neighboring settlements separated by a distance of only a few kilometers. The combatants used bows and arrows and, at several points, firearms; the skirmishing took place over two days and resulted in three deaths. The planning and counterplanning involved numerous people and occurred over a matter of months. In short, the Blackwater skirmish was a small version of a war, and it involved only members of the Pima tribe, people who on other occasions would have joined forces in repelling the attacks of Apaches or Yumans.

For the Pima, the definition of enemy depended on the context, which is one characteristic of societies with complementary opposition. The historic accounts of the Pima and Maricopa do not describe a perfectly nested arrangement of such contexts, although ethnographers in the early twentieth century did not attempt to elicit such relationships. Spier and Russell each dealt with only one tribe and did not focus on the close interdependency of the two tribes as part of one settlement system. Nonetheless, these accounts show the Pima using the same technology and tactics to engage in combat at different scales. At the lowest level the hostilities were between villages of the same tribe on neighboring canals, and at the highest level hostilities joined the members of two separate tribes into a single military force. Although this is not a perfect description of complementary opposition, it has some of the characteristics of such organizations and is certainly a very different approach to fielding a force than that commonly found in tribal organizations.

The Implications of Armament and Tactics for Fortification Design

The battlefield technology of the Hohokam was probably similar to that still being used by the Pima and other southern Arizona tribes in the late nineteenth century. A description of the weapons deployed in historic times provides insights into how the Hohokam might have used a similar range of implements. Although there are no descriptions of nineteenth-century fortifications, an understanding of Pima and Maricopa weaponry and tactics is valuable for establishing the requirements such fortifications would have had to serve had they been constructed. These principles can be used to evaluate the defensive potential of Hohokam settlements in terms of either constructed features or characteristics of the natural setting. Such an evaluation proves useful in identifying fortified Hohokam settlements and differentiating them from unfortified settlements.

The basic armament of the Pima and Maricopa consisted of the compound bow, rawhide shield, and wooden club (Russell 1975; Spier 1933; Webb 1959:22–27). The lance did not appear until after the introduction of metal by the Spaniards, and then it was used primarily by the Yuma on the Lower Colorado River (Russell 1975:95). Rawhide armor was not worn by the O'Odham and their allies (Russell 1975; Spier 1933), although it was employed on occasion by the Apache (Russell 1975:39). The Apache also sometimes made clubs by wrapping stone balls in rawhide and fixing them to the end of wooden handles (Opler 1941:390, 392); stone balls occur in Hohokam sites, but there are no ethnographic accounts of clubs with stone heads among the Pima or their allies (see Spier 1933:131).

The Pima used a compound (double curve) bow made of mulberry wood for war (Russell 1975:95) and free bows of willow for hunting. Both kinds of bows measured about 1.5 m in length. The bow was an important weapon, and among the Maricopa it was the desired weapon of war (Spier 1933:132), but it was not particularly lethal. With a hunting bow (not a compound bow), an arrow shot at a range of 30 m penetrated only about 1 cm into the side of a deer (Spier 1933:132). Although compound bows very likely had a greater range, it is nonetheless clear that shields and armor made of rawhide were very effective defense against the bow (Russell 1975:39), and combatants could survive battle with several arrow wounds (Spier 1933:132).

Shields measured 45 to 50 cm in diameter and were made by stretching rawhide over both sides of a wooden hoop (Russell 1975:120; Spier 1933:136). This size was sufficient to cover the upper torso and head (Spier 1933:136), although Pima warriors were capable of advancing in a crotched position such that much of the body was hidden by the shield (Webb 1959:39–40; Russell 1975:120). It is possible that the shields described in the early–twentieth-century ethnographic accounts were smaller than the shields used in actual battles in the first half of the nineteenth century, although none of the ethnographic accounts suggests this might have been the case. As long as both sides employed bows and shields, there was a balance of force between opposing groups.

To inflict more than an occasional casualty in war it was necessary to engage in hand-to-hand combat, which was done with clubs. War clubs were made of ironwood or mesquite, measured 38 to 48 cm in length, weighed about 1 kg, and had a large knob carved at one end. The knobs on the Piman clubs frequently had shoulders, giving the clubs the appearance of potato mashers (Russell 1975:96; Spier 1933:135). On some clubs the end of the handle opposite the knob was pointed so it could also be used as a jabbing instrument. The war clubs were hung on the wrist with a cord to keep them from being dropped. The shields, held in the opposite hand, were used to parry blows from the opponent's war club (Spier 1933:136).

The most lethal blow with the war club was to the cranium, and combatants attempted to grab the enemy by the hair and bring the club in a downward blow delivered to the temple (Spier 1933:135). The club could also be brought up in an underhand blow while the head of the enemy was held down. Piman combatants in the front line also sought to grab and fling the enemy over their shoulders; a person in the second line would then club the enemy as he hung with his head facing the ground. Lances or other kinds of piercing instruments would have delivered lethal blows to the torso, but they were not used, possibly because a stone point on a lance would quickly break in the repeated thrust and withdrawal action. The sharpened end of the handle on the war club could be used in an upward thrusting motion to the torso if the blow to the cranium was deflected, but this was obviously a secondary use of the primary weapon.

Hand-to-hand fighting with clubs was most effective when blows could be delivered to the head of the opponent; a slight increase in elevation of a meter would provide considerable advantage. Combatants standing on higher ground could bring their clubs down on the heads of the enemy while keeping their own heads beyond reach of the opposing clubs. Added height also allowed the clubs to be swung through a longer arc, providing more momentum. Combatants using war clubs and standing on a slope, the top of a wide wall, a platform, or the berm of a canal would have the advantage over their opponents.

Reasons for Going to War

The Pima (Akimel O'Odham) and Tohono O'Odham, known collectively as the O'Odham, believed that their enemies had powerful magicians who sought to deprive them of rain and good growing conditions; the enemy used magical means to direct the clouds and rain away from the O'Odham. Going to war was thus a means of restoring their world, to make it lush and to return the whirlwinds, clouds, and butterflies that come with moisture (Underhill 1938b:86). War was essentially a struggle against the evil magicians of the enemy (Underhill 1938b:85), and the attack was intended to destroy their power (Russell 1975:201–202). The Pima war speeches given on the nights before an attack talk about destroying the enemies' wind, clouds, springs, and trees and stealing their turquoise, bird down, and other objects of power (Russell 1975:361–367); these were figurative objectives that were accomplished when the enemy forces were defeated. The consequence of victory is fertility; success in war brings rain (Russell 1975:362; Underhill 1938b:68).

Combatants returned from battle with the scalps of those they had killed, although they seem for the most part to have removed only hair with no skin attached (Russell 1975:44). Immediately on their return, every combatant who had slain an enemy warrior went into a 16-day period of seclusion for purposes of purification. During this time other members of the community placed the trophies, sometimes referred to as ravens, on poles and performed dances (Spier 1933:184; Underhill 1938a:46). This process of dancing with the scalps acted to change the scalp from an enemy into a relative (Spier 1933; Underhill 1938a:46). On the eighth day of the purification period the trophies of enemy hair were given to the combatants to be washed, fashioned into a fetish shaped like a human being, wrapped with eagle down, and placed in a special basket (Underhill 1938a:47; Russell 1975:205). The baskets went home with the warriors and were fed with cornmeal; they provided the warrior with power. Among the O'Odham the scalps were used to call clouds and bring rain (Underhill 1938a:44), but among the Maricopa they were kept in the main council house of the tribe, where they brought dreams to a person called the "scalp keeper"; the dreams warned the Maricopa of approaching enemies or impending catastrophes (Spier 1933).

The O'Odham and Maricopa also gave practical reasons for going to war, such as to retaliate against the Apache for the theft of horses. Many of the encounters against the Apache were simply skirmishes in which a small party of Apache might be found in the vicinity of a village and was attacked by a small party of Pima. The more formal attacks of the Yuma, though couched in ideological terms, frequently took place in times of Yuman hardship and were motivated by a desperate need to obtain food (Stone 1981). The Pima and Maricopa held that winter was the most dangerous time for an enemy attack, but the greatest number of recorded battles took place in the spring and summer (Spier 1933:163). Economic hardships would be the greatest at these times, when winter stores had been depleted and crops for the current year were still ripening.

The O'Odham and Maricopa engaged in war for the practical purposes of defending their resources or retaliating for past loss of resources to the enemy, whereas the Yuma, Mohave, Apache, and Yavapai usually engaged in war so that they could deprive the O'Odham and Maricopa of their food, livestock, and women. But there was also an explicit ideology that saw war as the mechanism for restoring balance to the natural world by eliminating the sorcerers among the enemy. This was achieved by meeting the enemy in formal battle and returning with the scalps of the enemy dead. The practical and ideological reasons for going to war frequently coincided, but the power of ideology ought not to be minimized for that reason.

In one sense the ideology helped circumscribe the scale of battle by placing a considerable burden on those who were successful in slaying the enemy and by identifying the destruction of a single individual (an enemy who practiced sorcery) as a sufficient claim to victory. Engagements between the Pima and the Yuma could end with only a minor loss of life, although there were also occasions on which hundreds of combatants were killed.

Nevertheless, by identifying war as a pursuit necessary for the well-being of the subsistence system, ideology generalized the definition of the enemy and broadened the scope of war beyond the immediate recovery of food and resources from the enemy. This ideology essentially deferred gratification to the next planting seasons; going to war and defeating the enemy might not result in the short-term gain of very much food (captured food was usually consumed by the warriors), but it would help ensure that the rains would come at the necessary times to bring abundant crops in the next season.

It is difficult to determine how early the basic elements of this ideology were in place and what role they played in Hohokam warfare. But with some such belief, members of Hohokam settlements on a canal system could perceive settlements in the foothills or in other basins to be a threat to their irrigated fields, even though from the perspective of ecological and anthropological science there was no such relationship. This possibility illustrates that arguments for the absence of war cannot be based on the indirect evidence that no economic grounds can be found for engaging in war. Hohokam populations living in settlements on the canals could produce far more food than the people living in the settlements in the surrounding desert, and attacks on the desert settlements would not have provided the irrigation farmers with tangible resources. But a generalizing ideology concerning the balance of nature could have given the irrigation farmers sufficient reasons for attacking the peripheral populations, not for the resources that they could gain immediately but because they believed that doing so would increase their own productivity in the future.

ARCHAEOLOGICAL COMPARISONS

The ability of the Pima and Maricopa villages on the Gila River to act as a single unit in fielding a military force was an organizational legacy of the Hohokam. The massing of people in defense of a common territory, rather than a single community, is more a characteristic of states than of tribal or village society. Some tribal groups, however, have the ability to mass on a large scale using the principle of complementary opposition (Sahlins 1961; Evans-Pritchard 1940) without much if any form of centralized leadership and governmental institutions.

Complementary opposition refers to a society composed of segments that are capable of joining into larger segments such that the new units continue to constitute a single geographical bloc (Sahlins 1961). The Hohokam irrigation system (Figure 11.3) was an organization in which the opposition between complementary parts was structured by ecology rather than kinship (Rice 1998); indeed, ecological factors of some kind

Figure 11.3. The
thirteenth- and four-
teenth-century
Hohokam irrigation
system on the Gila
and Salt Rivers.

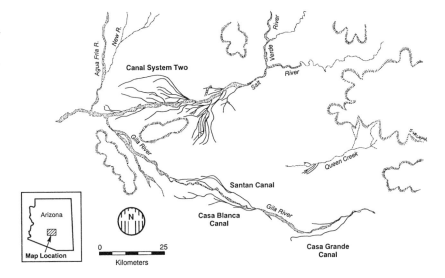

may be the primary elements underlying the origins of such systems
(Sahlins 1961). The scale of the Hohokam irrigation system created conditions in which solidarity in war was based on the location in which an
individual resided rather than membership in a particular kinship unit.
The reasons for this had in large part to do with the scarcity of good locations for canal headgates, which on the Salt and Gila Rivers numbered
fewer than two dozen (Gregory and Nials 1985; Gregory 1991). By the
early part of the Hohokam tradition (A.D. 700 or 800) most of these
good locations had been occupied; canal users could not risk being dis-
lodged from their headgate since they could not establish a new headgate
somewhere else on the river.

A sizable number of people also lived in the desert beyond the irrigated fields bordering the Salt and Gila Rivers, and these populations
used runoff techniques or water from small springs for their fields.
(Archaeologists assign these populations to the Hohokam tradition as
well.) There were, in short, groups of people living in the desert who had
good economic reasons for trying to capture a headgate location on the
river, and there were equally good economic reasons for the people already on the canals to band together in mutual self-interest. Since an attack could come from any direction, the populations on the canals had
little to gain in aggregating into a single large settlement; the strategy was
instead to mass into a large enough fighting force and move as a force to
whatever part of the canal was under attack. Settlement dispersal was
also productive in that it facilitated monitoring the full length of the
canal. Aggregating into large communities did not address the real defense needs of the people living on the canal systems, who had to be prepared to defend their control of a vital and limited ecological niche, the
territory containing their canal and headgate.

The populations living on the canals also needed a mechanism for ensuring the equitable distribution of water to all points on the canals.

Researchers have suggested that some level of centralized decision-making authority was required to perform this administrative function. The same ends could be achieved through the use of force, however (Rice 1998). During periods of low water the people at the ends of the canals ran the greatest risk of not receiving their allocation. They could handle this problem by marching up the canal, attacking those near the headgate, and taking their share of the water. To ensure the necessary outcome, of course, it would help if the final settlement was as large as all the other settlements on the canal combined. So if force, or the threat of the use of force, also characterized relationships between the settlements on the same canal system, we would expect to find (a) that the largest settlements were located at the ends of the canals and (b) that conflict began occurring at settlements on canals once the canals were long enough to accommodate two or more settlements (in many areas this could be as early as A.D. 800 or 700). Both expectations are supported by the archaeological evidence.

Conflict also took place between settlements on the canals and those in the surrounding desert, but for reasons not having to do with the distribution of canal water. Villages located in the surrounding desert, which did not use irrigation, or used much shorter canals, were organized very differently. These settlements did not have an ecological basis for joining as territorial units with their immediate neighbors and therefore were less capable of massing and fielding large military forces drawn from multiple settlements. Moreover, the populations living in the desert experienced agricultural shortages far more frequently than the irrigation farmers and therefore would have often sought food (obtained by either trade or raids) from the canal settlements. This exchange would not have been symmetrical: the people on the canals would have provided far more resources to the desert settlements than they received in return. Over the period of several centuries (A.D. 900 to 1100) the settlements in the desert grew in number and size, so there was a gradual rise in the frequency and scale of the demands for resources from the irrigated areas. The populations on the canals also experienced growth during this period, however, and they built longer canals, raising the number of settlement groups per canal, and thus the scale of the military forces that could be rapidly massed from various parts of the canal systems also increased.

As the desert settlements became progressively more needy for food from the canal populations, the canal-based settlements became progressively more capable of fielding overwhelmingly large military forces. The asymmetry of this relationship erupted finally in a protracted period of warfare (starting in the late A.D. 1100s) during which the canal-based populations would have been victorious more often than the desert populations. The desert populations reacted initially by moving into defensive retreats on high hilltops or by fortifying their settlements with walled compounds, but by the late twelfth or thirteenth century they had been driven completely from the desert regions surrounding the irrigated zones in the Salt and Gila river valleys (Spoerl 1979; Spoerl and Gumerman 1984; Wilcox 1989, this volume). And in pushing their desert neighbors into more distant regions, the Hohokam initiated a series of reactive responses that eventually extended well beyond their own area (Wilcox this volume; Oliver this volume).

The Hohokam irrigation system was by its very nature a catalyst for war. Hohokam populations living on large irrigation networks used war to manage the distribution of water through their canals, and at the same time the scale of their canal systems gave them considerable success in waging war against their less organized neighbors. In the twelfth century A.D. the Hohokam exercise of war had become so extensive that it was triggering military responses in very distant areas; in the thirteenth and fourteenth centuries populations throughout the Hohokam, much of the Sinaguan, and part of the Mogollon region were on a war footing, very likely in response to the culmination of developments that had begun sometime in the eighth or ninth century A.D. in the Hohokam core area.

As we have seen, this model of the mechanisms underlying Hohokam warfare and of the gradual widening of the scale of that warfare has three major points:

1. Relationships between settlements on the same canal system were structured by the principle of complementary opposition.

2. War and/or feuds occurred at Hohokam settlements on large canal systems once the canals were long enough to accommodate two or more distinct settlements; in many areas these conditions existed as early as A.D. 800, and conflict should have occurred periodically throughout the remainder of the Hohokam tradition, to about 1400 or 1450. The period between 800 and 1100 was one of peace in other parts of the Southwest, as discussed by LeBlanc (1998, this volume), so the expectation of warfare on the canal systems at an early date is unusual.

3. By the late twelfth and early thirteenth centuries, warfare pitted entire canal systems against sets of settlements located in the neighboring desert regions; the intensity of warfare declined as the desert periphery was abandoned (creating an unoccupied zone), and settlements on the canal were fortified.

I next review the archaeological data to support these points.

Massing for Common Defense

The assertion that relationships among settlements sharing the use of one or more canals were structured by the principle of complementary opposition has been treated at length elsewhere (Rice 1998, 2000) and is reviewed only briefly here. The notion is that populations sharing the use of a canal would show considerable solidarity when dealing with similar

Figure 11.4.
Hohokam Canal
System Two in the
Phoenix metropoli-
tan area, showing
the distribution of
thirteenth- and four-
teenth-century settle-
ments with platform
mounds.

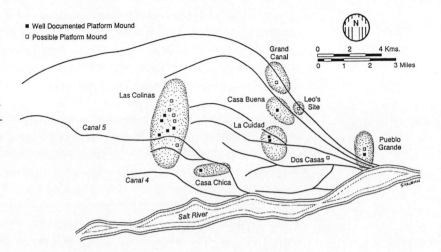

groups beyond their local canal; that is, they would act as a single segment in opposition to other comparable segments on other canals. It is
also possible that several neighboring canals might form a higher-order
unit in opposition to more distant enemies, such as settlements in the surrounding desert regions. When dealing internally, however, such as in
matters having to do with the allocation of water, the settlement at the
end of the canal formed a minor segment in opposition to the settlements
closer to the headgate, which constituted the opposing minor segment.
For that reason, the final settlement needed to be considerably larger and
include roughly as many people as all the other settlements lying between
it and the headgate.

Archaeological data support the various implications of this model.
Settlements sharing the use of a canal did, in fact, tend to interact with
one another to a greater degree than other settlements, forming a social
unit coincident with the canal or canals originating from the same headgate location. In a study that included the use of electron microscopy to
characterize the paste and temper constituents of a large sample of ceramic artifacts, Abbott (1994a) showed that Classic period settlements
on Canal System Two in the Phoenix Basin (Figure 11.4) exchanged
plainware vessels with one another more regularly than they did with
settlements on different canal systems, even if those other settlements
were closer. Since this evidence is observed in the distribution of utilitarian vessels, the interaction probably occurred at the level of individual
households. This expression of intracanal cohesiveness did not exist during the Preclassic period, suggesting that before about A.D. 1100 the populations on the canal were seldom called on to act as a single segment
against an external foe.

The archaeological data also support the proposition that the largest
settlements occurred at the ends of the canal, which is the expected pattern if force was also used to retain a balance of power within each set of

canals. With the largest settlements at the ends of the canals there was considerable motivation to arrive at consensus over the distribution of water; with a balance of power between the two ends of the canals the possibility of warfare between the settlement at the end of the canal and those closer to the headgate was greatly reduced. Eva and Robert Hunt observed this pattern among small-scale irrigation systems in the Cuicatec region of Mexico; the intensity of disputes (resolved in civil courts since these systems and communities operated within a state organization) was much less when the settlement at the end of the water delivery system was "superior in political might, population size, etc., to the upstream community" (Hunt and Hunt 1974:112). Among the Hohokam it was likely the threat of war, rather than actual fighting, that was important to the operation of the canal systems. Conflicts that occurred among settlements of the same canal system might have been on the order of feuds such as the one previously described that took place in 1879 between residents of Santan and Blackwater on the Gila River.

Data pertaining to Hohokam settlement size could be collected from only five canals or canal systems (the latter refers to sets of parallel canals sharing a single headgate location) because many Hohokam sites were destroyed by the growth of the Phoenix metropolitan area before they could be adequately recorded. Settlement size was measured indirectly by looking at the number and sizes of the compounds that contained platform mounds, a kind of public architecture in use from about A.D. 1250 to 1450. The settlements with the most and largest compounds around platform mounds occurred consistently at the end of the canal systems. On Canal System Two (Figure 11.4) the site of Las Colinas, at the end of the system, contained more platform mounds than the settlement of Pueblo Grande, located near the headgates. The largest known Classic period compound in the entire Salt and Gila basins occurred at Los Colinas; it covered more than 1.2 ha and enclosed two platform mounds (see Figure 11.10 below). In four other cases (Figure 11.5) the settlements with the largest platform mound compounds occurred at the ends of the canals (Rice 1998). The archaeological data satisfy the test expectation of the hypothesis; settlements at the ends of the canals needed to be large enough to balance the size of opposing settlements on the same canal system.

Clearly, canal systems would not have operated efficiently if the settlements on the same system were continuously at war with one another, and there may even have been strong cultural methods for limiting conflict to feuds and nonlethal displays of force. For instance, the settlements at the ends of the canals could simply make their presence known by posting people along the entire length of the canal when water was being delivered to their fields, but even such a relatively benign display would still require that they have more personnel than the other settlements on the canal.

Figure 11.5. The
sizes of compounds
with platform
mounds compared
to distance from
canal headgates on
four Hohokam canal
systems.

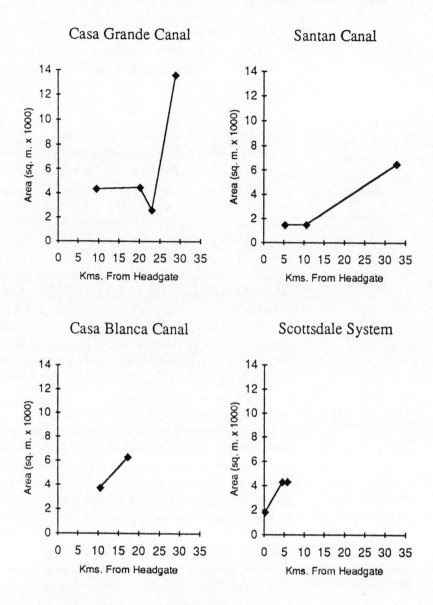

Evidence of Conflict on a Canal System

Another implication of this notion of complementary opposition on the
Hohokam canal systems is that evidence for conflict should be found in
Preclassic as well as Classic period sites. If war and lesser forms of hostility were instrumental to the operation of the Hohokam irrigation canals,
then such evidence should occur at least as early as the Colonial period,
when multiple settlements first began to appear on the same canal.

Canal System Two was located in the area that is now the city of
Phoenix, and the construction of a series of freeways and expressways
over a 15-year period has provided detailed excavated data sets from
seven settlements on the largest of the Hohokam canal systems. Evidence

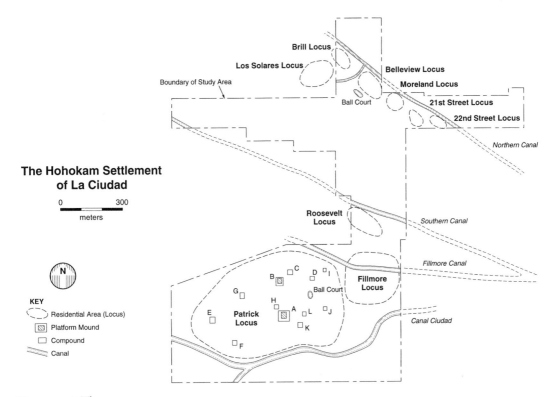

Figure 11.6. The mapped extent of the Hohokam settlement of La Ciudad, showing distribution of loci along separate canals. The northern loci were abandoned by A.D. 1100; occupation of the Patrick locus continued to 1400 (from Rice 1987b; Wilcox 1987).

for conflict among these sites is seen in the frequencies of burned structures during the Preclassic period and in the development of walled compounds during the Classic period. I begin with a focused examination of burned Preclassic period houses at La Ciudad, a data base that is familiar to me (Henderson 1987; Rice 1987b). There are good reasons for thinking that conflict is at least one factor contributing to the burning of structures at settlements on Canal System Two. Burning by accident or as part of burial ceremonies may also have been a contributing factor but could not alone have generated the distributional patterns observed at La Ciudad.

The settlement plan for La Ciudad at about A.D. 1000 illustrates the dispersed organization of Preclassic Hohokam villages in general (Henderson 1987; Rice 1987b), an organization that also characterized Pima and Maricopa villages some eight centuries later. The houses were freestanding wattle-and-daub structures built in shallow pits with short ramps leading to the entrance. Groups of two to five houses were arranged around the edges of a yard (sometimes also called a courtyard, although there was no surrounding wall) that served as the minimal residential unit. Residential yards were in turn arranged in groups surrounding cemeteries, units referred to as *loci*.

The settlement of La Ciudad was built along the edges of four parallel canals, each lined with residential yards arranged around cemetery loci (Figure 11.6). (The Patrick and Fillmore loci were occupied longer than the other loci, and the platform mounds were constructed after the northern loci had been abandoned.) Distances of up to 500 m, very likely devoted to agricultural fields, separated neighborhoods from one another. The four canals that passed through La Ciudad did not have separate origins on the river but rather were branches that bifurcated from the main canal just east of the settlement. One of the larger branches is shown on the map of Canal System Two in Figure 11.4.

The data used in this analysis come from excavations conducted among the northern loci of the settlement (Henderson 1987). The low percentage of burned structures (31 percent) in the northern area is not in itself suggestive of a high level of conflict. Nevertheless, both the temporal clustering and the spatial distribution of burned structures indicate the village was periodically attacked and houses were burned.

The northern canal that formed the northeast boundary of the settlement, was an effective defensive barrier for the community even when no water flowed through it. A hostile group approaching the settlement from the opposite side of the canal could certainly shoot arrows across the canal into the settlement, but this would have little lethal effect on the occupants. Given the strength of the bows, people would be protected by hiding behind structures. But if the enemy attempted to cross the canal to engage in hand-to-hand combat, the defenders would have the advantage of holding the higher ground on the canal bank. This canal was 4 to 5 m wide, a distance too wide to jump, and had a depth of at least 1.5 m. Standing in the canal, the attackers would be well below the shoulders of defenders standing on the bank of the canal; the heads of the attackers would be exposed to club blows from above, but the attackers would be limited to striking at the knees and feet of the defenders.

Hostile groups with serious intent of engaging in combat would be far more likely to approach the settlement from the southwest, the side away from the canal. There they would be met by the defenders of the village, and the two groups would form opposing lines along the southwest side of the settlement. Unless the settlement was completely overrun, the greatest amount of fighting would take place on the southwest side of the village, away from the canal.

The distribution of burned houses at La Ciudad is very consistent with this expectation. There is a distinct pattern in the spatial distribution of the numbers of houses that burned over a 300-year period (Figure 11.7). In the Belleview and Moreland loci some of the houses were located in the space between the canal and the cemeteries; other groups of houses were in the area to the southwest of the cemeteries. The houses between the cemeteries and the canals were protected from attack by the canal on one side and by intervening houses on the other; only 13 to 25 percent of these houses were burned. Houses located on the southwestern edge of the settlement were the first to be encountered on entering the settlement, and between 38 and 63 percent of those houses burned.

The variation in the percentage of burned houses through time is also

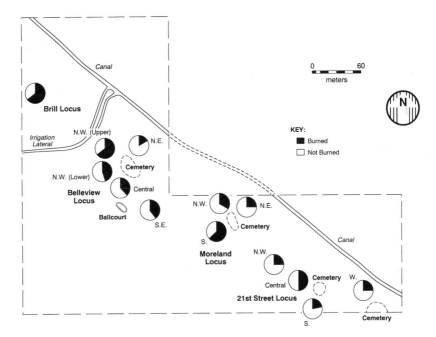

Figure 11.7. The northern loci of the Hohokam site of La Ciudad, showing the frequency and distribution of burned structures in different courtyard groupings of each locus (data from Henderson 1987b).

informative. The Preclassic wattle-and-daub houses probably had a use-life of not more than 10 to 20 years, and new houses were being constantly rebuilt as old ones were abandoned (Henderson 1987). Haury (1976:75) also reported that the use of Pima houses was limited to under 25 years. This regular turnover in houses makes it possible to study changes in the frequency of burning through time. Ceramic seriations and stratigraphic analyses were combined with radiocarbon and archaeomagnetic dates to establish the relative ages of features and to identify groups of contemporary structures (Henderson 1987:79–122).

The earliest houses at La Ciudad date to the Snaketown phase of the Pioneer period, around A.D. 750. They were isolated, only rarely occurring in pairs, and of a dozen houses dating to the first century of occupation, fully two-thirds had burned (Figure 11.8). (The houses in the Brill locus, shown in Figure 11.7, are not included in the graph because the lack of a cemetery and other data suggests that they may have been primarily field houses and thus functionally different from the residential loci.) During the second century (850–950) of the occupation the number of houses in the settlement increased, and the characteristic courtyard pattern developed. A ball court was built in the Belleview locus of La Ciudad sometime between 870 and 930, and the size of the population (as reflected in the number of structures) of all the loci along the northern canal began to grow. Few structures burned during the period that the ball court was in use; in the middle of the tenth century less than a third of the houses at the site burned, even as the total number of houses in the settlement approached an all-time maximum (17 houses dated to the decades between 940 and 960).

Figure 11.8.
Temporal patterns in
the frequency of
burned houses at La
Ciudad (data from
Henderson 1987b;
McGuire 1987).

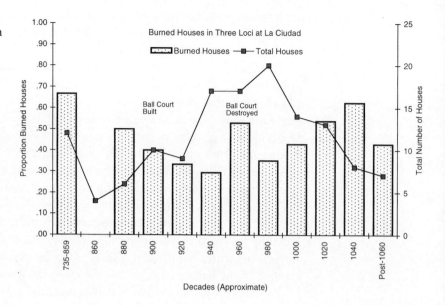

The ball court in the Belleview locus was intentionally destroyed around A.D. 960; dirt from its berms and from elsewhere on the site was thrown onto the floor of the ball court, and the area was used thereafter for trash disposal (McGuire 1987). This act was closely accompanied or shortly followed by the burning of more than 50 percent of the houses in the settlement; the greatest burning occurred in the vicinity of the ball court. Ball courts continued to be used in the more southern parts of La Ciudad, and it is possible that the purpose of destroying the Belleview ball court was to pull this part of the settlement into a more centralized and larger ball-court organization (McGuire 1987). There was a temporary respite in the frequency of burned structures in the closing decades of the tenth century, but as the size of the settlement declined, the percentage of burned structures began to increase again, and by about 1030 had risen above 50 percent. As the size of the northern loci declined, an increasingly greater number of houses stood as single structures rather than as groups around a common courtyard or part of a cemetery locus. The northern loci were abandoned by about 1100, but the Patrick locus at the site persisted, possibly even growing in size, well into the 1300s.

The incidence of burning at La Ciudad was not a function of the density of structures; some of the lowest levels of burning coincided with periods in which the density of structures was greatest (first half of the tenth century A.D.). Conversely, houses that occurred as solitary structures on the landscape were frequently burned, as seen in the first century (735–860) and last decades (1040–60) of the occupation. In addition to safety in numbers, there apparently was safety in the presence of a ball court, possibly because it represented an organization of a large group of people who could gather for purposes of defense as well as ceremony. After the destruction of the ball court this northern part of the Ciudad settlement appears to have been less capable of defending itself; the incidence of burning increased steadily over the course of the next century until the site was finally abandoned.

The timing and location of burned structures suggest that the northern part of La Ciudad was threatened on occasion by displays of force, but displays that stopped short of the destruction of all the houses. Certainly some houses burned for reasons not associated with war, either by accident or perhaps as part of a mortuary ritual such as was common among the Pima and Tohono O'Odham (Underhill 1938a). Such processes ought to result, however, in a relatively uniform spatial distribution of burned structures in the settlement and a relative constant rate of burning over time. What we find at La Ciudad is a spatial distribution of burning that corresponds to the unintended fortification advantage provided by the canal and a temporal pattern in which a sudden increase in burned structures happens to coincide with another destructive act, the leveling of the ball court. This has the appearance of conflict conducted at the level of a feud, over issues that apparently had to do with the relative prestige and centrality of different parts of the settlement. Since only parts of the settlement were burned, the application of force was relatively restrained.

The Ciudad case illustrates that, although multiple factors were probably responsible for the burning of structures in Preclassic Hohokam villages, warfare was at least an important factor. Periods with high numbers of burned structures, especially when the structures are distributed across contiguous areas of a village, can be attributed to hostile attacks; the accidental and/or ceremonial burning of houses would result in noncontiguous distributions of burned houses and in lower overall frequencies of burning.

Data on burned structures are available from seven other excavated sites on Canal System Two (Table 11.1), and inspection of the combined data sets shows several interesting temporal and spatial patterns. More than 50 percent of the structures burned at one or more settlements during each phase from A.D. 700 to 1450. Hostilities involving the burning of structures occurred throughout much of the long history of the occupation of the canal.

What is particularly interesting about these data sets, however, is the evidence of canalwide burning events during the Sacaton and the Soho phases. During the Sacaton phase the settlements of Las Colinas, La Ciudad, and La Lomita Pequeña burned repeatedly. Given the resolution of the dating methods, it is not possible to determine whether the burning events were concurrent, but the Sacaton phase was a period in which nearly every part of the canal system was subject to hostilities leading to burned structures.

During the Soho phase, settlements at the headgate (Pueblo Grande), middle portion (Casa Buena), and end (Las Colinas) of the canal system burned; during this phase 55 percent of all houses on the canal system

TABLE 11.1 Variation through Time in the Frequency of Burned Structures on Canal System Two (in Percent; Values above 50 Percent in Italic).

Phase	Age Range	Pueblo Grande (a)	Pueblo Grande Monument (b)	La Lomita Pequena (c)	La Lomita (d)	El Caeserio (e)	La Ciudad (f)	La Ciudad, Brill Locus (f)	Casa Buena (g)	Grand Canal Ruin (h)	Las Colinas Residential (i)	Las Colinas Mound (i)
Late Classic	1380(?)–1450	39								*67*		0
Civano	1300–1380(?)	25	33						50	*80*		13
		44							43			
Soho	1200–1300	*64*	31						*60*			*75*
												100
Transition			50								38	*100*
							53			*67*		
Sacaton	1000–1150		27	*83*			*54*				38	
				56	23		43				*78*	
Transition				0	33	25						
				10	50		35					
Santa Cruz	900–1000		67			20	*53*					
							33	*83*				
							50	*100*				
Gila Butte	800–900		25			25	20	50				
							67					
							33					
Snaketown	700–800		20				*80*					
			0									

(a) Mitchell (ed.) 1994
(b) Downum and Bostwick 1993:50–54
(c) Mitchell (ed.) 1988:25–83
(d) Mitchell (ed.) 1990
(e)Mitchell (ed.) 1989a:24 and 1989b
(f) Henderson (ed.) 1987:149–153
(g) Howard 1988:68–112
(h) Mitchell (ed.) 1989a
(i) Layhe 1988:174–177 and Teague 1988:43–76 (remnants of floors excluded from counts)

burned, the highest for any phase. The burning of houses during this phase is particularly interesting in that it coincides with the appearance for the first time of fortified retreats in the desert regions surrounding the irrigation systems, discussed in greater detail below. The Soho phase was also a period during which houses were free-standing and dispersed in

Figure 11.9. The dispersed arrangement of walled compounds at the Pueblo Grande ruin.

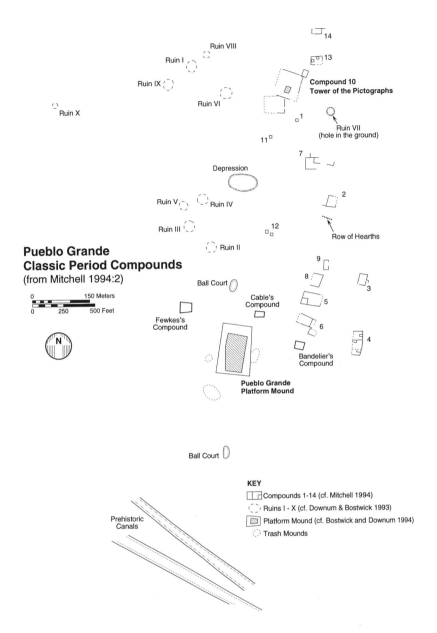

Pueblo Grande
Classic Period Compounds
(from Mitchell 1994:2)

KEY
Compounds 1-14 (cf. Mitchell 1994)
Ruins I - X (cf. Downum & Bostwick 1993)
Platform Mound (cf. Bostwick and Downum 1994)
Trash Mounds

low density across broad areas; settlements on the canal system were not yet fortified.

In the following Civano phase only 29 percent of houses burned, and only one small settlement had more than 50 percent burned houses. The decline in frequencies of burned structures during the Civano phase (Table 11.1) coincided with the appearance of walled compounds on the canal system and of the depopulation of much of the desert region surrounding Canal System Two. The drop in the rate of burning does not necessarily reflect a return to a period of peace; it could show that the irrigation farmers on Canal System Two had gained the military advantage over their enemies by building fortified villages and by driving the opposing forces out of the basin.

The fortification of settlements by the Hohokam is consistent with their practice of engaging in conflict at both local and regional levels, that is, their fortifications reflect the amalgamation of complementarily opposed segments at different levels of inclusiveness. The plan map of the Pueblo Grande site (Figure 11.9) shows a typical arrangement for a Hohokam platform mound settlement during the Civano phase; some two dozen walled compounds were dispersed over a distance of a kilometer. Each compound had 5 to 20 rooms, sufficient in size for a few households.

No residential compound was large enough to hold more than a fraction of a force defending the settlement from external attack. A withdrawal into the residential compounds would serve to divide the defending force into small groups, thus defeating (if I may be excused the play on words) the purpose of massing to defend a common location. The walled compounds of the Civano phase closely resembled in size and organization the unwalled residential yards of the Preclassic village (Sires 1987; Jacobs 1994:287–329). The walls had the effect of breaking the settlement into a series of very small units. Only the compound with the platform mound (and possibly Compound 10, although it has been mostly destroyed by modern construction) was of sufficient size to protect all or a sizable portion of the population of the community.

Although walled, settlements of the Civano phase were not aggregated. In discussing a similar layout at the Marana site, Paul and Suzanne Fish (1989:121) conclude that the individual compounds were too vulnerable to "siege, burning, and missiles" to be defended from a determined enemy force, and they feel the compound walls are "better explained as physical and symbolic delimitation of social space for the personnel of particular residential units and ceremonial precincts about public architecture." We can wonder, however, why the Hohokam felt it necessary to go to such efforts in delineating social space.

The layout of the typical Civano phase Hohokam settlement is fully consistent with the proposal of a segmentary organization with complementary opposition, however; indeed, it is quite difficult to conceive of any other fortification strategy that would apply to such a system. These are fortified villages, and the fortifications are designed to provide protection against two different scales of hostility. The individual walled compounds provide protection for individual residential units feuding against comparable residential units within the same village or perhaps a neighboring settlement, whereas the walled public precincts of the platform mounds provide protection for the entire community against attacks from more distant enemies. This arrangement recalls the events of the nineteenth century (discussed above) in which the Gila River Pima engaged in feuds pitting individual households against one another as well as full-scale battles in which their entire tribe and their Maricopa allies fought against the Yuma and Mohave alliance.

The walled compounds around residential areas would have been effective in minimizing the extent of actual destruction between feuding households and would have tended to limit engagements to exchanges of arrow shots. The barrier provided by the compound walls (fallen walls show they were about 2 m in height) would keep feuding factions from engaging in club combat, a much more lethal form of fighting. This leads to a second observation that there are indeed many situations in which excavators are unable to trace the compound wall around the full perimeter of the residential unit. Rather than a problem of poor preservation, it is possible that such incomplete compounds were part of an intentional strategy of providing protection against attacks from the rear and flanks, thereby forcing attacking groups to engage from only one direction and face the prospect of dealing with clubs as well as arrows.

Fortifications around the platform mounds are also consistent with the tactical requirement of warfare as practiced in the Southwest. In a technology dependent on the use of clubs, and in which leather shield and armor were capable of stopping arrows, parapets and thick walls were not necessary to protect combatants from hostile fire. But walls were useful as fortification if they were wide enough so that two lines of defenders, a front line of warriors with clubs and shields and a second row of archers, could stand on top of the wall. During an exchange of arrows the front row would protect the archers with their shields. If the attackers attempted to storm the wall, the front row of defenders would use their clubs and by standing on a higher surface would have a considerable advantage over the attackers.

The Cline Terrace platform mound in the Tonto Basin (Jacobs 1997) is an example of such a fortified platform mound; it was enclosed by a compound wall measuring about 2 m in width (Figure 11.10). Entry to the compound was through four gateways, two of which were just wide enough to allow passage of one person at a time. The other two entries had originally been several meters wide, but toward the end of the occupation they were partially walled in to narrow the passage to the width of a single person. Although there were rooms located in various parts of this compound (not shown in Figure 11.10), the amount of available plaza space was nonetheless far greater than at other settlements that formed part of the same dispersed complex. Extramural features such as hearths, roasting pits, and burial crypts were limited to only a few plazas on the southeast side of the platform mound. Many of the rooms in the other plazas served only as temporary structures and may have actually been little more than well-constructed ramadas. These facilities were sufficient to allow the gathering of a large group of noncombatants inside the compound while combatants stood two deep on the walls to repel attacking enemy forces.

Figure 11.10. Two examples of fortified platform mounds. The outer defensive walls are 2–3 m wide, providing defenders sufficient room to stand in double ranks during combat.

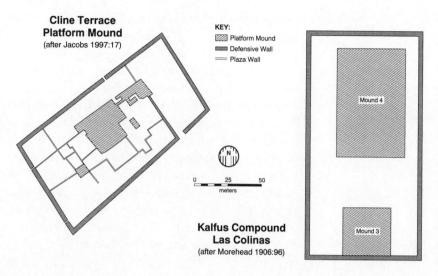

Cline Terrace
Platform Mound
(after Jacobs 1997:17)

KEY:
▨ Platform Mound
▰ Defensive Wall
═ Plaza Wall

Mound 4

Mound 3

0   25   50
meters

Kalfus Compound
Las Colinas
(after Morehead 1906:96)

A similar fortified platform mound occurred at the site of Las Colinas on Canal System Two. This was the compound that enclosed platform mounds 3 and 4 (Figure 11.10), sometimes referred to as the Kulfus ruin (Fewkes 1910). The outer wall of the compound was 3 m wide (Morehead 1906:96), and although the compound included two large platform mounds, they took up only a quarter or at most a third of the space within the 1.2-ha enclosure (Fewkes 1910:421; Morehead 1906; Turney 1929:93). The compound was of sufficient size to have held a large number of people, noncombatants as well as warriors, during an attack. It was also located at the end of the canal system, on the border between the systems of irrigated fields and the desert, in a location that required the greatest massing of people both for maintenance of power on the canal system and for protection from more distant populations.

At other platform mounds researchers have found pairs of parallel walls around the edge of the compound, leading to speculations about racetracks or secret passageways for processions (Fewkes 1912b; Craig and Clark 1994). These walls could, however, represent a variant defensive strategy if wooden platforms were constructed across the relatively narrow distances between the parallel walls. There was no need for the 2-m-wide platform to be a solid wall, since the military technology in the twelfth- to fifteenth-century Southwest did not include cannons and battering machines. This may have been a more expedient way of constructing a wide platform on which warriors could stand. The parallel walls were frequently not continuous all the way around the compound perimeter, although they took up large sections of each side of the compound. These kinds of double-wall features are found at the platform mounds of Casa Grande, which, like Las Colinas, is the final as well as the largest settlement on its canal system and therefore in a position with multiple requirements for defense.

Platform mounds, especially by the Late Classic period, were also elite residences. Rooms built on top of the platform mounds were used as residences and included assemblages of domestic artifacts and refuse comparable to those found in residential rooms at any other Hohokam settlement (Doyel 1981; Rice 1995, 1997b; Wilcox 1987), but rooms on the platforms required ten times more effort to construct than comparable size rooms built at ground level (Rice 1997b:453). Platform mounds also included rooms used in ceremonial functions with assemblages of pigments, crystals, shell tinklers, and shrine stones, which suggests the elites living in the rooms on the mounds were religious specialists (Bostwick and Downum 1994; Jacobs and Rice 1997; Lindauer 1995; Rice 1995).

The addition of a wide compound wall around a platform mound made it into a fortified elite residence that functioned as a keep. In the event of a hostile attack the population of the surrounding settlements could withdraw for protection into the spacious plazas of the fortified platform mound compound. Keeley (1996:58) observes that in nonstate societies the fortification of an elite residence is extremely unusual, but then so is the use of massing. It is possible these unusual traits go hand in hand. In a system that makes use of massing and a dispersed settlement pattern, there is likely to be considerable motivation to fortify the elite households for the use of the entire community.

Escalation of Warfare beyond the Canal Systems

A third expectation of the model is that groups of settlements on the larger irrigation canals would have an organizational advantage in massing large military forces against populations living in the surrounding desert. The intersettlement network of relationships that made possible the coordinated use of the irrigation canal could be turned outward and employed in launching military operations against settlements elsewhere on the landscape. Settlements located in the desert regions surrounding the large irrigation systems lacked the ecological basis for joining in large groups through complementary opposition, and each independent settlement could not match in size the military forces capable of being fielded by the populations living on the canal systems. Their self-sufficiency in agricultural pursuits put them at a numerical and organizational disadvantage when it came to war.

The evidence for the escalation of warfare into the areas surrounding the irrigation systems first appears in the archeological record of the twelfth century. By the thirteenth century residential settlements both within the canal systems and in the surrounding periphery were being fortified, and by the fourteenth century broad expanses of the desert periphery adjacent to the largest of the irrigation systems had been abandoned. Archaeological evidence from sites in two different parts of the Hohokam region illustrate the overall similarity in processes despite the considerable differences in settlement patterns. The

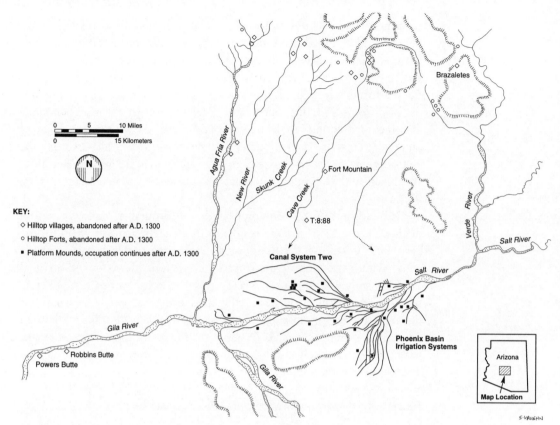

Figure 11.11.
Distribution of
Classic period hill-
top sites around the
irrigation systems in
the Phoenix Basin.

first example is drawn from the Phoenix Basin and deals with the desert periphery surrounding Canal System Two on the Salt River (Figure 11.11). The second example has to do with settlement pattern changes on the Santa Cruz River to the south of the Casa Grande irrigation system (Figure 11.13 below).

During the Colonial and Sedentary periods a number of settlements were established in the desert region bordering the Hohokam irrigation systems in the Phoenix Basin. They relied on short irrigation canals fed by seasonally active drainages such as the Agua Fria, New River, Skunk Creek, Cave Creek, and Verde River to irrigate fields or employed runoff techniques in good locations on the pediments of local mountain ranges. Settlements also existed on the Gila River to the west of the Agua Fria confluence (Robbins Butte, Powers Butte), but a restricted floodplain in that stretch of the river prevented the construction of overly long irrigation canals, and the associated settlements were under the same ecological constraints as those in other parts of the desert periphery around the Phoenix Basin canal systems.

In the twelfth century A.D. a significant change occurred in the distribution of settlements. Communities that had previously been located on the flat valley floor shifted to new locations on the crests and sides of high buttes (Spoerl 1979, 1984; van Waarden 1984; Wilcox et al. this volume, Chapter 6). The changing settlement patterns in the vicinity of

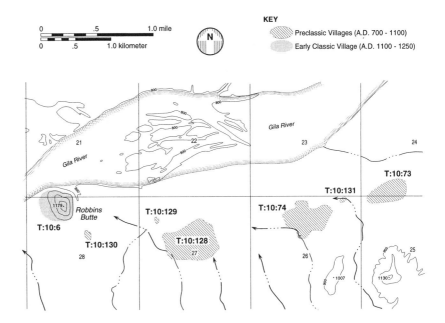

Figure 11.12.
Change in Preclassic
to Early Classic set-
tlement patterns in
the Robbins Butte
area.

Robbins Butte area (Figure 11.12) on the Gila River (Rice and Smith
1999) illustrate this process. Several large and small Colonial and
Sedentary villages were situated on the valley floor on the edge of the second river terrace of the Gila River; the narrow alluvial terraces had prevented the establishment of a long canal system. At the end of the
Sedentary period these sites were abandoned and a new village was established on the slopes of Robbins Butte itself (Rice and Smith 1999).
Changes of this kind took place throughout the western and northern
parts of the Phoenix Basin. In areas of greater population density several
settlements would be clustered on the valley floor around the base of a
hilltop retreat so that everyone could withdraw quickly to the higher
ground when the need arose.

The layout of the hilltop villages varied considerably, suggesting that
several different groups of people occupied the periphery of the Phoenix
Basin. For instance, the Robbins Butte and Powers Butte sites at the
western edges of the basin are trincheras-style settlements with structures
built on small terraces scattered across the sides and crests of the hills.
Similar sites occur in the Tucson Basin (Downum 1993) and farther
downstream on the Gila River (Greenleaf 1975). The Brazaletas Pueblo
at the eastern edge of the Phoenix Basin is, as the name implies, an
arrangement of several large blocks of contiguous rooms around the
edges of plazas (Valehrach and Valehrach 1971). Brazaletas resembles
other large "pueblo" sites in the Sinagua, Mogollon, and Anasazi regions
to the north and west.

The hilltop sites include loopholes in walls for shooting arrows and
corridor-like entryways that force groups to walk in single lines when entering the settlement (Spoerl 1979, 1984; van Waarden 1984). A single

room excavated at Brazaletas Pueblo (Valehrach and Valehrach 1971) exposed 14 human burials that appear to have been the victims of a battle (see Wilcox et al. this volume, Chapter 6). Four lacked skulls, three had badly crushed skulls, and six individuals were missing limbs or portions of their torsos. Two individuals were represented by the torso and arm limbs only. Certainly it is possible that these individuals had been placed in an ossuary and the desiccated bodies were disturbed by animals following abandonment of the site, but it seems likely that they were interred in a mass burial following an attack on the site (Valehrach and Valehrach 1971:8) and that the dismemberment occurred during the course of hand-to-hand combat. The burials were laid out in a formal manner and were accompanied by artifacts such as beads, turquoise-inlaid stone cylinders, pendants, shell jewelry, projectile points, and vessels. However, many of these accompaniments appear to have been attached to clothing or worn as adornment in the hair or as necklaces, and only the vessels may have been intended specifically as burial offerings. The use of a room as a location for the interments could reflect the urgency of the event and might indicate a decision by the remaining population to abandon the settlement.

A second example of the escalation of warfare beginning in the twelfth century is found in the archaeological record of the area surrounding the Casa Grande irrigation system (Figure 11.13). The Casa Grande canal was one of the longest in the Hohokam region, measuring more than 20 km from headgate to end. It was also associated with seven platform mounds, exceeded only by the number of platform mounds (10 or more) on Canal System Two and matched by the number on Canal System One (Rice 1998). Four platform mounds located in the desert to the south of the Casa Grande site (Figure 11.13 shows three of these four sites) were probably associated with those on the canal (Doelle and Wallace 1991; Bayman 1996; Wilcox 1988; Fish et al. 1992; Wallace and Doelle this volume) and formed a regional settlement cluster that Bayman (1996) has termed the Casa Grande supracommunity. This proposal of a settlement cluster is currently based on a spatial gap that developed in the fourteenth century between it and a group of contemporary settlements in the southern Tucson Basin and by a gap in the distribution of platform mounds (but not of individual walled compounds) between the Casa Grande and the Casa Blanca canal systems (Figure 11.13).

The platform mound settlement complexes around the Picacho Mountains may have played a role analogous to that provided by the Maricopa for the Pima; they could have buffered the Casa Grande and other settlements on the Gila River against direct attacks from the south. The Gila River settlements would come to the aid of the Picacho group during an attack not from a sense of altruism or cultural affinity but as a military tactic to maintain the buffer between them and people living to the south. For this reason, the populations in the Picacho-area settlements

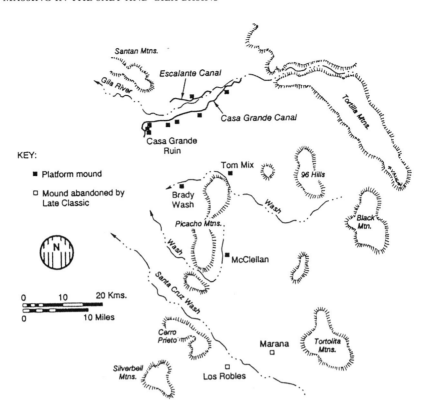

Figure 11.13.
Distribution of settlements with platform mounds in the Casa Grande supracommunity, plus two abandoned platform mounds in the unoccupied zone that developed after A.D. 1300.

need not have had strong historic ties with the populations on the Gila River; like the Maricopa and Pima, they could have spoken different languages and had different cultural beliefs. The relationships among the settlements comprising the Casa Grande supracommunity have yet to be studied in any detail.

The segment of the Santa Cruz Valley (see the Marana and Los Robles platform mounds in Figure 11.13) lying to the south of the Picacho Mountains was occupied continuously from the late Archaic through the Early Classic period. Fields were well watered by short irrigation canals on the Santa Cruz, and the pediment at the base of the Picacho Mountains was used for runoff and flood water for agricultural fields. By the Early Classic period the Marana and Los Robles site complexes were spread out over distances of 10 to 20 km. From the location of the platform mound, the Marana settlement complex extended almost 20 km upstream (southeast) and about 15 km northeast across the pediment toward the Tortolita Mountains (Fish et al. 1992). The Los Robles settlement complex extended about 5 km in both the upstream and downstream directions from the platform mound location (Downum 1993).

Despite the favorable conditions for agriculture and the historic stability of occupation, the Marana and Los Robles sites became the locus of considerable conflict starting in the early twelfth century and continuing into the thirteenth century; by the early fourteenth century this por-

TABLE 11.2. Proportion of Burned Structures in Sites of the Marana Settlement Complex.

Site Designation	Pithouses	Total Burned (%)	Adobe-lined Pithouses	Total Burned (%)	Adobe Rooms	Total Burned (%)	All Structures	Total Burned (%)
AA:12:2, Locus A	7	100					7	100
AA:12:2, Locus D	5	100	4	100	2	100	11	100
AA:12:2, Locus E	13	77	4	100	6	67	23	78
AA:12:2, Locus H	3	33					3	33
AA:12:3, Locus 1	2	50	2	0			4	25
AA:12:1	4	100					4	100
Total	34	82	10	80	8	75	52	75

Source: Henderson 1987(ed.):66, 89, 123, 153, 162, 180.

tion of the Santa Cruz Valley had been abandoned, apparently in response to the fighting. There is no indication that the move was triggered by economic difficulties associated with an inability to conduct agriculture (Fish et al 1992:39–40). Increases in the size of the McClellan Wash settlement complex at the start of the fourteenth century suggest that major portions of the populations at Marana and Los Robles moved northward to the Picacho Mountains (Fish et al. 1992:103). The abandonment of the Marana and Los Robles settlements complexes created a 40-km unoccupied zone between the southern perimeter of the Casa Grande supracommunity (the platform mounds around Picacho Peak) and a cluster of settlements in the south Tucson Basin (Wallace and Doelle this volume).

The gradual intensification of warfare is observable in the archaeology of these sites. During the twelfth century 75 percent of the structures in the Marana cluster of sites burned (Table 11.2; also Henderson, ed. 1987; Rice 1987a). Large assemblages of ceramic vessels, implements, household items, and metates and manos on the floors of the structures (Rice 1987a: 79–142; Kisselburg 1987:143–159) suggest the burning was a precipitous action with expensive consequences. The superimposition of burned structures (with de facto floor assemblages) indicates that the villages had burned on more than one occasion.

By the thirteenth century rooms were enclosed by walled compounds, and the distribution of houses along the edge of the valley floor had contracted from the 20 km of the previous century to about 1.5 km in the area of the platform mound (Fish et al. 1992). Although the community pattern continued to be quite dispersed, efforts were being taken to fortify the settlements of the complex. By the early fourteenth century the Marana community complex had been abandoned (Fish et al. 1992:27–30).

Two partially burned wooden artifacts recovered from one of the Marana structures (Figure 11.14) might be war clubs. The knobs lack the

Figure 11.14.
Possible war clubs
recovered from
burned structures in
the Marana settle-
ment complex.

sharp contours that make Pima war clubs resemble wooden potato
mashers (Russell 1975:96), although tapered knobs similar to these were
observed on Maricopa war clubs (Spier 1933:135). (The knobs on both
artifacts are incomplete because portions have burned off, leaving flat
edges that slice diagonally through the spherical shape of the knob.) Two
Late Classic period clubs recovered from the Tonto National Monument
lack knobs completely, although one has a row of protrusions at one end
(Steen et al. 1967:20, 84). The pointed hook at the end of one of the handles of the Marana clubs recalls the Piman descriptions of a difficult but
highly valued maneuver in which the combatant struck the enemy on the
head with a downward movement of the club and slashed his abdomen
with the pointed end of the club on the return upswing. A Pima war club
illustrated by Russell (1975:96) is sharpened at the end but does not have
a barb.

It is unclear why the populations on the irrigation district began to
pose a threat to the peripheral populations in the twelfth century, since
they did not appear to have been much of a danger before that time.
From the twelfth century on, however, the pressure seems to have been
maintained, and by the fourteenth century many parts of the periphery
were abandoned. Wilcox and others (this volume) describe what appears
to be a gradual movement out of the northern periphery of the Phoenix
Basin, resulting in a withdrawal of populations into a series of settlements on the easily defended Perry Mesa.

The irrigation agriculturalists probably gained few real resources in
terms of food supplies or captives by attacking the populations living in
the desert periphery, but their motives may have been based on ideological principles similar to those held by the nineteenth-century Pima. The
Pima needed trophies of hair (usually without any skin attached) taken
from slain enemies to use as power bundles to bring rain. This or a related belief may have been the basis for attacks by the Hohokam irrigation farmers on the desert populations; the objectives for going to war
need not be apparent in the archaeological record. But whatever the reasons, once engaged in war, the populations on the irrigation systems
could field much larger forces than any of the small, fragmented groups
living on the periphery. Faced with these much larger forces, the popula-

tions in the periphery withdrew into the fortified refuges and somewhat later were driven farther into the mountains away from the irrigation systems on the Salt and Gila.

MASSING VS. AGGREGATING STRATEGIES IN WAR

A basic distinction can be made in the way societies field large forces for war; some populations aggregate into large settlements for defense whereas others mass their forces in defense of a common territory. In historic times this was the difference between puebloan groups on the Colorado Plateau and ranchería settlements of the Pima on the Gila River, and it is a distinction with considerable antiquity in the Southwest.

The Pima and Maricopa strategy in war differed markedly from that of other tribal groups in the Southwest. Among the Hopi, for instance, the maximal defensive group was a closely grouped set of villages on a mesa (Voth 1905:258–268); archaeologically, some of these mesa groupings might be considered one site with multiple room blocks. Even though large Hopi villages were located on other mesas only 12 to 15 km away, and there was invariably ample warning (a full day) of the approach of an enemy (Voth 1905:258, 267), the Hopi appear not to have rallied to the aid of their neighbors on other mesas. In a Navajo attack on Oraibi, people from the Hopi settlement of Walpi (about 26 km from Oraibi) are thought to have secretly joined with the Navajo forces against their fellow Hopi (Voth 1903:259, 264). The Hopi were remarkably capable fighters, and their use of buckskin armor gave them an advantage against superior enemy forces, but they apparently were unaccustomed to coming to the defense of villages on other mesas. Hopi mesas at times joined forces in offensive attacks but only after considerable negotiation and in fairly exceptional circumstances. Under these conditions the size of the settlement was important since it established the upper limit of the force that could be fielded in the event of an attack.

These differences between the Pima and Hopi in how they responded to attacks are not attributable to environmental factors; the distance between Hopi villages on the various mesas (12 to 26 km) is much less than the maximum distance (42 km) separating Pima villages on the Gila River. Although the Hopi villages were located on mesas tops, the terrain between the mesas was flat and easily traversed, and travel between Hopi villages was not particularly more difficult than between the Pima villages. Both the Hopi and the Pima placed high value on long-distance runners, who played important roles in certain kinds of ceremonial occasions and were also used to convey messages between villages (Voth 1905:256–258; Russell 1975:171–175). The Pima were accustomed to massing into a single territorial bloc comprising the entire tribe, and the Hopi were not.

For the Hopi, the individual mesa group was the maximal level of defensive effort. This priority is seen in the layout of their villages. In Hopi villages, as in most prehistoric "pueblo" settlements after about A.D. 1300, rooms were built in compact blocks and single settlements might include hundreds of rooms. Population density was high, and different households frequently occupied adjoining rooms.

One effect of aggregating into large settlements is that all members of the community are committed to the defense of that settlement because all have placed their resources, including their food, in the same location. Aggregation ensures individuals will not, at the critical moment, abandon the cause of common defense. This defensive principle of aggregating into large settlements had developed among puebloan groups on the Colorado Plateau and the central mountains at least as early as A.D. 1200 and was still in operation among puebloan groups in historic times.

A considerably different strategy is used by populations with the ability to mass for purposes of defense. The standing organizational commitment to gather for the common defense of a territory frees the population to continue living in a dispersed settlement pattern, which can be useful if dispersion facilitates subsistence activities. Dispersion can also aid defense, primarily because the attacking party must work harder to loot and destroy houses that are widely spread apart. If the attackers are repelled soon enough, only a few of the houses will be burned, and the defending parties have greater flexibility in selecting a location for a counterattack. Obviously, this strategy works only if there is a total commitment by the population to gather for a common defense, even when the threat still lies 40 km away. This kind of mobilization is nearly the rule in state-level societies but is extremely rare among tribes; it was, nonetheless, a characteristic of the nineteenth-century Pima and Maricopa on the Gila River.

The contrast between the Hopi and Pima settlement types has direct parallels to the prehistoric settlement patterns in the two regions extending back to at least the thirteenth century A.D. Large aggregated room blocks built around central plazas occurred on the Colorado Plateau and in the central mountains whereas dispersed settlements made up of small compounds dotted the desert valleys of the Hohokam region. The Hohokam retained a dispersed settlement system even as the intensity of war increased because they tended to mass in defense of a common territory rather than a common settlement.

With dispersed settlements the size of the population that might be massed for the purpose of war was not limited to the size of the population that could successfully live in face-to-face proximity in a single village. Mechanisms for reducing scalar stress (Johnson 1982) within a single community were not of great importance for people who lived in dispersed settlements. Thus a society with the ability to mass (draw combatants from multiple settlements) in defense of a common territory could be capable of fielding a larger military force than a society that aggregated into a single community. Archaeological researchers need to consider the possibility that the Hohokam, rather than being peaceful irrigation farmers, loomed large on the prehistoric landscape as an intimidating military presence, a presence made possible precisely because of their use of irrigation agriculture.

Finally, the Hohokam and Pima examples provide an interesting contrast to the expectations of "conflict theories" of social evolution. This subset of neo-evolutionary models cites war as a major factor in the evolution of political systems from tribes to chiefdoms and from chiefdoms to states (e.g., Carneiro 1970, 1978; Fried 1978; Haas 1982). War disrupts the equilibrium of a society and leads to increased centralization of leadership roles as victors take over and administer progressively larger units of territory (Cohen 1978:5–7; Fried 1978; Carneiro 1970, 1978).

For the Hohokam, war or the threat of war was instrumental to the operation of the irrigation system as a mechanism that maintained equilibrium on each canal system. (War was less important in this regard for the small scale of the Pima irrigation systems with only a single village per canal.) Lacking a system of centralized courts within a state-level organization, the Hohokam depended on intrasocietal warfare as a means of resolving disputes over water. In an odd way, therefore, intrasocietal warfare acted as an integrative mechanism in Hohokam societies and may well have contributed to the 700-year stability of the Hohokam irrigation systems on the Salt and Gila Rivers.

The Hohokam and the O'Odham irrigation agriculturalists also engaged in intersocietal warfare for the control of adjacent territory, although again not exactly in the manner modeled by conflict theories. The Hohokam irrigation farmers fought against the populations living in the surrounding desert and mountains, and the Gila River Pima, against Apache and Yavapai populations living in the mountains. From the historic case of the Pima we know that Apache and Yavapai theft of food from planted fields was a threat to both Pima lives and food supplies. The incessant raiding was of sufficient intensity that it led the Pima to abandon a portion of the Gila River during the nineteenth century. The intent on the part of the Hohokam and Pima was not to gain use of the enemy land itself but rather to rid the enemy land of its inhabitants so as to create an unoccupied zone to act as a protective barrier around their irrigation systems. This was a different objective than that of subjugating neighboring populations, the assumption made in most conflict theories (e.g., Carneiro 1978:207; Cohen 1978:141–142), and not surprisingly, the outcome differed from the expectation of the models.

Neither the Hohokam nor the Gila River Pima ever attained the full scale of a state-level organization, but both societies had some of the characteristics of states and are examples of one kind of nonstate system that might eventually evolve into a more complex state (Cohen 1978: 142). In both time periods populations massed in defense of a common territory and waged aggressive war on the populations occupying the desert areas beyond their irrigated fields. In the historic period the Gila River Pima incorporated a different ethnic group, the Maricopa, into their polity and territorial unit, and in the prehistoric period the Hoho-kam built fortifications around elite residences and successfully moved into already occupied areas such as the Tonto Basin (Rice 1998).

What the Hohokam and Pima societies lacked, however, were systems of strongly centralized leadership roles. The Classic period Hohokam had elites with certain religious functions, but the evidence is that these individuals did not manage or encourage economic activities, not even those having to do with the distribution of irrigation water (Rice 1998, 2000; Rice, ed. 1998). The Pima had tribal chiefs, but there were other highly valued leadership positions including war leaders, orators, several categories of diviners and healers, and ditch bosses. Moreover, there was no leader, not even nominally, for the combined Pima and Maricopa polity, although archaeologically the settlements of the ethnically distinct groups would appear to be part of a single regional pattern, and the two groups acted as a single body in matters of war. Leadership roles among the Hohokam and certainly among the Pima were not particularly more differentiated or hierarchically structured than those in other tribes of the Southwest. What set the Hohokam and Pima apart from other south-western tribes were their abilities with respect to war; in things to do with war, the Hohokam and their Piman descendants exhibited many of the characteristics of states. It is possible that the evolution of states need have little to do with changes in the institution of leadership but rather has to do with the role of war in selecting for settlement systems capable of acting as territorial blocs.

ACKNOWLEDGMENTS

This chapter benefited greatly from the comments of Steven LeBlanc, Steve Plog, and three anonymous reviewers. Thanks to Alan Ferg for guiding me to some of the references on prehistoric clubs. Christopher Garraty assisted with the compilation of data on burned structures on Canal System Two, for which I am grateful. My thanks as well to Kimberley Vivier for her excellent editing and clarification of the text. My thinking on the topics of war and segmentary organizations has de-veloped through numerous conversations I have had over the years with Christopher Garraty, David Jacobs, Owen Lindauer, Chris Loendorf, Ted Oliver, Julie Solometo, and Arleyn Simon; my thanks to all of you.

CHAPTER TWELVE

Giving War a Chance

Lawrence H. Keeley

The chapters in this volume address a topic long neglected in the literature concerning the pre- and protohistoric peoples of the American Southwest—warfare. This iconoclastic focus makes these contributions automatically interesting for three reasons: (1) the American Southwest is one of the most intensively studied and widely published archaeological regions in the world; (2) the methodological quality of archaeological research that has been done there has long been recognized, worldwide, by other archaeologists as "cutting-edge"; and (3) the neglect of prehistoric warfare by archaeologists is not peculiar to southwestern archaeologists but is universal. Rightly, I have been asked to comment on these chapters regarding only the larger issues they raise because I am not a southwestern archaeologist and cannot critique the detailed evidence adduced in this book. I can comment on some points raised here that are of general anthropological and archaeological interest. In decreasing generality, these topics are the postwar pacification of the past, some common and worldwide features of all warfare, and the archaeology of warfare (i.e., documenting warfare in the archaeological record).

PACIFICATION OF THE PAST

All the contributions to this volume swim against one of the most pervasive intellectual currents of the late twentieth century. Since the late

1940s, historians (including military historians), ethnohistorians, anthropologists (including archaeologists), and other social scientists have "pacified the past" by both commission and, more commonly, omission. These neo-Rousseauian academicians have claimed or implied that prehistoric and recent nonstate societies were much more peaceful and much less homicidal than the states, nations, and empires of ancient and modern Europe, the Near East, and China. Their pacifications have been accomplished via three avenues: by definition, by special pleading interpretation or reinterpretation, and by ignorance. The most common technique for artificially pacifying past or recent tribal peoples involves defining *war* as an activity that only states or civilized (i.e., urban) states can conduct. By such definitions, *war*, *real war*, or *true war* is conducted only by armies, that is, by hierarchically organized collections of "units" of several thousand men led by (if not consisting wholly of) full-time craft specialists (soldiers) who fight battles or conduct sieges against similarly organized and specialized foes. This true or real "War" is contrasted with the "ritualized" battles, raids, ambushes, and seldom mentioned "massacres" of nonstate and prehistoric peoples. It is then claimed or implied that war so defined (that is, a possibility only for societies organized as states) is deadly and destructive, terrible and thus effective, whereas the mild "submilitary combat" of "primitives" is none of these things.

The primary result of this narrow and ethnocentric definition of war is that its promulgators can then blithely claim that nonstate peoples, prehistoric or historic, do not "make war." They further claim or imply that whatever fighting nonstate peoples may conduct is ineffective and unimportant. This pacification by definition ignores three universal facts: (1) the number of fighters any society can field depends entirely on its population; (2) the population size and density of all known societies are directly, if roughly, correlated with occupational specialization, social hierarchy and subordination, technological elaboration and logistical capacity; and (3) the "submilitary combat" of nonstate societies is just as deadly, terrible, and effective as that of states and empires, perhaps more so (Keeley 1996). Pacifying the warfare of nonstate societies "by definition" is analogous to defining a human "nose" as something that must be absolutely large. That is, to be called a "nose" it must have an arbitrarily large volume, extend relatively (by ratio) some arbitrary distance from the plane of the face, and show those allometric features that are correlated with a nose large in size and projection. With such a scale-dependent definition, one could claim that no children and only a tiny minority of adult humanity had noses. But a scientific critic would observe that in physical fact, all humanity had "midfacial projections" in the same location, with the same basic structures and serving the same functions as these narrowly defined "noses." So it is with war: the fatality, destructiveness, effectiveness, and social importance of tribal warfare cannot be defined away.

Another ploy for pacifying the past involves interpreting the activities of prestate warfare or their material effects under such peaceful rubrics as "symbolic," "ceremonial," or "economic." Thus obvious fortifications are claimed to be only symbols of possession or status, an epidemic of burned houses often with corpses inside is supposed to evidence a new "mortuary practice," battle axes become money, and so on. Some of these reinterpretations are just silly. For example, the "new mortuary ritual" that results in the destruction of houses and property, the violent deaths of their inhabitants, and the abandonment of their corpses is called, on planet Earth anyway, "war." Most other of these reinterpretations ignore the prosaic and obvious for the problematic and the arcane. There are few human artifacts and actions that are not invested with some symbolic content, but this overlay of symbolism does not mean that these items and acts do not primarily serve prosaic functions. Dollars do not just symbolize wealth; they are wealth because they are a medium of exchange. A bow symbolizes male power because men use it to kill animals and other men. A fortification symbolizes power and possession because it enhances the military power of its users to retain possession of their lives, territory, and property. Military weapons, paraphernalia, and structures are often loaded with symbolism precisely because they are used in a most terrible and dangerous activity. When not absurd, such symbolic interpretations ironically evidence the very behavior—warfare—and its importance that they are attempting to dismiss or disguise.

The most common way that archaeologists have pacified the past is through ignorance: that is, by ignoring the evidence of warfare they do uncover or by regarding such evidence as insignificant and unworthy of further attention. In my earlier career I was as guilty as any of such a blindness (Keeley 1996:viii–ix). One can document this process by comparing site reports with more synthetic works mentioning the same sites. The site reports frequently describe finding human skeletons with embedded projectile points, fortification ditches and walls, "destruction horizons," and other evidence of violent social conflicts. Yet these finds are often tucked away in appendices and go unremarked in the conclusions. One reason for this disregard is ignorance of comparisons, especially regarding the relative significance of violent deaths. For example, if only 3 to 5 percent of the skeletal remains exhibit traumas from violent death, most archaeologists seem to regard this rate as insignificant. Yet at Gettysburg, one of the acmes of civilized violence, 3 to 5 percent of the soldiers engaged were actually killed. If such prehistoric homicide rates are compared with those recorded in modern warfare, they are very high (Keeley 1996:90, 196–198). When it is further considered that relying only on embedded projectile points will underestimate the number of those killed by projectiles by perhaps four times, the nonchalance of archaeologists in the face of such evidence of a high level of violence is even more censurable. In any case, when syntheses are written, such bellicose evidence is usually never mentioned or is reinterpreted in peaceful terms. In general textbooks on archaeology and prehistory, with few exceptions (e.g., Hayden 1993), warfare is never even mentioned except in discussions of civilized states, implying either that warfare did not exist or that it was unimportant before the emergence of urban states in any region. The contributions to this volume, as well as others dealing with the prehistoric Southwest (e.g., Wilcox and Haas 1994; Haas and Creamer 1993) and elsewhere (e.g., Milner et al. 1991; Martin and Frayer 1997), indicate that the scales are beginning to fall from archaeologists' eyes.

One can now foresee that future archaeological research will gradually eliminate "pacification by ignorance," which in turn will highlight the absurdities and special pleadings of "pacification by interpretation." "Pacification by definition" is unlikely to disappear anytime soon, however. This sophistry serves too many academic and political agendas, especially those discomfited by, and thus anxious to ignore or dismiss, anthropology and the comparative data anthropologists have so painstakingly accumulated.

COMMON ASPECTS OF WARFARE IN THE ANCIENT SOUTHWEST

One of the most important points implied or stated in most of the chapters of this book is that warfare is a variable, not a constant. All available ethnographic and historical evidence indicates that all modern *H. sapiens sapiens*, and all the economies and societies they have lived in, are capable of conducting warfare. Indeed, several cross-cultural ethnological and historical surveys indicate that more than 90 percent of all known societies have been at war at least once a generation (see references in Keeley 1996 to the works of the Embers, Marc Ross, Keith Otterbein, and Quincy Wright). But this same evidence also shows that the incidence and intensity of warfare is highly variable in space and over relatively short time periods (i.e., a century or two). The historical record is replete with examples of societies, nations, cultures, and peoples changing in a short period of time, sometimes only a single generation, from bellicose to pacific or vice versa. Millions of individuals in many places and times have made parallel psychological transitions from peace to war and back again within a few years.

Everywhere and among every kind of people we know, bitter enemies have become friends and close allies have become enemies with a sometimes bewildering rapidity. In the few regions of the world where archaeological and/or historical records are adequate for us to make a judgment on this point (e.g., western Europe, the Near East, and the American Midwest and Eastern Woodlands), evidence is reemerging that there have been periods of relative peace as well as times of intense, extensive, and brutal warfare. The warfare executed by humans over the last forty thousand years has varied not merely in its incidence and intensity but also in its contexts, "causes," weaponry, social correlates, and effects. In the present intellectual climate, analysis of this variability requires first the recognition that warfare was, in fact, relatively common among prehistoric nonstate societies. All the contributors to this volume acknowledge this fact. They all realize that this known variability of warfare requires them to document its existence and importance in the regions and time periods of their particular expertise and interest. Most of these authors address more than just the existence and incidence of warfare—many of their chapters variously ask why warfare was more common and intense in some regions and periods than others. Some of them also ask how warfare, when and where it was common and intense, might have affected other aspects of social behavior and how these social effects might have affected, in turn, how warfare was conducted. Whatever the scientific validity of the hypotheses presented here, they are all predicated on the established scientific fact of warfare's variability.

Several chapters refer to military elements that I have concluded are the fundamental predicates of the only universal "law" of warfare: larger numbers, fortifications, and better logistics will win, in the long run and in most cases, over unfortified smaller numbers with poorer logistics. Military logistics involve creating, moving, massing, and sustaining fighting men, weapons, ammunition, food, fuel, and militarily useful structures (such as fortifications, depots, and means of transport) to, and then at, the loci of potential or actual combat. But logistics are key because all military activities ultimately and immediately depend on them. For this very reason, military officers have long used and appreciated the adage "Amateurs discuss tactics while professionals discuss logistics."

The predicates of this universal principle are closely interdependent. A numerically superior mass of soldiers, especially if thirsty, hungry, or short of ammunition, will usually be defeated by far smaller numbers of better supplied or fortified foes. Fortifications are excellent "force multipliers" that allow tiny numbers of defenders to fight off larger forces outnumbering them by 10 to 25 times. But fortifications have severe limitations: they are immobile; they can defend only the tiny areas encompassed by the lethal range of their defenders' weapons; and they are dependent on the people, supplies, and ammunition they contain when besieged. Unless a fort's supplies are superior to those of its attackers, or a friendly mobile (i.e., unfortified) force large enough to defeat its besiegers comes to its relief, like all forts it will succumb to a siege by superior numbers. Superior logistics, if directed to war parties or armies outnumbered by well-supplied adversaries or attacking an equal number of fortified foes, will likely be unavailing. Other axiomatic military desiderata, such as "interior lines," "the defensive," and "firepower," are merely derivative of one or more of the three predicates of this general principle.

Most of the contributions to this volume focus on such essential military issues as fortifications, the numbers of warriors potentially available, and the possible means by which they could have been alerted, amassed, and supplied. Several discuss the military efficacy of the natural and artificial fortifications at some settlements. Others consider the ability of some groups of settlements to signal one another so that they might at least warn, if not summon reinforcements from, one another when one was attacked. Rice suggests that during periods of increased warfare some prehistoric southwesterners aggregated into larger and/or fortified settlements while others in that region instead clustered their small unfortified settlements within "hailing" distance of one another. Both strategies would have mustered larger numbers of warriors or would have "multiplied" the force of the warriors mustered. Neither ancient southwesterners nor most modern archaeologists have been trained in even the rudiments of modern military "science." Yet, as modern archaeologist have belatedly recognized, the "Old Ones" once used the first principles of war.

Several chapters acknowledge or imply that exchange (or trade) and warfare are closely related. This trade-raid linkage was first noted by Claude Lévi-Strauss (1943) more than 50 years ago and has been documented worldwide by many other ethnologists and historians (see discussion and references in Keeley 1996:121–126, 218). Universally, exchange has been a productive source of war—for all kinds of societies, trade partners have been the most common enemies. Many, if not most, civilized and tribal wars have been fought to obtain trade items, to possess the sources of items of exchange, or to control trade routes. And even the bitterest wars have been interrupted or immediately followed by eager trade between late adversaries. Exchange and war seem to be two sides of the same coin, a coin that is usually and universally flipped frequently. The goods and people moved from one group to another by these alternate means seem to be the coin itself. Some of the contributors to this volume recognize at least that exchange between two societies does not preclude war nor does war preclude trade between them. Ethnology and history suggest a stronger association: people fight those they usually trade with and trade with those they usually fight. As Lévi-Strauss (1948:367) noted half a century ago (speaking of the Nambicuara of Amazonia), "Warfare . . . is closely connected with barter."

Specifying *the* cause any particular war, or even all wars, has been and is a popular academic pastime among historians and ethnographers. A cynic may suspect that this pursuit has been so fashionable for so long precisely because it is impossible: opponents claim different reasons for fighting, as do the participants even on one side; external observers often see causes different from those claimed by participants, and so on. Alas, the data available to archaeologists do not permit them to join in such vain and obviously entertaining debates. Instead, they have been stuck analyzing warfare in terms of its drab "contexts" and "associations." History and ethnography as well as archaeology indicate that some regional circumstances seem to intensify warfare: hard times and moving frontiers, for example. These two contexts are noted in several chapters here.

In the Southwest, as in many parts of the world, droughts and/or periods with increased likelihood of droughts were apparently marked by increased warfare. For example, Libyan and Asiatic pastoralists raided the Nile Valley of ancient Egypt especially during dry years (Aldred 1984:117, 120–121, 151). A series of droughts is implicated in the decades of sanguinary warfare fought among Bantu chiefdoms in the early 1800s in southern Africa (Thompson 1990:81–87) known as the "Mfecane." Decreasing rainfall was also correlated with evidence of increased warfare in the Upper Missouri region during the first half of the 1300s (Bamforth 1994). Other kinds of ecological "hard times" have had similar effects in other regions (see Keeley 1996:138–141). Just as was the case in the prehistoric Southwest, the desperate and the anxious will fight to get what they need or anticipate needing in hard times, making others fight to keep what they have. Like the south African Mfecane, the increased warfare typical of such periods makes bad times worse and may lead to the depopulation, even abandonment, of entire regions. Moving cultural frontiers are violent places where the risk of warfare is much higher than within cultures or on static frontiers. As noted above, exchange encourages warfare. Exchange across cultural frontiers is common but faces greater than normal risks because it must be conducted with "others," outsiders who do not share one's own ethics and values, social system, methods for resolving disputes, language, or economy.

Frontiers are most vulnerable to raids because they are easier for raiders to get to and retreat from and are less densely populated. A moving cultural frontier means that one way of life and/or "people" is replacing another. Although such a change may be accomplished by peaceful voluntary means, dramatic cultural and economic change always breeds resentments and often violent resistance, especially on frontiers where there is no overawing power to suppress these responses or mutually agreed mechanisms to ameliorate them. In fact, moving cultural frontiers are precisely those regions where violence is most likely but where the cultural and social restraints against the escalation of violence between individuals into warfare are minimal or absent (Keeley 1996:130–138).

Another factor that seems to exacerbate warfare in a region is the introduction of new weapons. In Chapter 2 LeBlanc discusses the apparent increase in the frequency and intensity of warfare attending the introduction of the sinew-backed bow to the Southwest, which was more powerful and longer-ranged than the self bow that had appeared a number of centuries earlier. The general question is a universal one: Has the introduction or invention of new weapons or weapon systems increased and intensified warfare even temporarily? This is a favorite topic among Western military historians (Parker 1988, O'Connell 1989, and Van Creveld 1989 are some well-written and thoughtful recent examples) but one long neglected by anthropologists, including myself. I judge that a systematic survey of the ethnographic, ethnohistorical, and archaeological data on this question needs to be done and will give an affirmative answer. The military advantages conferred by better new weapons will usually be readily exploited by their possessors. But such advantages will not last long because foes will soon acquire such weapons and all will learn how to counter or avoid them.

Several chapters here discuss the development of "no-man's-lands" (that is, the unpopulated zones between warring groups). Such no-man's-lands are the universal effect of warfare because inhabitants flee war-torn and heavily raided frontiers. However, the width of these depopulated zones depends on local land usage and population density (Keeley 1996:112, 198)—the more intensive the land use and the higher the human density, the narrower such no-man's-lands. Estimations of prehistoric population densities are fraught with problems, but the widths of the apparent no-man's-lands discussed here are reasonable for the associated probable population densities. As noted in Chapter 1, the appearance of such areas where they did not exist previously is an excellent indicator of warfare.

In Chapter 11 Rice suggests that "segmentary" organization, very useful in and probably an adaptation to frequent warfare, was present prehistorically in the Gila Basin. An old proverb (Arab, as I recall) succinctly expresses the segmentary principle: "I against my brother, my brother and I against our family, our family against our tribe, our tribe against the world." Rice proposes that such a segmentary social military adaptation gave rise to the tightly clustered settlement pattern of small unfortified villages and hamlets that characterize the Gila Basin. Other regions in the Southwest seem to have adapted to periods of frequent warfare by aggregating into larger and/or fortified towns and villages. Rice has tried to confirm this proposal by showing that burned houses within one such settlement cluster were those most militarily vulnerable, making a strong case. I found this hypothesis exciting because it may also apply to the peculiarly "clustered" settlement pattern of the Early Neolithic LBK farmers that I study. My social anthropologist colleague, Waud Kracke, noted in our discussion of this hypothesis that the segmentary principle is ubiquitous and apparently "adaptive" in all human social life, not just warfare. In the ethnology of warfare such "segmentation" has been associated only with patrilineages (Sahlins 1961). In this southwestern instance this association would lead one to expect that the farmers of the late prehistoric Gila Basin were patrilineal whereas their Pueblo contemporaries were matrilineal or bilineal. Inferring the kin reckoning of prehistoric peoples is so difficult as to be practically impossible; at best, archaeologists may occasionally infer related continuities in postmarital residence. Decades ago, using ceramic analyses, it was argued that several late prehistoric Pueblos were matrilocal, a trait correlated with matrilineally oriented forms of kin reckoning. If there is no evidence of major changes, it is not improbable that late prehistoric ancestors had kinship systems similar to those of their early historic descendants. My scan of the ethnohistorical descriptions of the Contact period societies of the Southwest in volumes 9 and 10 of *The Handbook of North American Indians* indicates that the Puebloans were usually matri- or bilineal whereas the Pima-Papago and Maricopa-Cocopa of the Gila and Salt Rivers were patrilineal. In any case, the military utility of segmentary patrilineages is well attested in ethnology (e.g., Ember and Ember 1990:239–240).

Many of the hypotheses and interpretations presented in this volume reflect some of the most universal and fundamental aspects of warfare. If these hypotheses and interpretations are or prove to be scientifically true, then the prehistoric peoples of the Southwest conducted their wars in the same basic ways and under the same basic conditions that all other humans have for tens of thousands of years. Judging from history, ethnology, and comparative prehistory, there is nothing observed or inferred in these contributions about prehistoric southwestern warfare that is unrealistic, improbable, or inhuman. Whether correct in all particulars or not, these chapters ring true.

ARCHAEOLOGY OF WARFARE

Most of the contributors to this volume recognize the importance of and artfully use multiple lines of evidence and multiple competing hypotheses. These methods are, of course, common in all good archaeology, but they are especially crucial when dealing with a contested, even denied, phenomenon such as prehistoric warfare. Several independent lines of evidence are important because warfare is an activity that involves the behavior of many individuals and affects several aspects of social life. On the one hand, one skeleton with embedded arrow points does not make a war. On the other hand, fortifications, defensive site locations, no-man's-lands, burned houses, representations of combat or warriors, mass graves, abandoned corpses, and several skeletons with weapons traumas or war-related mutilations, when found in the same area during the same time, do mean war. It is not sufficient to show that warfare, or the threat of war, accounts for some feature of the archaeological record; alternative hypotheses must be excluded or shown to be less probable. For example, as Rice argues in Chapter 11, the mortuary practice of burning houses in which a death occurred would result in a large number of burned houses, but they should be widely distributed, not concentrated on the militarily vulnerable peripheries of a settlement cluster. The use of multiple lines and competing hypotheses avoids circularities—for example, warfare creates depopulated zones, thus depopulated zones are evidence of warfare—by adducing independent evidence of warfare where and when such zones appear and excluding alternative explanations. Southwestern archaeologists, like their colleagues worldwide, are in the early stages of a revival of interest in warfare such that few independent lines of evidence for warfare are available and few alternatives have been decisively excluded. These chapters are nevertheless good evidence that change is coming and that in the near future southwestern archaeologists will be able to call on more diverse bodies of evidence relevant to the opposed questions of war and peace.

The most unequivocal evidence for warfare is found on human remains. I was surprised how rarely weapons traumas on burial remains were mentioned in these contributions. LeBlanc, in Chapter 1, claims that this lack of attention exists because such traumas are "relatively uncommon in the Southwest." As I noted above, if unequivocal evidence of homicide is found on more than 1 or 2 percent of the human remains from a prehistoric burial population, then this ancient population was more violent than twentieth-century Europe. I suspect the "rarity" of prehistoric homicides in the Southwest, especially during periods when there is other evidence of warfare, has more to do with decades of inattention by archaeologists and neglect of paleopathology than with any actual absence of evidence.

One source of evidence for prehistoric warfare is the depiction of warriors and/or combat in paintings, engravings, and sculpture. Such iconographic evidence is addressed in one chapter. If such representations are interpreted very cautiously, indeed simplistically, they can provide clear evidence that members of a prehistoric group were at least familiar with combat and can document the weapons, armor, and regalia known to the artists and their audiences and, sometimes, those they regarded as enemies. Attempting to read anything more from such art, such as the motives, frequency, casualty rates, or "warlikeness" of prehistoric peoples, is not recommended. "Artistic" representations, however realistic in style, are never snapshots. At best, they are sketches from memory. They may depict visions and dreams, legends and myths. The safest course for archaeologists is to take literally only those aspects that are realistic: that is, that depict items or behaviors familiar from other archaeological, ethnographic, or historical evidence. The proportion of combat or warrior representations in the corpus of artwork from a particular region or period bears no necessary relationship to the actual frequency of fighting. For example, the proportion of combat scenes in Classic Athenian painted vases actually declines as warfare becomes more frequent and intense during the Persian and Peloponnesian wars (Vencl 1984:19). Like high-school bathroom graffiti concerning sexual intercourse, common artistic depictions of warfare imply only familiarity and preoccupation, not necessarily an abundance of experience. Even if such representations are of legendary or mythological events, they are invariably anachronistic; that is, they depict the military equipment and techniques known firsthand by the artists. For example, the combat scenes on Classic Greek vases were commonly meant to represent legendary events that occurred 600 years earlier in the Homeric Bronze Age, yet the arms and tactics depicted were those of the Classic period hoplites (Hanson 1989:50). Even with these limitations, ancient depictions of warriors and combat possess an extraordinary value—they cannot be ignored or bowdlerized away. Their creators and audiences had to know war weapons, warriors, and combat to depict and appreciate them. Overly bellicose interpretations of such prehistoric military iconography can be naive or exaggerated, but they can never be completely wrong.

A majority of the chapters in this book argue either that warfare determined a particular settlement pattern or that particular settlement patterns are evidence of warfare, or both. Most of these arguments seem at least plausible, even convincing, to an archaeologist unfamiliar with the detailed geography of the relevant regions of the Southwest. Therefore, I can only suggest some vague and probably irrelevant cautions. Some locations are militarily important precisely because they are "strategic" for peaceful surveillance, transportation, trade, and production. It is more militarily desirable to be able to see your enemies than your allies. The most easily defended natural positions rarely encompass the water sources, fields, pastures, fishing stations, and the like that a group must defend to survive. For these reasons, military explanations of settlement patterns especially require independent evidence of warfare and strong arguments against alternative peaceful explanations. Because war always involves such enduring physical effects as homicide with weapons, vandalism, and destruction, warfare is difficult to document archaeologically only when archaeologists refuse to look for it. But when archaeologists search for and try to document warfare, as do the authors in this volume, only the strongest evidence and arguments should be used.

CONCLUSIONS

Allowing warfare back into prehistory helps archaeologists understand data patterns that were incomprehensible in pacific terms. Why did ancient southwesterners move their settlements to uneconomic and inaccessible locations at some periods? Why were burned houses and unburied or cremated bodies so common in some places and times but not others? Why were some swaths of densely occupied territory abandoned for a few generations while similar lands immediately adjacent to them were not? Why were some towns and villages walled and others not? What was the purpose of *trincheras*? If history and ethnohistory repeatedly attest that warfare has been a frequent but variable occurrence among the socially and culturally diverse peoples inhabiting the Southwest for the past five hundred years, why were their prehistoric ancestors so different in being always peaceful? How could the mere gaze of some wandering Spanish friars turn the descendants of four hundred generations of pacifists instantly into fierce warriors? It is clear that I regard the contributions to this volume as signaling a healthy return to our scientific senses about prehistoric and "primitive" warfare after four decades of increasingly irrational meandering in a neo-Rousseauian, postmodernist "woo-woo land." To shift metaphors, these contributions are evidence that one of the intellectual pendulums of our century has reached a limit of absurdity and falsity and begun swinging back toward reason and reality. But a few passages in a few of these chapters make me uneasy—they are too eager to see warfare in ambiguous archaeological data and adduce weak arguments in their support. There is, I fear, a danger that the metaphorical intellectual pendulum will swing back too far. Future archaeologists might see war everywhere and in every facet of prehistoric life. Other social scientists, following archaeologists' lead, might come to regard universal, endless, and genocidal warfare among humans as a necessity rather than a capacity, a constant rather than a variable. But this qualm of mine is, in fact, rhetorical and affected. Past humans have left behind unequivocally real, material remains of their actions. This physical archaeological record exists independent of our hypotheses, interpretations, wishes, fears, and delusions. If future anthropologists, like those of this volume, treat the archaeological record as the final arbiter of their interpretations, the return swing of this pendulum will be dampened.

The common message of the chapters in this book is that prehistoric war is too frequent and effective to be glibly dismissed but too variable to be glibly assumed. All archaeologists need to look for evidence of warfare in their particular regions and time periods and to consider its significance and ramifications whether they find it or not. In short, they should try to do no less and no more than the contributors to this book have done—give war a chance.

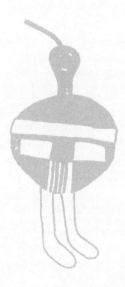

REFERENCES

Abbott, David R.

1994a   *Hohokam Social Structure and Irrigation Management: The Ceramic Evidence from the Central Phoenix Basin.* Unpublished Ph.D. dissertation, Department of Anthropology, Arizona State University, Tempe.

1994b   *The Pueblo Grande Project, Vol. 3: Ceramics and the Production and Exchange of Pottery in the Central Phoenix Basin.* Soil Systems Publications in Archaeology No. 20. Phoenix.

Adams, E. Charles

1991   *The Origin and Development of the Pueblo Katsina Cult.* University of Arizona Press, Tucson.

Adams, R. McC.

1966   *The Evolution of Urban Society: Early Mesopotamia and Prehistoric Mexico.* Aldine, Chicago.

Adler, Michael A. (editor)

1996   *The Prehistoric Pueblo World, A.D.1150–1350.* University of Arizona Press, Tucson.

Ahlstrom, R. V. N., and Heidi Roberts

1995   *Prehistory of Perry Mesa: The Short-Lived Settlement of a Mesa-Canyon Complex in Central Arizona, ca. A.D.1200–1450.* The Arizona Archaeologist No. 28. Phoenix.

Ahlstrom, R. V. N., C. R. Van West, and J. S. Dean

1995   Environmental and Chronological Factors in the Mesa Verde–Northern Rio Grande Migration. *Journal of Anthropological Archaeology* 14:125–142.

Aldred, C.

1984   *The Egyptians.* Thames and Hudson, London.

Allen, W. H, C. F. Merbs, and W. H. Birkby

1985   Evidence for Prehistoric Scalping at Nuvakwewtaqa (Chavez Pass) and Grasshopper Ruin, Arizona. In *Health and Disease in the Prehistoric Southwest,* edited by C. Merbs and R. Miller, pp. 23–34. Anthropological Research Papers No. 34. Arizona State University, Tempe.

Altschul, Jeffrey H., and Bruce A. Jones
1990   *Settlement Trends in the Middle San Pedro: A Cultural Resources Sample Survey of the Fort Huachuca Military Reservation.* Technical Series No. 19. Statistical Research, Inc., Tucson.

Altschul, Jeffrey H., Rein Vanderpot, Robert A. Heckman, and Cesar A. Quijada
1998   The Periods Between: Archaic and Formative Cultures of the Upper and Middle San Pedro Valley. Paper presented at the Amerind Foundation, Inc., seminar "The Archaeology of a Land Between: Prehistory and History of Southeastern Arizona," Dragoon, Arizona.

Anderson, Keith M.
1971   Excavations at Betatakin and Keet Seel. *The Kiva* 37:1–29.

Anyon, Roger, Susan M. Collins, and Kathryn H. Bennett
1983   *Archaeological Investigations between Manuelito Canyon and Whitewater Arroyo, Northwest New Mexico.* Zuni Archaeology Program Report No. 185. Zuni, New Mexico.

Ardrey, R.
1966   *The Territorial Imperative.* Athenaeum, New York.

Arizona Miner
1875   Old Arizona Ruins—Who Built Them? *Arizona Miner*, April 2, 1875, p. 2, col. 2.

Austin, Ken
1977   The Mountain Patayan People of West Central Arizona. Ms. on file, Sharlot Hall Museum, Prescott, Arizona.
1979a   Cummings Site. Ms. on file, Sharlot Hall Museum, Prescott, Arizona.
1979b   Linda Gilpin Sites A, B, and C. Ms. on file, Sharlot Hall Museum, Prescott, Arizona.
2000   The Mountain Patayan People of West Central Arizona. In *Archaeology in West Central Arizona: Proceedings of the 1996 AAC Prescott Conference,* edited by Thomas Motsinger, Douglas R. Mitchell, and James M. McKie, pp. 63–74. Sharlot Hall Museum Press, Prescott, Arizona.

Bailey, L. R.
1964   *The Long Walk: A History of the Navajo Wars, 1846–68.* Westernlore Press, Los Angeles.

Bamforth, D.
1994   Indigenous People, Indigenous Violence: PreContact Warfare on the North American Great Plains. *Man* 29:95–115.

Bandelier, Adolph F.
1892   *Final Report of Investigations among the Indians of the Southwestern United States,*

Part 2. Papers of the Archaeological Institute of America. American Series, Vol. 4. Cambridge, Massachusetts.

Barnes, Will C.
1935   *Arizona Place Names.* University of Arizona General Bulletin No. 2. University of Arizona, Tucson.

Barnett, Franklin
1974a   *Excavation of Main Pueblo at Fitzmaurice Ruin—Prescott Culture in Yavapai County, Arizona.* Museum of Northern Arizona Special Publication. Museum of Northern Arizona, Flagstaff.
1974b   *Sandstone Hill Pueblo Ruin: Cibola Culture in Catron County, New Mexico.* Albuquerque Archaeological Society, Albuquerque.

Basso, Keith (editor)
1971   *Western Apache Raiding and Warfare.* University of Arizona Press, Tucson.

Bayman, James M.
1994   *Craft Production and Political Economy at the Marana Platform Mound Community.* University Microfilms, Ann Arbor.
1996   Reservoirs and Political Integration in the Hohokam Classic Period. In *Debating Complexity Proceedings of the 26th Annual Chacmool Conference,* edited by D. A. Meyer, P. C. Dawson, and D. T. Hanna, pp. 304–311. The Archaeological Association of the University of Calgary, Calgary.

Bayman, James W., Manuel R. Palacios-Fest, and Lisa W. Huckell
1977   Botanical Signatures of Water Storage Duration in a Hohokam Reservoir. *American Antiquity* 62(1):103–111.

Bernard-Shaw, Mary
1989   *Archaeological Investigations at the Redtail Site, AA:12:149 (ASM), in the Northern Tucson Basin.* Technical Report No. 89-8. Center for Desert Archaeology, Tucson.

Berndt, Ronald M.
1964   Warfare in the New Guinea Highlands. *American Anthropologist* 66(4):183–203.

Berry, D. R.
1983   *Disease and Climatic Relationship among Pueblo III and Pueblo IV Anasazi of the Colorado Plateau.* Unpublished Ph.D. dissertation, University of California, Los Angeles.

Billideau, Jenny
1986   On the Trail of the Turquoise Toad. Ms on file, Museum of Northern Arizona Library, Flagstaff.

Black, Andrew T., and Margerie Green (editors)
1995   *The San Carlos Reservoir Cultural Resources Survey.* Archaeological Consulting Services, Tempe.

Blanton, Richard E., Gary M. Feinman, Stephen A. Kowalewski, and Peter N. Peregrine

1996   A Dual-Processual Theory for the Evolution
        of Mesoamerican Civilization. *Current
        Anthropology* 37(1):1–14.

Blick, J. P.
1988   Genocidal Warfare in Tribal Societies as a
        Result of European-Induced Culture
        Conflict. *Man* (n.s.) 23:654–670.

Blitz, John H.
1999   Mississippi Chiefdoms and the Fission-
        Fusion Process. *American Antiquity*
        64(4):577–592.

Bock, K.
1980   *Human Nature and History: A Response to
        Sociobiology.* Columbia University Press,
        New York.

Boehm, C.
1992   Segmentary "Warfare" and the
        Management of Conflict: Comparison of
        East African Chimpanzees and Patrilineal-
        Patrilocal Humans. In *Coalitions and
        Alliances in Humans and Other Animals,*
        edited by A. H. Harcourt and F. B. M. de
        Waal, pp. 137–173. Oxford University
        Press, Oxford.

Bostwick, Todd W., and Christian E. Downum
1994   *Archaeology of the Pueblo Grande Platform
        Mound and Surrounding Features, Vol. 2:
        Features in the Central Precinct of the
        Pueblo Grande Community.* Pueblo Grande
        Museum Anthropological Papers No. 1.
        Parks, Recreation, and Library Department,
        Phoenix.

Bostwick, Todd, and Stan Plum
1996   The Shaw Butte Hilltop Site: A Prehistoric
        Hohokam Observatory. Paper presented at
        the Oxford V Conference, "Cultural
        Aspects of Astronomy: An Intersection of
        Disciplines," Santa Fe. Ms. on file, Pueblo
        Grande Museum, Phoenix.

Bradley, Ronna J. E.
1996   *The Role of Casas Grandes in Prehistoric
        Shell Exchange Networks within the
        Southwest.* Unpublished Ph.D. dissertation,
        Department of Anthropology, Arizona State
        University, Tempe.

Bradley, Ronna J., and Glen E. Rice
1997   Shell Artifacts from U:4:33/132, the Cline
        Terrace Mound. In *A Salado Platform
        Mound on Tonto Creek, Roosevelt Platform
        Mound Study: Report on the Cline Terrace
        Mound, Cline Terrace Complex,* by David
        Jacobs, pp. 455–464. Roosevelt Monograph
        Series No. 7, Anthropological Field Studies
        No. 36. Office of Cultural Resource
        Management, Department of Anthropology,
        Arizona State University, Tempe.

Brew, Susan A., and Bruce B. Huckell
1987   A Protohistoric Piman Burial and a
        Consideration of Piman Burial Practices.
        The Kiva 52:163–191.

Brody, J. J.
1964   *Design Analysis of the Rio Grande Glaze
        Pottery of Pottery Mound, New Mexico.*
        Unpublished Master's thesis, Department of
        Art History, University of New Mexico,
        Albuquerque.

Brown, Gary M.
1991   Embedded and Direct Lithic Resource
        Procurement Strategies on Anderson Mesa.
        The Kiva 56(4):359–386.

Bruder, J. Simon
1982   *Prehistoric Settlement and Subsistence
        Strategies in the Carefree Area, South
        Central Arizona.* Ph.D. dissertation,
        Arizona State University, Tempe. University
        Microfilms, Ann Arbor.

Burrus, Ernest J., S.J.
1971   *Kino and Manje: Explorers of Sonora and
        Arizona.* Sources and Studies for the
        History of the Americas No. 10. Jesuit
        Historical Institute, Rome and St. Louis,
        Missouri.

Cameron, Catherine M.
1995   Migration and the Movement of
        Southwestern Peoples. *Journal of
        Anthropological Archaeology*
        14(2):104–124.

Carneiro, R.
1970   A Theory of the Origin of the State. *Science*
        169:733–738.
1978   Political Expansion as an Expression of the
        Principle of Competitive Exclusion. In
        *Origins of the State: The Anthropology of
        Political Evolution,* edited by Ronald
        Cohen and Elman R. Service, pp. 205–224.
        Institute for the Study of Human Issues,
        Philadelphia.
1981   The Chiefdom: Precursor of the State. In
        *The Transition to Statehood in the New
        World,* edited by G. D. Jones and R. R.
        Kautz, pp. 37–79. Cambridge University
        Press, Cambridge.
1990   Chiefdom-Level Warfare as Exemplified in
        Fiji and the Cauca Valley. In *The
        Anthropology of War,* edited by Jonathan
        Haas, pp. 190–211. Cambridge University
        Press, Cambridge.

Castleton, Kenneth B.
1978   *Petroglyphs and Pictographs of Utah, Vol.
        1: The East and Northeast.* Utah Museum
        of Natural History, Salt Lake City.
1979   *Petroglyphs and Pictographs of Utah, Vol.
        2: The South, Central, West, and
        Northwest.* Utah Museum of Natural
        History, Salt Lake City.

Chaffee, Scott D., Marian Hyman, Marvin W. Rowe,
Nancy J. Coulam, Alan Schroedl, and Kathleen
Hogue
1994   Radiocarbon Dates on the All American

Man Pictograph. *American Antiquity* 59:769–781.

Chagnon, Napoleon A.
1968 Yanomamö Social Organization and Warfare. In *War: The Anthropology of Armed Conflict and Aggression*, edited by Morton Fried, Marvin Harris, and Robert Murphy, pp. 85–91. Natural History Press, Garden City, New York.

1992 *Yanomamö: The Last Days of Eden.* Harcourt, Brace, Jovanovich, New York.

Chamberlin, T. C.
1965 The Method of Multiple Working Hypotheses. *Science* 148(3671):754–759.

Ciolek-Torrello, Richard
1997 Prehistoric Settlement and Demography in the Lower Verde Region. In *Vanishing River, Landscapes, and Lives of the Lower Verde Valley: The Lower Verde Archaeological Project*, edited by Stephanie M. Whittlesey, Richard Ciolek-Torrello, and Jeffrey H. Altshul, pp. 531–596. SRI Press, Tucson.

Ciolek-Torrello, Richard S., and Richard C. Lange
1990 The Gila Pueblo Survey of the Southeastern Sierra Ancha. *The Kiva* 55(2):127–154.

Ciolek-Torrello, Richard, Steven D. Shelly, and Su Benaron (editors)
1994 *The Roosevelt Rural Sites Study, Vol. 2: Prehistoric Rural Settlements in the Tonto Basin.* Technical Series No. 28. Center for Desert Archaeology, Tucson.

Ciolek-Torrello, Richard S., and David R. Wilcox (editors)
1988 *Hohokam Settlement along the Slopes of the Picacho Mountains: The Brady Wash Sites, Tucson Aqueduct Project.* 2 vols. Research Paper No. 35. Museum of Northern Arizona, Flagstaff.

Clark, Jeffery J.
1995 The Role of Migration in Social Change. In *The Roosevelt Community Development Study: New Perspectives on Tonto Basin Prehistory*, edited by M. D. Elson, M. T. Stark, and D. A. Gregory, pp. 369–384. Anthropological Papers No. 15. Center for Desert Archaeology, Tucson.

Clark, Jeffery J., M. Kyle Woodson, and Mark C. Slaughter
1998 Those Who Went to the Land of the Sun. Paper presented at the Amerind Foundation, Inc., seminar "The Archaeology of a Land Between: Prehistory and History of Southeastern Arizona," Dragoon, Arizona.

Clark, John E., and Michael Blake
1994 The Power of Prestige: Competitive Generosity and the Emergence of Rank Societies in Lowland Mesoamerica. In *Factional Competition and Political Development in the New World*, edited by E. M. Brunfiel and J.W. Fox, pp. 17–30. Cambridge University Press, Cambridge.

Clark, Tiffany
1998 Faunal Resources Depletion and Nutritional Stress in Aggregated Pueblo IV Communities. In *Migration and Reorganization: The Pueblo IV Period in the American Southwest*, edited by Katherine Spielmann, pp. 193–207. Arizona State University, Tempe.

Cline, Joanne, and Earl Cline
1983 The Storm Site NA13407: Excavation of Two Small Prescott Culture Ruins. *The Arizona Archaeologist* 18:1–102.

Coe, Michael D.
1992 *Breaking the Maya Code.* Thames and Hudson, New York.

Cohen, Ronald
1978 Introduction to *Origins of the State: The Anthropology of Political Evolution*, edited by Ronald Cohen and Elman R. Service, pp. 1–20. Institute for the Study of Human Issues, Philadelphia.

Cole, S. J.
1990 *Legacy on Stone: Rock Art of the Colorado Plateau and Four Corners Region.* Johnson Books, Boulder, Colorado.

Cordell, Linda S.
1984 *Prehistory of the Southwest.* Academic Press, Orlando, Florida.

1994 *Ancient Pueblo Peoples.* Remy Press and Smithsonian, Washington, D.C.

1997 *Archaeology of the Southwest.* 2nd ed. Academic Press, Orlando, Florida.

Craig, Douglas B., and Jeffery J. Clark
1994 The Meddler Point Site, AZ V:5:4/26 (ASM/TNF). In *The Roosevelt Community Development Study, Vol. 2: Meddler Point, Pyramid Point, and Griffin Wash Sites*, edited by Mark D. Elson, Deborah L. Swartz, Douglas B. Craig, and Jeffery J. Clark, pp. 1–198. Anthropological Papers No. 13. Center for Desert Archaeology, Tucson.

Crary, Joseph S.
1991 An Archaeological Survey of the Lower Verde Area: A Preliminary Report. Paper presented at the 64th Pecos Conference, Nuevo Casas Grandes, Chihuahua, Mexico. Ms. on file, Museum of Northern Arizona Library, Flagstaff.

2000 The Chronology and Culture of Upper (Northern) Southeastern Arizona: The Formative and Classic Periods. In *Between Mimbres and Hohokam: Exploring the Archaeology and History of Southeastern Arizona and Southwestern New Mexico*, edited by Henry D. Wallace. Amerind Foundation, Dragoon, Arizona, and

University of New Mexico Press, Albuquerque, in press.

Crary, Joseph S., Stephen Germick, and David E. Doyel
1994   Exploring the Gila Horizon. Paper presented at the 8th Mogollon Conference, El Paso, Texas.

Creamer, Winifred
1996   Developing Complexity in the American Southwest: Constructing a Model for the Rio Grande Valley. In *Emergent Complexity: The Evolution of Intermediate Societies (Archaeological Series No. 9)*, edited by Jeanne Arnold, pp. 91–106. International Monographs in Prehistory. University of Michigan, Ann Arbor.

Crotty, Helen K.
1995   *Anasazi Mural Art of the Pueblo IV Period, A.D.1300–1600: Influences, Selective Adaptation, and Cultural Diversity in the Pueblo Southwest.* Ph.D. dissertation, University of California, Los Angeles. University Microfilms, Ann Arbor.

Crown, P. L.
1981   *Variability in Ceramic Manufacture at the Chodistaas Site, East-Central Arizona.* Unpublished Ph.D. dissertation, University of Arizona, Tucson.
1987   Classic Period Hohokam Settlement and Land Use in the Casa Grande Ruins Area, Arizona. *Journal of Field Archaeology* 14:147–162.
1994   *Ceramics and Ideology: Salado Polychrome Pottery.* University of New Mexico Press, Albuquerque.

Crown, Patricia L., Larry A. Schwalbe, and J. Ronald London
1988   X-Ray Fluorescence Analysis of Materials Variability in Las Colinas Ceramics. In *The 1982–1984 Excavations at Las Colinas, Vol. 4: Material Culture,* by D. R. Abbott, K. E. Beckwith, P. L. Crown, R. T. Euler, D. A. Gregory, J. R. London, M. B. Saul, L. A. Schwalbe, M. Bernard-Shaw, C. R. Szuter, and A. W. Vokes, pp. 29–72. Archaeological Series No. 162. Arizona State Museum, University of Arizona, Tucson.

Danson, E. B.
1957   *An Archaeological Survey of West Central New Mexico and East Central Arizona.* Papers of the Peabody Museum of Archaeology and Ethnology Vol. 44, No. 1. Harvard University, Cambridge.

Dean, Jeffrey S.
1970   Aspects of Tsegi Phase Social Organization: A Trial Reconstruction. In *Reconstructing Prehistoric Pueblo Societies*, edited by William A. Longacre, pp. 140–174. School of American Research, Santa Fe, and

University of New Mexico Press, Albuquerque.
1988   Dendrochronology and Paleoenvironmental Reconstruction on the Colorado Plateau. In *The Anasazi in a Changing Environment*, edited by George J. Gumerman, pp. 119–167. Cambridge University Press, Cambridge.
1994   The Medieval Warm Period on the Southern Colorado Plateau. *Climatic Change* 26:225–241.
1996   Demography, Environment, and Subsistence Stress. In *Evolving Complexity and Environmental Risk in Prehistoric Southwest*, edited by J. Tainter and B. B. Tainter, pp. 25–56. Santa Fe Institute Studies in Scientific Complexity XXIV. Addison-Wesley, Reading, Massachusetts.

Dean, Jeffrey S., William H. Doelle, and Janet D. Orcutt
1994   Adaptive Stress, Environment, and Demography. In *Themes in Southwest Prehistory*, edited by G. Gumerman, pp. 53–86. School of American Research Press, Santa Fe.

Dean, Jeffrey S., Robert C. Euler, George J. Gumerman, Fred Plog, Richard H. Hevly, and Thor N. V. Karlstrom
1985   Human Behavior, Demography, and Paleoenvironment on the Colorado Plateau. *American Antiquity* 50:537–554.

Dean, J. S., and W. J. Robinson
1982   Dendrochronology of Grasshopper Pueblo. In *Multidisciplinary Research at Grasshopper Pueblo*, edited by W. A. Longacre, S. J. Holbrook, and M. W. Graves, pp. 46–60. Anthropological Papers of the University of Arizona No. 40. University of Arizona Press, Tucson.

DeBoer, Warren R.
1981   Buffer Zones in the Cultural Ecology of Aboriginal Amazonia: An Ethnohistorical Approach. *American Antiquity* 46(2):364–377.

Debowski, S., A. George, R. Goddard, and D. Mullon
1976   *An Archaeological Survey of the Buttes Reservoir.* Archaeological Series No. 93. Arizona State Museum, University of Arizona, Tucson.

Di Peso, Charles C.
1956   *The Upper Pima of San Cayetano del Tumacacori: An Archaeohistorical Reconstruction of the Ootam of Pimeria Alta.* Amerind Foundation No. 7. The Amerind Foundation, Dragoon, Arizona.
1958   *The Reeve Ruin of Southeastern Arizona: A Study of Prehistoric Western Pueblo Migration into the Middle San Pedro Valley.* Amerind Foundation Series No. 8.

The Amerind Foundation, Dragoon, Arizona.

Dittert, Alfred E. Jr.

1959   *Culture Change in the Cebolleta Mesa Region, Central Western New Mexico.* Ph.D. dissertation, Department of Anthropology, University of Arizona. University Microfilms, Ann Arbor.

Dobyns, Henry F.

1963   Indian Extinction in the Middle Santa Cruz River Valley, Arizona. *New Mexico Historical Review* 38(2):163–181.

Dockstader, F. J.

1979   Hopi History, 1850–1940. In *Handbook of North American Indians*, Vol. 9, edited by A. Ortiz, pp. 524–532. Smithsonian Institution, Washington, D.C.

Doelle, William H.

1995   The Centuries before Coronado: The Classic Period on the San Pedro River. *Archaeology in Tucson* 9(2):1–6.

Doelle, William H., David A. Gregory, and Henry D. Wallace

1995   Classic Period Platform Mound Systems in Southern Arizona. In *The Roosevelt Community Development Study: New Perspectives on Tonto Basin Prehistory*, edited by Mark D. Elson, Miriam T. Stark, and David A. Gregory, pp. 385–440. Anthropological Papers No. 15. Center for Desert Archaeology, Tucson.

Doelle, William H., and Henry D. Wallace

1986   *Hohokam Settlement Patterns in the San Xavier Project Area, Southern Tucson Basin.* Technical Report No. 84-6. Institute for American Research, Tucson.

1990   The Transition to History in Pimería Alta. In *Perspectives on Southwestern Prehistory*, edited by P. E. Minnis and C. L. Redman, pp. 239–257. Westview Press, Boulder, Colorado.

1991   The Changing Role of the Tucson Basin in the Hohokam Regional System. In *Exploring the Hohokam: Prehistoric Desert Peoples of the American Southwest*, edited by G. J. Gumerman, pp. 279–345. Amerind Foundation New World Studies Series No. 1. Amerind Foundation, Dragoon, Arizona, and University of New Mexico Press, Albuquerque.

Dove, Donald E.

1970   A Site Survey along the Lower Agua Fria River, Arizona. *The Arizona Archaeologist* 5:1–36.

Downum, Christian E.

1986   The Occupational Use of Hill Space in the Tucson Basin: Evidence from Linda Vista Hill. *The Kiva* 51:219–232.

1995   Archaeological Investigations at Linda Vista Hill, 1980–1987. In *Archaeological Investigations at Los Morteros, a Prehistoric Settlement in the Northern Tucson Basin.* Anthropological Papers No. 17. Center for Desert Archaeology, Tucson.

Downum, Christian E. (editor)

1993   *Between Desert and River: Hohokam Settlement and Land Use in the Los Robles Community.* Anthropological Papers of the University of Arizona No. 57. University of Arizona Press, Tucson.

Downum, Christian E., and Todd W. Bostwick

1993   *Archaeology of the Pueblo Grande Platform Mound and Surrounding Features, Vol. 1: Introduction to the Archival Project and History of Archaeological Research.* Pueblo Grande Museum Anthropological Papers No. 1. Parks, Recreation, and Library Department, Phoenix.

Downum, Christian E., John E. Douglas, and Douglas B. Craig

1993   The Cerro Prieto Site. In *Between Desert and River: Hohokam Settlement and Land Use in the Los Robles Community*, edited by C. E. Downum, pp. 53–95. Anthropological Papers of the University of Arizona No. 57. University of Arizona Press, Tucson.

Downum, Christian E., Paul R. Fish, and Suzanne K. Fish

1994   Refining the Role of *Cerros de Trincheras* in Southern Arizona Settlement. *The Kiva* 59(3):271–296.

Downum, Christian E., and John H. Madsen

1993   Classic Period Platform Mounds South of the Gila River. In *The Northern Tucson Basin Survey: Research Directions and Background Studies*, edited by J. H. Madsen, P. R. Fish, and S. K. Fish, pp. 125–142. Arizona State Museum, University of Arizona, Tucson.

Doyel, David E.

1981   *Late Hohokam Prehistory in Southern Arizona.* Contributions to Archaeology No. 2. Gila Press, Scottsdale, Arizona.

1991   Hohokam Cultural Evolution in the Phoenix Basin. In *Exploring the Hohokam: Prehistoric Desert Peoples of the American Southwest*, edited by George J. Gumerman, pp. 231–278. Amerind Foundation New World Studies Series No. 1. Amerind Foundation, Dragoon, Arizona, and University of New Mexico Press, Albuquerque.

Doyel, David E., and Mark D. Elson (editors)

1985   *Hohokam Settlement and Economic Systems in the Central New River Drainage, Arizona.* Soil Systems Publications in Archaeology No. 4, Phoenix.

Drennan, Robert

1984   Long-Distant Transport Costs in Pre-

Hispanic Mesoamerica. *American Anthropologist* 86(1):105–112.

Duff, Andrew I.
1995   Excavations at Rattlesnake Point Pueblo on the Upper Little Colorado River. Paper presented at the 60th Annual Meeting of the Society for American Archaeology, Minneapolis.
1996   When Is a Region? Issues for Late Pueblo Prehistory. Paper presented at the Southwest Symposium, February, Tempe, Arizona.

Duffen, William A.
1936   Development of Human Culture in the San Pedro River Valley, Arizona. Unpublished Master's thesis, University of Arizona. On file, Arizona State Museum Library, Tucson.

Dutton, Bertha P.
1963   *Sun Father's Way: The Kiva Murals of Kuaua, A Pueblo Ruin, Coronado State Monument, New Mexico.* University of New Mexico Press, Albuquerque.

Earle, Timothy K.
1997   *How Chiefs Come to Power.* Stanford University Press, Stanford.

Ehrenreich, B.
1997   *Blood Rites: Origins and History of the Passions of War.* Metropolitan, New York.

Ellis, Christopher J.
1997   Factors Influencing the Use of Stone Projectile Tips: An Ethnographic Perspective. In *Projectile Technology*, edited by Heidi Knecht, pp. 37-74. Plenum Press, New York.

Ellis, Florence Hawley
1951   Patterns of Aggression and the War Cult in Southwestern Pueblos. *Southwestern Journal of Anthropology* 7(2):177–201.

Elson, Mark D.
1992   Settlement, Subsistence, and Cultural Affiliation within the Upper Tonto Basin. In *The Rye Creek Project: Archaeology in the Upper Tonto Basin, Vol. 3: Synthesis and Conclusions*, by Mark D. Elson and Douglas B. Craig, pp. 55–78. Anthropological Papers No. 11. Center for Desert Archaeology, Tucson.
1998   *Expanding the View of Hohokam Platform Mounds: An Ethnographic Perspective.* Anthropological Papers of the University of Arizona No. 63. University of Arizona Press, Tucson.

Elson, Mark D., and David A. Gregory
1995   Tonto Basin Phase Chronology. In *The Roosevelt Community Development Study: New Perspectives on Tonto Basin Prehistory*, edited by Mark D. Elson, Miriam T. Stark, and David A. Gregory, pp. 61–77. Anthropological Papers No. 15. Center for Desert Archaeology, Tucson.

Elson, Mark D., David A. Gregory, and Miriam T. Stark
1995   New Perspectives on Tonto Basin Prehistory. In *The Roosevelt Community Development Study: New Perspectives on Tonto Basin Prehistory*, edited by Mark D. Elson, Miriam T. Stark, and David A. Gregory, pp. 441–480. Anthropological Papers No. 15. Center for Desert Archaeology, Tucson.

Elson, Mark D., Miriam T. Stark, and David A. Gregory (editors)
1995   *The Roosevelt Community Development Study: New Perspectives on Tonto Basin Prehistory.* Anthropological Papers No. 15. Center for Desert Archaeology, Tucson.

Elson, Mark D., and Deborah L. Swartz
1994   *The Roosevelt Community Development Study, Vol. 1: Introduction and Small Sites.* Anthropological Papers No. 13. Center for Desert Archaeology, Tucson.

Elson, Mark D., Deborah L. Swartz, Douglas B. Craig, and Jeffery J. Clark
1994   *The Roosevelt Community Development Study, Vol. 2: Meddler Point, Pyramid Point, and Griffin Wash Sites.* Anthropological Papers No. 13. Center for Desert Archaeology, Tucson.

Ember, C.
1978   Myths about Hunter-Gatherers. *Ethnology* 17:439–448

Ember, Carol R., and Melvin Ember
1990   *Cultural Anthropology.* 6th ed. Prentice-Hall, Englewood Cliffs, New Jersey.
1992   Resource Unpredictability, Mistrust, and War: A Cross-Cultural Study. *Journal of Conflict Resolution* 36(2):242–262.

Evans-Pritchard, Edward W.
1940   *The Nuer.* Clarendon Press, Oxford.

Ezzo, J. A.
1992   Dietary Change and Variability at Grasshopper Pueblo, Arizona. *Journal of Anthropological Archaeology* 11:219–289.
1993   *Human Adaptation at Grasshopper Pueblo, Arizona: Social and Ecological Perspectives.* International Monographs in Prehistory, Archaeological Series No. 4. Ann Arbor.

Ezzo, J. A., C. M. Johnson, and T. D. Price
1997   Analytical Perspectives on Prehistoric Migration: A Case Study from East-Central Arizona. *Journal of Archaeological Science* 24:447–466.

Fairchild-Parks, J., and J. S. Dean
1993   Analysis of Tree-Ring Dates from Balcony House—Mesa Verde National Park, Colorado. Ms. on file, Laboratory of Tree-Ring Research, Tucson, Arizona.

Farmer, M. F.
1957   A Suggested Typology of Defense Systems

of the Southwest. *Southwestern Journal of Anthropology* 13(3):249–266.

Ferg, Alan

1979   The Petroglyphs of Tumamoc Hill. *The Kiva* 45(1–2):95–118.

Ferguson, R. Brian

1984   Introduction: Studying War. In *Warfare, Culture, and Environment*, edited by R. B. Ferguson, pp. 1–82. Academic Press, New York.

1992   A Savage Encounter: Western Contact and the Yanomami War Complex. In *War in the Tribal Zone: Expanding States and Indigenous Warfare*, edited by R. Brian Ferguson and Neil L. Whitehead, pp. 199–227. School of American Research Press, Santa Fe.

1997   Violence and War in Prehistory. In *Troubled Times: Violence and Warfare in the Past*, edited by D. L. Martin and D. W. Frayer, pp. 321–355. Gordon and Breach, London.

Ferguson, R. Brian (editor)

1984   *Warfare, Culture, and Environment*. Academic Press, Orlando, Florida.

Ferguson, R. Brian, and Neil L. Whitehead (editors)

1992   *War in the Tribal Zone: Expanding States and Indigenous Warfare*. School of American Research Press, Santa Fe.

Ferguson, T. J.

1996   *Historic Zuni Architecture and Society: An Archaeological Application of Space Syntax*. Anthropological Papers of the University of Arizona No. 60. University of Arizona Press, Tucson.

Fetterman, J., and L. Honeycutt

1987   *The Mockingbird Mesa Survey*. Colorado State Office, Bureau of Land Management Cultural Resource Series No. 22. Denver.

1990   *In the Fremont-Anasazi Transition Zone: Excavations in Verdure Canyon*. Woods Canyon Archaeological Consultants. Submitted to the Bureau of Land Management, San Juan Resource Area Office, Moab, Utah.

Fewkes, Jesse Walter

1893   A-Wa-To-Bi: An Archaeological Verification of a Tusayan Legend. *American Anthropologist* 6:363–375.

1898   The Winter Solstice Ceremony at Walpi. *American Anthropologist* (n.s.) 11 (3):65–87 and (n.s.) 11(4):101–115.

1904   *Two Summers' Work in Pueblo Ruins*. 22nd Annual Report of the Bureau of American Ethnology for 1900–1901, Part 1. Washington, D.C.

1908   *Excavations at Casa Grande, Arizona, in 1906–1907*. Smithsonian Miscellaneous Collections No. 50, Quarterly Issue 4, Part 3:289–329.

1910   *Prehistoric Ruins of the Gila Valley*. Smithsonian Miscellaneous Collections No. 52, Quarterly Issue 5, Part 4:403–436.

1912a   Antiquities of the Upper Verde River and Walnut Creek Valleys, Arizona. In *Twenty-Eighth Annual Report of the Bureau of American Ethnology, 1906–1907*, pp. 181–220. Government Printing Office, Washington, D.C.

1912b   Casa Grande, Arizona. In *Twenty-Eighth Annual Report of the Bureau of American Ethnology, 1906–1907*, pp. 25–179. Government Printing Office, Washington, D.C.

Fish, Paul R.

1989   The Hohokam: 1,000 Years of Prehistory in the Sonoran Desert. In *Dynamics of Southwest Prehistory*, edited by Linda S. Cordell and George J. Gumerman, pp. 19–63. Smithsonian Institution Press, Washington, D.C.

Fish, Paul R., and Suzanne K. Fish

1989   Hohokam Warfare from a Regional Perspective. In *Cultures in Conflict: Current Archaeological Perspectives*, edited by D. C. Tkaczuk and B. C. Vivian, pp. 112–129. Proceedings of the 20th Annual Chacmool Conference. Archaeological Association of the University of Calgary, Calgary.

1993   An Assessment of Abandonment Processes in the Hohokam Classic Period of the Tucson Basin. In *Abandonment of Settlements and Regions: Ethnoarchaeological and Archaeological Approaches*, edited by Catherine M. Cameron and Steve A. Tomka, pp. 99–109. Cambridge University Press, Cambridge.

1994   Multisite Communities as Measures of Hohokam Aggregation. In *The Ancient Southwestern Community*, edited by W. H. Wills and Robert D. Leonard, pp. 119–130. University of New Mexico Press, Albuquerque.

Fish, Paul R., Suzanne K. Fish, George Gumerman, and J. Jefferson Reid

1994   Toward an Explanation for Southwestern "Abandonments." In *Themes in Southwestern Prehistory*, edited by M. Gell-Mann and G. Gumerman. School of American Research Press, Santa Fe.

Fish, Paul R., Suzanne K. Fish, Austin Long, and Charles H. Miksicek

1986   Early Corn Remains from Tumamoc Hill, Southern Arizona. *American Antiquity* 51:563–572.

Fish, Suzanne K.

1996   Dynamics of Scale in the Southern Deserts. In *Interpreting Southwestern Diversity: Underlying Principles and Overarching*

Patterns, edited by Paul R. Fish and J. Jefferson Reid, pp. 107–114. Anthropological Research Papers No. 48, Arizona State University, Tempe.

Fish, Suzanne K., and Paul R. Fish
1992   The Marana Community in Comparative Context. In *The Marana Community in the Hohokam World*, edited by Suzanne K. Fish, Paul R. Fish, and John H. Madsen, pp. 97–105. Anthropological Papers of the University of Arizona No. 56. University of Arizona Press, Tucson.

Fish, Suzanne K., Paul R. Fish, and Christian E. Downum
1984   Hohokam Terraces and Agricultural Production in the Tucson Basin, Arizona. In *Prehistoric Agricultural Strategies in the Southwest*, edited by Suzanne K. Fish and Paul R. Fish, pp. 55–71. Arizona State University Anthropological Research Paper No. 33. Arizona State University, Tempe.

Fish, Paul R., Suzanne K. Fish, Austin Long, and Charles Mikisicek
1986   Early Corn Remains from Tumamoc Hill, Southern Arizona. *American Antiquity* 51(3):563–572.

Fish, Suzanne K., Paul R. Fish, and John H. Madsen
1992   *The Marana Community in the Hohokam World*. Anthropological Papers of the University of Arizona No. 56. University of Arizona Press, Tucson.

Fontana, Bernard L., J. Cameron Greenleaf, and Donnelly D. Cassidy
1959   A Fortified Arizona Mountain. *The Kiva* 25(2):41–53.

Fowler, Andrew P., John R. Stein, and Roger Anyon
1987   An Archaeological Reconnaissance of West-Central New Mexico: The Anasazi Monuments Project. Ms. on file, New Mexico Historic Preservation Division, Santa Fe.

Fox, John W.
1987   *Maya Postclassic State Formation*. Cambridge University Press, Cambridge.

Fox, Richard G.
1977   *Urban Anthropology: Cities in Their Cultural Settings*. Prentice-Hall, Englewood Cliffs, New Jersey.

Franklin, Hayward H.
1980   *Excavations at Second Canyon Ruin, San Pedro Valley, Arizona*. Contributions to Highway Salvage Archaeology in Arizona No. 60. Arizona State Museum, University of Arizona, Tucson.

Fried, Morton H.
1978   The State, the Chicken, and the Egg, or What Came First. In *Origins of the State: The Anthropology of Political Evolution*, edited by Ronald Cohen and Elman R. Service, pp. 35–48. Institute for the Study of Human Issues, Philadelphia.

Fried, Morton, Marvin Harris, and Robert Murphy
1968   *War: The Anthropology of Armed Conflict and Aggression*. Natural History Press, Garden City, New York.

Frisbie, Theodore R.
1973   Field Report: The Newton Site, Catron County, New Mexico. *Awanyu* 1(4):31–36.

Geib, Phil R., and Helen C. Fairley
1996   A Pueblo III Community in Glen Canyon. In *Glen Canyon Revisited*, edited by Phil R. Geib, pp. 185–194. University of Utah Anthropology Papers No. 119. University of Utah Press, Salt Lake City.

Germick, Stephen, and Joseph S. Crary
1992   From Shadow to Substance: An Alternative Perspective on the Roosevelt Phase. In *Proceedings of the Second Salado Conference, Globe, Arizona, 1992*, edited by Richard C. Lange and Stephen Germick, pp. 286–303. Occasional Paper. The Arizona Archaeological Society, Phoenix.

Gladwin, Harold S.
1930   An Outline of Southwestern Prehistory. *Arizona Historical Review* 3(1):71–87.

Glennie, Gilbert D., and William D. Lipe
1984   Replication of an Early Anasazi Pithouse. Paper presented at the 49th Annual Meeting of the Society for American Archaeology, Portland, Oregon.

Goodwin, G.
1942   *The Social Organization of the Western Apache*. University of Chicago Press, Chicago.

Gosden, C.
1989   Debt, Production, and Prehistory. *Journal of Anthropological Archaeology* 8:355–387.

Gould, S. J.
1996   The Diet of Worms and the Defenestration of Prague. *Natural History*, September: 18–67.

Graves, M. W.
1982   Apache Adaptation to the Mountains. In *Cholla Project Archaeology: The Q Ranch Region*, edited by J. J. Reid, pp. 193–215. Archaeological Series No. 161, Vol. 3. Arizona State Museum, Tucson.

Graybill, D. A., and J. J. Reid
1982   Cholla Project Chipped Stone Identification Procedures. In *Cholla Project Archaeology: The Q Ranch Region*, edited by J. J. Reid, pp. 27–34. Archaeological Series No. 161, Vol. 1. Arizona State Museum, Tucson.

Grebinger, Paul F.
1976   Salado Perspectives from the Middle Santa Cruz Valley. *The Kiva* 42(1):39–46.

Greenleaf , J. Cameron
1975   The Fortified Hill Site near Gila Bend, Arizona. *The Kiva* 40:213–282.
Gregg, J. B., L. J. Zimmerman, J. P. Steele, H. Ferwerda, and P. S. Gregg
1981   Ante-Mortem Osteopathology at Crow Creek. *Plains Anthropologist* 25:287–300.
Gregory, David A.
1987   The Morphology of Platform Mounds and the Structure of Classic Period Hohokam Sites. In *The Hohokam Village: Site Structure and Organization*, edited by David E. Doyel, pp. 183–210. Southwestern and Rocky Mountain Division of the American Association for the Advancement of Science, Glenwood Springs, Colorado.
1991   Form and Variation in Hohokam Settlement Patterns. In *Chaco and Hohokam: Prehistoric Regional Systems in the American Southwest*, edited by Patricia L. Crown and W. James Judge, pp. 159–194. School of American Research Press, Santa Fe.
1995a   *A Cultural Resources Overview of the Rye Creek Geographic Study Area, Payson and Tonto Basin Ranger Districts, Tonto National Forest, Gila County, Arizona.* Technical Report No. 95-10. Center for Desert Archaeology, Tucson.
1995b   Prehistoric Settlement Patterns in the Eastern Tonto Basin. In *The Roosevelt Community Development Study: New Perspectives on Tonto Basin Prehistory*, edited by Mark D. Elson, Miriam T. Stark, and David A. Gregory, pp. 127–184. Anthropological Papers No. 15. Center for Desert Archaeology, Tucson.
Gregory, David A. (editor)
1988   *The 1982–1984 Excavations at Las Colinas: The Mound 8 Precinct.* Archaeological Series No.162, Vol. 3. Arizona State Museum, University of Arizona, Tucson.
Gregory, David A., and Fred L. Nials
1985   Observations Concerning the Distribution of Classic Period Hohokam Platform Mounds. In *Proceedings of the 1983 Hohokam Symposium*, Part 1, edited by Alfred E. Dittert Jr., and Donald E. Dove, pp. 373–388. Arizona Archaeological Society Occasional Paper No. 2. The Arizona Archaeological Society, Phoenix.
Griffin, P. B.
1967   A High Status Burial from Grasshopper Ruin, Arizona. *The Kiva* 33:37–53.
Grove, Jean
1990   *The Little Ice Age.* Routledge, London.
Gumerman, George J., and Jeffrey S. Dean
1989   Prehistoric Cooperation and Competition in the Western Anasazi Area. In *Dynamics of Southwest Prehistory*, edited by Linda S. Cordell and George J. Gumerman, pp. 99–148. Smithsonian Institution Press, Washington, D.C.
Haas, Jonathan
1982   *The Evolution of the Prehistoric State.* Columbia University Press, New York.
1990   Warfare and the Evolution of Tribal Polities in the Prehistoric Southwest. In *The Anthropology of War*, edited by Jonathan Haas, pp. 171–189. Cambridge University Press, New York.
Haas, Jonathan (editor)
1990   *The Anthropology of War.* Cambridge University Press, New York.
Haas, Jonathan, and Winifred Creamer
1993   *Stress and Warfare among the Kayenta Anasazi of the Thirteenth Century A.D.* Fieldiana Anthropology, New Series, No. 21, Publication No. 1450. Field Museum of Natural History, Chicago.
1995   A History of Pueblo Warfare. Paper presented at the 60th Annual Meeting of the Society for American Archaeology, Minneapolis.
1996   The Role of Warfare in the Pueblo III Period. In *The Prehistoric Pueblo World, A.D. 1150–1350*, edited by Michael A. Adler, pp. 205–213. University of Arizona Press, Tucson.
1997   Warfare among the Pueblos: Myth, History, and Ethnology. *Ethnohistory* 44(2):235–261.
Haase, W. R.
1985   Domestic Water Conservation among the Northern San Juan Anasazi. *Southwestern Lore* 51(2):15–27.
Hackbarth, Mark R.
1993   Implications of the SCFAP Mortuary Data. In *Classic Period Occupation on the Santa Cruz Flats: The Santa Cruz Flats Archaeological Project, Part 2*, edited by T. Kathleen Henderson and Richard J. Martynec, pp. 566–577. Northland Research, Inc., Flagstaff, Arizona.
1997   *Archaeological and Archival Investigations of Las Canopas: The Esteban Park Project.* Pueblo Grande Museum Anthropological Papers No. 6. Pueblo Grande Museum, Phoenix.
Hackenberg, Robert A.
1974a   *Aboriginal Land Use and Occupancy of the Pima-Maricopa Indians, Vol. 1.* Garland Publishing, New York.
1974b   *Aboriginal Land Use and Occupancy of the Pima-Maricopa Indians, Vol. 2.* Garland Publishing, New York.
Hage, Per, and Frank Harary
1983   *Structural Models in Anthropology.* Cambridge University Press, Cambridge.

Hally, David J.
1993   The Territorial Size of Mississippian
        Chiefdoms. In *Archaeology of Eastern
        North America: Papers in Honor of Stephen
        Williams*, edited by James B. Stoltman, pp.
        143–168. Archaeological Report No. 25.
        Mississippi Department of Archives and
        History, Jackson.

Hanson, V.
1989   *The Western Way of War*. Oxford
        University Press, New York.

Hard, Robert J., and John R. Roney
1998   A Massive Terraced Village Complex in
        Chihuahua, Mexico, 3000 Years before
        Present. *Science* 279:1661–1664.

Hardy, William H.
1888   Early Trouble with Indians—1866. *Mohave
        County Miner*, December 8, 1888. Copy in
        Munk Library of Arizoniana, Southwest
        Museum, Los Angeles.

Harrill, Bruce G.
1967   Prehistoric Burials near Young, Arizona.
        The Kiva 33(2):54–59.

Harry, Karen G.
1997   Ceramic Production, Distribution, and
        Consumption in Two Classic Period
        Hohokam Communities. Unpublished
        Ph.D. dissertation, Department of
        Anthropology, University of Arizona,
        Tucson.

Hartmann, Gayle H., and William K. Hartmann
1979   Prehistoric Trail Systems and Related
        Features on the Slopes of Tumamoc Hill.
        The Kiva 45:29–70.

Haury, Emil W.
1934   *The Canyon Creek Ruin and the Cliff
        Dwellings of the Sierra Ancha*. Medallion
        Paper No. 14. Gila Pueblo, Globe, Arizona.
1945   *The Excavation of Los Muertos and
        Neighboring Ruins in the Salt River Valley,
        Southern Arizona*. Papers of the Peabody
        Museum of American Archaeology and
        Ethnology Vol. 24, No. 1. Harvard
        University, Cambridge. Reprint. Kraus
        Reprint Co., Millwood, New York, 1975.
1958   Evidence at Point of Pines for a Prehistoric
        Migration from Northern Arizona. In
        Migrations in New World Culture History,
        edited by R. H. Thompson, pp. 1–18.
        University of Arizona Bulletin 29(2).
        University of Arizona Press, Tucson.
1976   *The Hohokam: Desert Farmers and
        Craftsmen: Excavations at Snaketown,
        1964–1965*. University of Arizona Press,
        Tucson.
1985   *Mogollon Culture in the Forestdale Valley,
        East-Central Arizona*. University of Arizona
        Press, Tucson.
1986   Evidence at Point of Pines for a Prehistoric
        Migration from Northern Arizona. In *Emil

*Haury's Prehistory of the American
        Southwest*, edited by J. Jefferson Reid and
        David E. Doyel, pp. 414–421. University of
        Arizona Press, Tucson. Originally published
        1958.
1989   *Point of Pines, Arizona: A History of the
        University of Arizona Archaeological Field
        School*. Anthropological Papers of the
        University of Arizona No. 50. University of
        Arizona Press, Tucson.

Haury, Emil W., and Lyndon Hargrave
1931   *Recently Dated Pueblo Ruins in Arizona*.
        Smithsonian Miscellaneous Collections
        82(11). Washington, D.C.

Haury, E. W., and E. B. Sayles
1947   *An Early Pithouse Village of the Mogollon
        Culture*. Social Science Bulletin No. 16.
        University of Arizona, Tucson.

Hayden, B.
1993   *Archaeology: The Science of Once and
        Future Things*. W. H. Freeman, New York.

Hayden, Julian D.
1957   *Excavations, 1940, at the University Indian
        Ruin, Tucson*. Technical Series No. 5.
        Southwestern Monuments Association,
        Globe, Arizona.

Hayes, Alden C.
1964   *The Archeological Survey of Wetherill
        Mesa, Mesa Verde National Park,
        Colorado.* Archeological Research Series
        No. 7-A. National Park Service,
        Washington, D.C.
1981   *Contributions to Gran Quivira Archeology,
        Gran Quivira National Monument, New
        Mexico*. Publications in Archeology No. 17.
        National Park Service, Washington, D.C.

Hayes, Alden C., Jon N. Young, and A. Helene
Warren
1981   *Excavation of Mound 7, Gran Quivira
        National Monument, New Mexico*.
        Publications in Archeology No. l6. National
        Park Service, Washington, D.C.

Heacock, Laura A., and Martha M. Callahan
1988   Ceramics. In *Hohokam Settlement along the
        Slopes of the Picacho Mountains, Vol. 4:
        Material Culture*, edited by M. M.
        Callahan, pp. 1–127. Cultural Resource
        Mitigative Data Recovery Studies—Phase
        A, Tucson Aqueduct Project, Central
        Arizona Project. Museum of Northern
        Arizona, Flagstaff.

Heider, Karl
1979   *Grand Valley Dani: Peaceful Warriors*.
        Holt, Rinehart, and Winston, New York.

Heidke, James M.
1995   Ceramic Analysis. In *Archaeological
        Investigations at Los Morteros, a
        Prehistoric Community in the Northern
        Tucson Basin*, by H. D. Wallace, pp.

263–442. Anthropological Papers No. 17. Center for Desert Archaeology, Tucson.

2000 Utilitarian Ceramic Production and Distribution in the Prehistoric Tonto Basin. In *A Tonto Basin Perspective on Ceramic Economy*, edited by J. M. Vint and J. M. Heidke. Anthropological Paper No. 23. Center for Desert Archaeology, Tucson, in press.

Heidke, James M., and Miriam T. Stark
1995 Ceramic Chronology, Technology, and Economics in the Roosevelt Community Development Study Area. In *The Roosevelt Community Development Study, Vol. 2: Ceramic Chronology, Technology, and Economics*, edited by J. M. Heidke and M. T. Stark, pp. 395–407. Anthropological Papers No. 14. Center for Desert Archaeology, Tucson.

Heidke, James M., and Miriam T. Stark (editors)
1995 *The Roosevelt Community Development Study, Vol. 2: Ceramic Chronology, Technology, and Economics*. Anthropological Papers No. 14. Center for Desert Archaeology, Tucson.

Henderson, T. Kathleen
1987 *Structure and Organization at La Ciudad*. Anthropological Field Studies No. 18. Office of Cultural Resource Management, Department of Anthropology, Arizona State University, Tempe.

1993 Perspectives on the Classic Period Occupation of the Santa Cruz Flats. In *Classic Period Occupation on the Santa Cruz Flats: The Santa Cruz Flats Archaeological Project*, edited by T. Kathleen Henderson and Richard J. Martynec, pp. 579–596. Northland Research, Inc., Flagstaff.

1996 Time and Event in Southern Arizona Prehistory. Paper presented at the 61st Annual Meeting of the Society for American Archaeology, New Orleans.

Henderson, T. Kathleen (editor)
1987 *Field Investigations at the Marana Community Complex*. Anthropological Field Studies No. 14. Office of Cultural Resource Management, Arizona State University, Tempe.

Hensler, Kathy Niles
1992 Intrusive Ceramic Exchange within the Tonto Basin. In *Proceedings of the Second Salado Conference, Globe, Arizona, 1992*, edited by Richard C. Lange and Stephen Germick, pp. 238–247. Occasional Paper. The Arizona Archaeological Society, Phoenix.

1998 Social Boundaries Set in Clay: Trade Ware Patterning in the Tonto Basin of East-

Central Arizona. *Journal of Anthropological Research* 54(4):477–496.

Hensler, Vern Harris
1993 Paints, Slips, and Firing of Decorated Ceramics of the Roosevelt Platform Mound Study. Paper presented at the Arizona Archaeological Council Spring 1993 Meeting, Flagstaff. Ms. on file, Archaeological Research Institute, Arizona State University, Tempe.

Hibben, F. C.
1948 The Gallina Architectural Forms. *American Antiquity* 14(1):32–36.

1975 *Kiva Art of the Anasazi at Pottery Mound*. Reprint. KC Publications, Las Vegas, 1984.

Hickerson, Harold
1962 *The Southwestern Chippewa: An Ethnohistorical Study*. American Anthropological Association Memoir No. 92. Menasha, Wisconsin.

1965 The Virginia Deer and Intertribal Buffer Zones in the Upper Mississippi Valley. In *Man, Culture, and Animals*, edited by A. Leeds and A. P. Vayda, pp. 43–65. Monograph of the AAAS No. 78. Washington, D.C.

Hillier, Bill, and Julienne Hanson
1984 *The Social Logic of Space*. Cambridge University Press, Cambridge.

Hinkes, M. J.
1983 *Skeletal Evidence of Stress in Subadults: Trying to Come of Age at Grasshopper Pueblo*. Unpublished Ph.D. dissertation, University of Arizona, Tucson.

Hinsley, Curtis M., and David R. Wilcox (editors)
n.d. Vol. 2 in the series "Frank Hamilton Cushing and the Hemenway Expedition, 1886–1889," edited by Curtis M. Hinsley and David R. Wilcox. University of Arizona Press, Tucson, in preparation.

Hodge, Hiram C.
1877 *Arizona as It Is; or, The Coming Country*. Hurd and Houghton, New York.

Hohmann, John W.
1985 *Hohokam and Salado Hamlets in the Tonto Basin: Site Descriptions*. Office of Cultural Resource Management Report No. 64. Office of Cultural Resource Management, Department of Anthropology, Arizona State University, Tempe.

Hohmann, John W., and Linda B. Kelley
1988 *Erich F. Schmidt's Investigations of Salado Sites in Central Arizona*. Museum of Northern Arizona Bulletin No. 56. Flagstaff.

Holliday, William G.
1974 *Archeological Investigations in the Cave Creek Drainage, Tonto National Forest, Arizona*. Archeological Report No. 1. USDA

Forest Service, Southwest Region, Albuquerque.

Holmes, W. H.
1981   Report on the Ancient Ruins of Southwestern Colorado, Examined during the Summers of 1875 and 1876. In *Hayden Survey, 1874–1876: Mesa Verde and the Four Corners*, by W. H. Jackson and W. H. Holmes, pp. 383–408. Bear Creek Publishing, Ouray, Colorado.

Hough, Walter
1903   *Archeological Field Work in Northeastern Arizona: The Museum-Gates Expedition of 1901*. Government Printing Office, Washington, D.C.
1907   *Antiquities of the Upper Gila and Salt River Valleys in Arizona and New Mexico*. Bureau of American Ethnology Bulletin No. 35. Washington, D.C.

Howard, Ann Valdo
1993   Marine Shell Artifacts and Production Processes at Shelltown and the Hind Site. In *Shelltown and the Hind Site: A Study of Two Hohokam Craftsman Communities in Southwestern Arizona, Vol. 1*, edited by W. S. Marmaduke and R. J. Martynec, pp. 321–423. Northland Research, Inc., Flagstaff.

Howard, Jerry
1987   The Lehi Canal System: Organization of a Classic Period Community. In *The Hohokam Village: Site Structure and Organization*, edited by David E. Doyel, pp. 211–221. Southwestern and Rocky Mountain Division of the American Association for the Advancement of Science, Glenwood Springs, Colorado.
1988   *Excavations at Casa Buena: Changing Hohokam Land Use along the Squaw Peak Parkway*. Soil Systems Publications in Archaeology No. 11. Phoenix.
1993   A Paleohydraulic Approach to Examining Agricultural Intensification in Hohokam Irrigation Systems. In *Economic Aspects of Water Management in the Prehispanic New World*, edited by Vernon L. Scarborough and Barry L. Isaac, pp. 263–324. Research in Economic Anthropology, Supplement No. 7. JAI Press, Cincinnati.

Howard, Robertson
1993   A Paleohydraulic Approach to Examining Agricultural Intensification in Hohokam Irrigation Systems. In *Economic Aspects of Water Management in the Prehispanic New World*, edited by Vernon L. Scarborough and Barry L. Isaac, pp. 263–324. Research in Economic Anthropology, Supplement No. 7. JAI Press, Cincinnati.

Howell, Todd L.
1996   Identifying Leaders at Hawikku. *The Kiva* 62(1):61–82.

Hudson, Charles, and Carmen Chavez Tesser (editors)
1994   *The Forgotten Centuries: Indians and Europeans in the American South, 1521–1704*. University of Georgia Press, Athens.

Hunt. Eva, and Robert C. Hunt
1974   Irrigation, Conflict, and Politics: A Mexican Case. In *Irrigation's Impact on Society*, edited by T. E. Downing and McGuire Gibson, pp. 129–158. Anthropological Papers of the University of Arizona No. 25. University of Arizona Press, Tucson. Reprinted in *Origins of the State: The Anthropology of Political Evolution*, edited by Ronald Cohen and Elman R. Service. Philadelphia: Institute for the Study of Human Issues, Philadelphia, 1978.

Hunter-Anderson, R.
1979   Explaining Residential Aggregation in the Northern Rio Grande: A Competition Reduction Model. In *Archaeological Investigations in Cochiti Reservoir, New Mexico, Vol. 4: Adaptive Change in the Northern Rio Grande Valley*, edited by J. V. Biells and R. C. Chapman, pp. 56–67. Office of Contract Archaeology, University of New Mexico, Albuquerque.

Huntington, Ellsworth
1914   *The Climatic Factor as Illustrated in Arid America*. Publication No. 192. Carnegie Institution of Washington, Washington, D.C.

Huntley, Deborah, and Gregson Schachner
1999   The Los Gigantes Community: Post-Chacoan Settlement in the Zuni Region of the American Southwest. Poster presented at the 64th Annual Meeting of the Society for American Archaeology, Chicago.

Hurst, W. B., and J. Pachak
1989   *Spirit Windows: Native American Rock Art of the Southwest*. Spirit Windows Project, Blanding, Utah.

Hurst, Winston B., and Christy G. Turner II
1993   Rediscovering the "Great Discovery": Wetherill's First Cave 7 and Its Record of Basketmaker Violence. In *Anasazi Basketmaker: Papers from the 1990 Wetherill–Grand Gulch Symposium*, edited by Victoria M. Atkins, pp. 143–191. Bureau of Land Management, Cultural Resource Series No. 24. Salt Lake City, Utah.

Ives, Gay Allyn
1980   Rock Art in Cliff Palace, Mesa Verde

National Park, Colorado. Paper presented at the American Rock Art Research Association 7th Annual Rock Art Symposium, Albuquerque.

Jacka, Robertson D.
1980   Prehistoric Sites of Perry Mesa. In *The Navajo Project: Archaeological Investigations, Page to Phoenix 500 KV Southern Transmission Line*, by Donald C. Fiero, Robert W. Munson, Martha T. McClain, Suzanne M. Wilson, and Anne H. Zier, pp. 271–282. MNA Research Paper No. 11. Museum of Northern Arizona, Flagstaff.

Jackson, Earl
1933   A Survey of the Verde Drainage. Unpublished Master's thesis, University of Arizona, Tucson.

Jackson, W. H.
1981   Ancient Ruins in Southwestern Colorado. In *Hayden Survey, 1874–1876: Mesa Verde and the Four Corners*, by W. H. Jackson and W. H. Holmes, pp. 369–381. Bear Creek Publishing, Ouray, Colorado.

Jacobs, David
1997   *A Salado Platform Mound on Tonto Creek, Roosevelt Platform Mound Study: Report on the Cline Terrace Mound, Cline Terrace Complex*. Roosevelt Monograph Series No. 7, Anthropological Field Studies No. 36. Office of Cultural Resource Management, Department of Anthropology, Arizona State University, Tempe.

Jacobs, David (editor)
1994   *Archaeology of the Salado in the Livingston Area of Tonto Basin, Roosevelt Platform Mound Study: Report on the Livingston Management Group, Pinto Creek Complex*. 2 parts. Roosevelt Monograph Series No. 3, Anthropological Field Studies No. 32. Office of Cultural Resource Management, Department of Anthropology, Arizona State University, Tempe.

Jacobs, David, and Glen E. Rice
1997   The Function of U:4:33/132, The Cline Terrace Mound. In *A Salado Platform Mound on Tonto Creek, Roosevelt Platform Mound Study: Report on the Cline Terrace Mound, Cline Terrace Complex,* by David Jacobs, pp. 577–586. Anthropological Field Studies No. 36. Office of Cultural Resource Management, Department of Anthropology, Arizona State University, Tempe.

James, H. C.
1990   *Hopi History*. University of Arizona Press, Tucson.

Jewett, Roberta A.
1989   Distance, Integration, and Complexity: The Spatial Organization of Pan-Regional Settlement Clusters in the American Southwest. In *The Sociopolitical Structure of Prehistoric Southwestern Societies*, edited by Steadman Upham, Kent G. Lightfoot, and Roberta A. Jewett, pp. 363–388. Westview Press, Boulder, Colorado.

Johnson, Gregory A.
1982   Organizational Structure and Scalar Stress. In *Theory and Explanation in Archaeology: The Southampton Conference*, edited by C. Renfrew, M. J. Rowlands, and B. Abbott Segraves, pp. 389–421. Academic Press, New York.
1989   Dynamics of Southwestern Prehistory: Far Outside—Looking In. In *Dynamics of Southwest Prehistory*, edited by Linda S. Cordell and George J. Gumerman, pp. 371–389. Smithsonian Institution Press, Washington, D.C.

Jorgensen, Joseph G.
1980   *Western Indians: Comparative Environments, Languages, and Cultures of 172 Western American Indian Tribes*. W. H. Freeman, San Francisco.

Katzer, Keith
1985   A Geomorphic Evaluation of the Agricultural Potential of Cerros de Trincheras. Ms. on file, Desert Archaeology, Inc., Tucson.
1993   A Geomorphic Evaluation of the Agricultural Potential of Cerros de Trincheras. In *Between Desert and River: Hohokam Settlement and Land Use in the Los Robles Community*, by C. E. Downum, pp. 91–95. Anthropological Papers of the University of Arizona No. 57. University of Arizona Press, Tucson.

Keeley, Lawrence H.
1996   *War before Civilization: The Myth of the Peaceful Savage*. Oxford University Press, New York.

Keeley, Lawrence H., and D. Cahen
1989   Early Neolithic Forts and Villages in Northeastern Belgium: A Preliminary Report. *Journal of Field Archaeology* 16:157–176.

Keller, Donald R., and Carl D. Halbirt
1979   An Archaeological Survey of 3,435 Acres of Proposed Agricultural Lands and 2,790 Acres of Proposed Forest Development Lands, San Carlos Indian Reservation. Arizona. Museum of Northern Arizona Project A79-24. Ms. on file, Museum of Northern Arizona, Flagstaff.

Kenzle, S. C.
1995   Enclosing Walls in the Northern San Juan: Defensive Walls or Sociophysical Boundaries. Paper presented at the January 1995 Big Meeting, Crow Canyon.

Kidder, A. V.
1924   *An Introduction to the Study of Southwestern Archaeology, With a Preliminary Account of the Excavations at Pecos.* Papers of the Phillips Andover Academy Southwestern Expedition. Yale University Press, New Haven.
1949   The Pendleton Ruin, Hidalgo County, New Mexico. Carnegie Institution of Washington Publication No. 585. *Contributions to American Anthropology and History* 50:107–152.

Kintigh, Keith W.
1980   An Archaeological Clearance Survey of Miller Canyon and the Southeast Boundary Fence Line, Zuni Indian Reservation, McKinley County, New Mexico. Ms. on file, Zuni Archaeology Program, Pueblo of Zuni, New Mexico.
1985   *Settlement, Subsistence, and Society in Late Zuni Prehistory.* Anthropological Papers of the University of Arizona No. 44. University of Arizona Press, Tucson.
1996   The Cibola Region in the Post-Chacoan Era. In *The Prehistoric Pueblo World, A.D. 1150–1350,* edited by Michael A. Adler, pp. 131–144. University of Arizona Press, Tucson.
1998   Leadership Strategies in Protohistoric Zuni Towns. Paper presented at the 63rd Annual Meeting of the Society for American Archaeology, Seattle.

Kintigh, Keith W., Todd L. Howell, and Andrew I. Duff
1995   Post-Chacoan Social Integration at the Hinkson Site, New Mexico. *The Kiva* 61(3):257–274.

Kirch, P.
1984   *The Evolution of Polynesian Chiefdoms.* Cambridge University Press, Cambridge.

Kisselburg, JoAnn E.
1987   Economic Specialization in the Community System at Marana. In *Studies in the Hohokam Community of Marana,* edited by G. E. Rice, pp. 143–160. Anthropological Field Studies No. 15. Office of Cultural Resource Management, Arizona State University, Tempe.

Kleidon, J. H.
1999   Castle Rock Pueblo. In *The Sand Canyon Archaeological Project: Site Testing* [HTML title], edited by M. D. Varien, chap. 14. Available: http://www.crowcanyon.org/researchreports/sitetesting/start.htm. Date of use: 1 September 2000.

Knauft, Bruce M.
1991   Violence and Sociality in Human Evolution. *Current Anthropology* 32:391–428.
1992   Warfare, Western Intrusion, and Ecology in Melanesia. *Man* (n.s.) 27:399–403.

Kroeber, Clifton B., and Bernard L. Fontana
1986   *Massacre on the Gila: An Account of the Last Major Battle between American Indians, with Reflections of the Origin of War.* University of Arizona Press, Tucson.

Kuckelman, K. A. (editor)
2000   *The Archaeology of Castle Rock Pueblo: A Thirteenth-Century Village in Southwestern Colorado* [HTML title]. Available: http://www.crowcanyon.org/researchreports/castlerock/start.htm. Date of use: 1 September 2000.

Lamb, Hubert H.
1995   *Climate, History, and the Modern World.* 2nd ed. Routledge, London.

Lambert, Patricia M.
1997   Patterns of Violence in Prehistoric Hunter-Gatherer Societies of Coastal Southern California. In *Troubled Times: Violence and Warfare in the Past,* edited by Debra L. Martin and David W. Frayer, pp. 77–110. Gordon and Breach, Amsterdam.

Lancaster, J. A., and J. M. Pinkley
1954   Excavation at Site 16 of Three Pueblo II Mesa-Top Ruins. In *Archeological Excavations in Mesa Verde National Park, Colorado, 1950,* by J. A. Lancaster, J. M. Pinkley, P. F. Van Cleave, and D. M. Watson, pp. 23–86. Archeological Research Series No. 2. National Park Service, Washington, D.C.

Lange, Charles H., and Carroll L. Riley (editors)
1970   *The Southwestern Journals of Adolph F. Bandelier.* Vol. 2. University of New Mexico Press, Albuquerque.

Lange, Richard C.
1989   Feature Descriptions. In *The 1979–1983 Testing at Los Morteros (AZ AA:12:57 ASM), A Large Hohokam Village Site in the Tucson Basin,* by R. C. Lange, and W. L. Deaver, pp. 83–146. Archaeological Series 177. Arizona State Museum, University of Arizona, Tucson.

Larson, Stephen M.
1972   The Tumamoc Hill Site near Tucson, Arizona. *The Kiva* 38:95–101.
1979   The Material Culture Distribution on the Tumamoc Hill Summit. *The Kiva* 45(12):7181.

Layhe, Robert W.
1988   The Analysis of Site Structure: House Groups and House Clusters. In *The 1982–1984 Excavations at Las Colinas: The Site and Its Features,* by David A. Gregory, William L. Deaver, Suzanne K. Fish, Ronald Gardiner, Robert W. Layhe, Fred L. Nials, Lynn S. Teague, and W. Bruce Masse, pp. 191–242. Archaeological Series 162, Vol. 2. Cultural Resource

Management Division, Arizona State Museum, University of Arizona, Tucson.

LeBlanc, Steven A.

1976 Temporal and Ceramic Relationships between Some Late PIII Sites in the Zuni area. *Plateau* 48:75–84.

1978 Settlement Patterns in the El Morro Valley, New Mexico. In *Investigations of the Southwestern Anthropological Research Group*, edited by Robert Euler and George Gumerman, pp. 45–52. Museum of Northern Arizona, Flagstaff.

1989 Cibola: Shifting Cultural Boundaries. In *Dynamics of Southwestern Prehistory*, edited by Linda S. Cordell and George J. Gumerman, pp. 337–369. Smithsonian Institution Press, Washington, D.C.

1997 Modeling Warfare in Southwestern Prehistory. *North American Archaeologist* 18(3):235–276.

1998 Settlement Consequences of Warfare during the Late Pueblo III and Pueblo IV Period. In *Migration and Reorganization: The Pueblo IV Period in the American Southwest*, edited by Katherine A. Spielmann, pp. 115–135. Arizona State University Anthropology Papers No. 51. Arizona State University, Tempe.

1999 *Prehistoric Warfare in the American Southwest*. University of Utah Press, Salt Lake City.

2000 The Impact of Warfare on Southwestern Regional Systems after A.D. 1250. In *The Archaeology of Regional Interaction in the American Southwest*, edited by Michelle Hegmon, pp. 41–70. University of Colorado Press, Boulder.

Lerner, Sheeren A.

1984 Modeling Spatial Organization in the Hohokam Periphery. Unpublished Ph.D. dissertation, Arizona State University, Tempe.

Le Roy Ladurie, Emmanuel

1971 *Times of Feast, Times of Famine: A History of Climate since the Year 1000*. Translated by Barbara Brey. Reprint. Noonday Press, New York, 1988.

Lévi-Strauss, C.

1943 Guerre et commerce chez les Indiens de l'Amérique Sud. *Renaissance* 1:122–139.

1948 The Nambicuara. In *Handbook of South American Indians, Vol. 3: The Tropical Forest Tribes*, edited by J. Steward, pp. 361–369. Government Printing Office, Washington, D.C.

Lightfoot, Ricky R.

1993 Abandonment Processes in Prehistoric Pueblos. In *Abandonment of Settlements and Regions: Ethnoarchaeological and Archaeological Approaches*, edited by

Catherine M. Cameron and Steve A. Tomka. Cambridge University Press, Cambridge.

Lightfoot, R. R., and K. A. Kuckelman

1994 Warfare and the Abandonment of the Mesa Verde Region. Paper presented at the 59th Annual Meeting of the Society for American Archaeology, Anaheim, California.

1995 Ancestral Pueblo Violence in the Northern Southwest. Paper presented at the 60th Annual Meeting of the Society for American Archaeology, Minneapolis.

Lindauer, Owen

1995 *Where the Rivers Converge, Roosevelt Platform Mound Study: Report on the Rock Island Complex*. Roosevelt Monograph Series No. 4, Anthropological Field Studies No. 33. Office of Cultural Resource Management, Department of Anthropology, Arizona State University, Tempe.

1996 *The Place of the Storehouses, Roosevelt Platform Mound Study: Report on Schoolhouse Point Mound, Pinto Creek Complex*. Roosevelt Monograph Series No. 6, Anthropological Field Studies No. 35. Office of Cultural Resource Management, Department of Anthropology, Arizona State University, Tempe.

1997 *The Archaeology of Schoolhouse Point Mesa, Roosevelt Platform Mound Study: Report on the Schoolhouse Point Mesa Sites, Schoolhouse Management Group, Pinto Creek Complex*. Roosevelt Monograph Series No. 8, Anthropological Field Studies No. 37. Office of Cultural Resource Management, Department of Anthropology, Arizona State University, Tempe.

2000 A Classic Period Village Perspective from Schoolhouse Point Mesa. In *Salado,* edited by Jeffrey Dean, pp. 219–240. University of New Mexico Press, Albuquerque.

Lindauer, Owen, and John H. Bliss

1997 Higher Ground: The Archaeology of North American Platform Mounds. *Journal of Archaeological Research* 5(2):169–207.

Lindsay, Alexander Johnston Jr.

1969 The Tsegi Phase of the Kayenta Cultural Tradition in North-Eastern Arizona. Unpublished Ph.D. dissertation, Department of Anthropology, University of Arizona, Tucson.

1987 Anasazi Population Movements to Southern Arizona. *American Archaeology* 6(3):190–198.

1992 Tucson Polychrome: History, Dating, Distribution, and Design. In *Proceedings of the Second Salado Conference*, edited by Richard C. Lange and Stephen Germick, pp.

230–237. Occasional Paper. The Arizona Archaeological Society, Phoenix.

Lindsay, Alexander J. Jr., Richard Ambler, Mary Anne Stein, and Philip M. Hobler
1968   *Survey and Excavations North and East of Navajo Mountain, Utah, 1959–1962.* Bulletin No. 45. Museum of Northern Arizona, Flagstaff.

Lister, Florence C.
1964   *Kaiparowits Plateau and Glen Canyon Prehistory.* University of Utah Anthropological Papers No. 71, Glen Canyon Series No. 3. University of Utah Press, Salt Lake City.

Loendorf, Chris
1996   Burial Practices at Schoolhouse Point Mound. In *The Place of the Storehouses, Roosevelt Platform Mound Study: Report on Schoolhouse Mound, Pinto Creek Complex*, Part 2, by Owen Lindauer, pp. 681–760. Roosevelt Monograph Series No. 6, Anthropological Field Studies No. 35. Office of Cultural Resource Management, Department of Anthropology, Arizona State University, Tempe.
1997a Burial Practices at U:4:33/132, the Cline Terrace Mound. In *A Salado Platform Mound on Tonto Creek, Roosevelt Platform Mound Study: Report on the Cline Terrace Mound, Cline Terrace Complex*, by David Jacobs, pp. 465–504. Roosevelt Monograph Series No. 7, Anthropological Field Studies No. 36. Office of Cultural Resource Management, Department of Anthropology, Arizona State University, Tempe.
1997b Burial Practices at the Cline Mesa Sites. In *Salado Residential Settlements on Tonto Creek, Roosevelt Platform Mound Study: Report on Cline Mesa Sites, Cline Terrace Complex, Part 2*, by Theodore J. Oliver and David Jacobs, pp. 769–834. Roosevelt Monograph Series No. 9, Anthropological Field Studies No. 38. Office of Cultural Resource Management, Department of Anthropology, Arizona State University, Tempe.

Longacre, W. A.
1962   Archaeological Reconnaissance in Eastern Arizona. In *Chapters in the Prehistory of Eastern Arizona*, by Paul S. Martin and others, pp. 148–169. Fieldiana: Anthropology 55:148–169. Chicago Natural History Museum.

Longacre, William A., Sally J. Holbrook, and Michael W. Graves (editors)
1982   *Multidisciplinary Research at Grasshopper Pueblo, Arizona.* Anthropological Papers of the University of Arizona No. 40. University of Arizona Press, Tucson.

Longacre, W. A., and J. J. Reid
1974   The University of Arizona Archaeological Field School at Grasshopper: Eleven Years of Multidiciplinary Research and Teaching. *The Kiva* 40:3–38.

Lorentzen, L. H.
1993   From Atlatl to Bow: The Impact of Improved Weapons on Wildlife in the Grasshopper Region. Master's paper, University of Arizona, Tucson.

Lowell, J. C.
1989   Flexible Social Units in the Changing Communities of Point of Pines, Arizona. In *Households and Communities*, edited by S. MacEachern, D. J. W. Archer, and R. D. Garvin, pp. 186–195. Proceedings of the 21st Annual Conference of the Archaeological Association of the University of Calgary, Calgary.
1991   *Prehistoric Households at Turkey Creek, Arizona.* Anthropological Papers of the University of Arizona No. 54. University of Arizona Press, Tucson.

Lundin, Richard J.
1993   A Preliminary Review of the Data Base on the Role of Monumental Masonry Structures in the Prehistoric Prescott Culture of North Central Arizona. Wondjina Research Institute, Prescott, Arizona. Ms. on file, MNA Site Files, Flagstaff, Arizona.

Lutonsky, Anthony F.
1992   Anasazi Wooden "Paddles" Sometimes Called "Digging Sticks." Paper presented at the Third Southwestern Symposium, "Interpreting Southwestern Diversity: Underlying Principles and Overarching Patterns," Tucson, Arizona.

Mackey, J., and R. C. Green
1979   Largo-Gallina Towers: An Explanation. *American Antiquity* 44:144–154.

Manje, Juan D.
1954   *Unknown Arizona and Sonora, 1693–1701.* Translated by Harry J. Karns. Arizona Silhouettes, Tucson.

Marquardt, William
1974   A Temporal Perspective on Late Prehistoric Societies in the Eastern Cibola Area: Factor Analytic Approaches to Short-Term Chronological Investigation. Unpublished Ph.D. dissertation, Department of Anthropology, Washington University, St. Louis.
1978   Advances in Archaeological Seriation. In *Advances in Archaeological Method and Theory*, vol. 1, edited by M. B. Schiffer, pp. 257–314. Academic Press, New York.

Martin, D. L., N. J. Akins, A. H. Goodman, W. Toll III, and A. Swedlund
2001   *Harmony and Discord: Bioarchaeology of*

the La Plata Valley. Museum of New Mexico Press, Santa Fe.

Martin, D., and D. Frayer
1997   *Troubled Times: Violence and Warfare in the Past*. Gordon and Breach, Amsterdam.

Martin, Paul S., and Fred Plog
1973   *The Archaeology of Arizona*. Doubleday–Natural History Press, New York.

Martin, Paul S., and Christine R. Szuter
1999   War Zones and Game Sinks in Lewis and Clark's West. *Conservation Biology* 13(1):36–45.

Martynec, Richard J.
1987   Black Mountain Trincheras Site. In *The San Xavier Archaeological Project, Vol. 5*, by Peter L. Steere, Boyd Johns, Aphrodite Ploumis, James Copus, Richard J. Martynec, Henry D. Wallace, Douglas E. Kupel, Linda Roth, and Scott T. Clay-Poole, pp. 1–37. Southwest Cultural Series No. 1. Cultural and Environmental Systems, Inc., Tucson.
1993   Decorated and Intrusive Ceramics from the SCFAP Sites. In *Classic Period Occupation on the Santa Cruz Flats: The Santa Cruz Flats Archaeological Project, Part 2*, edited by T. Kathleen Henderson and Richard J. Martynec, pp. 277–311. Northland Research, Inc., Flagstaff, Arizona.

Marwitt, John P.
1970   *Median Village and Fremont Culture Regional Variation*. University of Utah Anthropology Papers No. 95. University of Utah Press, Salt Lake City.

Masse, W. Bruce
1974   The Peppersauce Wash Project: Excavations at Three Multicomponent Sites in the Lower San Pedro Valley, Arizona. Contributions to Highway Salvage Archaeology in Arizona No. 53. Ms. on file, Arizona State Museum Library, University of Arizona, Tucson.
1979   An Intensive Survey of Prehistoric Dry Farming Systems near Tumamoc Hill in Tucson, Arizona. *The Kiva* 45:141–186.

Masse, W. Bruce, Linda M. Gregonis, and Mark C. Slaughter
1998   Corridor, Frontier, or Cultural Crossroads: Pre-Classic Period Archaeology of the Lower San Pedro Valley, A.D. 700–1200. Paper presented at the Amerind Foundation, Inc., seminar "The Archaeology of a Land Between: Prehistory and History of Southeastern Arizona," Dragoon, Arizona.

Maus, Marcel
1967   *The Gift*. W. W. Norton, New York.

McGarry, Thomas
1975   Cibola Corrugated: A Proposed New Pottery Type from the Southwest. Unpublished Master's thesis, Department of Anthropology, Wichita State University, Wichita, Kansas.

McGimsey, Charles R. III
1980   *Mariana Mesa: Seven Prehistoric Sites in West Central New Mexico*. Papers of the Peabody Museum of Archaeology and Ethnology Vol. 72. Harvard University, Cambridge.

McGregor, John C.
1951   *The Cohonina Culture of Northwestern Arizona*. University of Illinois Press, Urbana.
1965   *Southwestern Archaeology*. 2nd ed. University of Illinois Press, Urbana.

McGuire, Randall H.
1985   The Role of Shell Exchange in the Explanation of Hohokam Prehistory. In *Proceedings of the 1983 Hohokam Symposium*, Part 2, edited by Alfred E. Dittert Jr., and Donald E. Dove, pp. 473–482. Occasional Paper No. 2. The Arizona Archaeological Society, Phoenix.
1987   A Gila Butte Ballcourt at La Ciudad. In *The Hohokam Community of La Ciudad*, edited by Glen E. Rice, pp. 69–110. OCRM Report No. 69. Office of Cultural Resource Management, Department of Anthropology, Arizona State University, Tempe.
1991   On the Outside Looking In: The Concept of Periphery in Hohokam Archaeology. In *Exploring the Hohokam: Prehistoric Desert Peoples of the American Southwest*, edited by George J. Gumerman, pp. 347–382. Amerind Foundation New World Studies Series No. 1. Amerind Foundation, Dragoon, Arizona, and University of New Mexico Press, Albuquerque.

McKusick, Charmion R., and Jon Nathan Young
1997   *The Gila Pueblo Salado*. Salado Chapter, Arizona Archaeological Society, Globe.

Mearns, Edgar A.
1890   Ancient Dwellings of the Rio Verde Valley. *The Popular Science Monthly* 37:747–763.

Meggitt, Mervyn J.
1977   *Blood Is Their Argument*. Mayfield, Palo Alto, California.

Mera, H. P.
1935   *Ceramic Clues to the Prehistory of North Central New Mexico*. Laboratory of Anthropology Technical Series, Bulletin No. 8. Santa Fe.

Merton, Robert K.
1993   *On the Shoulders of Giants*. University of Chicago Press, Chicago.

Mills, Barbara J.
1998   Migration and Pueblo IV Community Reorganization in the Silver Creek Area, East-Central Arizona. In *Pueblo IV*

Migration and Community Reorganization, edited by Katherine A. Spielmann, pp. 65–80. Arizona State University Anthropological Papers No. 51. Arizona State University, Tempe.

Mills, Jack P., and Vera M. Mills
1975   The Meredith Ranch Site, VIV Ruin: A Prehistoric Salado Pueblo in the Tonto Basin, Central Arizona. Ms. on file, Tonto National Forest, Phoenix Office.

Milner, Claire M.
1991   Localization in Small-Scale Societies: Late Prehistoric Social Organization in the Western Great Lakes. In *Between Bands and States*, edited by Susan A. Gregg, pp. 35–57. Occasional Paper No. 9. Center for Archaeological Investigations, Southern Illinois University, Carbondale.

Milner, G. R., E. Anderson, and V. G. Smith
1991   Warfare in Late Prehistoric West-Central Illinois. *American Antiquity* 56:581–603.

Mindeleff, Cosmos
1896   Aboriginal Remains in the Verde Valley, Arizona. *Bureau of American Ethnology, Thirteenth Annual Report*, pp. 179–261. Washington, D.C.

Mindeleff, Victor
1891   A Study of Pueblo Architecture in Tusayan and Cibola. In *8th Annual Report of the Bureau of American Ethnology for the Years 1886–1887*, pp. 3–228. Washington, D.C.

Mitchell, Douglas R. (editor)
1988   *Excavations at La Lomita Pequeña, a Santa Cruz/Sacaton Phase Hamlet in the Salt River Valley*. Soil Systems Publications in Archaeology No. 10. Phoenix.
1989a   *Archaeological Investigations at the Grand Canal Ruins, a Classic Period Site in Phoenix, Arizona*. Soil Systems Publications in Archaeology No. 12. Phoenix.
1989b   *El Caserio: Colonial Period Settlement along the East Papago Freeway*. Soil Systems Publications in Archaeology No. 14. Phoenix.
1990   *The La Lomita Excavations: 10th Century Hohokam Occupation in South-Central Arizona*. Soil Systems Publications in Archaeology No. 15. Phoenix.
1994   *The Pueblo Grande Project, Vol. 2: Feature Descriptions, Chronology, and Site Structure*. Soil Systems Publication in Archaeology No. 20. Phoenix.

Montgomery, B. K.
1992   Understanding the Formation of the Archaeological Record: Ceramic Variability at Chodistaas Pueblo, Arizona. Unpublished Ph.D. dissertation, University of Arizona, Tucson.

Montgomery, B. K., and J. J. Reid
1990   An Instance of Rapid Ceramic Change in the American Southwest. *American Antiquity* 55:88–97.

Morehead, Warren King
1906   *A Narrative of Exploration in New Mexico, Arizona, Indiana, etc*. Phillips Andover Academy Department of Anthropology Bulletin No. 3.

Morley, S. G.
1908   The Excavation of the Cannonball Ruins in Southwestern Colorado. *American Anthropologist* (n.s.) 10:596–610.

Morren, George E. B. Jr.
1984   Warfare on the Highland Fringe of New Guinea: The Case of the Mountain Ok. In *Warfare, Culture, and Environment*, edited by R. Brian Ferguson, pp. 169–208. Academic Press, Orlando, Florida.

Morris, Donald H.
1970   Walnut Creek Village: A Ninth-Century Hohokam-Anasazi Settlement in the Mountains of Central Arizona. *American Antiquity* 35(1):49–61.

Morris, E. H.
1939   *Archaeological Studies in the LaPlata District, Southwestern Colorado and Northwestern New Mexico*. Carnegie Institution of Washington Publication No. 519. Washington, D.C.

Morris, Earl, and Robert Burgh
1941   *Anasazi Basketry, Basket Maker II through Pueblo III: A Study Based on Specimens from the San Juan River Country*. Carnegie Institution of Washington Publication No. 533. Washington, D.C.

Muller, Jon, and David R. Wilcox
1999   Powhatan's Mantle as Metaphor: Comparing Macroregional Integration in the Southwest and Southeast. In *Great Towns and Regional Polities*, edited by Jill E. Neitzel, pp. 159–164. University of New Mexico Press, Albuquerque.

Murdock, G., and C. Provost
1973   Measurement of Cultural Complexity. *Ethnology* 9:302–330.

Naroll, Raoul
1962   Floor Area and Settlement Population. *American Antiquity* 27:587–588.
1966   Does Military Deterrence Deter? *Trans-Action* 3(2):14–20.

Neily, R. B.
1983   The Prehistoric Community on the Colorado Plateau: An Approach to the Study of Change and Survival in the Northern San Juan Area of the American Southwest. Unpublished Ph.D. dissertation, Department of Anthropology, Southern Illinois University, Carbondale.

Neitzel, Jill
1991   Hohokam Material Culture and Behavior: The Dimensions of Organizational Change. In *Exploring the Hohokam: Prehistoric Desert Peoples of the American Southwest*, edited by George J. Gumerman, pp. 177–230. Amerind Foundation New World Studies Series No. 1, Amerind Foundation, Dragoon, Arizona, and University of New Mexico Press, Albuquerque.

Newberry, J. S.
1876   Geological Report. In *Report of the Exploring Expedition from Santa Fé, New Mexico, to the Junction of the Grand and Green Rivers of the Great Colorado of the West, in 1859*. Engineer Department, U.S. Army, Government Printing Office, Washington D.C.

Nordenskiöld, G.
1979   *The Cliff Dwellers of the Mesa Verde, Southwestern Colorado: Their Pottery and Implements*. Reprint. Rio Grande Press, Glorieta, New Mexico. Originally published 1893, P. A. Norstedt & Söner, Stockholm.

O'Connell, R.
1989   *Of Arms and Men*. Oxford University Press, New York.

Oliver, Theodore J.
1997   *Classic Period Settlement in the Uplands of Tonto Basin, Roosevelt Platform Mound Study: Report on the Uplands Complex*. Roosevelt Monograph Series No. 5, Anthropological Field Studies No. 34. Office of Cultural Resource Management, Department of Anthropology, Arizona State University, Tempe.

Oliver, Theodore J., and David Jacobs
1997   *Salado Residential Settlements on Tonto Creek, Roosevelt Platform Mound Study: Report on the Cline Mesa Sites, Cline Terrace Complex, Parts 1 and 2*. Roosevelt Monograph Series No. 9, Anthropological Field Studies No. 38. Office of Cultural Resource Management, Department of Anthropology, Arizona State University, Tempe.

Olson, Alan P.
1954   An Archaeological Survey of the Payson Region. Ms. on file, Museum of Northern Arizona Library, Flagstaff.

Opler, Morris Edward
1941   *An Apache Life-Way: The Economic, Social, and Religious Institutions of the Chiricahua Indians*. University of Chicago Press, Chicago.

Otterbein, Keith F.
1970   *The Evolution of War: A Cross-Cultural Study*. Human Relations Area Files Press, New Haven.

1989   *The Evolution of War: A Cross-Cultural Study*. 3rd ed. Human Relations Area Files, New Haven.

1994   *Feuding and Warfare: Selected Works of Keith F. Otterbein*. Gordon and Breach, Lanhorne.

1997   The Origins of War. *Critical Reviews* 11:251–277.

2000   Historical Essay: A History of Research on Warfare in Anthropology. *American Anthropologist* 101(4):794–805.

Owsley, D. W., H. Berryman, and W. Bass
1977   Demographic and Osteological Evidence for Warfare at the Lawson Site, South Dakota. *Plains Anthropologist Memoir* 13:119–131.

Owsley, D. W., and R. L. Jantz
1994   *Skeletal Biology in the Great Plains: Migration, Warfare, Health, and Subsistence*. Smithsonian Institution Press, Washington, D.C.

Parker, G.
1988   *The Military Revolution*. Cambridge University Press, Cambridge.

Peck, Fred R.
1956   An Archaeological Reconnaissance of the East Verde River in Central Arizona. Unpublished Master's thesis, University of Arizona, Tucson.

Peckham, Barbara A.
1981   Pueblo IV Murals at Mound 7. In *Contributions to Gran Quivira Archeology, Gran Quivira National Monument, New Mexico*, by Alden C. Hayes, pp. 15–38. Publications in Archeology No. 17. National Park Service, Washington, D.C.

Petersen, K. L.
1988   *Climate and the Dolores River Anasazi: A Paleoenvironmental Reconstruction from a 10,000-Year Pollen Record, La Plata Mountains, Southwestern Colorado*. University of Utah Anthropology Papers No. 113. University of Utah Press, Salt Lake City.

1994   A Warm and Wet Little Climatic Optimum and a Cold and Dry Little Ice Age in the Southern Rocky Mountains. *Climatic Change* 26:243–269.

Pilles, Peter J. Jr.
1976   Sinagua and Salado Similarities as Seen from the Verde Valley. *The Kiva* 42(1):113–124.

1994   Rock Art of the Red Rock Canyons, Sedona, Arizona. Paper presented at the 1994 International Rock Art Congress, "Rock Art—World Heritage." Northern Arizona University, Flagstaff.

1996   The Pueblo III Period along the Mogollon Rim: The Honanki, Elden, and Turkey Hill

Phases of the Sinagua. In *The Prehistoric
Pueblo World, A.D. 1150–1350*, edited by
Michael A. Adler, pp. 59–72. University of
Arizona Press, Tucson.

Pilles, Peter J. Jr., and James M. McKie
1998   Conquest, Replacement, or Transition? The
Prehistoric and Historic Period Yavapai in
Central Arizona. Paper presented at the
conference "Transition between History
and Prehistory," Albuquerque.

Plog, Stephen
1997   *Ancient Peoples of the American Southwest.*
Thames and Hudson, London.

Polzer, Charles M.
1971   *Kino's Biography of Francisco Javier Saeta,
S.J. Translated, with an Epilogue.* Jesuit
Historical Institute, St. Louis.

Polzer, Charles M., and Thomas Naylor
1986   *The Presidio and Militia on the Northern
Frontier of New Spain, Vol. 1: 1570–1700.*
University of Arizona Press, Tucson.

Potter, James M.
1997   Communal Ritual Feasting and Social
Differentiation in Late Prehistoric Zuni
Communities. Unpublished Ph.D. disserta-
tion, Department of Anthropology, Arizona
State University, Tempe.

Power, M.
1991   *The Egalitarians—Human and Chimpanzee:
An Anthropological View of Social
Organization.* Cambridge University Press,
Cambridge.

Price, T. Douglas, Anne Birgitte Gebauer, and
Lawrence H. Keeley
1995   The Spread of Farming into Europe North
of the Alps. In *Last Hunters—First Farmers:
New Perspectives on the Prehistoric
Transition to Agriculture*, edited by T.
Douglas Price and Anne Birgitte Gebauer,
pp. 95–126. School of American Research
Press, Santa Fe.

Ravesloot, J. C.
1988   *Mortuary Practices and Social
Differentiation at Casas Grandes,
Chihuahua, Mexico.* Anthropological
Papers of the University of Arizona No. 49.
University of Arizona Press, Tucson.

Ravesloot, John, and Patricia M. Spoerl
1989   The Role of Warfare in the Development of
Status Hierarchies at Casas Grandes,
Chihuahua, Mexico. In *Cultures in Conflict:
Current Archaeological Perspectives*, edited
by D. C. Tkaczuk and B. C. Vivian, pp.
130–137. Proceedings of the 20th
Chacmool Conference, Department of
Archaeology, University of Calgary,
Calgary.

Reagan, Albert B.
1930   Archeological Notes on the Fort Apache

Region, Arizona. *Transactions of the
Kansas Academy of Science* 33:111–132.

Redman, Charles L.
1978   *The Rise of Civilization: From Early
Farmers to Urban Society in the Ancient
Near East.* W. H. Freeman, San Francisco.
1993   *People of the Tonto Rim: Archaeological
Discovery in Prehistoric Arizona.*
Smithsonian Institution Press, Washington,
D.C.

Reed, Erik K.
1953   Human Skeletal Remains from Te'ewi. In
*Salvage Archaeology in the Chama Valley,
New Mexico*, edited by Fred Wendorf, pp.
104–118. School of American Research,
Santa Fe.

Regan, Marcia H.
1997   Physical Anthropology of the Cline Mesa
Sites. In *Salado Residential Settlements on
Tonto Creek, Roosevelt Platform Mound
Study: Report on the Cline Mesa Sites,
Cline Terrace Complex*, by Theodore J.
Oliver and David Jacobs, pp. 835–868.
Anthropological Field Studies No. 38.
Office of Cultural Resource Management,
Department of Anthropology, Arizona State
University, Tempe.

Reid, J. J.
1989   A Grasshopper Perspective on the Mogollon
of the Arizona Mountains. In *Dynamics of
Southwestern Prehistory*, edited by Linda S.
Cordell and George J. Gumerman, pp.
65–97. Smithsonian Institution Press,
Washington, D.C.

Reid, J. J. (editor)
1982   *Cholla Project Archaeology.* Archaeological
Series No. 161. Arizona State Museum,
Tucson.

Reid, J. J. and H. D.Tuggle
1988   Settlement Pattern and System in the Late
Prehistory of the Grasshopper Region,
Arizona. Paper presented at the seminar
"From Pueblo to Apache: The Peopling of
the Arizona Mountains," Grasshopper,
Arizona.

Reid, J. Jefferson, John R. Welch, Barbara K.
Montgomery, and María Nieves Zedeño
1996   A Demographic Overview of the Late
Pueblo III Period in the Mountains of East-
Central Arizona. In *The Prehistoric Pueblo
World, A.D. 1150–1350*, edited by Michael
A. Adler, pp. 73–85. University of Arizona
Press, Tucson.

Reid, J. J., and S. M. Whittlesey
1982   Households at Grasshopper Pueblo.
American Behavioral Scientist 25(6):
687–703.
1990   The Complicated and the Complex:
Observations on the Archaeological Record

of Large Pueblos. In *Perspectives on Southwestern Prehistory*, edited by P. Minnis and C. Redman, pp. 184–195. Westview Press, Boulder.

1997   *The Archaeology of Ancient Arizona.* University of Arizona Press, Tucson.

1999   *Grasshopper Pueblo: A Story of Archaeology and Ancient Life.* University of Arizona Press, Tucson.

Rice, Glen E.

1974   Were the Early Mogollon Sedentary Agriculturists? Paper presented at the 73rd Annual Meeting of the American Anthropological Association, Mexico City.

1975   *A Systemic Explanation of Mogollon Settlement Pattern Changes.* Ph.D. dissertation, Department of Anthropology, University of Washington, Seattle. University Microfilms, Ann Arbor.

1990   Toward a Study of the Salado of the Tonto Basin. In *A Design for Salado Research*, edited by Glen E. Rice, pp. 1–20. Roosevelt Monograph Series No. 1, Anthropological Field Studies No. 22. Office of Cultural Resource Management, Department of Anthropology, Arizona State University, Tempe.

1995   Special Artifacts and Evidence for the Differentiation of Residential and Ritual Rooms at the Bass Point Mound. In *Where the Rivers Converge, Roosevelt Platform Mound Study: Report on the Rock Island Complex*, by Owen Lindauer, pp. 331–350. Roosevelt Monograph Series No. 4, Anthropological Field Studies No. 33. Office of Cultural Resource Management, Department of Anthropology, Arizona State University, Tempe.

1997a   The Distribution of Special Artifacts at the Cline Mesa Sites. In *Salado Residential Settlements on Tonto Creek, Roosevelt Platform Mound Study: Report on the Cline Mesa Sites, Cline Terrace Complex*, by Theodore J. Oliver and David Jacobs, pp. 757–768. Roosevelt Monograph Series No. 9, Anthropological Field Studies No. 38. Office of Cultural Resource Management, Department of Anthropology, Arizona State University, Tempe.

1997b   Special Artifacts and the Uses of Rooms at U:4:33/132, The Cline Terrace Mound. In *A Salado Platform Mound on Tonto Creek, Roosevelt Platform Mound Study: Report on the Cline Terrace Mound, Cline Terrace Complex*, by David Jacobs, pp. 431–454. Anthropological Field Studies No. 36. Office of Cultural Resource Management, Department of Anthropology, Arizona State University, Tempe.

1998   War and Water: An Ecological Perspective on Hohokam Irrigation. *The Kiva* 63(3):263–301.

2000   Hohokam and Salado Segmentary Organization: The Evidence from the Roosevelt Platform Mound Study. In *Salado*, edited by Jeffrey Dean, pp. 143–166. University of New Mexico Press, Albuquerque.

Rice, Glen E. (editor)

1987a   *Studies in the Hohokam Community of Marana.* Anthropological Field Studies No. 15. Office of Cultural Resource Management, Department of Anthropology, Arizona State University, Tempe.

1987b   *The Hohokam Community of La Ciudad.* OCRM Report No. 69. Office of Cultural Resource Management, Department of Anthropology, Arizona State University, Tempe.

1990   *A Design for Salado Research.* Anthropological Field Studies No. 22. Office of Cultural Resource Management, Department of Anthropology, Arizona State University, Tempe.

1998   *A Synthesis of Tonto Basin Prehistory: The Roosevelt Archaeology Studies, 1989 to 1998.* Anthropological Field Studies No. 41. Office of Cultural Resource Management, Department of Anthropology, Arizona State University, Tempe.

Rice, Glen E., John C. Ravesloot, and Christy G. Turner II

1992   Salado Ethnic Identity and Social Complexity: The Biocultural Approach. Paper presented at the 57th Annual Meeting of the Society for American Archaeology, Pittsburgh.

Rice, Glen E., Arleyn W. Simon, and Christopher Loendorf

1998   Production and Exchange of Economic Goods. In *A Synthesis of Tonto Basin Prehistory: The Roosevelt Archaeology Studies, 1989 to 1998*, edited by Glen E. Rice, pp. 105–130. Roosevelt Monograph Series No. 12, Anthropological Field Studies No. 41. Office of Cultural Resource Management, Department of Anthropology, Arizona State University, Tempe.

Rice, Glen E., and Annette Joye Smith

1999   *An Archaeological Survey of a Portion of the Robbins Butte Wildlife Area.* OCRM Report No. 97. Office of Cultural Resource Management, Department of Anthropology, Arizona State University, Tempe.

Richardson, Stacy L.

1994   An Analysis of Specialization in the Production of Salado Plain Wares from the Tonto Basin. Unpublished Master's thesis, Department of Anthropology, Arizona State University, Tempe.

Riley, Carroll L.
1976   *Sixteenth-Century Trade in the Greater Southwest.* Mesoamerican Studies No. 10. University Museum, Southern Illinois University, Carbondale.

Rinaldo, J. B.
1964   Notes on the Origin of the Historic Zuni Culture. *The Kiva*: 29(4):86–98.

Roberts, Frank H. H. Jr.
1932   *The Village of the Great Kivas on the Zuni Reservation, New Mexico.* Bulletin No. 111. Smithsonian Institution, Washington, D.C.

Rodgers, James B.
1978   The Fort Mountain Complex, Cave Buttes, Arizona. In *Limited Activity and Occupation Sites*, edited by Albert E. Ward, pp. 147–165. Contributions to Anthropology Studies No. 1. Albuquerque.

Rohn, A. H.
1977   *Cultural Change and Continuity on Chapin Mesa.* Regents Press of Kansas, Lawrence.

Roney, John R.
1996   The Pueblo III Period in the Eastern San Juan Basin and Acoma-Laguna Areas. In *The Prehistoric Pueblo World, A.D. 1150–1350*, edited by Michael A. Adler, pp. 145–169. University of Arizona Press, Tucson.

Ross, Marc Howard
1983   Political Decision Making and Conflict: Additional Cross-Cultural Codes and Scales. *Ethnology* 22:169–192.

Ruppé, Reynold J. Jr.
1953   The Acoma Culture Province: An Archaeological Concept. Unpublished Ph.D. dissertation, Department of Anthropology, Harvard University, Cambridge.

Russell, Frank
1975   *The Pima Indians.* Reprint. University of Arizona Press, Tucson. Originally published 1908, *26th Annual Report of the Bureau of American Ethnology to the Secretary of the Smithsonian Institution*, 1904–1905, Government Printing Office, Washington, D.C.

Russell, J. Townsend Jr.
1930   Notes on Ruins in the Tonto National Forest Reserve of Arizona Visited by J. Townsend Russell, Jr., April 1930. Ms. on file, Pueblo Grande Museum, Phoenix.

Sackett, James R.
1985   Style and Ethnicity in the Kalahari: A Reply to Wiessner. *American Antiquity* 50(1):154–159.

Sahlins, Marshall D.
1961   The Segmentary Lineage: An Organization of Predatory Expansion. *American Anthropologist* 63:322–345.

1968   *Tribesman.* Prentice-Hall, Englewood Cliffs, New Jersey.

Saitta, Dean J.
1991   Room Use and Community Organization at the Pettit Site, West Central New Mexico. *The Kiva* 56(4):385–409.

1994   The Political Economy and Ideology of Early Population Aggregation in Togeye Canyon, A.D. 1150–1250. In *Exploring Social, Political, and Economic Organization in the Zuni Region*, edited by T. L. Howell and T. Stone, pp. 47–60. Anthropological Research Papers No. 46. Arizona State University, Tempe.

Sauer, Carl O., and Donald R. Brand
1930   Pueblo Sites in Southeastern Arizona. *University of California Publications in Geography* 3(7):415–458.

1931   Prehistoric Settlement of Sonora with Special Reference to *Cerros de Trincheras*. *University of California Publications in Geography* 5:67–148.

Schaafsma, Polly
1965   Kiva Murals from Pueblo del Encierro (LA 70). *El Palacio* 72(3):7–16.

1966   A Survey of Tsegi Canyon Art. Ms. on file, Laboratory of Anthropology, Museum of New Mexico, and National Park Service, Region 3 Office, Santa Fe.

1971   *The Rock Art of Utah from the Donald Scott Collection.* Papers of the Peabody Museum of Archaeology and Ethnology Vol. 65. Harvard University, Cambridge.

1978   Rock Art in the White Canyon Basin. In *Antiquities Section Selected Papers*, Vol. 5, No. 13, pp. 67–72. Department of Development Services, Division of State History, Utah State Historical Society, Salt Lake City.

1980   *Indian Rock Art of the Southwest.* School of American Research, Santa Fe, and University of New Mexico Press, Albuquerque.

1992a   Imagery and Magic. In *Archaeology, Art, and Anthropology: Papers in Honor of J. J. Brody*, edited by Meliha H. Duran and David T. Kirkpatrick, pp. 157–174. Archaeological Society of New Mexico, Albuquerque.

1992b   *Rock Art in New Mexico.* Rev. ed. Museum of New Mexico Press, Santa Fe. Originally published 1972, New Mexico State Planning Office.

Schiffer, Michael B.
1987   *Formation Processes of the Archaeological Record.* University of New Mexico Press, Albuquerque.

Schlanger, Sarah H., and Richard H. Wilshusen
1993   Abandonment in the North American Southwest. In *Abandonment of Settlements*

and Regions: Ethnoarchaeological and Archaeological Approaches, edited by Catherine M. Cameron and Steve A. Tomka, pp. 85–98. Cambridge University Press, Cambridge.

Schroeder, Albert H.

1954   Four Prehistoric Sites near Mayer, Arizona, Which Suggest a New Focus. *Plateau* 26(3):103–107.

1979   Prehistory: Hakataya. In *Handbook of North American Indians*, edited by William Sturtevant, Vol. 9, *Southwest*, edited by Alfonso Ortiz, pp. 100–107. Smithsonian Institution, Washington D.C.

Schulman, A.

1950   Pre-Columbian Towers in the Southwest. *American Antiquity* 4:288–297.

Service, Elman R.

1962   *Primitive Social Organization: An Evolutionary Perspective*. Random House, New York.

1975   *Origins of the State and Civilization: The Process of Cultural Evolution*. Norton, New York.

Shackley, Steven M.

1988   Sources of Archaeological Obsidian in the Southwest: An Archaeological, Petrological, and Geochemical Study. *American Antiquity* 53(4):752–772.

1995   Sources of Archaeological Obsidian in the Greater American Southwest: An Update and Quantitative Analysis. *American Antiquity* 60(3):531–551.

1998   Obsidian Procurement in Early Classic and Classic Contexts, Tonto Basin, Arizona: An Energy-Dispersive X-Ray Fluorescence Analysis of Archaeological Obsidian. Report prepared for Office of Cultural Resource Management and Archaeological Research Institute, Department of Anthropology, Arizona State University, Tempe. Ms. on file, Archaeological Research Institute, Tempe.

Shankman, Paul

1991   Culture Contact, Cultural Ecology, and Dani Warfare. *Man* (n.s.) 26:229–321.

Shaw, Anna Moore

1974   *A Pima Past*. University of Arizona Press, Tucson.

Shelley, Steven D., and Richard Ciolek-Torrello

1994   Grapevine Recreations and Stockpile Areas. In *The Roosevelt Rural Sites Study, Vol. 2: Prehistoric Rural Settlements in the Tonto Basin*, Part 1, edited by Richard Ciolek-Torrello, Steven D. Shelley, and Su Benaron, pp. 223–344. Technical Series No. 28. Statistical Research, Tucson.

Shipman, J. H.

1980   Basic Data on Skeletal Remains from the Salmon Site (LA 8846), New Mexico:

Sitewide and Room 64W (the Tower Kiva). In *Investigations at the Salmon Site: The Structure of Chacoan Society in the Northern Southwest*, vol. 4, part 12, edited by C. Irwin-Williams and P. H. Shelley, pp. 249–259. Eastern New Mexico University, Portales.

Shreve, F.

1951   *Vegetation of the Sonoran Desert*. Carnegie Institution, Washington, D.C.

Sillitoe, Paul

1977   Land Shortage and War in New Guinea. *Ethnology* 16:71–81.

Simon, Arleyn W.

1996   Pottery and Pigments in Arizona: Salado Polychrome. MRS *Bulletin* 21(12):38–47.

Simon, Arleyn W. (editor)

1998   *Salado Ceramics and Social Organization: Prehistoric Interactions in the Tonto Basin*. Roosevelt Platform Mound Study. Roosevelt Monograph Series No. 11, Anthropological Field Studies No. 40. Office of Cultural Resource Management, Department of Anthropology, Arizona State University, Tempe.

Simon, Arleyn W., James H. Burton, and David R. Abbott

1998   Intraregional Connections in the Development and Distribution of Salado Polychromes in Central Arizona. *Journal of Anthropological Research* 54(4):519–547.

Simon, Arleyn W., and David Jacobs

2000   Salado Social Dynamics: Networks and Alliances in the Tonto Basin. In *Salado*, edited by Jeffrey Dean, pp. 193–218. University of New Mexico Press, Albuquerque.

Simon, Arleyn W., and John C. Ravesloot

1995   Salado Ceramic Burial Offerings: A Consideration of Gender and Social Organization. In *The Archaeology of Gender in the American Southwest*, edited by Katherine A. Spielmann, pp. 103–124. *Journal of Anthropological Research* 51(2).

Simon, Arleyn W., Glen E. Rice, and M. Steven Shackley

1997   Trade Items at Salado Platform Mounds: Ritual or Managerial Control? Paper presented at the 62nd Annual Meeting of the Society for American Archaeology, Nashville.

Simpson, Claudette

1982   Arizona's "King" Left His Mark on Ruins. *Prescott Courier, Westward Supplement*, December 10, pp. 4–8.

Sires, Earl

1987   Hohokam Architectural Variability and Site Structure during the Sedentary-Classic Transition. In *The Hohokam Village: Site Structure and Organization*, edited by

David E. Doyel, pp. 171–182. Southwestern and Rocky Mountain Division of the American Association for the Advancement of Science, Glenwood Springs, Colorado.

Skibo, James M.
1988   Large Site Reconnaissance in the Lower Santa Cruz Basin. In *Recent Research on Tucson Basin Prehistory: Proceedings of the Second Tucson Basin Conference,* edited by W. H. Doelle and P. R. Fish, pp. 241–251. Anthropological Papers No. 10. Institute for American Research, Tucson.

Skinner, Elizabeth
1981   A Systematic Analysis of Chipped Stone Industries from the El Morro Valley, New Mexico. Unpublished Ph.D. dissertation, Department of Anthropology, Washington University, St. Louis.

Slaughter, Mark C.
1996   Occupation of the Gibbon Springs Site: Summary and Concluding Thoughts. In *Excavation of the Gibbon Springs Site: A Classic Period Village in the Northeastern Tucson Basin,* edited by Mark C. Slaughter and Heidi Roberts, pp. 523–534. Archaeological Report No. 94-87. SWCA, Inc., Environmental Consultants, Tucson.

Smith, Fay Jackson, John L. Kessell, and Francis J. Fox, S.J.
1966   *Father Kino in Arizona.* Arizona Historical Society, Tucson.

Smith, J. E.
1987   *Mesas, Cliffs, and Canyons: The University of Colorado Survey of Mesa Verde National Park, 1971–1977.* Mesa Verde Research Series No. 3. Mesa Verde Museum Association, Mesa Verde National Park, Colorado.

Smith, Watson
1952   *Kiva Mural Decoration at Awatovi and Kawaka-a with a Survey of Other Wall Paintings in the Pueblo Southwest.* Papers of the Peabody Museum of American Archaeology and Ethnology No. 37. Harvard University, Cambridge.
1971   *Painted Ceramics of the Western Mound at Awatovi.* Papers of the Peabody Museum of American Archaeology and Ethnology No. 38. Harvard University, Cambridge.
1972   *Prehistoric Kivas of Antelope Mesa.* Papers of the Peabody Museum of American Archaeology and Ethnology No. 39(1). Harvard University, Cambridge.

Spicer, Edward H., and Louis P. Caywood
1936   *Two Pueblo Ruins in West Central Arizona.* University of Arizona Bulletin 7(1). Social Science Bulletin No. 10. University of Arizona, Tucson.

Spielmann, Kate (editor)
1998   *Environment and Subsistence in the Classic Period Tonto Basin.* Roosevelt Monograph Series No. 10, Anthropological Field Studies No. 40. Office of Cultural Resource Management, Department of Anthropology, Arizona State University, Tempe.

Spier, Leslie
1917   *An Outline for a Chronology of Zuni Ruins.* Anthropological Papers of the American Museum of Natural History 18:205–331. New York.
1918   *Notes on Some Little Colorado Ruins.* Anthropological Papers of the American Museum of Natural History 17 (4):337–362. New York
1919   *Ruins in the White Mountains, Arizona.* Anthropological Papers of the American Museum of Natural History 18(5). New York.
1933   *Yuman Tribes of the Gila River.* University of Chicago Press, Chicago. Reprinted 1970.

Spoerl, Patricia M.
1979   *Prehistoric Cultural Development and Conflict in Central Arizona.* Ph.D. dissertation, Southern Illinois University at Carbondale. University Microfilms, Ann Arbor.
1984   Prehistoric Fortifications in Central Arizona. In *Prehistoric Cultural Development in Central Arizona: Archaeology of the Upper New River Region,* edited by Patricia M. Spoerl and George J. Gumerman, pp. 261–276. Center for Archaeological Investigations Occasional Papers No. 5. Southern Illinois University, Carbondale.

Spoerl, Patricia M., and George J. Gumerman (editors)
1984   *Prehistoric Cultural Development in Central Arizona: Archaeology of the Upper New River Region.* Center for Archaeological Investigations Occasional Paper No. 5. Southern Illinois University, Carbondale.

Stacy, V. K. Pheriba
1974   Cerros de Trincheras in the Arizona Papagueria. Unpublished Ph.D. dissertation, Department of Anthropology, University of Arizona, Tucson.

Stark, Miriam T.
1995a   Commodities and Interaction in the Prehistoric Tonto Basin. In *The Roosevelt Community Development Study: New Perspectives on Tonto Basin Prehistory,* edited by Mark D. Elson, Miriam T. Stark, and David A. Gregory, pp. 307–341. Anthropological Papers No. 15. Center for Desert Archaeology, Tucson.
1995b   Cultural Identity in the Archaeological Record: The Utility of Utilitarian Ceramics. In *The Roosevelt Community Development*

Study, Vol. 2: Ceramic Chronology, Technology, and Economics, edited by J. M. Heidke and M. T. Stark, pp. 331–362. Anthropological Papers No. 14. Center for Desert Archaeology, Tucson, Arizona.

Stein, Charlie R., Lloyd M. Pierson, Vorsila L. Bohrer, and Kate Peck Kent
1962   *Archaeological Studies at Tonto National Monument, Arizona.* Southwestern Monuments Association, Technical Series, Vol. 2. Gila Pueblo, Globe, Arizona.

Stein, John, and Andrew P. Fowler
1996   Looking beyond Chaco: The San Juan Basin and Its Peripheries. In *The Prehistoric Pueblo World, A.D. 1150–1350*, edited by Michael A. Adler, pp. 114–130. University of Arizona Press, Tucson.

Stevenson, Marc G.
1982   Toward an Understanding of Site Abandonment Behavior: Evidence from Historic Mining Camps in the Southwest Yukon. *Journal of Anthropological Archaeology* 1:237–265.

Stone, Connie L.
1981   Economy and Warfare along the Lower Colorado River. *Anthropological Research Papers* 24:183–197. Arizona State University, Tempe.

Stone, Tammy
1992   The Process of Aggregation in the American Southwest: A Case Study from Zuni, New Mexico. Ph.D. dissertation, Department of Anthropology, Arizona State University, Tempe.

Sussman, R. W. (editor)
1997   *The Biological Basis of Human Behavior: A Critical Review.* Prentice-Hall, New York.

Swartz, Marc J., Victor W. Turner, and Arthur Tuden (editors)
1966   *Political Anthropology.* Aldine, Chicago.

Tainter, Joseph A., and David A. Gillio
1980   *Cultural Resources Overview: Mt. Taylor Area, New Mexico.* USDA Forest Service, Southwestern Region and Bureau of Land Management, New Mexico State Office, Albuquerque and Santa Fe.

Tanner, Clara Lee
1936   Blackstone Ruin. *The Kiva* 2(1):9–12.

Teague, Lynn S.
1984   Role and Ritual in Hohokam Society. In *Hohokam Archaeology along the Salt-Gila Aqueduct, Central Arizona Project, Vol. 9: Synthesis and Conclusions*, edited by Lynn S. Teague and Patricia L. Crown, pp. 155–185. Archaeological Series No. 150. Cultural Resource Management Division, Arizona State Museum, University of Arizona, Tucson.

1985   The Organization of Hohokam Exchange. In *Proceedings of the 1983 Hohokam Symposium*, edited by A. E. Dittert and D. E. Dove, pp. 397–419. Occasional Paper No. 2. The Arizona Archaeological Society, Phoenix.

1988   The History of Occupation at Las Colinas. In *The 1982–1984 Excavations at Las Colinas: The Site and Its Features*, by David A. Gregory, William L. Deaver, Suzanne K. Fish, Ronald Gardiner, Robert W. Layhe, Fred L. Nials, Lynn S. Teague, and W. Bruce Masse, pp. 121–152. Archaeological Series 162, Vol. 2. Cultural Resource Management Division, Arizona State Museum, University of Arizona, Tucson.

1989   Production and Distribution at Las Colinas. In *The 1982–1984 Excavations at Las Colinas: Synthesis and Conclusions*, by Lynn S. Teague and William L. Deaver, pp. 89–131. Archaeological Series No. 162, Vol. 6. Cultural Resource Management Division, Arizona State Museum, University of Arizona, Tucson.

1993   Prehistory and the Traditions of the O'Odham and Hopi. *The Kiva* 58(4):435–454.

Teague, Lynn S., and William L. Deaver
1989   *The 1982–1984 Excavations at Los Colinas: Synthesis and Conclusions.* Archaeological Series No. 162, Vol. 6. Cultural Resource Management Division, Arizona State Museum, University of Arizona, Tucson.

Thompson, L.
1990   *A History of South Africa.* Yale University Press, New Haven.

Thompson, R. H., and W. A. Longacre
1966   The University of Arizona Archaeological Field School at Grasshopper, East-Central Arizona. *The Kiva* 31:255–275.

Tkaczuk, D. C., and B. C. Vivian (editors)
1989   *Cultures in Conflict.* Proceedings of the 20th Chacmool Conference. Department of Archaeology, University of Calgary, Calgary.

Triadan, D.
1997   *Ceramic Commodities and Common Containers: Production and Distribution of White Mountain Red Ware in the Grasshopper Region, Arizona.* Anthropological Papers of the University of Arizona No. 61. University of Arizona Press, Tucson.

Topic, John, and Theresa Topic
1987   The Archaeological Investigation of Andean Militarism: Some Cautionary Observations. In *The Origins and Development of the Andean State*, edited by Jonathan Haas, Shelia Pozorski, and Thomas Pozorski, pp. 47–55. Cambridge University Press, Cambridge.

Tuden, Arthur
1966   Leadership and the Decision-Making
        Process among the Ila and the Swat
        Pathans. In *Political Anthropology*, edited
        by Marc J. Swartz, Victor W. Turner, and
        Arthur Tuden, pp. 275–284. Aldine,
        Chicago.
Tuggle, H. D.
1970   Prehistoric Community Relationships in
        East-Central Arizona. Unpublished Ph.D.
        dissertation, University of Arizona, Tucson.
1982   Settlement Patterns in the Q Ranch Region.
        In *Cholla Project Archaeology: The Q
        Ranch Region*, edited by J. J. Reid, pp.
        151–164. Archaeological Series No. 161,
        Vol. 3. Arizona State Museum, Tucson.
Tuggle, H. D., K. W. Kintigh, and J. J. Reid
1982   Trace Element Analysis of White Wares. In
        *Cholla Project Archaeology: Ceramic
        Studies*, edited by J. J. Reid, pp. 22–38.
        Archaeological Series No. 161, Vol. 5.
        Arizona State Museum, Tucson.
Tuggle, H. D., J. J. Reid, and R. C. Cole
1984   Fourteenth-Century Mogollon Agriculture
        in the Grasshopper Region of Arizona. In
        *Prehistoric Agriculture Strategies in the
        Southwest*, edited by S. F. Fish and P. R.
        Fish, pp. 101–111. Anthropological
        Research Papers No. 33. Arizona State
        University, Tempe.
Turner, Christy G. II, Marcia H. Regan, and Joel D.
Irish
1994   Physical Anthropology and Human
        Taphonomy. In *The Roosevelt Rural Sites
        Study, Vol. 2: Prehistoric Rural Settlements
        in the Tonto Basin*, Part 2, edited by
        Richard Ciolek-Torrello, Steven D. Shelley,
        and Su Benaron, pp. 559–584. Technical
        Series No. 28. Statistical Research, Tucson.
Turner, Christy G. II, and Jacqueline A. Turner
1999   *Man Corn: Cannibalism and Violence in
        the Prehistoric American Southwest*.
        University of Utah Press, Salt Lake City.
Turney, Omar
1929   *Prehistoric Irrigation in Arizona*. Arizona
        Historian, Phoenix. *Arizona Historical
        Review* 1(2):2–52, 1(3):9–45, 1(4):33–73.
Turney-High, H.
1949   *Primitive War: Its Practice and Concepts*.
        Reprint. University of South Carolina Press,
        Columbia, 1971.
Tyler, Hamilton A.
1964   *Pueblo Gods and Myths*. University of
        Oklahoma Press, Norman.
Underhill, Ruth Murray
1938a   *Papago Woman*. American Anthropological
        Association, Memoir No. 46. Reprint.
        Waveland Press, Prospect Heights, Illinois,
        1979.
1938b   *Singing for Power: The Song Magic of the

        Papago Indians of Southern Arizona*.
        Reprint. University of Arizona Press,
        Tucson, 1993.
1939   *Social Organization of the Papago Indians*.
        Contributions to Anthropology, Vol. 30.
        Columbia University, New York.
Upham, Steadman
1982   *Polities and Power: An Economic and
        Political History of the Western Pueblo*.
        Academic Press, New York.
Upham, Steadman, and Lori Stevens Reed
1989   Regional Systems in the Central and
        Northern Southwest: Demography,
        Economy, and Sociopolitics Preceding
        Contact. In *Columbian Consequences:
        Archaeological and Historical Perspectives
        on the Spanish Borderlands West*, edited by
        David Hurst Thomas, pp. 57–76.
        Smithsonian Institution Press, Washington,
        D.C.
Upham, Steadman, and Glen E. Rice
1980   Up the Canal without a Pattern: Modeling
        Hohokam Interaction and Exchange. In
        Current Issues in Hohokam Prehistory,
        edited by David E. Doyel and Fred Plog, pp.
        78–105. Arizona State University
        Anthropological Research Papers No. 23.
        Arizona State University, Tempe.
Valehrach, E. M., and B. S. Valehrach
1971   Excavations at Brazaletes Pueblo. *The
        Arizona Archaeologist* 6:1–45.
Van Creveld, M.
1989   *Technology and War*. Free Press, New York.
van der Dennen, J. M. G.
1995   *The Origin of War: The Evolution of a
        Male-Coalitional Reproductive Strategy*.
        Origin Press, Groningen, Netherlands.
van Waarden, Nora
1984   Hilltop Sites in Central Arizona: An
        Analysis of Their Functional Relationships.
        Unpublished Master's thesis, Arizona State
        University, Tempe.
Van West, C. R.
1999   Did the Iceman Cometh? A Review of Data
        Concerning Drought, the Little Ice Age, and
        Chaotic Precipitation and Their
        Relationship to the Mesa Verde Regional
        Abandonment. Paper presented at the 64th
        Annual Meeting of the Society for American
        Archaeology, Chicago.
Varien, M. D.
1997   New Perspectives on Settlement Patterns:
        Sedentism and Mobility in a Social
        Landscape. Unpublished Ph.D. dissertation,
        Department of Anthropology, Arizona State
        University, Tempe.
Varien, M. D. (editor)
1999   *The Sand Canyon Archaeological Project:
        Site Testing* [HTML Title]. Available:
        http://www.crowcanyon.org/researchreports

/sitetesting/start.htm. Date of use: 1
September 2000.

Varien, M. D., W. D. Lipe, M. A. Adler, I. M.
Thompson, and B. A. Bradley
1996   Southwestern Colorado and Southeastern
        Utah Settlement Patterns: A.D. 1100 to
        1300. In *The Prehistoric Pueblo World, A.D.
        1150–1350*, edited by M. A. Adler, pp.
        86–113. University of Arizona Press,
        Tucson.

Vayda, Andrew P.
1960   *Maori Warfare*. The Polynesian Society,
        Wellington, New Zealand.
1968   Hypotheses about Functions of War. In
        *War: The Anthropology of Armed Conflict
        and Aggression*, edited by Morton Fried,
        Marvin Harris, and Robert Murphy, pp.
        85–91. Natural History Press, Garden City,
        New York.
1976   *War in Ecological Perspective*. Plenum
        Press, New York.

Vencl, S.
1984   War and Warfare in Archaeology. *Journal of
        Anthropological Archaeology* 3:116–132.

Vokes, Arthur W.
1995   The Shell Assemblage. In *The Roosevelt
        Community Development Study, Vol. 1:
        Stone and Shell Artifacts*, edited by Mark
        D. Elson and Jeffery J. Clark, pp. 151–212.
        Anthropological Papers No. 14. Center for
        Desert Archaeology, Tucson.

Voth, Henry R.
1905   *Traditions of the Hopi*. Anthropological
        Series No. 8. Field Museum of Natural
        History Publication No. 96. Field Museum
        of Natural History, Chicago.

Wallace, Henry D.
1983   The Mortars, Petroglyphs, and Trincheras
        on Rillito Peak. *The Kiva* 48(3):137–246.
1987   Regional Context of the Prehistoric Rancho
        Vistoso Sites: Settlement Patterns and
        Socioeconomic Structure. In *Settlement in
        the Cañada del Oro Valley, Arizona: The
        Rancho Vistoso Survey Project*, by D. B.
        Craig and H. D. Wallace, pp. 117–166.
        Anthropological Papers No. 8. Institute for
        American Research, Tucson.
1988   Ceramic Boundaries and Interregional
        Interaction: New Perspectives on the
        Tucson Basin Hohokam. In *Recent
        Research on Tucson Basin Prehistory:
        Proceedings of the Second Tucson Basin
        Conference*, edited by W. H. Doelle and P.
        R. Fish, pp. 313–348. Anthropological
        Papers No. 10. Institute for American
        Research, Tucson.
1995a   *Archaeological Investigations at Los
        Morteros, a Prehistoric Settlement in the
        Northern Tucson Basin*. Anthropological

Papers No. 17. Center for Desert
        Archaeology, Tucson.
1995b   Decorated Buffware and Brownware
        Ceramics. In *The Roosevelt Community
        Development Study, Vol. 2: Ceramic
        Chronology, Technology, and Economics*,
        edited by J. M. Heidke and M. T. Stark, pp.
        19–84. Center for Desert Archaeology,
        Anthropological Papers No. 14. Tucson.
1996   *Documentation of a Platform Mound
        Compound and Monitoring of the
        Excavation of a Septic System Leach Field
        within AZ BB:13:8, San Xavier District,
        Tohono O'odham Reservation*. Letter
        Report No. 96128. Desert Archaeology,
        Inc., Tucson.
1998   Presence or Parlance? The Meaning of
        "Hohokam" and Concepts of Culture, A.D.
        800 to 1050, in Southeastern Arizona.
        Paper presented at the Amerind
        Foundation, Inc., seminar "The
        Archaeology of a Land Between: Prehistory
        and History of Southeastern Arizona,"
        Dragoon, Arizona.

Wallace, Henry D., and William H. Doelle
1997   From Ballcourts to Platform Mounds to
        Rancherias: A Comparison of Three
        Organizational Strategies on the Lower San
        Pedro River. Paper presented at the 62nd
        Annual Meeting of the Society for American
        Archaeology, Nashville.

Wallace, Henry D., William H. Doelle, and John
Murray
2000   *An Archaeological Survey of the Lower San
        Pedro Valley, Arizona, 1990 to 1995*.
        Center for Desert Archaeology, Tucson, in
        press.

Wallace, Henry D., James M. Heidke, and William
H. Doelle
1995   Hohokam Origins. *The Kiva*
        60(4):575–618.

Wallace, Henry D., and James P. Holmlund
1984   The Classic Period in the Tucson Basin. *The
        Kiva* 49:167–194.

Warren, A. Helene
1979   The Pottery of Pueblo del Encierro. In
        *Archaeological Excavations at Pueblo del
        Encierro, LA 70, Cochiti Dam Salvage
        Project, Cochiti, New Mexico, Final
        Report: 1964–1965 Field Season JC3580
        (66), USNPS Southwest Region, Santa Fe*,
        edited by David H. Snow, Section B, pp.
        1–58. Museum of New Mexico Laboratory
        of Anthropology Notes No. 78. Museum of
        New Mexico, Santa Fe.

Warren, Claude N.
1984   The Desert Region. In *California
        Archaeology*, edited by Michael J. Moratto,
        pp. 115–430. Academic Press, New York.

Wasley, William W., and Blake Benham
1968   Salvage Excavation in the Buttes Dam Site,
        Southern Arizona. *The Kiva* 33(4):244–279.
Waters, Michael R.
1987   Holocene Alluvial Geology and
        Geoarchaeology of AZ BB:13:14 and the
        San Xavier Reach of the Santa Cruz River,
        Arizona. In *The Archaeology of the San
        Xavier Bridge Site (AZ BB:13:14), Tucson
        Basin, Southern Arizona*, edited by J. C.
        Ravesloot, pp. 39–60. Archaeological Series
        No. 171. Arizona State Museum, University
        of Arizona, Tucson.
1988   The Impact of Fluvial Processes and
        Landscape Evolution on the Archaeological
        Sites and Settlement Patterns along the San
        Xavier Reach of the Santa Cruz River.
        Geoarchaeology 3(3):205–219.
Watson, Patty Jo, Steven A. LeBlanc, and Charles
        Redman
1980   Aspects of Zuni Prehistory: Preliminary
        Report on Excavations and Survey in the El
        Morro Valley of New Mexico. *Journal of
        Field Archaeology* 7:201–218.
Weaver, Donald E. Jr.
1978   Prehistoric Population Dynamics and
        Environmental Exploitation in the
        Manuelito Canyon District, Northwestern
        New Mexico. Unpublished Ph.D. disserta-
        tion, Department of Anthropology, Arizona
        State University, Tempe.
Webb, George
1959   *A Pima Remembers*. University of Arizona
        Press, Tucson.
Welch, John Robert
1996   The Archaeological Measures and Social
        Implications of Agricultural Commitment.
        Unpublished Ph.D. dissertation, University
        of Arizona, Tucson.
Welch, John R., and Daniela Triadan
1991   The Canyon Creek Turquoise Mine,
        Arizona. *The Kiva* 56(2):145–164.
Wendorf, Fred
1953   *Salvage Archaeology in the Chama Valley,
        New Mexico*. Monograph of the School of
        American Research No. 17. School of
        American Research, Santa Fe.
Whipple, Amiel W.
1856   Report of Explorations for a Railway
        Route, Near the Thirty-fifth Parallel of
        North Latitude from the Mississippi River
        to the Pacific Ocean. In *Reports of
        Explorations and Surveys to Ascertain . . .
        Route for Railroad from Mississippi River
        to Pacific Ocean . . . , 1853–1860, Vol. 3*,
        pp. 1–136. U.S. War Department,
        Washington D.C.
White, Christopher W.
1974   Lower Colorado River Tribal Warfare and

        Alliance Dynamics. In *?Antap California
        Indian Political and Economic
        Organization*, edited by Lowell John Bean
        and Thomas F. King, pp. 111–136. Ballena
        Press Anthropological Papers No. 2.
        Ramona, California.
White, T. D.
1992   *Prehistoric Cannibalism at Mancos
        5MTUMR-2346*. Princeton University
        Press, Princeton.
Whittlesey, S. M., E. Arnould, and W. Reynolds
1982   Archaeological Sediments: Discourses,
        Experiment, and Application. In
        *Multidisciplinary Research at Grasshopper
        Pueblo*, edited by W. A. Longacre, S. J.
        Holbrook, and M. W. Graves, pp. 28–35.
        Anthropological Papers of the University of
        Arizona No. 40. University of Arizona
        Press, Tucson.
Wilcox, David R.
1979a   The Hohokam Regional System. In *An
        Archaeological Test of Sites in the Gila
        Butte-Santan Region*, by Glen Rice, David
        Wilcox, Kevin Rafferty, and James
        Schoenwetter, pp. 77–116. Arizona State
        University Anthropological Research Papers
        No. 18. Arizona State University, Tempe.
1979b   The Warfare Implications of Dry-Laid
        Masonry Walls on Tumamoc Hill. *The Kiva*
        45(1–2):15–38.
1981   Changing Perspectives in the Protohistoric
        Pueblos, A.D. 1450–1700. In *The
        Protohistoric Periods in the North
        American Southwest*, edited by D. R.
        Wilcox and W. B. Masse, pp. 378–409.
        Research Paper No. 24. Arizona State
        University, Tempe.
1987   *Frank Midvale's Investigation of the Site of
        La Ciudad*. Anthropological Field Studies
        No. 19. Office of Cultural Resource
        Management, Department of Anthropology,
        Arizona State University.
1988   The Regional Context of the Brady Wash
        and Picacho Area Sites. In *Hohokam
        Settlement along the Slopes of the Picacho
        Mountains: Synthesis and Conclusions,
        Tucson Aqueduct Project*, edited by Richard
        Ciolek-Torrello and David R. Wilcox, pp.
        244–267. MNA Research Paper No. 35,
        Vol. 6. Museum of Northern Arizona,
        Flagstaff.
1989   Hohokam Warfare. In *Cultures in Conflict:
        Current Archaeological Perspectives*, edited
        by Diana Claire Tkaczuk and Brian C.
        Vivian, pp. 163–172. Proceedings of the
        20th Annual Chacmool Conference.
        University of Calgary, Calgary.
1991a   Changing Contexts of Pueblo Adaptations,
        A.D. 1200–1600. In *Farmers, Hunters, and*

Colonists: Interaction between the
Southwest and the Southern Plains, edited
by Katherine A. Spielmann, pp. 128–154.
University of Arizona Press, Tucson.

1991b   Hohokam Religion: An Archaeologist's
Perspective. In The Hohokam, Ancient
People of the Desert, edited by David Grant
Noble, pp. 47–59. School of American
Research Press, Santa Fe.

1991c   Hohokam Social Complexity. In Chaco and
Hohokam: Prehistoric Regional Systems in
the American Southwest, edited by Patricia
L. Crown and W. James Judge, pp.
253–276. School of American Research
Press, Santa Fe.

1993   The Evolution of the Chaco Polity. In The
Chimney Rock Archaeological Symposium,
edited by J. McKim Malville and Gary
Matlock, pp. 76–90. Rocky Mountain
Forest and Range Experiment Station. USDA
Forest Service, General Technical Report
RM-227. U.S. Department of Agriculture,
Fort Collins, Colorado.

1995a   A Processual Model of Charles D. Di Peso's
Babocomari Site and Related Systems. In
The Gran Chichimeca: Essays on the
Archaeology and Ethnohistory of Northern
Mesoamerica, edited by Jonathan E.
Reyman, pp. 281–319. Ashgate Publishing
Co., Brookfield, Vermont.

1995b   The Wupatki Nexus:
Chaco-Hohokam-Chumash Connectivity,
A.D.1150–1225. Ms. on file, Museum of
Northern Arizona Library, Flagstaff.

1996   Pueblo III: People and Polity in Relational
Context. In The Prehistoric Pueblo World,
A.D. 1150–1350, edited by Michael Adler,
pp. 241–254. University of Arizona Press,
Tucson.

1999   A Peregrine View of Macroregional Systems
in the North American Southwest, A.D.
750–1250. In Great Towns and Regional
Polities, edited by Jill Neitzel, pp. 115–142.
University of New Mexico Press,
Albuquerque.

2000   Restoring Authenticity: Judging Frank
Hamilton Cushing's Veracity. Paper
presented at the symposium "Hohokam
Political Organization," Annual Meeting of
the Society for American Archaeology,
Philadelphia.

Wilcox, David R., Donald Keller, and David Ortiz
2000   Long-Distance Exchange, Warfare, and the
Indian Peak Ruin, Walnut Creek, Arizona.
In Archaeology in West Central Arizona:
Proceedings of the 1996 AAC Prescott
Conference, edited by Thomas Motsinger,
Douglas R. Mitchell, and James M. McKie,
pp. 119–144. Sharlot Hall Museum Press,
Prescott.

Wilcox, David R., Stephen Larson, W. Bruce Masse,
Gayle H. Hartmann, and Alan Ferg
1979   A Summary of Conclusions and
Recommendations of the Tumamoc Hill
Survey. The Kiva 45:187–195.

Wilcox, David R., Gerald Robertson Jr., and J. Scott
Wood
1999   Perry Mesa, a Fourteenth-Century Gated
Community in Central Arizona. Plateau
Journal (Summer): 44–61.

Wilcox, David R., and Charles Sternberg
1983   Hohokam Ballcourts and Their
Interpretation. Arizona State Museum
Archaeological Series No. 160. University
of Arizona, Tucson.

Wilshusen, Richard H.
1986   The Relationship between Abandonment
Mode and Ritual Use in Pueblo I Anasazi
Protokivas. Journal of Field Archaeology
13:245–254.

Wiseman, Regge N.
1997   A Preliminary Look at Evidence for Late
Prehistoric Conflict in Southeastern New
Mexico. In Layers of Time: Papers in
Honor of Robert H. Weber, edited by
Melitha S. Duran and David T. Kirkpatrick,
pp. 135–146. Paper No. 23. Archaeological
Society of New Mexico, Albuquerque.

Wolf, Eric R.
1982   Europe and the People without History.
University of California Press, Berkeley.

Wood, J. Scott
1978   An Archeological Survey of the Battle Flat
Watershed Experimental Chaparral
Conversion Project, Crown King Ranger
District, Prescott National Forest: Culture
History and Prehistoric Land Use in the
Bradshaw Mountains of Central Arizona.
Cultural Resources Report No. 24. USDA
Forest Service, Southwestern Region,
Albuquerque.

1980   The Gentry Timber Sale: Behavioral
Patterning and Predictability in the Upper
Cherry Creek Area, Central Arizona. The
Kiva 16:99–119.

1987   Checklist of Pottery Types for the Tonto
National Forest: An Introduction to the
Archaeological Ceramics of Central
Arizona. The Arizona Archaeologist 21.
Phoenix.

1992   Field Trip to Perry Mesa. Ms. on file,
Museum of Northern Arizona Library,
Flagstaff.

2000   Vale of Tiers Palimpsest: Salado Settlement
and Internal Relationships in the Tonto
Basin Area. In Salado, edited by Jeffrey S.
Dean, pp. 107–142. University of New
Mexico Press, Albuquerque.

Woodall, Gregory R., David D. Barz, and Michael P. Neeley (editors)
1998   *Rocks, Roasters, and Ridgetops: Data Recovery across the Pioneer Road Landscape, State Route 87-Segment F, Maricopa and Gila Counties, Arizona.* Archaeological Research Services Project Report No. 94:77B. Tempe.

Woodbury, Richard
1956   The Antecedents of Zuni Culture. *Transactions of the New York Academy of Sciences,* series 2, 18:557–563.
1959   A Reconsideration of Pueblo Warfare in the Southwestern United States. *Actas del XXXIII Congreso Internacional de Americanistas* 2:124–133. Editorial Lehmann, San José, Costa Rica.

Woodbury, Richard, and Natalie F. S. Woodbury
1956   Zuni Prehistory and El Morro National Monument. *Southwestern Lore* 21:56–60.

Woodson, Michael Kyle
1995   The Goat Hill Site: A Western Anasazi Pueblo in the Safford Valley of Southeastern Arizona. Unpublished Master's thesis, Department of Anthropology, University of Texas, Austin.

Wormington, H. M.
1955   *A Reappraisal of the Fremont Culture.* Proceedings of the Denver Museum of Natural History No. 1. Denver Museum of Natural History, Denver.

Wrangham, Richard W., and D. Peterson
1996   *Demonic Males: Apes and the Origins of Human Violence.* Houghton-Mifflin, Boston.

Wright, Barton
1976   *Pueblo Shields from the Fred Harvey Fine Arts Collection.* Northland Press, Flagstaff, Arizona.

Zedeño, María Nieves
1994   *Sourcing Prehistoric Ceramics at Chodistaas Pueblo, Arizona: The Circulation of People and Pots in the Grasshopper Region.* Anthropological Papers of the University of Arizona No. 58. University of Arizona Press, Tucson.
1998   Defining Material Correlates for Ceramic Circulation in the Prehistoric Puebloan Southwest. *Journal of Anthropological Research* 54(4):461–476.

Zier, Christian J.
1976   *Excavations near Zuni, New Mexico, 1973.* Museum of Northern Arizona Research Paper 2.

CONTRIBUTORS

HELEN K. CROTTY, PH.D. art history, has been researching and documenting prehistoric southwestern rock art and kiva murals for more than 20 years.

WILLIAM H. DOELLE, PH.D., is president of Desert Archaeology, Inc., Tucson.

DENNIS C. GOSSER is a graduate associate at the Archaeological Research Institute, Department of Anthropology, Arizona State University, Tempe.

LAWRENCE H. KEELEY, PH.D., is professor of anthropology at the University of Illinois at Chicago.

KRISTIN A. KUCKELMAN, M.A. anthropology, is a research archaeologist at Crow Canyon Archaeological Center, Cortez, Colorado.

STEVEN A. LEBLANC, PH.D., is director of collections, Peabody Museum of Archaeology and Ethnology. He is the author of *Prehistoric Warfare in the American Southwest* (Utah 1999).

RICKY R. LIGHTFOOT, PH.D. anthropology, is president and chief executive officer of Crow Canyon Archaeological Center, Cortez, Colorado.

THEODORE J. OLIVER, B.A., is database manager at Desert Archaeology, Inc., Tucson.

J. JEFFERSON REID, PH.D., is professor of anthropology at the University of Arizona.

GLEN E. RICE, PH.D., is head of the office of cultural resource management at Arizona State University.

ARLEYN W. SIMON, PH.D., is associate research professor and curator, Archaeological Research Institute, Department of Anthropology, Arizona State University, Tempe.

H. DAVID TUGGLE, PH.D., is a senior archaeologist with International Archaeological Research Institute, Inc.

HENRY D. WALLACE, M.A., is senior research archaeologist at Desert Archaeology, Inc., Tucson.

DAVID R. WILCOX, PH.D. anthropology, is senior curator of anthropology at the Museum of Northern Arizona.

Index

abandonment: and Classic Period sites in San Pedro Valley, 274; of fortified villages in Tucson Basin, 256, 259, 282; of Pueblo IV sites in Grasshopper region, 102–103; of Roosevelt and Gila phase sites in Tonto Basin, 208–15, 216, 217; of Scribe S site in El Morro Valley, 28, 30; of smaller sites in El Morro Valley, 46. *See also* settlement patterns

Abbott, David R., 170n10, 233, 306

Acoma Pueblo, 31, *33*

Adams, E. Charles, 221

Africa, and examples of climate change and warfare, 337

age, and skeletal remains: and Castle Rock Pueblo, 62–63; and Roosevelt and Gila phase sites in Tonto Basin, 201, *203*

aggregation: as defensive strategy, 290; and Castle Rock Pueblo, 58–59; and conflict in El Morro Valley, 45–46; and conflict in Grasshopper region, 89–95, 101; and Hohokam sites in Salt and Gila Basins, 327–29; and Late Classic period in Tucson Basin, 257; and Pima and Maricopa warfare, 326–27; and platform mound sites in San Pedro Valley, 265–66, 267, 271, 278, 280–81; and Roosevelt and Gila phases in Tonto Basin, 203–205, 237. *See also* settlement patterns

agriculture: and canal systems in San Pedro Valley, 265; and fortification of sites in Tucson Basin, 248–50; and Grasshopper Pueblo, 94; and Perry Mesa region, 155, 169n3–4. *See also* irrigation; subsistence and subsistence strategies

Agua Fria, and Perry Mesa settlement system in Pueblo III, 121, 122, 124, *128–31*

Alder Wash site, 267, 272

Alkire, Frank & George, 125n4

alliances: lack of attention to in archaeological literature of Southwest, 16; and platform mound sites in Tonto Basin, 223; and site clusters in El Morro Valley, 39

Altschul, Jeffrey H., 278

Amerind Foundation, 266

Anasazi: Fremont influence on art of, 67–69; and militaristic imagery in rock art and kiva murals, 65–67, 69–83; and Sinagua shield form pictographs, 69

Apache, 8, 123, 241, 243, 290, 293, 294–95, 297, 299, 301, 328

archaeology: and comparison of Pima and Maricopa villages to Hohokam sites, 302–26; and defensive sites in Arizona, 142–43; and evidence for warfare, 14–18, 49n2, 85, 195, 196, 239, 339–41; and